The Wakefield Mystery Plays

The Wakefield Mystery Plays

EDITED BY MARTIAL ROSE

DOUBLEDAY & COMPANY, INC.
GARDEN CITY, NEW YORK
1962

Library of Congress Catalog Card Number 62–11380

Printed in the United States of America
First Edition in the United States of America

Author's Note

In 1954 I was asked to make a contribution to a course on Environmental Studies at Woolley Hall, near Wakefield, by producing three plays from the Wakefield cycle of mystery plays. In consequence the Bretton Hall Drama students presented *The Salutation, The Second Shepherds' Play,* and *The Flight into Egypt.* The plays were performed in the original language by a remarkable group of students whose own vernacular was not so very far removed from that of the original. They realized to the full both the lyricism and the buffoonery. More significant, the lyricism and the buffoonery were revealed not as independent features of the drama but as integrally related. And for once *The Second Shepherds' Play* also became integrally related to the cycle of plays from which it is so frequently torn. Even within the context of the three plays performed at Woolley it was set in a new perspective: it was not the only jewel in the Wakefield Plays; there were others, and some with as many facets.

The opportunity of presenting the major part of the cycle came in 1958, when the Principal and staff of Bretton Hall determined to focus the main work of the year on the study and production of the Wakefield Plays. An abbreviated version of twenty of the plays was made, and this formed the basis of the present edition. The production employed both mobile pageants and a stationary three-tier structure representing heaven, middle-earth and hell. The music throughout was live, sung and played from a *heavenly* tower. The running time of the twenty abbreviated plays was six and a half hours. The whole college was divided into craft groups, each group being responsible for the presentation of one or more plays. The overall production was managed by the staff.

My present endeavour to produce a complete acting version of the Wakefield Plays has been greatly assisted by the liberal provision of the Ministry of Education, the University of Leeds, and the governors of Bretton Hall in granting me sabbatical leave in which to pursue my studies. I am especially indebted to Kay Hudson, Frances Stevens (University of Leeds) and John Stevens (University of Cambridge), and to the West Riding County Library for the more than generous supply of books. Above all, my thanks are due to the Principal, staff, and students of Bretton Hall who first gave support to the project and finally achieved, in a memorable performance, the revival after four hundred years of the most dramatic of the medieval mystery cycles.

Lastly, the enthusiasm and guidance of Lionel Hale and Peter Richards have brought this matter to print. Their conviction that this was an enterprise of some magnitude has been of the greatest encouragement, and their attention to detail has stirred me to an unwonted alertness.

MARTIAL ROSE

Contents

Part One

Part Two

Part Three

Part Four

An Introduction to The Wakefield Plays

WHY WAKEFIELD?

The unique manuscript of the *Towneley Plays* now rests in the Huntington Library, San Marino, California. It comprises thirty-two plays all but one of which, *The Hanging of Judas,* are written in a mid-fifteenth-century hand. Five plays are in parts identical with the corresponding plays in the York cycle. The scope of the plays encompassing the creation, fall, redemption and judgement of man, approximates to that found in the other English cycles. There are, however, a few plays, *Caesar Augustus* and *The Talents* for instance, which are unique in the records of English medieval drama. It is true that the Chester *Annunciation* introduces the character of Octavian and that the other cycles include mention, if not dramatization, of the dicing for Christ's garment, but the extended treatment of this material in the Towneley Plays argues an indigenous source. The name Towneley has been given to the plays because the manuscript was for a great number of years in the possession of the Towneley family of Towneley Hall, near Burnley, Lancashire. It was sold by the family in 1814 but was returned in May, 1819, where it remained until the second sale of the Towneley library in June, 1883.

There has been so far no satisfactory explanation of how the manuscript found its way into the Towneley library. Are the plays after all a mystery cycle indigenous to Lancashire? Certainly other Lancashire names appear in the manuscript: James Blakebourn (folio 90a); Thomas Hargraves (folios 73b and 90a); moreover, against Hargraves' name (folio 90a) are the words 'of Burnley'. Associations with Lancashire are further strengthened by the 1822 introduction to the *Iudicium* (*The Judgement*), a publication for the Roxburgh Club, written by Francis Douce who attributed the original possession of the manuscript to the Abbey of Whalley from where, at the dissolution, 'it passed into the library of the neighbouring family of Towneley'.

'Wakefeld', however, is included in the heading of two of the plays. *The Creation* begins with the words '*In dei nomine amen. Assit Principio, Sancta Maria, Meo. Wakefeld*'. *Noah* is entitled '*Processus Noe cum filiis. Wakefeld*'. This satisfactorily establishes that these two plays belong to Wakefield, but on this evidence alone it would be rash to assume that the whole cycle has its origin in Wakefield. Indeed Louis Wann asks 'If the entire cycle of plays was produced at Wakefield, why are these two alone–and these not in consecutive order–designated as Wakefield plays? Does not the mention of Wakefield in the case of these two plays establish a presumption that the others were not connected with Wakefield?' ('A New Examination of the Manuscript of the *Towneley Plays*', P.M.L.A., 1928, 151–152.) Perhaps this question would not have arisen had 'Wakefeld' appeared at the beginning of *The Creation* only. Had this been the case the whole cycle, since it is substantially the work of one scribe, might reasonably have been assigned to Wakefield, but the repetition in the *Noah* title complicates the issue. The essential difference between the appearance of 'Wakefeld' in the first and the third play of the cycle is that whereas in the third play it clearly stands as part of the title, in the first play it is the conclusion of the scribe's invocation. In compliance with literary convention and in anticipation of the great task that lies ahead of him, that of copying out the whole cycle which extends to one hundred and thirty-two leaves of vellum, the scribe asks a blessing on his work which, as the last word signifies, will be undertaken in Wakefield.

In examining this problem, then, the first question to be asked is not why 'Wakefeld' does not appear in the heading of all the plays, but rather why it should have appeared as part of the heading of *Noah*. A possible answer is that the scribe is handling a heterogeneous group of plays, some in their pristine fourteenth-century state, some revisions of plays from other cycles and some, five in all, brilliant new plays, written in a vigorous nine-line stanza, this last the work of a dramatic genius usually known as the Wakefield Master. The first play in the cycle written in this characteristic stanza is *Noah.* The scribe copies faithfully the text before him, and when he comes to *Noah* he copies the author's title, who includes the word 'Wakefeld' because this is the first of a set of plays he has written especially for the *Corpus Christi* celebrations of the people of Wakefield.

Apart from the five completely new plays (*Noah, The First Shepherds' Play, The Second Shepherds' Play, Herod the Great*, and *The Buffeting*) contributed to the cycle by the Wakefield Master, he shows his hand also in a number of revisions and interpolations. *The Killing of Abel,* the second play in the Cycle, is commonly associated with the work of the Master. 'The extraordinary boldness of the play' writes A. W. Pollard in his Introduction to '*The Towneley Plays*' (O.U.P. 1897) xxii, 'and the character of its humour, make it difficult to dissociate it from the work of the author of *Shepherds' Plays.*' A. C. Cawley supports this judgement and includes *The Killing of Abel* in his edition of *The Wakefield Pageants in the Towneley Cycle* (Manchester U.P. 1958). Whoever the author, *The Killing of Abel* is indelibly stamped as a Wakefield play. Cain pleads for a Wakefield burial:

Bery me in Gudeboure at the quarell hede. (367)

Matthew Peacock, in Anglia Vol. xii, 1901, pointed out that 'the Grammar School was built in Goodybower Close, and the stone came from the adjacent quarry. . . . Perhaps it was in the quarry that the plays were performed'. There is then consecutive evidence in the first three plays of the cycle that the Towneley Plays are concerned with Wakefield.

Other local allusions are found in *The First Shepherds' Play* (244) 'Have good ayll of Hely' (Have good ale of Healey), 'possibly a township of this name lying between Ossett and Horbury, about four miles south-west of Wakefield' (Cawley, op. cit., 101); 'the crokyd thorne' [*The Second Shepherds' Play* (403)], was most likely the outstanding landmark of the village of Thornes that lies between Horbury and Wakefield; 'Horbery shrogys' [*The Second Shepherds' Play* (455)], the bushy countryside near Horbury, a town three miles south-west of Wakefield; 'Watlyn strete' [*The Judgement* (126)], the Roman road which crossed the parish of Wakefield. This reference to Watling Street is found in one of the Wakefield Master's interpolations in *The Judgement*. Dr. Cawley argues 'Although these local allusions are confined to certain of the pageants belonging to the Wakefield Group in the Towneley cycle, it will be seen that the homogeneity of the pageants and parts of the pageants written in the Wakefield nine-line stanza allows us to infer that *all* of them have associations with the Wakefield area' (op. cit., xv.). In all this would account for thirteen plays, including all the most important plays in the Passion sequence. If we accept the first three plays of the cycle as belonging to Wakefield, the three plays of the Nativity sequence in the nine-line stanza, all the Passion plays, *The Pilgrims, The Ascension,* and *The Judgement,* we might with some justification rename the cycle the Wakefield Plays.

The references to the crafts, Tanners, Glovers, Dyers, Fishers, appearing in the manuscript on the first pages of *The Creation, The Killing of Abel, Pharaoh,* and *The Pilgrims* respectively, afford no additional evidence of Wakefield authorship. The names of the crafts are written in a sixteenth-century hand. Certainly only a wealthy town with a powerful and flourishing fraternity of guilds could have accepted responsibility for staging the plays, which in their entirety would have matched the length of the York cycle. Yet it is the very paucity of reference to the guilds that contrasts so sharply with the York and Chester plays, and in this the Wakefield cycle resembles the *Ludus Coventriae*.

THE AUTHOR?

In the notice for the 1814 sale of Towneley books and manuscripts Francis Douce wrote that the plays 'belonged to the Abbey of Widkirk, near Wakefield'. No explanation has been offered why eight years later he should have ascribed them to Whalley Abbey. Widkirk is generally accepted as Woodkirk, four miles north of Wakefield, where in the Middle Ages a cell was kept by Augustinian monks, dependent on Nostell Priory, and it is indeed possible that the scribe was a man in holy orders, living in or near Wakefield, and attached to the greatest monastic house in the area. The task he undertook was to copy a wide variety of manuscripts which at that time comprised the latest collection of the Wakefield Plays: some, such as *Isaac* and *Jacob*, were already nearly a hundred years old, their dramatic structure was crude and their versification gauche; some such as *The Harrowing of Hell* followed the York text closely throughout and might have been borrowed from that cycle; some, indigenous and borrowed, had been substantially altered through revision, as in the case of *The Killing of Abel*, or through interpolation (378 lines) in the case of *The Judgement;* and in the last group were the five new plays written by the Wakefield Master. The plays, then, are the work of many authors whose labours probably extended over a hundred years. These authors remain anonymous, and even the identity of the last great reviser of the cycle, who also made such a spectacular and original contribution to the drama, has escaped detection. Oscar Cargill put forward the theory ('The Authorship of the *Secunda Pastorum*', P.M.L.A., Dec., 1926) that Gilbert Pilkington, no more of whom is known than his association with one manuscript of *The Northern Passion*, was the Wakefield Master. The main evidence was based on the colophon at the end of *The Northern Passion:*

Explicit Passio Domini
nostri ihesu christi Quod Dominus Gilbertus
Pylkyngton Amen.

The Cambridge manuscript in which this version of *The Northern Passion* appears contains, among twenty-seven other pieces of verse, a poem entitled *The Turnament of Totenham*, a satire on chivalry written in the nine-line stanza which Cargill identifies as the Wakefield Master's. In brief, his conclusions are that Gilbert Pilkington was the author of *The Northern Passion, The Turnament of Totenham,* and those plays of the Wakefield cycle written in the nine-line stanza. His argument involves him in asserting that all three works were composed about 1355, an acceptable date for *The Northern Passion* but a virtually impossible date for the Wakefield Plays. Frances A. Foster has disposed of Cargill's case ('Was Gilbert Pilkington the Author of the *Secunda Pastorum*?' P.M.L.A., 1928) and Hardin Craig ('English Religious Drama', O.U.P. 1955, 234) recording Cargill's inability to substantiate his theory, writes '. . . it is rather a pity that he had no evidence'. It is strange that both Cargill and his critics have overlooked the essential difference between *The Turnament of Totenham* stanza and that of *The Second Shepherds' Play.* It is that the internal rhyme scheme of the first four lines in each stanza, the hall-mark of the Wakefield Master's verse, is nowhere to be found in *The Turnament of Totenham.*

A pity indeed, Mr. Cargill's lack of evidence! But what a fund of coincidences is revealed by an investigation of his case. Firstly, we know *The Northern Passion* exerted an influence on the formation of the fourteenth-century mystery cycles (*The Northern Passion,* vol. ii. edited by Frances A. Foster, E.E.T.S., 81–101); secondly, *The Turnament of Totenham,* although not in the identical stanza as that used by the Wakefield Master, nevertheless has many of its characteristics, and its satirical tone and mock-heroic theme calls for comparison with the Master's work, especially in view of the northern linguistic similarities; thirdly Mr. Cargill's suggestion that *The Turnament of Totenham* may once have been a satire of Tottington, the adjacent town to Pilkington in Lancashire, while no more than an outrageous guess, might nevertheless give us pause when, on examining Thomas Whitaker's *History of Whalley,* we find such frequent reference to the Manor of Tottington. Large tracts of the forest of Tottington which reached northward into the parish of Whalley were granted by thirteenth-century charters to the priory of Monk Bretton, about nine miles south-east of Wakefield, founded as a Cluniac house about 1154 and becoming a Benedictine establishment from 1281. These lands with an immense quantity of others were regranted to John Braddyll of Whalley by letters patent of Henry VIII in 1546. In this *History of Whalley* we read that in 1469 a licence was granted to Thomas Pilkington to kernel and embattle his manor house at Bury (Towneley MSS G 13), and that a Thomas Pilkington was a generous donor to Whalley Abbey, among whose monks was one Brother John of Wakefield. Mr. Cargill had stressed that a branch of the Lancashire Pilkingtons had established themselves in Wakefield and had built there, early in the fifteenth century, Pilkington Hall. Many of the manuscripts studied by Thomas Whitaker were made accessible to him at the Towneley Hall library, and it was to Charles Towneley that he dedicated his work in 1800.

No fresh evidence for the authorship of *The Second Shepherds' Play* has been adduced, but the territorial associations between Whalley and Wakefield have been strengthened, and in both areas the Pilkington family exerted its influence. Furthermore the Pilkingtons and the Towneleys were related families: Sir John Towneley, a ward of Sir Charles Pilkington, married in 1480 Isabella, Sir Charles' daughter and heiress. The coats of arms of both families appeared in the fifteenth-century glass in the Wakefield Parish Church (J. W. Walker, *The Cathedral Church of Wakefield,* 1888, 86–88).

THE TOWNELEY POSSESSION OF THE MANUSCRIPT

In the east window of the north chancel of what was Wakefield Parish Church and is now the Cathedral appeared the Towneley coat of arms impaled by the coat of arms of the house of Nowell. This signified the marriage between the two houses of Roger Nowell and Grace Towneley in 1488. J. W. Walker in his *History of Wakefield* suggests that the plays might have found their way into the possession of the Towneley family in consequence of this marriage. Roger Nowell was an extremely affluent and influential man, founding the Nowell Chantry in the Parish Church in 1478, and owning many acres of land in Wakefield, Stanley, Bradford, Sandal, and Wentbridge.

(J. W. Walker, *The Cathedral Church of Wakefield,* 67–71). But he was also the son and heir of Alexander Nowell of Read Hall, two miles south-east of Whalley, lying in fact on the route between Towneley Hall and Whalley Abbey. The families of Nowell and Towneley were further connected by Elizabeth Kay of Rochdale marrying first John, the son of Roger Nowell, and then, after her husband's death, Charles Towneley, the heir of Towneley Hall. It is in all probability her first husband whose name appears in the records of the Wakefield Parish Church as patron of the Nowell Chantry Chaplains: 'April 8, 1511 . . . John Nowell de Whalley Armiger.' (Walker, ibid. 71.) John Towneley, the son by Elizabeth's second marriage, was a staunch Roman Catholic who suffered for his faith a life of intermittent imprisonment. By her first marriage Elizabeth had four sons, the two eldest, Alexander and Laurence, held high office in the church, the former becoming Dean of St. Paul's (1560–1602) and the latter Dean of Lichfield (1559–1576), in whose diocese Whalley lay. [R. Churton, *The Life of Alexander Nowell* (1809).]

Alexander Nowell, a life-long friend of Edmund Grindal, Archbishop of York (1570–1576) was a member of the 1576 commission to look into ecclesiastical abuses while Grindal was still Archbishop of York. Grindal's appointment to York was made on the understanding that he would root out Romish superstition in the north, and part of his campaign was waged against performances of mystery plays. In 1568 Matthew Hutton, Dean of York Minster, called in the York Creed Play for perusal, and after that date no more is heard of it. Archbishop Grindal on 30th July, 1572, asked for a copy of the York *Pater Noster* Play, after which date no record remains of it. No doubt the York Mystery Plays were similarly examined, and although their performance was discontinued, at least the manuscript has survived. 'The correction, indeed the abolition, of the plays' writes Hardin Craig (op. cit., 201), 'is attributed to the influence of Edmund Grindal, Archbishop of York, and of Matthew Hutton, the Dean of the Minster. A complete overhauling of the plays was projected for 1579, but fortunately not carried out, and we have the plays pretty much as they were written down at some time before the middle of the fifteenth century. Apparently the Dean and the Archbishop, by 1579 Edwin Sandys, took the prudent course of keeping the register in their own possession and temporizing with the citizens, who obviously still wanted the plays performed'.

That the Wakefield Plays were subject to Protestant revision there is no doubt. In *John the Baptist* (197) a passage referring to the sacraments is first altered and then the whole stanza is struck through, and in the margin is written 'corectyd and not playd'. The word 'pope' seems literally to have been dug out of the text of *Herod the Great* (263), and it is practically certain, from analogy with the other cycles, that the twelve leaves missing from the manuscript between *The Ascension* and *The Judgement* contained plays dealing with the death, assumption and coronation of the Blessed Virgin Mary, details from which are depicted over the west portal of the fourteenth-century façade of the Chantry Bridge Chapel. (This façade now graces the boat-house of Kettlethorpe Hall.) Positive evidence of the Ecclesiastical Commission suppressing the Wakefield Plays is derived from the Diocesan Court of High Commission.

> xxvij° die Maii Anno dni 1576 cora Com eccle Ebor. Cora Mrr. Matthew Hutton, John Gibson et W° Palmer Commissionarii et in pr mei Willim Fothergill notarii publici. This daie upon intelligence geven to the saide Commission that it is meant and purposed that in the towne of Wakefeld shalbe plaid this yere in Whitsonweke next or thereaboutes a plaie commonlie called *Corpus Christi* plaie which hath bene heretofore used there, wherein they are done t' understand that there be many thinges used which tende to the derogation of the Majestie and glorie of God, the prophanation of the sacramentes and the maunteynaunce of superstition and idolatrie, the said Commissioners decreed a lettre to be written and sent to the baylyffe, burgesses and other the inhabitantes of the said towne of Wakefeld that in the said playe no pageant be used or set furthe wherin the

> Ma[t]ye of God the Father, God the Sonne, or God the Holie Ghoste or the administration of either the Sacraments of baptisme or of the Lordes Supper be counterfeyted or represented, or anythinge plaied which tende to the maintenaunce of superstition and idolatrie or which be contrarie to the lawes of God (and) or of the realme.

The Commission, not content with the amendments of the Wakefield Plays on doctrinal issues, for instance the reducing of the seven sacraments to two in *John the Baptist* (197) and the subsequent deletion of the stanza and also of that stanza in *The Resurrection* (328–333) referring to transubstantiation, were obviously bent on establishing such inhibitions which made further performance of the plays impossible. Few plays were left the citizens of Wakefield to perform if no impersonations of God the Father, God the Son, and God the Holy Ghost were permitted, and if performance had been attempted of the few that remained they would, no doubt have been put down on grounds of 'superstition and idolatrie'. The York and Wakefield Cycles may well have shared the same fate as the York Creed and *Pater Noster* Plays, that is, once called in by the Commission they were not released again to the civic authorities. Provided there was but one original, or register [and such from the single surviving manuscripts of the York, Wakefield, and the *Hegge Plays* (*Ludus Coventriae*) seems probable] this was as effective a method of suppression as any. After 1576 we hear of no further attempt to perform the Wakefield Plays. At Chester, however, where the manuscript of the plays remained in the hands of the citizens, despite the contrary instructions received from the Archbishop of York, in 1575 Sir John Savage, Mayor of Chester, permitted their performance. He and his successor were later arrested and taken to London to await their trial. (H. C. Gardiner, *Mysteries' End,* Yale U.P. 1946, 81.) The defiance of the Chester citizens may well have encouraged the Commission to secure in the following year the manuscript of the Wakefield Plays to reinforce their inhibition.

It is then possible that Alexander Nowell, through his association with the Ecclesiastical Commission and through his long and intimate friendship with Grindal, who by May 1576 had been elected Archbishop of Canterbury, acquired the manuscript of the Wakefield Plays and at a later date bequeathed it to his uterine brother, John Towneley, a man who had maintained his Roman Catholicism under conditions of the bitterest adversity, and for whom these plays would have been as a testament of a people's faith in that old world of a less fragmented Christendom.

THE STAGING OF THE WAKEFIELD PLAYS

The reference concerning the suppression of the Wakefield Plays in the records of the Diocesan Court of High Commission at York is one of the very few pieces of external evidence that Wakefield possessed a cycle of mystery plays. The document tells us that the plays were planned for 'Whitsonweke . . . or thereaboutes', that the bailiff and burgesses of Wakefield were responsible for their organization, and that in the plays, as we have noticed earlier as, for instance, in *John the Baptist* and *The Resurrection*, certain references were made to the sacraments which were unacceptable to the reformed church.

The only other external evidence that Wakefield had its own cycle of *Corpus Christi* plays is the Wakefield Burgess Court Rolls which, in Queen Mary's reign (1553–1558), have the following entries:

> PAYNES LAYD BY THE BURGES QWEST AS FOLLOYT. IN ANNO 1554 Itm a payne is layd yt gyles Dolleffe shall brenge In or Causse to be broght ye regenall of *Corpus Xty* play before ys & wytsonday In pane. . . . Itm a payne layde yt ye mesters of ye *Corpus Xti* playe shall Come & mayke thayre a Count before ye gentyllmen burgessus of ye toun before this & may day next. In payne of everye one not so doynge 20s.
>
> PAYNES LAYDE BY THE BURGES ENQUESTS AT THE COURTE KEPTE AT WAKEFELDE NEXTE AFTER THE FEASTE OF SAYNTE MICHAELL THARCHAUNGELL IN THIRDE AND

FOURTE YEARE OF THE REIGNES OF OUR SOVERAIGNE LORDE AND LADYE KINGE PHILYPPE AND QUENE MARYE, 1556

Itm a payne is sett that everye crafte and occupation doo bringe furthe theire pagyaunts of *Corpus Christi* daye as hathe bene heretofore used and to give furthe the speches of the same in after holydayes in payne of everye one not so doynge to forfett xls.

Itm a payne is sett that everye player be redy in his pagyaunt at setled tyme before 5 of ye clocke in ye mornynge in payne of every one not so doynge to forfett vjs. viijd.

Itm a payne is sett yt ye players playe where setled and no where els in payne of no (sic) so doynge to forfett xxs.

Itm a payne is sett yt no man goe armed to disturb ye playe or hinder ye procession in payne of everye one so doynge vjs. viijd.

Itm a payne is sett yt everye man shall leave hys weapon att hys home or at hys ynne in payne of not so doynge vjs. viijd.

Ye summe of ye expens of ye Cherche mester for ye *Corpus Christi* playe xvijs. xd.

Item payd to ye preste	xijd.
Itm payd to ye mynstrells	xxd.
Itm payd to ye mynstrells of *Corpus Christi* playe	iijs. ivd.
Itm payde for ye *Corpus Christi* playe & wrytynge ye spechys for yt	iijs. viijd.
Itm payd for ye Baner for ye mynstrells	vjs. viijd.
Itm payd for ye ryngyng ye same day	vjd.
Itm payd for garlonds on *Corpus Christi* daye	xijd.

It is understandable that the return to the throne of Queen Mary, a Catholic monarch, should have provided the encouragement for the re-staging of the mystery plays which in the reigns of Henry VIII and Edward VI had been discredited through the anti-papal policies of the crown. The loss of the Wakefield plays dealing with the death, assumption, and coronation of the Blessed Virgin, which were probably contained in those twelve leaves, now missing, between *The Ascension* and *The Judgement,* may have coincided with the prohibition in 1548 of the corresponding York plays. H. C. Gardiner writes '. . . the excision of the plays on the Death, Assumption, and Coronation of the Blessed Virgin in York in 1548 shows that, apart from any official decree, the spirit of Protestantism was at work'. (Op. cit., 61.)

The time of year in 1554 when the Burgess Banns (Paynes) were laid down is not clear, but from the records of Norwich and Coventry we gather that the citizens set about preparing for their *Corpus Christi* plays at Easter or soon after. In these Wakefield Banns the phrase 'before this and may day next' may indicate that their meeting took place on or just after May 1st. According to the records of the York Diocesan Court the plays were performed during 'Whitsonweke . . . or thereaboutes'. The phrasing suggests that the plays were not presented on one day only but on two or more days. The Chester cycle, though called the *Corpus Christi* plays, was performed on Monday, Tuesday and Wednesday of Whit week; a procession was held on *Corpus Christi* day followed by a play presented by the clergy. (Glynne Wickham, *Early English Stages,* Routledge and Kegan Paul, 1959, 346–347; E. K. Chambers, *The Mediaeval Stage,* O.U.P. 1903, ii. 138.) The shifting of the plays from *Corpus Christi* day to Whit week took place at Chester as early as 1462; at York in 1569 they were performed on Whit Tuesday, and Norwich and New Romney also record performances of the *Corpus Christi* plays in Whit week.

The 1556 Banns were prepared at the first meeting of the Burgess Court following the feast of St. Michael (29th September, 1555). The frequency of the Burgess Court meetings is unknown, but by the contents of the Banns for 1556 this particular meeting could not have been too distant from the *Corpus Christi* festivities. It seems, from the hint given in the 1554 Banns, that the 1556 meeting was probably on May Day, and that this was the occasion of the Court recording the expense accounts of those responsible for the previous year's *Corpus Christi* play; that of the churchwarden's is one such account. The churchwarden's account must refer to the festivities of the previous year (1555) because all the 1556 Banns concern the preparations for the 1556 procession and play. Surely no accounts would be submitted until after performance, and we gather from the second item in the 1554 Banns that the wardens of the *Corpus Christi* play were allowed almost a year in which to make up their accounts and submit them 'before ye gentyllmen & burgessus' of Wakefield.

The very last item in the churchwarden's account, 'payd for garlonds on *Corpus Christi* day xijd.', seems to prove that the crafts brought forth their pageants 'of *Corpus Christi* daye' on *Corpus Christi* day. But there is more than a strong suggestion in the Banns that the procession and the plays took place on separate days. The crafts are asked to bring forth their pageants on *Corpus Christi* day —and it is for this day the garlands are required—but it is 'in after holydayes' that they are 'to give furthe the speches of the same'. Does this mean that the procession took place on *Corpus Christi* day, a Thursday, and that the following Friday and Saturday were treated as holidays on which the plays were performed? Does the bringing forth of pageants then mean the joining in the *Corpus Christi* day procession which moved from the parish church through the town returning again to the church? Was there singing on the way, and did the pageants at certain stations draw back their curtains to a dumb-show representation of the drama they were to perform 'in after holydayes'? Questions abound; answers supported by circumstantial evidence are scarce. But it is clear that the Banns suggest a separation of the procession and the plays. No man may go armed lest he 'disturb ye playe or hinder ye procession'; there are two separate payments to the minstrels, one of which specifies 'ye mynstrells of *Corpus Christi* playe'; the garlands, the ringing of bells, the minstrels in procession with their very expensive banner, and the officiating priest are indications of the procession. The playbook (regenall), the rewriting of parts, the injunction to play 'where setled and no where els' are obvious references distinguishing the plays from the procession. In York, where before 1426 the plays and the procession were undertaken on the same day, the Proclamation of 1394 introduces a difference of phrasing in its reference to the location of the plays which may be significant: 'And þat men þat brynges furth pagentes þat þai play *at the places* þat is assigned þerfore and nowere elles . . .' The Wakefield 'where setled' is ambiguous; obviously at York there were in 1394 many stations; at Wakefield in 1556 there may have been but one.

If the plays were not performed in Wakefield until after *Corpus Christi* day why should the Burgesses be asking for the master copy of the plays ('ye regenall' or original) to be returned to them before Whit Sunday? To whom did the churchwarden pay 3s. 8d. for the *Corpus Christi* play and for the writing of speeches for it? And who, anyway, was Giles Dolleffe that he should have the manuscript of the plays in his keeping? It may be that Whit Sunday marked the beginning of the preparations for the *Corpus Christi* festival when the master copy was called in to be, if necessary, 'corectyd', and to be the source for the copying out of parts and, possibly, of whole plays. The twelve days between Whit Sunday and *Corpus Christi* day might seem too inadequate a time in which to rehearse the whole cycle, but contemporary evidence points to very little time being spent on rehearsal: 'these pagente shulde be played after breeffe rehearsal' (The Banns of the Chester Plays, 60). The Coventry Smiths held their first rehearsal in Easter week and their second in Whit week. In the Coventry records there are seldom more than two rehearsals before performance; the outstanding exception is the Cappers' record of five rehearsals in 1584 for the new play *The Destruction of Jerusalem.* (Hardin Craig, 'Two Coventry *Corpus Christi* Plays', O.U.P. 1957, 98.) It is significant that this play was especially written for Coventry to replace the *Corpus Christi* cycle. If the craft-guilds who undertook the performance of this play, which from all accounts appears to have been of a similar length to the cycle it was displacing, required only five rehearsals,* it is reasonable to assume that two would have sufficed for the mystery plays which had been in existence for well over a hundred years, and which by annual performance had ingrained their contents in the mind and memory of spectators and players. It was traditional for the players to perform the same parts year after year. Only the rare change of cast would have necessitated a part being copied out. The scribe who undertook to copy parts out from the original, since he was paid by the churchwarden, was most probably one of the parish clergy. At Coventry in 1495 payment is made 'for copyyng of ij knyghts partes and demons', and in 1540 one penny is paid 'for writyng a parte for Herre Person'. (Hardin Craig, op. cit., 89, 94.) Apparently 'Herre Person' had a very small part; on the other hand the Wakefield scribe, if he earned his 3s. 8d., must have had either many parts to copy out or a new play to write. The Coventry Smiths, Cappers, and Mercers, each paid John Green five shillings for copying from the manuscript of *The Destruction of Jerusalem* the particular plays that were the responsibility of their respective companies. The 3s. 8d. in the Wakefield accounts may conceivably have been due, not only to the copying of parts but also for the writing of *The Hanging of Judas*, the only play in the manuscript which is written in a sixteenth-century hand. The scribe, it will be noticed, is paid 'for ye *Corpus Christi* playe & wrytynge ye spechys for yt'. It is obvious from his payment that he was not employed to copy out the whole master copy; he may however have copied out one play which, according to Coventry rates of pay in the sixteenth century, would have earned him about five shillings. But the scribe may also have been paid for 'bearing' the book, which E. K. Chambers (op. cit., ii. 140) interprets as acting as prompter. The Coventry Smiths in 1494 record that they 'paid to John Harryes for berying of the orygynall that day vjd'.

If the Wakefield scribe then had possession of the 'origi-

* Thomas Sharp asserts that 'no less than six rehearsals took place previous to the public exhibition of this new pageant.' (H. Craig, ibid. 90.)

nal' soon after Whit Sunday, when it was handed to him through the agency first of the Burgess Court and then of the churchwarden, what was the 'original' doing in the possession of Gyles Dolleffe until Whit Sunday? The Coventry Cappers in 1584 pay one shilling 'for the kepynge the boke', but it is not clear whether payment is for prompting or for safe-keeping of the play after performance. It is more likely that Gyles Dolleffe had the plays in his safe-keeping and that he was himself one of the wardens or producers. His, too, may have been the task to prepare the text for the 1556 performance and to submit it for approval to both the Burgess Court and the ecclesiastical authorities before rehearsals commenced. We know he was a prominent citizen of Wakefield, a burgess himself, attending the Burgess Court meetings, living in Kirkgate and by trade a draper. [J. W. Walker, *Wakefield, Its History and People,* Wakefield (1934), 133, 359, 380.] His wife's death is recorded in the Archbishop's Registry at York under March 25th, 1604: 'Agnis doliffe late wife of Giles Doliffe buried xxvijth daye' [J. W. Walker, *The Cathedral Church of Wakefield,* Wakefield (1888), 293]. It would be interesting to know a good deal more about Gyles Dolleffe, for he may have been, as Thomas Colclow was for the Coventry Smiths' play (Hardin Craig, TCCCP, 83), a highly paid producer whose contract extended over a number of years.

The 1556 Banns of the Wakefield Burgess Court order every player to be ready in his pageant by 5 a.m. The 1394 York Proclamation decreed 4.30 a.m. as the time when all should assemble. A town-clerk of York, Roger Burton, made two lists of the York Plays, one undated containing fifty-seven plays, and the other dated 1415 containing fifty-one: the unique manuscript contains forty-eight (L. T. Smith, op. cit., xviii). Assuming that only forty-eight plays are to be performed in the day, we have then a drama whose total length is 13,121 lines, the average length of each play being 273 lines. The plays, as tradition has it, were performed at a number of different stations in York, the whole cycle being presented at each successive station. The number of stations varied: in 1417 there were twelve, in 1519 there were fourteen, and in 1554 sixteen (L. T. Smith, ibid. xxxii, xxxiii). The playing of 273 lines, including the music and movement, would take about fifteen minutes. At the first station, allowing five minutes for the time taken between the end of one pageant and the beginning of another, the whole cycle would last for about fifteen hours; if it started at 4.30 a.m. it would finish at 7.30 p.m. At the second station, allowing five minutes for the journey and five minutes for the combined preparation for the journey at the first station and for the playing at the second—and we have to bear in mind that these are horse-drawn pageants making their way in procession not at a gallop—performance would begin at 4.55 a.m. and the cycle would finish at 7.55 p.m. At this rate the first pageant would begin at 9.05 a.m. at the twelfth station and the last would finish just after midnight. It must be recognized that these estimates are almost impracticably conservative, and the pace at which such a schedule could be maintained would put an intolerable strain on both performers and spectators. Yet records indicate that fifty-seven plays were performed at sixteen different stations. The processional street-pageant staging of the York cycle has been too readily accepted without due consideration given to the practical problems. Why, for instance, were *all* the players asked to assemble at 4.30 a.m. if at the first station the cast of *The Judgement Day* had to wait until 7 p.m. until they performed? And were performances continued after nightfall? The records indicate provision for lanterns, cressets, torches, tapers, iron lamps for the pageants, but since an important part of both the York Proclamation and the Wakefield Banns is concerned with minimizing the possibility of rowdiness and rioting, would not the normal curfew be stringently enforced? If not, how can we account for the fact that when Queen Margaret visited Coventry in 1457 she saw at the first station a performance of the whole cycle 'save domes-day, which myght not pleyde for lak of day'? Even for the Queen of England playing could not be permitted after sun-down. If this were true also of York, what happened to the fifty-seven plays at sixteen different stations?

A study of the extant cycles reveals general similarities but individual differences, and this applies to the staging as well as to the text of the plays. In making a statement concerning the staging of the Wakefield Plays, because of the scarcity of local external evidence, recourse is had to analogy. Of those towns whose mystery cycles have survived, York is the nearest to Wakefield. Furthermore the York and Wakefield cycles have certain plays in common, and their Banns also show concern for similar problems: the necessity of an early start; the danger of armed men at the procession or the plays; the need for the players to play 'where setled'. Furthermore the Wakefield cycle is of a comparable length to the York. It contains 12,276 lines; including the lines from the missing twenty-eight leaves the total number would approach 15,000, which would make it longer than the existing York manuscript. Wakefield then shares with York the practical problem, indeed the practical impossibility, of performing the whole cycle at a number of stations in the compass of a day.

At York in 1426, for the first time, the procession and the plays were separated. The plays were performed on *Corpus Christi* day and the procession took place the day following (R. Davies, *Extracts from the Municipal Records of the City of York during the Reigns of Edward IV, Edward V, and Richard III*, 1843). At Chester the three-day performance of the plays took place in Whit week, and the *Corpus Christi* procession in the following week on the day of the festival. At Norwich the plays were performed on the Monday and Tuesday of Whit week, and, as at Chester, the procession followed on *Corpus Christi* day (O. Waterhouse, *Non Cycle Mystery Plays* xxxii). The separation of the plays from the procession arose in the first place from their divergent origins—the liturgical drama predates the *Corpus Christi* procession—and in the second from the extreme difficulty of finding time for both on the same day. In consequence the plays were generally put first and the procession followed later, either the next day, as at York, or the next week, as at Chester and Norwich. Since the York schedule shown earlier for the station-to-station playing is scarcely practicable, the stations at some stage may have been used not as acting areas for performance of the whole cycle, but rather as stopping places during the procession at which each pageant presented its scene in tableau. After 1426 the York procession took place on the day following *Corpus Christi.* If the plays performed on *Corpus Christi* day began at 4.30 a.m. they would have lasted at least until nightfall at just one station, and if the procession began the following day at 4.30 a.m. it would take the most part of the day, if combined with the religious services and the singing, to thread its way from station to station through the town. This is purely conjectural, but all the pageants moving off together does at least make sense of that reference in the Proclamation to all players being ready at 4.30 a.m. It is difficult to believe that the actors in *The Judgement Day* waited from dawn to dusk before their first line was spoken.

A similar problem attends the presentation of the Wakefield cycle. A single performance at a single station is all that is possible in a day, and this makes no allowance for the procession. The procession had to be separated from the performance, and the first item in the 1556 Banns suggests such a separation. The crafts are asked to prepare their pageants for the procession on one day and to perform the plays ('to give furthe the speches of the same in after holydayes') on the days that follow. If this interpretation is correct then Wakefield reversed the order at York, where the procession preceded the plays. From the 1576 record of the Diocesan High Court at York we may gather that under a Protestant monarch, with the prohibition of Catholic festivals, performance of the plays at Wakefield was planned for Whit week.

The thirty-two plays of the Wakefield cycle average 384 lines each. If they were performed processionally they would have taken over fourteen hours at each station. If however they were performed at one station only, and by such an arrangement reducing the time spent in procession and in preparation before and after each performance, then the total playing time would have stretched from dawn to dusk. This playing time may at a later stage have been spread over two or more days. One possible explanation of there being two Shepherds' plays in the cycle is that *The First Shepherds' Play* was performed at the end of the first day's playing and *The Second Shepherds' Play* at the beginning of the second. It is certainly true that if the missing leaves of the manuscript are taken into account the play would be divided into three equal parts if breaks were made after *The First Shepherds' Play* and after *The Crucifixion.* (The Chester Plays which were performed on three successive days broke at *The Adoration of the Magi* and at *Christ's Descent into Hell;* the Ancient Cornish Drama, lasting also three days, broke at *The Execution of Maximilla* and *The Crucifixion.*) But whether the plays were performed on one, two, or three days, there is sufficient evidence to suggest that they were performed in the mid-fifteenth century at least, when the Wakefield Master had written his plays and made so many other revisions in the cycle, in one fixed locality, on a multiple stage, and in the round.

THE ONE FIXED LOCALITY

One particular feature of the manuscript of the Wakefield Plays, which sets it apart from the York and Chester cycles, is the sparse reference to the guilds. The names of four guilds—Barkers (Tanners), Glovers, Litsters (Dyers), and Fishers—are written on the title pages of four of the plays, but in a sixteenth-century hand. The fifteenth-century manuscript would, in its original state, have contained no reference to any of the guilds. In this the Wakefield Plays resemble the *Ludus Coventriae*. The strong case made by Hardin Craig (E.R.D. 239–280) to establish that the *Ludus Coventriae* and the Lincoln *Corpus Christi* plays are one and the same might lead us by analogy, through what we know were the conditions under which the Lincoln Plays were produced, to the organization and staging of the Wakefield cycle.

The *Corpus Christi* plays at Lincoln were the responsibility not of the trade-guilds but of a religious guild, either the *Corpus Christi* guild or that of St. Anne. Every man and woman of Lincoln was a member of the St. Anne guild, paying annually a minimum of four pence each towards the maintenance of their guild. The *Corpus Christi* procession after about 1470 took place not on *Corpus Christi* day but on St. Anne's day (26th July). Hardin Craig maintains that on this occasion the pageants passed in procession through the city but that there was no performance until they reached the Minster. 'All the pageants would be there. It should also be remembered that all the citizens of Lincoln were, failing good excuse, obliged to be there. It may be said also that the only place in the old city of Lincoln where there could be such a concourse of people was the cathedral with its close and the vacant areas around it. It is surely no wild conjecture to suggest that the plays were acted there. One play we know was regularly performed on St. Anne's day in the nave of the cathedral church, that is, the Assumption and Coronation of the Blessed Virgin Mary. And we are not without another plausible piece of evidence that plays were to be seen at the cathedral.' (Hardin Craig, E.R.D., 275.)

One established playing site in a large area, having scaffolds specially erected for the spectators, and with the pageants moving into the spaces left between the scaffolds to complete a circle, or a horse-shoe, tallies exactly with the staging arrangements which must have prevailed for the performance of the *Ludus Coventriae,* and if these were the Lincoln *Corpus Christi* plays performed outside the cathedral church, the upper windows of The Close houses would also have provided excellent viewing.

The *Ludus Coventriae* resembles the Wakefield cycle in that it is an apparent compilation of diverse material, later than either the York or Chester cycles, but showing marked signs, particularly in the Passion sequences, of continuity of action and actors. The forty-eight York plays, both in their brevity and in their insulation, tend to become fragments rather than dramas and this, perhaps, is due to their being broken down to the requirements of the numerous guilds. On the other hand the *Ludus Coventriae* and the Wakefield Plays show an overall design which might well indicate that both the editing—if not the writing—of the plays and their preparation for performance was directed by a single organization, whether religious guild or corporation, and that responsibility for the individual plays was not assumed by the trade-guilds.

In the late fourteenth and early fifteenth century the York guilds may well have numbered over sixty. The very fact that there were at one time fifty-seven plays in the York cycle points to the flourishing guild organizations in that city. On the other hand, Wakefield in 1377, when each person over sixteen had to pay a four-penny Poll Tax, could only muster £4. 15. 8d. 'The list for the town of Wakefield shows a population of 567 over the age of sixteen years, and among the traders are found 2 mercers, 4 walkers or fullers, 5 websters or weavers, 8 tailors, 3 barkers or tanners, 3 drapers, 2 cattle-dealers, 4 wool merchants, 1 franklin or gentleman, 2 butchers, 2 wheelwrights, 1 skinner, 2 ostlers (hotel-keepers), 4 smiths, 1 mason, 1 goldsmith, 1 glover. . . .' (J. W. Walker, *Wakefield, Its History and People,* Wakefield, 1934, 113.) We can assume then that in 1377, apart from beggars, there were approximately two hundred and eighty men living in Wakefield. But there are two hundred and forty-three different parts in the plays, and even if the population of Wakefield had doubled by 1425 it is extremely doubtful whether the plays would have been the responsibility of the guilds. For instance the Barkers would require at least eleven actors to perform *The Creation,* quite apart from the team to prepare the pageant for performance and to assist with properties and general problems of stage management. It may well have been the case that it was not until the sixteenth century that the guilds were large enough in Wakefield to undertake full production responsibilities. How then were they organized in the fifteenth century?

Performed on the trade-guild system existing in York and Chester there is the likelihood that two hundred and forty-three different actors would have been required to fill all the roles, but if the plays were performed on the basis of the *Ludus Coventriae* production, where there was one organization only to cast and direct the plays, far fewer actors would be required for, as so strongly indicated in the *Ludus Coventriae* Passion sequence, the same actors would almost certainly play the parts of the main characters throughout. In the York cycle there are twenty-seven plays in which Jesus appears. We are given to understand that in performance twenty-seven different actors played the part. Wakefield, through sheer lack of man-power, quite apart from any artistic consideration, could not support such a principle of production, at least not until well into the sixteenth century.

Where a religious guild undertook production of the plays, as at Lincoln, it was stoutly supported by the trade-guilds, without whose co-operation no progress could have been made. But the direction of the plays by a religious guild would have followed more closely the traditions laid down by the liturgical drama. The religious guild's close association with the drama still acted in the church is evident in the Lincoln example of the clergy performing *The Assumption* in the nave of the cathedral as the culmination of the St. Anne's day celebrations. Religious plays on the continent were less dependent on the trade-guilds than in England, and their staging derived more directly from liturgical drama.

> 'For most liturgical plays the so-called "simultaneous staging" was the rule. Thus in the Fleury *Conversion of St. Paul,* Jerusalem is on one side of the playing-space, Damascus on the other; in the Daniel plays, the *domus* of the hero to which he retires, the lions' den, and the throne occupied successively by Belshazzar and Darius, all are in view from the opening of the plays. Similarly the various St. Nicholas plays move the chief characters from one part of the playing-space to another, but always to stations visible to the audience from the beginning to the end of the performance. Only in such a highly organized spectacle as the *Presentation of the Virgin* do we find some provision for a distinct change of locale: in that *ordo* the two stages have a symbolical value, the second connoting Mary's reception into the church after her presentation. Processions were, of course, introduced at times to suggest journeys and

therefore scene-shifts, but once the actors had arrived at the playing-space, the stage-setting, however far-flung the action, remained fixed.'

(Grace Frank, *Medieval French Drama,* O.U.P. 1954, 70.)

If at Wakefield the plays were produced by a religious guild, and if shortage of man-power brought about continuity of actors (that is one actor playing Jesus, or Pilate, or Caiaphas, and so on, throughout), it is more than likely that continuity of action took place in a stage-setting which 'remained fixed'.

The Norwich cycle of plays was also the responsibility of a religious guild, St. Luke's, and here, too, although they went forward in procession on *Corpus Christi* day, performance on Whit Monday and Tuesday is considered to have been stationary (O. Waterhouse, op. cit., xxxii). When in 1527 the strain of maintaining the plays became too burdensome for the St. Luke's guild, its members 'petitioned the corporation to divide the responsibility and expense among the various guilds'. A similar shedding of responsibility for certain of the plays might have taken place at Wakefield, and the appearance in the manuscript in a sixteenth-century hand of the four guilds (Tanners, Glovers, Dyers, and Fishers) tends to confirm this.

The evidence suggests that where the religious guilds assumed responsibility for the plays, although the procession remained a regular feature of the *Corpus Christi* festival, the performance was given in a fixed locality. The *Ludus Coventriae* and the *Digby Plays,* none of which was associated with trade-guilds, were also given in fixed localities. Indeed, performance by pageants in procession is the exception rather than the rule, as the stationary presentation of plays at Louth, Reading, Bassingbourne, Chelmsford, Shrewsbury, Cornwall, Aberdeen, and Edinburgh prove. (E. K. Chambers, op. cit., ii. 135.) Furthermore, the staging of the Wakefield Plays calls for a fixed locality in which heaven, paradise, earth, limbo, and hell stand always in the same relationship to each other. Also the variety of levels, the repetition of the journey motif

(*Abraham*, the *Shepherds*, the *Magi*, Mary and Joseph, the road to Emmaus), and the frequent use of a messenger, crossing from one acting area to another (*Pharaoh, Caesar Augustus, Herod*), argue a complexity and spaciousness of staging which would be quite beyond the range of the processional pageant play, performed in the congestion of a medieval street. Above all, the continuity of action which informs the Passion sequence could only be realized through continuity of acting in one fixed locality.

MULTIPLE STAGING

The repeated requirement in the Wakefield Plays for staging a journey with two distinct acting areas, at the beginning and at the end, suggests the use of more than one pageant and lays considerable stress upon the acting area between the pageants. The journey motif is best exemplified in *The Second Shepherds' Play* and *The Offering of the Magi*. In the former Mak's house is opposed to the manger; the shepherds pass from one to the other and even sleep on the green (634) between the two mansions. *The Offering of the Magi* is similarly staged with Herod's palace replacing Mak's house; similarly, too, the kings sleep, but this time in a litter (590), between the two mansions. To suggest that the Wakefield Plays, which contain references to two or more mansions, could nevertheless be staged on the same pageant is to turn a blind eye to the stage directions, whether implicit in the dialogue or explicit in the rubrics, which, for instance, indicate that the three kings make separate entries from different directions on horseback, that their dialogue is continued on horseback for one hundred and forty lines, and that when they set off together to follow the star they are still mounted. On reaching Herod's palace they dismount and remount on leaving (492), but when they discover that the star they have been following is obscured—and this they attribute to Herod's malignant influence—they dismount ['here lyghtys the kyngys of thare horses' (504)] and pray. The star then appears over the mansion of the Nativity, where they go to present their gifts. This riding of horses between mansions would seem to dispose of the possibility that the mansions were placed on the same pageant. The very frequent references to characters riding horses in medieval drama suggest the use of real and not make-believe animals (the York *Flight into Egypt*, Chester *Abraham and Isaac*, the Ancient Cornish Drama, the *Ludus Coventriae Adoration of the Magi*, Caro's horse in *The Castle of Perseverance*, *The Conversion of St. Paul*). But horses were not the only animals used. In the Wakefield *Slaying of Abel*, for example, we have to account for Cain's plough-team of four oxen and four horses (25–43) [A. C. Cawley, *The Wakefield Pageants in the Towneley Cycle*, Manchester U.P. (1958), 91]. There are also Abraham's ass (*Abraham* 117), Pharaoh's chariots (*Pharaoh* 404), the Third Shepherd's mare (*The First Shepherds' Play*, 164), the ass on which Mary rides (*The Flight*, 151), and the Centurion's horse (*The Resurrection*, 44). It is certainly indisputable from the Norwich and Coventry records that live animals were used, at least for the drawing of the pageant, and by the extraordinary detail that was lavished on their decoration they may well have been used in the performance of the actual plays. There is a Canterbury record that 'the steeds of the Magi were made of hoops and laths and painted canvas' (E. K. Chambers, op. cit., ii. 142), but unfortunately the play is not extant. The probability is that where riding is indicated in the stage directions real horses were used. Given the acting area it would have been easier in the Middle Ages to have used a real horse rather than one made of hoops, laths, and canvas. It is interesting to note that when the animal is played by actors, as in the case of the ass in the Chester *Balaam and Balak*, it is specifically where the beast has a speaking part (Karl Young, *The Drama of the Medieval Church*, O.U.P. 1933, ii. 152).

The most weighty evidence, however, for the multiple staging of the Wakefield Plays lies in the Passion sequence, which sweeps on in continuous action from play to play and from stage to stage. For instance, *The Conspiracy*, the first play of this sequence, if divided into distinct acting areas would be represented as follows:

1. Pilate's hall (1–313)
2. Jesus and his disciples (314–333)
3. John and Peter on their way to Jerusalem, and
4. Their meeting with Paterfamilias outside his house (334–345)
5. The chamber of the Last Supper (strewn with rushes), the scene of the washing of feet (346–491)
6. The two levels of Olivet, one where Jesus prays and the other where the disciples sleep (492–599)
7. During which scene God appears in heaven's tower (528–555)
8. Pilate's hall (560–651)
9. From Olivet to the place of capture (652–707)
10. Pilate's hall (708–747)
11. Malcus and the soldiers lead Jesus to Caiaphas' hall (748–755).

This play is probably the combination of two plays, *The Conspiracy* and *The Capture,* and such a consideration underlines the unity of effect which the reviser of the Passion sequence, if not of the whole cycle, was striving to achieve. This unity could not be achieved by allowing one acting area to be used for a variety of scenes: Pilate's hall must be reserved exclusively for the scenes in which Pilate appears; God, as throughout the cycle, appears from heaven's tower; Mount Olivet is the hill on which Jesus prays, and below which his disciples sleep; the chamber strewn with rushes, set with table and benches to seat Jesus and the twelve disciples, is also most certainly a fixture throughout this play. The common area then appears to be the ground between this chamber and the other mansions, or stations; and there is every indication dramatically that the capture is staged on ground level midway between Mount Olivet and Pilate's hall.

In reconstructing the staging of *The Conspiracy* the picture that is formed is of four pageants set well apart representing heaven, Pilate's hall, Mount Olivet, and the chamber of The Last Supper, and whatever action does not take place on these pageants, such as the very first passage, in which Jesus dispatches John and Peter to find a room for the paschal feast, and the capture itself, takes place on the ground between the pageants. The pageants are placed at points on the circumference of circle so that the action between the pageants takes place in the centre of the circle. The spectators whether on raked scaffolds or thronging on the ground, fill the gaps on the circumference between the pageants.

IN THE ROUND

The manuscript of the Cornish Plays [*The Ancient Cornish Drama*, edited by Edwin Norris, O.U.P. (1859)] preserves the record of a performance in the round in which the stations in the three parts of the drama, performed on successive days, are designated as follows:

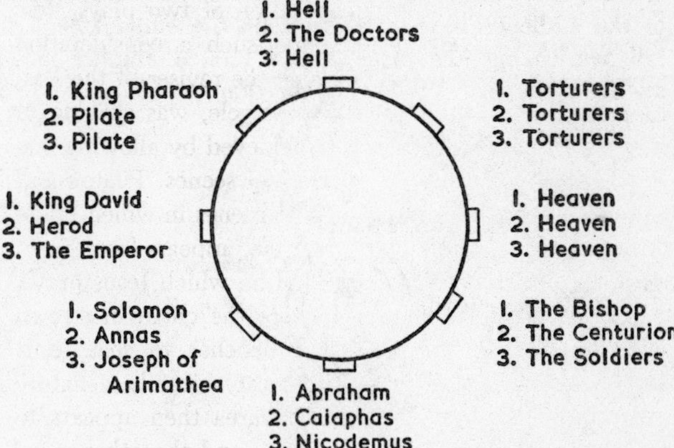

The stage directions refer frequently to the 'platea', 'the place', the central area separating the pageants, where a great deal of the action takes place and where on occasion an additional mansion is established, as for instance the prison in *The Resurrection* in which Nicodemus and Joseph of Arimathea are confined. The plays were performed in one of the Cornish amphitheatres which accommodated the audience on the tiered seats leading down to 'the place'. The audience and the established mansions, as shown in the diagram, were placed alternately on the circumference of the amphitheatre.

Another indisputable record of medieval drama in the round is the ground plan which appears in the manuscript of *The Castle of Perseverance,* a morality play of about 1425. Richard Southern in a detailed examination of the staging of this play (*The Medieval Theatre in the Round,* Faber and Faber, 1957) reconstructs the original use of the main acting areas which were the mansions on the circumference and 'the place' in the centre. We are given to understand that *The Castle of Perseverance* was not performed in an already established amphitheatre, but that such a theatre had to be made—an obscure procedure—but the event is clear. The castle stands on stilts in the centre of 'the place' with a bed beneath its long legs; there are five mansions or scaffolds on the circumference; part of the audience have fixed seats on the embankment or hill overlooking 'the place' and a limited number move about in 'the place' following the drama from scaffold to scaffold.

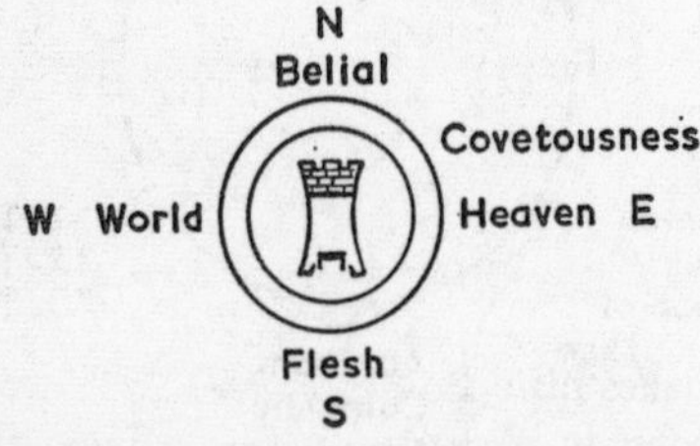

On the original plan it is the south scaffold which appears at the top but it will be more readily seen from the above diagram that the relationship of heaven to hell (east and north) corresponds exactly with that found in the Cornish Plays. Also omitted from the diagram are a great many details relative to the staging of *The Castle of Perseverance*. For example, a number of stewards (stytelerys) are required to keep the audience in order in 'the place', and to clear the way in front of the main characters when they have to cross from one scaffold to another.

Some of the plays in the Digby manuscript (*The Digby Mysteries,* edited by F. J. Furnivall, N. Trübner and Co. 1882) also provide strong evidence of their having been performed in the round. In *Herod's Killing of the Children* the knights and Watkin walking about 'the place' (232), the killing of the children in 'the place', the acting area frequently shifting to localities beyond 'the place', and the concluding dance of the virgins, suggest multiple staging in the round. 'The place' is also prominently used in *The Conversion of St. Paul,* where Saul rides with his servants 'about the place and out of the place' (140); the scaffolds of heaven (182), hell (411), Damascus (210), and Jerusalem (14) stand on the circumference of 'the place'. *Mary Magdalene,* which in itself comprises a miniature cycle, is generally accepted as having been played in the round, and J. Q. Adams has reconstructed the arrangement of the pageants around 'the place' (*Chief Pre-Shakespearean Dramas,* Boston, 1924).

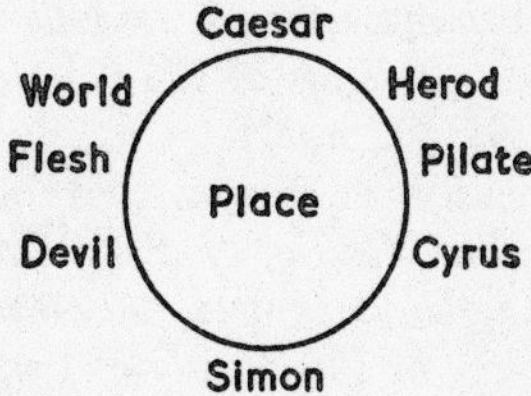

The devil makes his first entry (357) on a two-tier pageant which is probably pushed into and around 'the place' before being established in its stationary position for the rest of the play: 'Here xal entyr þe prynse of dylles In a stage, and Helle ondyr-neth þat stage. . . .' Heaven is also a two-tier pageant with a curtained upper stage (1348): 'her xall hevyne opyne and Iesus xall shew hymself'. The ship which features so regularly in the play is extremely mobile, shaped as a castle, and drawn or pushed about 'the place', but occupying no fixed station.

Is there any evidence to suggest that any of the four extant English *Corpus Christi* cycles were, as the Cornish Plays, *Mary Magdalene,* or *The Castle of Perseverance,* also played in the round? The *Ludus Coventriae* and *The Castle of Perseverance* have much in common: they share the same East Midland dialect; they are both strongly associated with Lincoln; they both contain analogous passages on an unusual subject in English medieval drama, *The Parliament in Heaven;* moreover the thirteen-line introductory stanzas of both plays, spoken by the banner-bearers (*vexillatores*), leave the name of the town, where the play is to take place, blank. This suggests that performances were given at a variety of towns in the neighbourhood and that the appropriate town was inserted as occasion demanded. This is consistent with the practice elsewhere. The Chelmsford *Corpus Christi* plays, for instance, were performed in a 'pightell', or enclosure, but were also performed at Malden and Braintree (E. K. Chambers, op. cit., ii. 122), and of Kent Hardin Craig writes 'There was much dramatic activity in that part of England, and the first interchange of performances among towns suggests that these towns must have had stationary stages and not the pageants of the *Corpus Christi* cycles'. (Hardin Craig, E.R.D., 142.)

It is the similarity of staging that brings the *Ludus Coventriae* and *The Castle of Perseverance* closest together. In the *Ludus Coventriae Adoration of the Magi* Herod, as does Caro of *The Castle of Perseverance,* enters on horseback. He retires to his pageant to dress himself more gorgeously and when he sits on his throne he commands his menials below him. His height above 'the place' is again emphasized when, after the children have been massacred, he congratulates the murderers:

wele have ȝe wrought
my ffo is sought
to deth is he brought
now come up to me.

(*Ludus Coventriae, The Massacre of the Innocents,* 125–128)

All initial entries in this play appear to be mounted: Herod, his dukes, and the three kings. The riding is stressed by stage directions and dialogue:

> Heyl be ȝe kyngys tweyne
> Fferre rydyng out of ȝour regne.
> (*The Adoration of the Magi*, 21–22)

The kings ride along a street or across a market square:

> Sere kyng in trone
> here comyth a-none
> by strete and stone
> kyngys thre. (*Ibid.* 135–138)

In this play the relationship of the scaffold to 'the place' corresponds to the use of these areas in both *The Castle of Perseverance* and in the Wakefield Plays. *The Trial of Joseph and Mary* (*Ludus Coventriae*) is preceded by the Summoner who undertakes the identical task of the stewards (stytelerys) of *The Castle of Perseverance*, clearing a path in 'the place' for the more important characters:

> A-voyd Serys And lete my lorde þe buschop come
> And syt in þe courte þe lawes ffor to doo
> And I xal gon in þis place them for to somowne
> tho þat ben in my book. . . .
> (*Prologue of the Summoner*, 1–3)

The two Passion plays of the *Ludus Coventriae*, in so many ways resembling the Wakefield Passion sequence, abound with references to the scaffolds of Annas and Caiaphas, to the castle representing Jerusalem, and to Mount Olivet. Particularly interesting is the use of an oratory in the centre of 'the place' which serves as a counsel house for the Jews. Setting a mansion in the middle of 'the place' corresponds to the use of the bed and the castle in *The Castle of Perseverance*. When not the focus of the action the curtains round the oratory are closed; when the action returns to the oratory they are opened:

'here Crist enteryth in-to þe hous with his disciplis and ete þe paschal lomb and in þe mene tyme þe cownsel hous beforn-seyd xal sodenly onclose shewyng þe buschopys prestys and jewgys syttyng in here Astat lyche as it were A convocacyone'

(*Ludus Coventriae, The First Passion Play,* 397.)

Similarly there are curtains round the pageant on which the Last Supper is played:

'Here The Buschopys partyn in þe place and eche of hem takyn here leve be contenawns resortyng eche man to his place with here meny to make redy to take cryst and þan xal þe place þer cryst is in xal sodeynly unclose rownd Abowtyn shewyng cryst syttyng at þe table and his dyscypulys eche in ere degre . . .'

(*Ibid.* 669.)

The scene is set for the capture of Jesus. The bishops and their men have dispersed to their various pageants on the circumference of 'the place', and when Jesus and his disciples re-enter 'the place' his enemies converge on him from all sides, 'weyl be-seen in white Arneys and breganderys (body armour) and some dysgysed in odyr garmentys with swerdys gleyvys and other straunge wepone as cressettys with feyr and lanternys and torchis lyth (lit) and judas formest of Al conveyng hem to jhesu be contenawns (signs)'

(*Ibid.* 972.)

The same system of staging is maintained in *The Second Passion Play* which begins with the following stage direction:

'What tyme þat processyon is enteryd in to þe place and þe herowdys takyn his schaffalde. and pylat and annas and cayphas here schaffaldys Also þan come þer An exposytour in doctorys wede þus seyng'

and goes on to clinch the case for performance in the round with that superb entry of the news-boy:

'here xal A massanger com in-to þe place rennyng and criyng Tydyngys tydyngys . and so rownd Abowth

þe place . jhesus of nazareth is take . Jhesus of nazareth is take . . .'
(*Ludus Coventriae, The Second Passion Play,* 69.)

The *Ludus Coventriae,* then, resembles *The Castle of Perseverance* in that it was presented as a stationary performance in the round in or near Lincoln during at least the middle part of the fifteenth century. Its use of scaffolds and 'the place' tallies in every way with the staging arrangements of the morality play. An essential difference, of course, is that whereas the *Ludus Coventriae* or Lincoln cycle was organized and performed in the main by members of a religious guild to celebrate a religious festival, *The Castle of Perseverance* was performed by a touring company of professional actors. The morality play is some 3,800 lines long and, although there may have been a fair amount of doubling, the main parts, such as Humanum Genus, Belial, and Covetousness, would have been played by the same actors throughout. Would this principle of casting have been so different in the *Ludus Coventriae*? At York, where the average length of each play is 273 lines, we assume from the records that twenty-seven different actors played the part of Jesus in the twenty-seven different plays in which the part occurs. But in the *Ludus Coventriae* the two *Passion* plays, which as far as we know were never played consecutively in the same year, each exceeds 1,000 lines, and their performance by the same group of actors would obviously achieve greater unity of dramatic effect. Indeed, it is difficult to believe how the York fragmentation of the great cycle was ever tolerated. Certainly, an audience used to the continuity of playing of the *Ludus Coventriae* and of *The Castle of Perseverance* would have taken hard the York division of plays, parts, and playing space.

Despite the many affinities of the York and Wakefield cycles, fundamental disparities preclude our assuming identical staging conditions. The Wakefield Plays are fewer but on average appreciably longer; their organization and direction were by a religious guild or the town corporation at least until the sixteenth century; and there is very strong evidence, especially in the *Passion* sequence, of continuity of playing: *The Conspiracy* runs straight into *The Buffeting, The Buffeting* into *The Scourging, The Scourging* into *The Crucifixion,* and *The Crucifixion* into *The Talents*. It is significant, too, that in this sequence which so clearly suggests a multiple stage, set in a circle round 'the place', none of the plays has any close association with those of York.

On the other hand, it is demonstrably on matters of staging that the Wakefield cycle reveals its affinities to the *Ludus Coventriae*. The fixed locality and the multiple stage have already been discussed as points of resemblance between the two cycles. This resemblance extends to performance in the round. Although the main setting for the *Ludus Coventriae* is stationary throughout there are two occasions on which pageants are moved into 'the place', in *Noah* (197) and in *The Trial of Joseph and Mary* (124). Such entries are not uncommon in plays performed in the round and in the Digby *Mary Magdalene* the ship on wheels and hell pageant make similar appearances. The Wakefield *Noah* also demands the drawing into 'the place' of a ship on wheels. The acting areas required are heaven for God, Noah's home, a station ('the place') beneath heaven where Noah stands to hear God's commands, and the ark itself. The producer's particular problem is that Noah has to build his ark in the full view of the audience in the course of a thirty-six line soliloquy. The ark has sail, mast, helm, and castle, a door, a window and three chambers. When Noah has finished building his ark he tries to persuade his wife to come aboard, but she persists in spinning on her hill (337). The 'hill' throughout the Wakefield Plays is referred to as the lowest level on the pageant above 'the place'. Mrs. Noah would scarcely refer to her position as 'this hill' if the ark were being constructed on the same pageant above where she was sitting. The following staging is suggested: Noah speaks to God beneath heaven's tower and God answers him giving him precise instructions for the building of the ark; Noah returns home, crossing 'the place' to his own pageant, where the first fight with his wife takes place; he then collects his tools and leaves the pageant (245) and draws into 'the place' a platform on wheels containing the ark in prefabricated sections, which Noah erects as he soliloquizes (253–288), commenting on each section of the ark as he puts it in position; he then returns home to fetch his family; Noah's wife inspects the ark; and returns to her hill in disgust; another fight ensues before all are aboard the ark, and after the waters have abated the family disembark and stand in 'the place' ('on this greyn' 534), and finally in procession lead their ark out of 'the place'.

The bringing of a pageant into 'the place' gives great flexibility to the movement of a production and echoes not only the instances quoted above from the *Ludus Coventriae* and *Mary Magdalene* but also the use of the oratory in the *Ludus Coventriae First Passion Play*. It will further be recalled that in *The Castle of Perseverance* the middle of 'the place' is occupied by the castle itself beneath which is a bed. The rubrics written on the ground plan suggest that the most important parts of the action of the play are to be seen in this area. An unusual detail in the Wakefield *Offering of the Magi* is the bed or litter in which the three kings sleep (590); its central position, between Herod's pageant and the Nativity pageant, tallies also with the placing of the bed of Ananias in the Fleury *Conversion of St. Paul* (Grace Frank, op. cit., 46) which is set in 'the place' between the main acting scaffolds.

The frequency of the journey motif is a characteristic of drama in the round, and the Wakefield Plays and the *Ludus Coventriae* share this characteristic to a high degree: *The Slaying of Abel, Abraham,* the two *Shepherds' Plays, The Offering of the Magi, The Flight, The Peregrini,* are a few of the many Wakefield Plays in which the action is dependent upon journeying. Such plays are much more satisfactorily staged in the round, and the whole Passion sequence gains greatly in dramatic power if 'the place' is used for the capture of Christ and for the procession of the cross in *The Scourging* and *The Crucifixion,* culminating in the climb (out of 'the place' and on to the pageant) to Mount Calvary.

RECONSTRUCTION

An attempt at reconstructing the staging of the Wakefield Plays, however controversial, is worth while. For the first time it takes into account the combined evidence of the Wakefield Burgess Court Banns of 1554 and 1556, the York Diocesan Court records of 1576, internal evidence from the plays themselves, and argument by analogy with other medieval plays performed in the round. The most uncertain feature of such a reconstruction is not how the plays were performed but when they were performed. Evidence points equally to either Whit week or *Corpus Christi* week. The probability is that the plays were not performed in Whit week until after Queen Mary's death in 1558, and also that they were performed not all on one day but on three.

In Wakefield then in the mid-fifteenth century, soon after dawn on *Corpus Christi* day, between twenty and thirty pageants, gaily painted and garlanded with flowers, set out on the *Corpus Christi* procession. The organization for the procession has been carried out by one of the religious guilds, that of St. Christopher or St. George. The trade guilds have given their full co-operation and now in their several liveries join the procession, each guild keeping close to the pageant with which it is most closely associated. Every citizen joins in the procession including all the clergy and the minstrels who are specially paid for their playing and singing on this occasion. The whole procession moves first to the parish church where at the service the Host of the Lord is raised and then carried out of the church, with the procession following, to various stations in the town. When the pageants reach these stations they reveal in dumb-show the climax of the play which they will perform in full on the days that follow. It is these tableaux that we see represented in all kinds of medieval iconography, in which, as for instance with the capture of Christ in the garden, so many incidents of the play are compressed within the one scene: the kiss of Judas, the soldiers seizing Christ, Peter striking off Malcus' ear, and Christ healing the wound. There are not as many pageants in the procession as there are plays in performance because many of the pageants are shared, as at Chester, by different plays. Some pageants therefore display two or more tableaux. But the whole procession winds on through the town until at last it returns to the parish church—a full day's journey.

The plays are performed on the three days that follow: the first day ends with *The First Shepherds' Play;* the second day begins with *The Second Shepherds' Play* and ends with *The Crucifixion;* the third day, which includes the (now missing) plays of Pentecost and of the death, assumption, and coronation of the Virgin, ends with *The Judgement*. The presentation takes place on the common, in the market place, or in the quarry, but each year there is only one place of performance, and here the audience gathers from far and near to secure a seat in the raked, circular auditorium that surrounds 'the place'. There are four or five gaps in the circle of the audience's scaffolds into which will be led the pageants. Heaven and hell are brought into position first and are left in place throughout the performance, heaven to the east and hell to the north. These two pageants are particularly more elaborate in design than the others. They are both two-tiered. On heaven's battlements God, the angels and the angelic choir appear. Beneath heaven's tower is paradise, and above it is the deep roof of the pageant which contains the winches, rope, and windlass, the lowering equipment required for such special effects as the ascension. It is on hell's tower that the devils set the watches on the walls [*The Deliverance* (121)] and beneath hell's tower that limbo is located. Close to limbo are the gaping jaws of hell through which the actors pass by trap-door to the ground level beneath the pageant. The hell pageant resembles that found in the *Ludus Coventriae*, *The Castle of Perseverance*, and *Mary Magdalene*. Access from the hell pageant to 'the place' is made through the jaws of hell; in the case of the other pageants it is made by sets of steps or ladders, such as we see in Fouquet's mid-fifteenth-century painting of the Martyrdom of St. Apollonia (*Le Livre d'heures d'Etienne Chevalier, Musée Condé, Chantilly*).

Although the pageants of heaven and hell are fixtures throughout the performance the other pageants are moved into place in the course of the cycle. For instance, the cycle begins with the pageants of *The Slaying of Abel* and *Noah* already in position, but during *Noah* the platform on which the ark is to be constructed is wheeled into the middle of 'the place', and by the time of the Nativity plays the earlier pageants have been replaced by those of the Shepherds or the Magi. During the latter play the litter for the Magi is located in the centre of 'the place'. During the Passion sequence the maximum number of pageants are in use simultaneously. Throughout a restricted number of the audience is permitted to sit or stand in 'the place'.

The players themselves are members of the religious guild which organizes and produces the play. Altogether there are about a hundred in the cast and there is a fair amount of doubling, but the main characters are played by the same actors throughout the cycle. If the itinerant professional players are available, and the funds run to it, they may take the main parts, as they do for other local religious festivals (Glynne Wickham, *Early English Stages*, Appendix C, 332–339). At the end of the third day's performance the *Te Deum* following the last words of *The Judgement* is sung by amateur and professional, by players and spectators, laymen and clergy, as a communal affirmation of faith in God and in that structured, hierarchical universe revealed in their cycle of mystery plays.

MUSIC

The liturgical roots of the mystery plays are clearly seen in the persistence of the identical church music at the various dramatic climaxes: God creates the world, and the angels sing the *Te Deum;* Gabriel hails Mary at the Annunciation; the *Gloria* is sung by the angel to the shepherds; the souls delivered from hell burst into a joyful *Salvator Mundi;* as Christ rises from the tomb the two angels sing *Christus Resurgens.* The Latin words of the liturgical music also persist into the sixteenth-century performances of the plays and the music itself, when it records a divine intervention, is played and sung by the angelic choir. The vernacular songs, such as the shepherds' 'As I rode out' or the lament of the Bethlehem mothers, 'Lully, lulla' (The Coventry Shearmen and Taylors' Play), are a later development.

A wide variety of instruments was used in liturgical drama, and records at Coventry, Lincoln, and Beverley indicate that an even greater variety was introduced for the performance of the mystery plays. The recent production by the New York Pro Musica of the thirteenth-century *The Play of Daniel* has stressed the range and effectiveness of medieval instrumentation. Noah Greenberg, the musical director of that production, has listed some of the medieval instruments and their possible modern substitutes:

straight trumpet	trumpet in C
rebec	oboe
recorders (soprano and sopranino)	soprano recorder
bowed vielle	viola
bell carillon	bell carillon or chimes
hand bells	hand bells
psaltery	zither or auto harp (without dampers)
portative organ	soprano recorder (or modern organ)
minstrel's harp	guitar

(*The Play of Daniel,* edited by Noah Greenberg, O.U.P., 1959.)

A particular feature of this production was the identification of each character with particular sounds: 'the Queen with finger cymbals, Darius with small cymbals, the envious counselors with sleigh bells. . . .' This, in a more general way, is true of the mystery plays: God and the angels are characterized by harmony; Satan and his rout by cacophony. In *The Judgement,* as the trump of doom issues intermittently from heaven's battlements, Tutivillus boasts of his own signature tune, and the mangled Latin that follows is but a verbal echo of his discordant blast:

Mi name is tutiuillus,
my horne is blawen;
ffragmina verborum tutiullus colligit horum,
Belzabub algorum belial belium doliorum.
(*The Judgement*, 249–250.)

Such a horn-blowing devil in hell's tower is included among Dr. W. L. Hildburgh's illustrations for his 'English Alabaster Carvings as Records of the Medieval Religious Drama' (*Archaeologia* 1949).

The main use of the instruments would be to accompany the singing, the ceremonial processions, and the entries, such as that of Herod or Pharaoh. In the *Ludus Coventriae Massacre of the Innocents,* for example, even the entry of a banquet dish is the occasion for a fanfare:

SENESCALLUS. now blowe up mynstrall with all ȝour
might þe servyse comyth in sone.
(153–154)

And at the grand climax of this play when Herod, swollen with pride, on the brink of an orgiastic celebration at the supposed slaughter of Christ, is touched by the finger of Death and received with his henchmen into the jaws of hell, the fanfare sounds his last farewell:

HEROD. Amonges all þat grett rowthe
he is ded I have no dowte
þerfore menstrell rownd a-bowte
blowe up a mery fytt. (229–232)

(*Hic dum buccinant mors interficiat herodem et duos milites subito et diabolus recipiat eos.*)

On the other hand, it is the ringing of bells that attend the Nativity and the Resurrection.

Who were the Wakefield minstrels who were paid 3s. 4d. for their part in the *Corpus Christi* plays in 1556? They were certainly a trained group of musicians, singers and instrumentalists, who could sing and play polyphonic music from memory; and since it was the churchwarden who was responsible for paying them, there can be little doubt of their close connection with the Wakefield Parish Church. They would represent a range of voices, men and boys together. The boys would have not only sung in the angel choir, but most probably would have spoken the angels' parts. One of the grand processional scenes in the York plays is Christ's entry into Jerusalem. A choir of boys, walking in front of the procession, as they sing lead Christ to the gates of the city:

FIRST BURGHER. Go we þan with processione
To mete þat comely as vs awe,
With myghtfull songes her on a rawe,
Our childir schall
Go synge before, þat men may knawe
To þis graunte we all.

(The York Plays, *The Entry into Jerusalem,* 260–266.)

It is evident from Roger Burton's 1415 list and synopsis of the York cycle that the part of the angel at the Resurrection was played by a boy:

'. . . *Juvenis sedens ad sepulcrum indutus albo, loquens mulieribus.*'

('York Plays', L. T. Smith, xxvi.)

Both angelic choir and angelic instruments are located in heaven's tower, which, when performances of religious drama left the precincts of the church, fulfilled largely the dramatic and ceremonial function that had previously been allotted to the '*pulpitum*', or rood screen loft.

The Wakefield Plays are not rich in reference to the playing or singing of music. The stage directions are appreciably less expansive than in the other cycles. Therefore in suggesting appropriate music for the plays recourse is had, at comparable stages of the drama, to information derived from the other cycles. For instance, Noah's psalm (432) is suggested by the singing included in the Chester play of *Noah,* the shepherds' song, 'As I Rode Out', and the Bethlehem women's lament, 'Lully lulla', are derived from the Coventry Shearmen and Taylors' Play, and the singing as Christ goes to sit in Judgement (88) is taken from York's *The Judgement Day* (216).

PLAY	MUSIC	SOURCE
The Creation	Creator of the Stars of Night	Plainsong
	Te Deum (18), Sanctus (60)	"
Noah	Psalm (432)	"
Abraham		
Pharaoh	Psalm 106 (431)	"
The Prophets	David sings as he plays his harp (109–156)	"
The Annunciation	Qui Natus Est (76)	Fayrfax Series
	Angelus ad Virginem (373)	English Gothic Music
The Salutation	Ave Regina	Fayrfax Series
The First Shepherds' Play	Gloria in excelsis (295)	Dunstable
	The Shepherds' imitation (430)	
	Nowell Sing We (502)	Medieval Carols
The Second Shepherds' Play	'As I Rode Out' (189)	Coventry Play
	Gloria (637)	Dunstable
	Shepherds' imitation (664)	
	Now Make We Merthe (754)	Medieval Carols
The Adoration of the Magi	Sanctus (594)	Roy Henry
The Flight into Egypt		
Herod the Great	Lully, Lulla (324)	Oxford Carols
John the Baptist	Benedictus (200)	Plainsong
The Crucifixion	Faithful Cross (666)	"

The Deliverance of Souls	Salvator Mundi (44)	Fauxbourdon
	Te Deum (404)	Plainsong
The Resurrection	Christus Resurgens (225)	Fauxbourdon
The Judgement	Salvator Mundi (88)	"
	Dies Irae played line by line (531–612) on the trombone	Plainsong
	Alleluia psallat (612)	English Gothic Music
	Gloria (612)	Dunstable
	Te Deum (620)	Plainsong

This list does not contain detailed directions concerning the fanfares. Furthermore the list does not imply that in each case the whole psalm, anthem, or hymn is to be sung. This practice would impede rather than enhance the drama.

Generally speaking the music here suggested is on the one hand the elaborate polyphonic music of the fourteenth and fifteenth centuries, which is more appropriate for the angelic choir, and on the other the plainsong hymns more suitable for a crowd response. The instrumentalists, a group of woodwind and brass, might play from *Six Instrumental Pieces for Wind Instruments* by H. Isaac *c.* 1500 (*Hortus Musicus* 29). Sources for the choral music are as follows:

The plainsong hymns will be found in 'Songs of Syon', edited by G. R. Woodward. Schott 1923.

Angelus ad Virginem } English Gothic Music Series
Alleluia psallat } Schott 1943

Gloria Musica Britannica, Vol. viii (Dunstable) edited by M. F. Bukofzer (Stainer and Bell 1953).

Old Hall MS Volume III—Plainsong and Medieval Music Society Publications 1933–1938.

Ave Regina Qui Natus Est	published in full in the Fayrfax Series of Early English Music. Stainer and Bell, edited A. T. Batts.
Lully, Lulla	Coventry Carol. The Oxford Book of Carols, reprinted 1956.
Nowell Sing We Now Make We Merthe	Musica Britannica, Vol. iv (Medieval Carols), edited by John Stevens. Stainer and Bell 1952.

THE PRESENT VERSION

The order of plays in this acting edition differs from that found in the manuscript and reproduced in George England's edition of 1897. *The Prophets* follows, instead of preceding, *Pharaoh;* and *Lazarus* and *The Hanging of Judas,* instead of following *The Judgement,* are returned to their usual places in the cycle, the former, as the only play representing Christ's ministry, following *John the Baptist,* and the latter following *The Scourging.* In performance *The Hanging of Judas,* since it is an incomplete, undramatic monologue, written at a much later date than the rest of the cycle, must be omitted, and the continuity of playing maintained between *The Scourging* and *The Crucifixion.*

Two plays, *The Creation* and *Abraham,* incomplete in the manuscript, have been completed in this edition with borrowings from the York play of *Man's Disobedience and Fall from Eden* and from the Brome play of *Abraham and Isaac* respectively. *The Creation* cries out for completion, and dramatically it seemed feeble to launch this great cycle with a fragment. *Abraham,* prefiguring God's sacrifice of his Son, is strategically placed in the cycle, and requires but a few borrowed lines to make it presentable. These are the only two instances of borrowing. The other incomplete plays in the cycle are *Isaac, The Prophets, The Purification of Mary, The Doctors, The Ascension,* and *The Judgement. Isaac* is too fragmentary for dramatic presentation. The other plays, some without heads and others without tails, have sufficient dramatic form to warrant presentation.

This version is complete and tallies line for line with the original. The principles underlying it are that it should be directed more towards the audience than the reader, that it should be generally intelligible without making any prerequisite demands on audience or reader of a knowledge of Middle English, and that the metrical and stanzaic structure, even where there was roughness and irregularity, should be retained. The obligation of, at times, maintaining complicated rhyme schemes has resulted in certain inconsistencies: 'thou', 'ye', 'you' are sometimes, as in the original, used indiscriminately; the Second Person Singular of the verb after 'thou' mostly appears without a final 't', and such was the fifteenth-century Yorkshire practice, but 'thou has' and 'thou shall' may sound strange to southern ears. 'Ay' (as in 'say') throughout carries the meaning of 'for ever', and 'aye' (as in 'eye') means 'yes'.

The stage directions which, in the original, are written mostly in Latin are here translated and many more added.

THE NOTES

The Notes are primarily for the producer. Their emphasis however is not so much on how the plays might be performed today, but rather through the illustration of guild accounts, iconography, and the collateral drama, on how they were performed in the Middle Ages.

Both in the Notes and the Introduction the *Ludus Coventriae* figures prominently. This is such a misleading title that I have hesitated long before adopting it. The alternatives, the Lincoln Plays, the Hegge Plays, the N-town Plays, might still bewilder the student who, if anxious to put his hand on the text of the plays, can do so only by consulting his library catalogue under *Ludus Coventriae*, K. S. Block, O.U.P., 1922.

Part One

THE FIRST PLAY

The Creation

GOD	1ST GOOD ANGEL
CHERUBIM	2ND GOOD ANGEL
LUCIFER	1ST DEVIL
1ST BAD ANGEL	2ND DEVIL
2ND BAD ANGEL	ADAM
	EVE

[GOD *sits upon his throne. His angels stand either side of him.*

GOD *Ego sum alpha et omega,*
I am the first, the last also,
One god in majesty;
Marvellous of might most,
Father, Son and Holy Ghost,
One god in trinity.

I am without beginning,
My godhead hath no ending,
And thus shall keep my throne;
One god in persons three,
Which may never parted be,
For I am God alone.

All manner of things is in my thought,
Without my power there may be nought,
All things are in my sight;
It shall be done after my will,
What I have planned I shall fulfil
And maintain with my might.

At the beginning of our deed
Make we heaven and earth with speed,
And fair lights for to see,

For it is good to be so;
Darkness from light we part in two,
In time to serve and be.

Darkness we shall call the night,
And the brightness be named light,
It shall be as I say;
After my will forth is brought,
Even and morn both are they wrought,
And thus is made a day.

Amidst the water we assent
Now be made the firmament,
Parted be they as is reckoned,
Be water from the land withdrawn,
Bring to pass both even and morn,
This day which is the second.

The waters that so wide have spread,
Be gathered together in one stead,
That dry the earth may seem;
Thereafter dry the earth shall be,
The waters shall I call the sea;
This work well done I deem.

Herbs out of the earth shall spring,
Trees shall flourish and fruit forth bring,
Of each kind at my word.
According to my will, so be
The even and morn at my decree
Of this day that is third.

Sun and moon set in the heaven,
With the stars and planets seven,
To stand in their degree.
The sun to serve the day with light,
The moon to minister at night;
The fourth day shall this be.

The fish shall dwell within the deep,
The earth shall nourish all beasts that creep,
That fly or stalk their way.

Multiply on earth, and be
Blessed abundantly by me;
    Thus then ends the fifth day.

CHERUBIM Our Lord God in trinity,
Joy and love are due to thee,
Our tribute before everything:
For thou hast made at thy bidding,
Heaven and earth and all that is,
That joy shall never come amiss.
Lord, thou art so full of might,
Thou hast made Lucifer so bright;
We love thee, Lord; bright are we
But none of us so bright as he:
Lucifer is that lord's name
For he bears so bright a flame.
He is so beauteous and so bright
It is great joy to see that sight;
We praise thee, Lord, with all our thought,
That such things could make of nought.

[GOD *withdraws from his throne.*

LUCIFER Certain it is a seemly sight,
Since that we are all angels bright,
    And ever in bliss to be;
If but ye behold me right,
    Worship is due to me.
I am so fair and bright,
From me comes all this light,
    This glamour and this glee;
Against so great a might
    May no resistance be.

As ye may well behold
I am a thousandfold
    Brighter than is the sun;
My strength may not be told,
Know of my might may none;
    In heaven, therefore, I hold
Myself above everyone.

For I am lord of bliss,
My toe the world may kiss,
My mirth is most of all;
Therefore, my will is this,
Master ye shall me call.
And when I come into my own,
How seemly may I mount the throne
As king of bliss;
I am so bright of blood and bone,
My seat shall be there as was his.

[LUCIFER *sits in* GOD's *throne.*

Say, fellows, how fits it me
To sit in seat of trinity?
I am so bright in every limb
I trust I seem as well as him.

1ST BAD ANGEL
In my sight thou art so fair,
Thou dost well to sit up there;
And so it seems to me.

1ST GOOD ANGEL
I warn you leave your vanity,
For none may sit therein but he
Who in his might all dooms decree.

2ND GOOD ANGEL
Cease your ill sport, I tell you plain,
For well I know you jest in vain;
He was never suited to that stall
So well as him that has made all.

2ND BAD ANGEL
Think you not Lucifer more fit,
He seems full worthy there to sit;
He is so fair without a lie,
Most worshipful to sit on high.
Therefore, fellow, hold your peace;
Prize first the sheep by its fine fleece.
He seems as worthy to sit there
As God himself if He were here.

LUCIFER
Dear fellows, think ye not so?

1ST BAD ANGEL
Yea, by God, and more we know.

1ST GOOD ANGEL Not us. His worship we forswear.

LUCIFER Now thereof not a leek I care.
Since I am myself so bright
Therefore will I take a flight.

[LUCIFER *tries to fly upwards above* GOD'S *throne but with the other* BAD ANGELS *is thrust down to hell. They all shout and wail as they are driven downwards. Immediately after the fall the* DEVILS *emerge howling from hell-mouth.*

1ST DEVIL Alas, alas, I wail for woe!
Lucifer, why fell you so?
We that were angels so fair,
And sat so high above the air,
Now we are made as black as coal,
And ugly, tattered as a foal.
What ailed thee, Lucifer, to fall?
Wast thou not fairest of angels all?
Brightest and best, and in the love
Of God himself that sits above?
Of orders ten now there are nine;
That face is dark that once did shine;
Fallen, who on God once leaned,
From an angel to a fiend.
Vile has been thy pride and vain,
To rob thy bliss and bring thee pain.
Alas there is nought else to say,
But we are beaten, now and ay.

2ND DEVIL Alas, the joy that we were in
Is lost forever for our sin.
Alas that ever came pride in thought,
For it has brought us all to nought.
With mirth and joy we were endowed
Till Lucifer waxed over proud.
Alas, we rue such wicked pride,
As may ye all that stand beside.
We listened to the lies he spread,
And now from us our peace is fled.

Our joy is lost and cannot mend,
And pain our lot without an end.

[*The* DEVILS *disappear into hell-mouth.* GOD *sits upon his throne. The* GOOD ANGELS *stand by him.*

GOD Creatures of earth that creep or fly,
Bring forth your young and multiply;
I see that it is good;
Now in our likeness make we man,
Who shall govern as he can
All fowl and fish in flood.

[GOD *stretches forth his hand.* ADAM *rises slowly until he stands beneath* GOD'*s throne, a little lower than the* ANGELS.

Spirit of life in thee I blow,
Good and ill both shalt thou know;
Rise up and stand by me.
All that is in water or land,
All shall bow unto thy hand,
And sovereign shalt thou be.

I give thee wit, I give thee strength,
Of all thou seest, the breadth and length,
Be wonderfully wise.
Mirth and joy to have at will,
And thy pleasure to fulfil,
And dwell in paradise.

[*During the following lines a heaviness comes upon* ADAM. *He lies down and sleeps.*

This I make thy living place,
Full of pleasure and solace,
And thee I set therein.
It is not good to be alone,
To enjoy this treasure on thine own
Without one of thy kin.

[*During what follows a* GOOD ANGEL *takes a rib coloured red from* ADAM'*s side, raises it aloft, then strikes the ground with it and* EVE *issues forth.*

Therefore a rib from thee I take,
And thereof a maid shall make
  To be thy helpmeet.
Ye both may govern what here is,
And evermore may live in bliss
  Close to my mercy-seat.

[ADAM *and* EVE, *standing, admire each other and the world around them.*

Ye shall have joy and bliss therein,
While ye keep yourselves from sin,
  And so your joy increase.
Rise up, mine angel Cherubim,
Take and lead them both therein,
  And leave them there in peace.

[*The* CHERUBIM *who has been kneeling by* GOD'S *throne, stands and listens attentively to* GOD'S *words but does not move towards* ADAM *and* EVE *until* GOD *has withdrawn.*

Hear thou Adam and Eve thy wife,
I forbid ye the tree of life,
And my commandment must be kept,
Take what ye will, that tree except.
Adam, if thou scorn my breath,
Thou shalt die a doleful death.

CHERUBIM Our Lord, our God, thy will be done,
To go with them I shall not shun.
Indeed, my Lord, I shall not rest
Till they be brought to that place blessed.
We thank thee, Lord, with full good cheer,
That man has made to share joy here.

[GOD *withdraws.* CHERUBIM *leads* ADAM *and* EVE *to a lower level—paradise.*

Come forth, Adam, I shall thee lead;
Now of my counsel take good heed.
Be mindful, man, how thou art made,
In praise ne'er leave the Lord unpaid,
He that made thee through his will,

The angels' place in heaven to fill.
Great bounty in his giving
Thee mastery of all things living.
He has forbad thee but a tree;
Look, Adam, that thou leave it be.
For if thou break his commandment,
No escape but punishment.
Walk here into paradise,
And warned ye be to be but wise;
And rest you well for I must go
Unto my Lord, his will is so.

[CHERUBIM *withdraws into heaven.*

ADAM Almighty Lord, thanks be to thee
That is, and was, and ay shall be,
For thy love and for thy grace,
For now is here a merry place.
Eve, my fellow, how find you this?

EVE A garden it seems of joy and bliss,
That God has given to thee and me;
Blessed everlastingly be he!

ADAM Eve, fellow, abide ye here,
I will go visit far and near
To see what trees have planted been;
For more is here than we have seen:
Grasses and other small flowers
That smell so sweet, of many colours.

EVE Here gladly, sir, I shall remain;
When you have seen them, come again.

ADAM But look well, Eve, my wife,
You come not near the tree of life,
For if you do we need have dread
That we be pained as he has said.

EVE Go forth, and wander all about;
I shall not near it while you are out,
For be you sure I were full loth
To do a thing to make Him wroth.

[ADAM *withdraws.* LUCIFER, *now changed to* SATAN, *comes out of hell-mouth followed by a rout of* DEVILS.

SATAN Who thought this time had ever been?
We that such mirth and joy have seen,
That we should suffer so much woe?
Whoever would have trusted so?
Ten orders in heaven have been
Of angels serving as was seen
Each in order of degree.
The tenth part fell down with me;
For they chose me as their guide,
And maintained me in their pride;
But hark now, fellows, what I say:
The joy that we have lost for ay,
God has fashioned man his friend,
To have that bliss without an end,
The fallen angels' place to fill,
Which we have left, such is his will.
And now are they in paradise,
But thence they shall, if we be wise.

My content I shall contrive,
If I might man betray,
His pleasure to deprive,
That soon I shall assay.
In a worm's likeness will I wend,
And lead astray with subtle lying.

[*Moves to paradise.*

Eve, Eve!

EVE Who is there?

SATAN I am a friend.
For thy good I am coming,
And thee have sought.
Of all the fruit that ye see hanging
In paradise, why eat ye nought?

EVE We may from every one
Take whate'er we thought,

But one tree we must shun,
Or into harm be brought.

SATAN And why that tree? that would I know,
More than others standing by?

EVE For God forbids us near it go
Nor eat thereof, Adam nor I,
We leave for fear;
And if we did we both should die,
He said, and end our pleasures here.

SATAN [*knowingly*]
Ssss! Eve, now be intent
To heed what thou shalt hear,
What matter is here meant,
That he should chill your cheer.
To eat thereof he you forbad,
I know it well, this was his will,
Because he would none other had
The virtues this tree may instil.
For wilt thou see,
Who eats the fruit, of good and ill
Shall knowledge have as well as he.

EVE Why what kind of thing art thou,
That tells this tale to me?

SATAN A worm that knows well how
That ye may worshipped be.

EVE What worship should we win thereby?
To eat thereof the need is nought;
Our lordship is in mastery
Of all things that on earth are wrought.

SATAN Woman, away!
To greater state ye may be brought,
If ye will do as I shall say.

EVE For no need do we long
That should our good dismay.

SATAN Nay, indeed it is no wrong,
Safely to eat ye may.

Sure, no peril therein lies,
 But worship for the winning.
For right as God ye shall be wise,
 And peer with him in everything.
Aye, Gods shall ye be!
 And of good and ill have knowing,
For to be as wise as he.

EVE Is this true that thou say?

SATAN Yea! why trust thou not me?
I never would in no way
 Tell ought but truth to thee.

EVE Thy words have won, my doubts are dashed,
 To fetch this fruit for our own food.

[EVE *bites, and* SATAN *writhes in exultation.*

SATAN Bite on boldly be not abashed,
 And take Adam to amend his mood,
  Also his bliss.

[SATAN *withdraws.* ADAM *approaches.*

EVE Adam! Have here the fruit full good.

ADAM Alas! Woman, why took thou this?
Our Lord commanded us both
 To shun this tree of his.
Thy work will make him wroth,
 Alas! Thou hast done amiss.

EVE Adam, by grief be nought beset,
 And I shall say the reason why;
Such wisdom hissed a worm I met,
 We shall as gods be, thou and I,
If that we ate
 Here of this tree; Adam, deny
Not such worship for to get.
 For we shall be as wise
As God that is so great,
 And so ourselves may prize;
So eat and earn that state.

ADAM To eat it I would not eschew,
 If certain of thy saying.

EVE Bite on boldly, for it is true,
As gods we shall know everything.

ADAM To win that name
I shall it taste at thy teaching.

[ADAM *bites the apple.*

Alas! What have I done for shame!
Ill counsel came from thee!
Ah! Eve, thou art to blame,
That thus enticed thou me;
My limbs against me exclaim,
For I am naked as I think.

EVE Alas, Adam, right so am I.

ADAM And for sorrow why might we not sink,
For we have grieved God almighty
That made me man,
Broken his bidding bitterly,
Alas! That ever we it began!
This work, Eve, thou hast wrought,
And made this bad bargain.

EVE Nay, Adam, chide me nought.

ADAM Alas, dear Eve, whom then?

EVE The worm of chiding is most worthy,
With tales untrue he me betrayed.

ADAM Alas! I listened to thy story,
And let with lies thou me persuade.
So may I bide,
For that rash act I am repaid,
For that deed done I curse my pride.
Our nakedness me grieves,
Wherewith shall we it hide?

EVE Let us take these fig-leaves
Since they grow here beside.

ADAM Right as thou say so shall it be,
For we are naked and all bare.

Full gladly now I would hide me,
From my Lord's sight, I know not where,
So I be not caught.

GOD [*in his throne*]
Adam! Adam!

ADAM Lord!

GOD Where art thou, there?

ADAM I hear thee, Lord, but see thee nought.

GOD Say, to whom does it belong,
This work that thou hast wrought?

ADAM Lord, Eve made me do wrong
And to this plight me brought.

GOD Say, Eve, why didst thou Adam make
To eat the fruit that should hang still,
Which was commanded none should take?

EVE A worm, Lord, beguiled my will,
So welaway!
That ever I did that deed so ill!

GOD Ah! Wicked worm, woe wait on thee for ay,
For thou in this manner
Hast caused such deep dismay;
My malediction have thou here,
With all the might I may.

And on thy belly shalt thou glide

[SATAN *grovels on his belly.*

And be ay full of enmity
To all mankind on every side,
And earth thy sustenance shall be
To eat and drink.
Adam and Eve, also ye
From work on earth ye shall not shrink,
But labour for your food.

ADAM Alas! For sorrow and care,
We that had all world's good,
Now thrust out as I think.

GOD Now, Cherubim, my angel bright,
    To middle-earth quick drive these two.

[CHERUBIM *descends from heaven to paradise and at the very end of the play drives* ADAM *and* EVE *to an even lower level, that of middle-earth.*

CHERUBIM All ready, Lord, as it is right,
    It is thy will I seek to do,
To thy liking.
    Adam and Eve, now go you two,
For here may ye make no dwelling.
    Go ye forth fast to fare;
Of sorrow may ye sing.

ADAM Alas! For sorrow and care,
Our hands now may we wring.

[CHERUBIM *returns to heaven.* ADAM *and* EVE *withdraw.*

THE SECOND PLAY

The Killing of Abel

BOY ABEL
CAIN GOD

BOY All hail, all hail, be blithe and glad,
For here come I, a merry lad;
Have done your din, my master bad,
  Or else the devil you speed.
Know you not I come before?
And he who jangles any more
Must on my black horn blow a score,
Both behind and before,
  Till his teeth bleed.
  Fellows, look you take good heed,
Never a noise to make nor cry;
Whoever dares to do that deed,
The devil hang him up to dry!

Fellows, I am a full great man,
My master's called a good yeoman.
  Full well ye all him ken;
If with you he starts to strive,
Then certainly you'll never thrive;
But as you hope to keep alive,
  Some of you are his men.
But still your lips and study when
  Best you may speak thereon.
If my master come welcome him then.

[*He indicates the sort of reception that should be given to* CAIN.

  Farewell, for I am gone.

[*The* BOY *runs off.* CAIN *enters ploughing.*

CAIN Get on, greenhorn, before I scream!
Draw on! Ill-fate may God ye deem.
Ye stand as though ye are in a dream;
  Will ye no farther fare?
Get up! Let's see how ye will draw;
Up bitch! Ye'd scarcely pull a straw.
What! Stand ye in no awe!
  Ye dun nag, why stay ye there?
  May God give ye sorrow and care!
Lo! Now heard she what I said;
  Now art thou the worst mare
To plough that ever I bred.

[CAIN *calls to the* BOY *who appears.*

How now, Pickbrain, must alone I strive?

BOY May God forbid that ever ye should thrive!

CAIN What, boy, must I both hold and drive?
  Hearst thou not how I cry?

BOY [*calling to* CAIN's *oxen and horses*]
Say, Mall and Stott, will ye not go?
Leming, Morrell, White-horn, oh!
  Now will ye not see how they hie?

CAIN God give thee sorrow, boy; and of meat a lack.

BOY Their food, sir, therefore, I lay on their back,
And tied the bags tight at the head,
Within not hay but stones instead.

CAIN Your tricks one day will cost your head.

BOY Not before I have done my spite.

CAIN I am thy master, wilt thou fight?

BOY Yea, I shall measure with thee my might;
What I borrow I shall requite.

[*They fight.*

CAIN Lo, now, no more! I would ere night
That we ploughed this land.

BOY Faster Morrell, step you light—
[*aside*]
And let the plough stand.

[ABEL *enters.*

ABEL God, as he both may and can,
Speed thee, brother, and thy man.

CAIN Come kiss my arse, God curse our clan,
Ye get from me no welcome hail.
Ye should have stayed till ye were called;
Come near and either drive or hold,
And kiss the devil's tail.
Go feed your sheep, man, in the dale,
And much ill luck achieve.

ABEL Brother, why thus on me ye rail?
Thee no one here would grieve.
But dear brother hear my speech:
The customs of our law us teach
All that work should take advice
And worship God with sacrifice.

Our fathers bad us, and our fathers knew,
That one tenth part to God was due.
Come forth, brother, and let us go
To worship God; why stay we so?
Part of our goods to God give we
Corn or cattle whatever it be.

And therefore, brother, let us go;
First cleanse us from the fiend, our foe,
Before we sacrifice
Then blessings forth shall flow,
Our service shall suffice.

CAIN Now, let forth your geese the fox will preach!
Thinkst thou me to appeach
With thy sermoning?
Hold still thy tongue, I say,
As any good wife may,
Or go the devil's way,
With thy vain carping.

Should I leave plough and everything
To make with thee an offering?
Nay, thou findst me not so mad.
Go to the devil, and say I bad!
What gives God thee to praise him so?
To me he gives but sorrow and woe.

ABEL Cain, leave this vain carping,
For God gives thee thy living.

CAIN Yet borrowed I never a farthing
Of him, by this hand.

ABEL Our elders have taught, and they understand,
To offer to God, each with his hand,
A tenth of his goods to be burnt with the brand.

CAIN In the priest's hand lies my farthing
Since last I offered.

ABEL Leave, brother, let us be walking;
I would our tithe were proffered.

CAIN Wait! Why should I give, dear brother?
For I am each year worse than another,
And by my troth it is none other;
My making is but mean,
No wonder I am lean;
Bitter my moans to him have been,
For, by him that has me saved,
I doubt he'll give what I have craved.

ABEL But all the goods you call your own,
By God's good grace are but a loan.

CAIN Lends he me as you thrive so?
For he has ever been my foe;
For had he my friend been
Otherwise it had been seen.
When all men's corn was fair in field,
Not a needle would mine yield;
When I should sow and wanted seed,
And of corn had full great need,
Then gave he me none of his,
No more will I give him of this;

Hardly hold me to blame
If I serve him with the same.

ABEL Dear brother, say not so,
But let us forth together go;
Good brother, let us go with speed,
To linger here we have no need.

CAIN Yea, yea, your jangling you waste;
The devil take me if I haste,
As long as I may live,
My goods to share or give
Either to God or man;
Keep I shall what goods I can;
For had I given away my wealth,
As beggar then with guile and stealth
My lot would be to save,
To go from door to door and crave.

ABEL Brother, come forth in God's name,
Afraid am I we are to blame:
Haste we now I thee implore.

CAIN Go! run on, in the devil's name, before!
By God, man, I hold thee mad!
Thinkst thou now that I would gad
To yield of all my treasures ought?

The devil speed him that me so taught!
Why should I my trouble lose,
And tear my socks while wearing shoes?

ABEL Dear brother, it were great wonder
That I and thou should part asunder.
Then would our father fain ask why;
Are we not brothers, thou and I?

CAIN No, but prate on till your wits are dazed,
Now, by my troth, I count thee crazed;
Whether he be blithe or wroth,
To give my goods I am full loth.

Oft have I stalked a better prize,
Whence more profit might arise.
But well I see go must I need;

Set on before, ill might thou speed!
Since notwithstanding we must go.

ABEL Dear brother, why say you so?
But go we forth both together;
Blessed be God we have fair weather.

[ABEL *with a sheep and* CAIN *with a stook of corn climb to a higher level.*

CAIN Lay down thy burden upon this hill.

ABEL Forsooth, brother, so I will.
God of heaven, take it for good.

CAIN Now offer first thy livelihood.

ABEL God that made both heaven and earth,
That has delivered us from dearth,
Now take in thanks if thy will be,
My tithe I offer here to thee;
For I give with good intent
To thee, my Lord, that all has sent.
I burn it now with steadfast thought,
In praise of him that all has wrought.

CAIN Rise, let me now, since thou hast done.
Lord, hear what boon I have begun!

The tithe that I here give to thee,
Of corn may scarce renew me;
But now begin I in my turn
Since I must needs my tithe now burn.
One sheaf, one, and this makes two,
Yet neither can I spare for you.
Two, two, now this is three,
Yea this also shall stay with me.
By saving all I spare my grief
And count it thrift to keep the sheaf.
Why, look now, four before you here!
Better grew I not this year.
In the spring I sowed fair corn,
Yet was it such when it was shorn:
Thistles and briers in great plenty,
And of weeds all kinds that could be.

Four sheaves, four, lo, this makes five—
The devil, I fast so long ere I thrive—
Five and six, now is this seven,
But this goes never to the God of heaven;
Nor none of these four from my right
Shall ever come within God's sight,
Seven, seven, now this is eight.

ABEL Cain, brother, come not in God's hate.

CAIN Therefore is it these things I say,
For I will not give my goods away.
Had I thought to give and not offend,
Then would thou say he were my friend;
But I think not, by my hood,
To forsake what does me good.
Why, eight, eight, and nine, and ten is this.
Yea, this may we best miss.
Give him that from out my store?
It goes against my heart full sore.

ABEL Cain, tithe rightly as you mean.

CAIN Yea, lo, twelve, fifteen sixteen.

ABEL Cain, you offer wrong and of the worst.

CAIN Come, hide my eyes that nothing is seen;
The waning moon is a time that's cursed;
Or else would you that I slept,
And that way I from wrong were kept?

Let me see now how it is—
Lo, I hold myself well paid,
My tithe I gave away by guess,
Even I an offering made.

ABEL Cain, of God it seems you take no heed.

CAIN If he get more the devil him speed!
As much in one swing one may reap
Was given to him—a bargain cheap;
Not as much great or small,
As he might wipe his arse withal.
For that and this that lies here
Have cost me full dear;

Ere it was shorn and made a stack,
Had I many a weary back;
Therefore ask me no more than this,
For I have given what my will is.

ABEL Cain, I warn thee, tithe aright,
For dread of his so powerful might.

CAIN The way I tithe tax not your head,
But tend thy scabby sheep instead;
If my tithes you think not true,
It will be the worse for you.
Would thou I gave him this sheaf or this sheaf?
But neither of these two will I leave;
But take this; now has he two,
By my soul, that's more than due,
But it goes sore against my will,
And he shall like this tithe but ill.

ABEL Cain, better tithe thou, to the end
That God of heaven rest your friend.

CAIN My friend? Nay not unless he will!
Reason only rules me still.
If I need not dread him sore,
I were a fool to give him more.

ABEL If right thou tithed, such must thou find.

CAIN Yea, kiss the devil's arse behind!
The devil hang thee by the neck!
How I may tithe never thou reck;
Wilt thou not yet hold thy peace?
Of this jangling I bid thee cease.
And tithed I well or tithed I ill,
To thee it's one; keep thy tongue still.
But now since thou hast offered thine,
Now will I set fire to mine.

[*Choking smoke comes from the offering.*

Alas! Harrow! Help to blow!
For me it burns no more than snow;
Puff! This smoke does me much shame—
Burn now in the devil's name!

Ah, what devil of hell is it!
Almost had my lungs been split.
Had I blown then one blast more
I had been choked to death full sore.
It stank like the devil in hell,
That longer there I might not dwell.

ABEL Cain, this is not worth one leek;
Such smoky offering who should seek?

CAIN Come kiss the devil right in the arse,
For this smoke is slow to pass;
I would that it were in thy throat,
Fire and sheaf, and wheat and oat.

[GOD *appears above.*

GOD Cain, why art thou such a rebel
Against thy brother, Abel?
To jeer and gibe there is no need,
If thou tithe right thou getst thy meed;
But be thou sure if thou tithe ill,
Repaid thou shalt be thy evil.

[GOD *withdraws.*

CAIN [*sarcastic*]
Why, who is that hob-over-the wall?
Alas, who was that that piped so small?
Come go we hence from perils all;
God is out of his wit.
Come forth, Abel, and let us go;
I find that God will be my foe,
From here then must I flit.

[*They leave the hill.*

ABEL Ah, Cain, brother, that is ill done.

CAIN No, but fast hence let us run;
And if I may, there shall I be
Where God's eye shall not see me.

ABEL Dear brother, I will be at hand
In the field where our beasts stand,
To see if they be well or sick.

CAIN Nay, nay, abide, we have a bone to pick.
Hark, speak with me ere thou go;
What, thinkst thou thus to escape so?
Nay a deep debt owe I thee by right,
And now is time I thee requite.

ABEL Brother, to me why show you so much spleen?

CAIN Out, thief, why burnt thy tithe so clean,
When mine but foully smoked
As if it would us both have choked?

ABEL God's will, I trust was here
That made mine burn so clear.
If thine smoked, am I to blame?

CAIN Why, yea, and thou shalt smart with shame;
With cheek-bone ere my hand I stay
I shall have torn thy life away.

[CAIN *strikes* ABEL *with a cheek-bone.*

So lie down there and take thy rest,
Thus braying curs are chastised best.

ABEL Vengeance, vengeance, Lord, I cry!
For I am slain and not guilty.

[ABEL *dies.*

CAIN Yea, lie thou there, wretch, lie there, lie;
[*to the* SPECTATORS]
And if any of you think I did amiss,
I shall amend it, worse than it is,
That all men may it see:
[*menacingly*]
Much worse than it is
Right so shall it be.
But now since he is brought to sleep
Into some hole I fain would creep;
For I fear I quake in so sore dread,
For be I taken I be but dead;
Here will I lie these forty days,
And curse him who may first me raise.

[GOD *appears above.*

GOD Cain, Cain!

CAIN Who is that that calls me?
Look, I am here, may thou not see?

GOD Where is thy brother, Abel?

CAIN Why ask of me? I think in hell,
I trust in hell he be—
As any there might see—
Or somewhere fallen a-sleeping;
When was he in my keeping?

GOD Cain, Cain, thou art caught in a fierce flood;
The voice of thy brother's blood
That thou hast slain in such false wise,
From earth to heaven vengeance cries.
And for thou hast brought thy brother down,
Under the flood of my fury drown.

CAIN Yea, deal out curses, I will none,
Or give them back when thou hast done.
Since I have done so great a sin,
That I may not thy mercy win,
And thus thou thrust me from thy grace,
I shall hide me from thy face;
And if any man may me find,
Let him slay me and not mind;
Wheresoever he may me meet,
Either by sty or in the street;
And harshly, when that I am dead,
Bury me in Goodybower at the Quarry Head;
If safe I can this place depart,
By all men set I not a fart.

GOD It is not so, Cain, nay.
No man may another slay,
For he that slays thee, young or old,
He shall be punished sevenfold.

[GOD *withdraws.*

CAIN No matter, I know where I shall go;
In hell for me the fire will glow;
For mercy now to wail is vain,

For that would but increase my pain;
But this corpse I would were hid,
For suddenly might come a swain
And cry "False wretch, now God forbid,
Thou hast thy very brother slain."
If only Pickbrain, my boy, were here,
We both should bury him without a tear.
How, Pickbrain, scape-grace, Pickbrain, how!

[BOY *enters*.

BOY Master, master!

CAIN [*striking him*] Hearest thou, boy?
There is a pudding in the pot,
Take thou that, boy, take thou that!

BOY I'd curse thy bones for that last thud,
Though thou wert my sire of flesh and blood;
All day for you I run till I sweat,
And never once your blows withstand,
Buffets as my reward I get.

CAIN Peace, man, I did it but to use my hand;
But hark, boy, I have counsel to thee to say:
I slew my brother this same day;
I prithee, good boy, if thou may,
To run with me away.

BOY Alas, out upon thee, thief!
Hast thou thy brother slain?

CAIN Peace, man, for God's pain!
I said it for a joke.

BOY Yea, but fearing such another stroke
Here I thee forsake;
The hangman's rope will make us choke,
If us the bailiffs take.

CAIN Ah, sir, I cry you mercy, cease!
And I shall give you your release.

BOY Wilt thou cry my peace
Throughout this land?

CAIN Yea, I give God a vow.

BOY What wilt thou do now?

CAIN Stand up, my good boy, on my life.
Peace be to them both man and wife;
And whoso will do after me,
Cunning in thrift then shall he be.
But thou must be my good boy,
And cry oyez, oyez, oy!

BOY Broth and dumplings for thy boy.

[CAIN *begins to call out like a town-crier. The* BOY *mocks him in asides.*

CAIN I command you in the King's name,

BOY And in my master's too, false Cain,

CAIN That no man find fault with them nor blame.

BOY Yea, this cold roast from his home came.

CAIN Neither with him nor with his boy,

BOY My master raves now, oyez, oy!

CAIN For they are true if all were told.

BOY My master eats no dish but cold.

CAIN The King writes thus unto you.

BOY But hot or cold, I lacked my due.

CAIN Them at least the King will save.

BOY Yea, for a draught of drink I crave.

CAIN At their own will let them stray.

BOY My belly's so empty it starts to bray.

CAIN Let no man challenge them, one or other.

BOY This same is he that slew his brother.

CAIN Bid them be loved the world throughout.

BOY Yea, ill-spun weft ay comes foul out.
You'll wear out your hose if you go thus about.

CAIN Bid every man them please to pay.

BOY Yea, do give thy horse a wisp of hay.

CAIN [*to the* BOY]
Now thou hast trod the devil's way,
May the fiend thy spirit snatch;
For, but for Abel, my brother,
Yet never I knew thy match.

BOY [*speaking from the hill to the* SPECTATORS]
Now old and young, before ye go,
The same blessing may God bestow
On all here in this place,
That he from heaven my master gave.
Cherish it well, your souls to save,
Granted was it through God's grace.

CAIN Come down yet in the devil's way,
And anger me no more;
And take yon plough, I say,
And press on fast before;
And I shall, if I may,
Teach thee a lesson sore;
I warn thee, lad, for ay,
For now and evermore,
That thou give me no gall;
For, by God, and if you do,
On this plough shalt thou rue,
Hanged by this rope, lad, too,
By him that died for all.

[*The* BOY *goes off pushing the plough.*

Now farewell, fellows all,
For now I needs must wend,
And to the devil be thrall,
World without end.
There ready is my stall,
With Satan, the foul fiend,
Ever ill might him befall

[*Shaking his fist at* GOD's *throne.*

That me thither did commend
This tide.

Farewell great, and farewell small,
Forever farewell, one and all,
  Accursed I needs must hide.

[*Exit* CAIN.

THE THIRD PLAY

Noah

NOAH	1ST SON	1ST SON'S WIFE
GOD	2ND SON	2ND SON'S WIFE
NOAH'S WIFE	3RD SON	3RD SON'S WIFE

NOAH To mighty God I pray, maker of all that is,
Three persons, no gainsay, one God in endless [bliss,
Thou made both night and day, beast, fowl, [and fish,
All creatures in thy sway, wrought thou at thy [wish,
As well thou might;
The sun, the moon, heaven's tent,
Thou made; the firmament,
The stars also full fervent,
To shine thou made full bright.

Angels thou made all even, all orders to bless,
To have the bliss in heaven, this did thou more [and less,
Now laid thereto the leaven, which fermented [faithlessness,
Marvels seven times seven than I can well [express;
And why?
Of all angels in brightness,
God gave Lucifer most lightness,
Who priding in his rightness,
By God himself sat high.

He thought himself as worthy as he that him [made,

In brightness and beauty, him God had to [degrade,—
Put him in low degree, swiftly from sun to [shade,
Him and his company, howling in hell were [laid,
    For ever.
They shall never get away
Hence until doomsday,
But burn in bale for ay,
    And never dissever.

Soon after, that gracious Lord in his likeness [made man,
That place to be restored, even as he began,
By the trinity in accord, Adam and Eve, that [woman,
To multiply without discord he gave them [space and span
    In paradise to both.
He gave in his command,
On the tree of life to lay no hand;
But yet the false fiend
    Made him with man wroth;

Enticed man to gluttony, stirred him to sin in [pride;
But in paradise surely, may no sin abide,
And therefore man full hastily was sternly [thrust outside,
In woe and wandering for to be, with all pains [plied
    Without ruth;
First on earth and then in hell
Fiercely with the fiends to dwell,
But to those no harm befell
    Who trusted in his truth.

Oil of mercy through his might he promised, [as is said,
To all that strove with right in peace his paths [to tread,

But now before his sight all people without [dread,
For most part day and night, in word and deed [they spread
Their sin full bold;
Some in pride, anger, and envy,
Some in covetousness and gluttony,
Some in sloth and lechery,
In ways manifold.

Therefore I dread lest God on us take venge- [ance,
For sin escapes the rod, without repentance;
Six hundred years and odd has been my [existence,
Daily on earth to plod, with great grievance
Each way;
And now I am old
Sick, sorry and cold,
As muck upon mould,
I wither away.

But yet I cry for mercy and call;
Noah, thy servant, am I, Lord over all!
Therefore me and my fry shall with me fall;
Save from villainy and bring to thy hall
In heaven;
And keep me from sin
This world within;
Mankind's comely king,
I pray morn and even.

[GOD *appears above.*

GOD Since I have made each thing that may live and [stand,
Duke, emperor, and king with my own hand,
To live to their liking by sea and by land,
Every man to my bidding should come at [command
Full fervent;
That made man such a creature,
Fairest of favour,

Man must heed me as a lover,
With reason and repent.

Methought I showed man love when I made [him to be
All angels above, like to the trinity;
And now in great reproof full low lies he,
On earth no jot aloof from sins which displease [me
Most of all;
Vengeance will I take,
On earth for sin's sake,
My grimness thus will wake
Both great and small.

I repent full sore that ever made I man,
By me he sets no store, and I am his sovereign;
I will destroy therefore both beast, man and [woman,
All shall perish less and more that so spurned [my plan,
And ill have done.
In earth I see right nought
But sin so dearly bought;
Of those that well have wrought
Find I but one.

Therefore shall I undo all people that are here,
With floods that shall subdue the land both far [and near,
I have good cause thereto for now no men me [fear,
As I say shall I do, the sword of vengeance rear,
And make an end–
Of all that bears life,
Save Noah and his wife,
They offered no strife,
Nor me did offend.

To him in great joy hastily will go,
Noah shall I not destroy, but warn him of his [woe.

Men on earth their sin enjoy, raging to and [fro,
Ever ill themselves employ, each the other's [foe,
With evil intent;
All shall I lay low
With floodings that shall flow,
I shall work them woe,
That will not repent.

Noah, my friend, I tell thee, saved be thou by [thy zeal,
But build a ship directly, of nail and board full [well.
Thou ever showed thy loyalty to me as true as [steel,
Still be obedient to me and friendship shalt [thou feel
My power provide.
Of length thy ship shall be
Three hundred cubits, warn I thee,
Of height even thirty,
Of fifty cubits wide.

Anoint thy ship with pitch and tar without, also [within,
The water to debar from flowing in;
Look no man it mar; three cabin rows begin,
Thou must use many a spar before this work [thou win
To end fully.
Make in thy ship also,
Of parlours even a row
And places more to stow
The beasts that there must be.

One cubit in height a window shall thou make;
A side door to fit tight, fashion without mistake;
With thee shall no man fight, nor harm thee [for my sake,
When all is done aright; thy wife see that thou [take

Into the ship with thee;
Thy sons of good fame,
Ham, Japhet, and Shem,
On board must remain,
With their wives three.

For all shall be destroyed, that lives on land, [but ye,
With floods that fill the void, and falling in [plenty;
The heavens shall be employed to rain [incessantly,
When days seven have cloyed, it shall last days [forty,
Without fail.
Take in thy ship also
Two beasts of each kind, so,
Male and female, see they go,
Before thou raise thy sail.

So thou may thee avail when all these things [are wrought,
Stuff thy ship with victual for hunger that ye [lack nought;
For beasts, fowl, and cattle keep them in your [thought
For them is my counsel, that some succour be [sought,
Uppermost;
They must have corn and hay,
And meat enough alway;
Do now, as I thee say,
In the name of the holy ghost.

NOAH Ah! Benedicite! What art thou thus,
That tells before what shall be? Thou art full [marvellous!
Tell me for charity thy name so gracious.

GOD My name is of dignity and also full glorious
To know.
I am God most mighty,

One God in trinity,
Made thee and each man to be;
  Love to me thou should show.

NOAH I thank thee, Lord, so dear, that would vouch- [safe
Thus low to appear to a simple knave;
Bless us, Lord, here for charity I it crave,
The better may we steer the ship that we have,
  Certain.

GOD Noah, to thee and to thy fry
My blessing grant I;
Ye shall work and multiply,
  And fill the earth again,
When all these floods are past and fully gone [away.

NOAH Lord, homeward will I fast in haste as that I [may;

[*Exit* GOD.

My wife will I ask what she will say,
And I am all aghast lest there be some fray
  Between us both;
For she is full tetchy,
For little oft angry,
If anything wrong be,
  Soon is she wroth.

[*He goes to his wife.*

God speed thee, wife, how fare ye?

WIFE Now, as ever might I thrive, the worse to see [thee;
Tell me, on your life, where thus long could [thou be?
To death may we drive, because of thee,
  Alack.
When work weary we sink,
Thou dost what thou think,
Yet of meat and drink
  Have we great lack.

NOAH Wife, we are hard pressed with tidings new.

WIFE But thou ought to be dressed in stafford blue;
For thou art always depressed, be it false or [true;
God knows I am oppressed, and that may I rue,
Full ill;
All I hear is thy crow,
From even till morrow,
Screeching ever of sorrow;
God send thee once thy fill.

We women may harry all ill husbands;
I have one, by Mary! That loosed me of my [bands;
If he twits I must tarry, however so it stands,
And seem to be full sorry, wringing both my [hands
For dread.
But in a little while,
What with game and guile,
I shall smite and smile
And pay him back instead.

NOAH Hush! Hold thy tongue, ramshit, or I shall thee [still.

WIFE As I thrive, if thou smite, I shall pay back with [skill.

NOAH We shall see who is right, have at thee, Gill!
Upon the bone shall it bite!

WIFE Ah, by Mary! Thou smitest ill!
But I suppose
I shall not in thy debt
Leave this place yet!
This strap is what you get
To tie up thy hose!

NOAH Ah! Wilt thou so? Mary, that is mine.

WIFE Have thou three for two, I swear, by God [divine,

NOAH I shall requite each blow, your skin will bear [my sign.

WIFE Out upon thee, ho!

NOAH Thou can both bite and whine
For all thou art worth.
For though she will strike,
Her shrieks my ears spike,
There is not her like
On all this earth.

WIFE But I will keep charity in this to-do
Here shall no man tarry thee; I pray thee go to!
Full well may we miss thee, as peace is our due;
To spin will I address me.

NOAH Farewell, then, to you;
But wife,
Pray for me busily,
Till again I come to thee.

WIFE Even as thou prayst for me,
As ever might I thrive.

NOAH I tarry full long, to my work I must go;
My gear take along and watch the work grow;
I may go all wrong, in truth, I it know;
If God's help is not strong I may sit in sorrow,
I ken;
Now assay will I
Something of carpentry,
In nomine patris, et filii,
Et spiritus sancti, Amen.
To begin with this tree, my bones will I bend,
I trust that the trinity succour will send;
The work prospers fairly to a fitting end;
Now blessed be he that this did commend.
Lo, here the length,
Three hundred cubits evenly,
Of breadth lo is it fifty,
The height is even thirty
Cubits full strength.

Now my gown will I cast and work in my coat
Make will I the mast to set in the boat,
Ah! My back breaks fast! This is a sorry note!
It is wonder that I last, so weak that I dote,
    Behold,
To begin this affair!
My bones are so bare,
No wonder they despair,
    For I am full old.

The top and the sail both will I make,
The helm and the castle also will I take,
To drive in each a nail without a mistake,
This way will never fail, that dare I undertake
    Right soon.
This was a noble plan,
These nails so swiftly ran
Through more or less the span
    Of these boards each one.

Window and door even as he said
Three cabins more, they are well made,
Pitch and tar full sure upon them have been [laid,
This will ever endure, I count myself well paid;
    And why?
It is better wrought
Than I could have thought;
Him, that made all of nought,
    I thank only.

Now will I hie me despite the ill weather
My wife and my family, to bring even hither.
Listen here carefully, wife, and consider,
Hence must we flee all together
    Right fast.

WIFE Why, sir, what ails you?
Who is it assails you?
To flee it avails you,
    Yet ye be aghast.

NOAH The yarn on the reel is otherwise, dame.

WIFE Tell me more and less, else ye be to blame.

NOAH He can cure our distress, blessed be his name.
Our dole he will redress to shield us from shame
And said,
All this world about
With fierce floods so stout,
That shall run in a rout,
Shall be overspread.

He said all shall be slain save only we,
Our bairns shall remain and their wives three;
A ship he bad me ordain to save our company,
Therefore with all our main that Lord thank we,
Saviour of our blood;
Get along fast, go thither.

WIFE I know not whither,
I daze and I dither,
For fear of that flood.

NOAH Be not afraid, have done, truss up our gear,
Lest we be undone, without more fear.

1ST SON Full soon it shall be done, brothers help me [here.

2ND SON My part I shall not shun, no matter how [severe,
My brother.

3RD SON Without any yelp
With my might shall I help.

WIFE I've a blow for each whelp,
If you help not your mother.

NOAH Now are we there, as we should be;
Go, get in our gear, cattle and company,
Into this vessel here, my children free.

WIFE Shut up was I never, so God save me,
In such an oyster as this.
In faith I cannot find
Which is before, which is behind;

Shall we here be confined,
Noah, as have thou bliss?

NOAH Dame, peace and still, we must abide grace;
Therefore, wife, with good will, come into this
[place.

WIFE Sir, for Jack nor for Gill, will I turn my face,
Till I have on this hill, spun a space
On my distaff;
Woe to him who moves me,
Now will I down set me,
And let no man prevent me,
For him will I strafe.

NOAH Behold in the heaven, the cataracts all
That are open full even, both great and small
And the planets seven, left have their stall,
The thunder downdriven, and lightnings now
[fall
Full stout,
On halls and bowers,
Castles and towers;
Full sharp are these showers,
That deluge about.

Therefore, wife have done, come in the ship
[fast.

WIFE Patch your shoes and run, the better they will
[last.

1ST WIFE Come, good mother, come, for all is overcast,
Both the moon and the sun.

2ND WIFE And many winds blast
Full sharp;
These floods may drown our kin,
Therefore, mother, come in.

WIFE In faith, still will I spin;
All in vain ye carp.

3RD WIFE If ye like, ye may spin, mother, in the ship.

NOAH Ye be twice bidden in, dame, in all friendship.

WIFE Whether I lose or I win, in faith, thy fellow-
[ship,
Set I not at a pin, this spindle will I slip
Upon this hill.
Ere one foot I stir.

NOAH By Peter, but ye err;
Without further spur
Come in if ye will.

WIFE Yea, the water nighs so near that I sit not dry,
Into the ship for fear quickly will I hie
For dread that I drown here.

NOAH Dame, but surely,
Paid ye have full dear, ye stayed so long by,
Out of the ship.

WIFE I will not at thy bidding,
Go from door to dunghill gadding.

NOAH In faith and for your long tarrying,
Ye shall taste of the whip.

WIFE Spare me not, I pray thee, do even as thou
[think,
These great words shall not flay me.

NOAH Abide dame and drink,
For beaten shalt thou be with this staff till thou
[stink;
Are these strokes good, say ye.

WIFE What say ye? Go sink!

NOAH Now quake!
Cry me mercy, I say!

WIFE To that say I nay.

NOAH If not, by this day,
Thy head shall I break.

WIFE Lord, I were at ease and heartily hale
With a pottage of pease and my widow's kale;
For thy soul it would please me to pay penny
[bail,

So would more than these I see in this dale,
Of the wives that here stir,
For the dance they are led,
Wish their husbands were dead,
For, as ever eat I bread,
So, would I our sire were.

NOAH Ye men that have wives, while they are young,
If ye love your lives, chastise their tongue:
Methinks my heart rives, both liver and lung,
To see such a strife, wedded men among;
But I,
As have I bliss,
Shall chastise this.

WIFE Yet may ye miss,
Nichol needy!

NOAH I shall make thee still as stone, beginner of [blunder!
I shall beat thee, back and bone, and break all [in sunder.

[*They fight.*

WIFE Out, alas, I am overthrown! Out upon thee, [man's wonder!

NOAH See how she can groan, and I lie under;
But wife,
Haste we, without ado,
For my back is near in two.

WIFE And I am beaten so blue
And wish for no more strife.

[*They enter the Ark.*

1ST SON Ah! Why fare ye thus? father and mother, [both!

2ND SON Your spite would scarce free us from such sin [as wroth.

3RD SON These scenes are so hideous, I swear on my [oath.

NOAH We will do as ye bid us, and that with no sloth.
Sons dear!
At the helm now I am bent
To steer the ship as is meant.

WIFE I see in the firmament
The seven stars here.

NOAH This is a great flood, wife, take heed.

WIFE So methought as I stood we are in great need;
That these waves be withstood.

NOAH Now God help us, we plead!
As thou art helmsman good, and best may [succeed
Of all;
Rule us in this race,
Thy word we embrace.

WIFE This is a parlous case:
Help God, when we call.

NOAH To the tiller, wife, see, and I shall assay
The deepness of the sea where we sail, if I may.

WIFE That shall I do full wisely, now go thy way,
For upon this flood have we fared many a day,
In pain.

[NOAH *lowers a plummet.*

NOAH Now the water will I sound:
Ah! It is far to the ground;
This labour I have found
Brings little gain.

Above the hills is seen the water risen of late
Of cubits full fifteen, but in no higher state
These waves of water green will spill with for- [mer spate,
Rain forty days has been, it will therefore abate
Its zeal.

[NOAH *again lowers the plummet.*

Again it is best,
The water to test;

Now I am impressed,
  It has waned a great deal.

Now have the storms ceased and cataracts quit,
Both the most and the least.

WIFE Methinks, by my wit,
The sun shines in the east, lo, is not yond it?
We should have a good feast when these floods [flit
  So stormy.

NOAH We have been here, all we,
Three hundred days and fifty.

WIFE Yea, look, now wanes the sea;
  Lord, well are we.

NOAH The third time will I try in what depth we [steer.

WIFE Too long will you ply, lay in thy line there.

NOAH With my hand touch I the ground even here.

WIFE Therefore be we spry and have merry cheer;
  But husband,
What hills may there be?

NOAH Of Armenia's country.

WIFE Now blessed be he
  That brings us to land!

NOAH The tops of the hills I see, many at a sight,
Nothing prevents me the sky is so bright.

WIFE Tokens of mercy these are full right.

NOAH Dame, now counsel me what bird best might
  Go forth,
With flight of wing
And bring without tarrying
Of mercy some tokening
  Either by south or north?

For this is the first day of the tenth moon.

WIFE The raven durst I lay will come again soon;
As fast as thou may, cast him forth, have done,

He may come back today and dispel before
[noon
Our dismay.

NOAH I will loose to the blue
Sky, doves one or two:
Go your way, do,
God send you some prey.

Now have these fowl flown to separate coun-
[tries;
Let our prayers be known, kneeling on our
[knees,
To him that is alone worthiest of dignities,
That he may not postpone their coming back
[to please
Us with a sign.

WIFE Land they should be gaining,
The water so is waning.

NOAH Thank we that God reigning,
That made both me and mine.

It is a wondrous thing most certainly,
They are so long tarrying, the fowls that we
Cast out in the morning.

WIFE Sir, it may be
They bide something to bring.

NOAH The raven is hungry
Alway;
He is without any reason,
If he find any carrion,
No matter the season,
He will not away.

The dove is more gentle, to her trust is due,
Like to the turtle to death she is true.

WIFE Hence but a little she comes now, look you!
She brings in her bill some tidings new.
Behold!
It is of an olive tree
A branch, it seems to me.

NOAH Yea sooth, verily,
  Right so is it called.

Dove, bird full blest, fair might thee befall,
Thou art true to thy quest, as stone in the wall;
Thou wert trusted as best to return to thy hall.

WIFE A true token to attest we shall be saved all:
  For why?
The depth, since she has come,
Of the water by that plumb,
Hast fallen a fathom
  And more, say I.

1ST SON These floods are gone, father, behold.

2ND SON There is left right none, and that be ye bold.

3RD SON As still as a stone, our ship has firm hold,

NOAH On land here has run; God's grace is untold;
  My children dear,
Shem, Japhet, and Ham,
With glee and with game,
Go we in God's name,
  No longer abide here.

WIFE Here have we been, Noah, long enough, now,
With grief as is seen and full furrowed brow.

NOAH Behold on this green, neither cart nor plough
Is left on the scene, neither tree nor bough,
  Nor other thing,
But all is away:
Many castles, I say
Great towns of array,
  Flit in this flooding.

WIFE These floods put in fright all this world so wide,
Which moved with great might the sea and the [tide.

NOAH But death was the plight of the proudest in [pride,
Each person in sight that ever was spied,
  With sin,

All are they slain,
And put to great pain.

WIFE From thence again
May they never win.

NOAH Win? No, indeed, save God turn his face,
Forgive their misdeed, and admit them to [grace;
As he may hardship heed, I pray him in this [space,
In heaven to hear our need, and put us in a [place,
That we,
With his saints in sight,
And his angels bright,
May come to his light:
Amen for charity.

THE FOURTH PLAY

Abraham

ABRAHAM	ISAAC
1ST BOY	GOD
2ND BOY	ANGEL

ABRAHAM Thou very god, Adonai,
Thou hear us when we to thee call,
As thou art he that best may,
Most succour and help art thou to all;
Mightiful Lord, to thee I pray,
Let once the oil of mercy fall,
I be unworthy to abide that day,
Truly yet I hope I shall.

Mercy, Lord omnipotent!
Thou long since this world has wrought;
Say whither all our elders went!
Such matter muse I in my thought.
Since Adam gave to Eve assent,
To eat that apple spared he nought,
For all the wisdom that he meant
Full dear that bargain has he bought.

God's angel drove him for that wrong
From paradise with full sad cheer,
And after lived he here full long,
More than three hundred year,
In sorrow and in travail strong,
And every day in doubt or fear;
His children angered him among,
Cain slew Abel, to Adam so dear.

Since Noah, that was true and good,
He and his children three,

Were saved when all was flood:
    That was a wonder thing to see.
And Lot from Sodom when he strode,
    Three cities burnt, yet escaped he;
Thus, for they moved God's angry mood,
    He smote their sin most vengefully.

When I think of our elders all,
    And of the marvels that have been,
No gladness in my heart may fall,
    My comfort goes away full clean.
Lord, when shall death make me his thrall?
    A hundred years certain have I seen;
Ma foi! Soon I hope he shall,
    For it is right high time I mean.

Yet Adam is to hell gone,
    And there has lain many a day,
And all our elders everyone,
    They are gone the same way,
Until God will hear their moan;
    Now help, Lord Adonai!
For certain no surer help I own,
    And there is none that better may.

[GOD *appears above.*

GOD I will help Adam and his kin,
    If any man be loyal within,
Tendering to me love and truth
    Shunning pride and showing ruth;
My servant will I try and test,
    Abraham, where his faith may rest;
In certain wise I will him prove,
    If he to me be true of love.

Abraham! Abraham!

ABRAHAM Who is that? lo! Let me see!
I heard one name my name.

GOD It is I, pay heed to me,
    That formed thy father Adam,
And everything in its degree.

ABRAHAM To hear thy will, ready I am,
  And to fulfil whatever it be.

GOD Of mercy have I heard thy cry,
  My ear thy devout prayers have won;
If thou love me, look that thou hie
  Unto the land of Vision;
And the third day be there, bid I,
  And take with thee Isaac, thy son,
As a beast to sacrify,
  To slay him look thou not shun.
In offering burn him as a brand.

ABRAHAM Ah, praised be thou, Lord, in thy throne!
  Hold over me, Lord, thy holy hand,
Full sure thy bidding shall be done.
  Blessed be that Lord in every land
To visit his servant thus so soon.
  Fain would I this deed were planned
No profit is God's will to shun.

This commandment must I needs fulfil,
  Though that my heart wax heavy as lead;
Should I offend against his will?
  Nay, I would rather my child were dead.
Whatso he bids me, good or ill,
  That shall be done in every stead;
Both wife and child if he bid kill
  That should I do without a dread.

If Isaac knew, whereso he were,
  He would be abashed now,
How that he is in danger.
  Isaac, son, where art thou?

[ISAAC *enters.*

ISAAC Already, father, see me here;
  Now was I coming unto you;
I love you greatly, father dear.

ABRAHAM And dost thou so? I would know how
  Thou lovest me, son, as thou hast said.

ISAAC Yea, father, with all my heart,
More than all that ever was made;
May God long life to you impart!

ABRAHAM Now who would not be glad that had
A child so loving as thou art?
Thy loving cheer makes my heart glad,
And loth am I that we must part.

Go home, son; come soon again,
And tell thy mother I come full fast.

[*Here* ISAAC *leaves his* FATHER.

Now God bless and save him pain!
And glad am I that he has passed!
Alone, right here in this plain,
Might I speak till my heart burst,
I would that all were well, full fain,
But it must needs be done at last.

And it is good I nothing mar
To be prepared full good it were;
The land of Vision is full far,
The third day's end must I be there,
My ass shall with us fare,
Our harness less and more to bear,
No nearer Isaac gets death's scar;
A sword must with us yet therefore.

And I shall briskly make me yare;
This night will I begin my way,
Though Isaac be never so fair,
And mine own son, the sooth to say,
And though he be my very heir,
And all should wield after my day,
God's bidding shall I never spare;
Should I that withstand? Ma foi! But nay!

Isaac!

ISAAC —Sir!

ABRAHAM Be ready, son;
For certainly thyself and I,
We two must now wend forth of town,

To sacrifice in far country,
For a certain cause and reason.
Take wood and fire in haste with thee;
By hill and dale both up and down,
Son, thou shalt ride, and by thee walk shall I.

Look thou forget not what thou shalt need;
Go make thee ready, my darling!

ISAAC I am ready to do this deed,
And ever to fulfil your bidding.

ABRAHAM My dear son, look thou have no dread,
We shall come home with great loving;
Both to and fro I shall us lead;
Come now, son, with my blessing.
[*to the* SERVANTS]
Ye two here with this ass abide,
For Isaac and I will to yond hill;
It is so high we may not ride,
Therefore ye two shall abide here still.

1ST BOY Sir, ye shall not be denied,
We are ready your bidding to fulfil.

2ND BOY Whatsoever to us betide
To do your bidding ay we will.

ABRAHAM God's blessing have ye both together;
I shall not tarry long from you.

1ST BOY Sir, we shall abide you here,
Out of this place shall we not go.

ABRAHAM Children, ye are ay to me full dear,
I pray God keep you ever from woe.

2ND BOY Thy bidding, sir, we keep for fear.

ABRAHAM Isaac, now are there but we two.

We must go a full good pace,
For it is further than I thought;
We shall make mirth and great solace,
When this thing to end be brought.
Lo, my son, here is the place.

ISAAC This wood and fire my hands have sought;
Tell me now, if ye have space,
Why beast for burning there is naught?

ABRAHAM Now son, I may no longer lie,
This work pierces my heart through;
Thou lived ever obediently,
Ever to yield thy duty as due.
But certainly thou now must die,
If my purpose hold but true.

ISAAC Now my heart as lead is heavy
My death thus hastily to rue.

ABRAHAM Isaac!

ISAAC Sir?

ABRAHAM Come hither, bid I;
Thou shalt be dead whatsoever betide.

ISAAC Ah, father, mercy! Mercy!

ABRAHAM That I say may not be denied;
Take thy death therefore meekly.

ISAAC Ah, good Sir, abide;
Father!

ABRAHAM What son?

ISAAC To do your will I am ready,
Wheresoever ye go or ride

If I may over-take your will,
Since I have trespassed I shall repent.

ABRAHAM Isaac!

ISAAC What, sir?

ABRAHAM Good son, be still.

ISAAC Father!

ABRAHAM What, son?

ISAAC Must my flesh be rent?
What have I done?

ABRAHAM Truly, no ill.

ISAAC And must I be slain?

ABRAHAM So have I meant.

ISAAC Sir, what may help?

ABRAHAM This must I fulfil.

ISAAC I ask mercy.

ABRAHAM Thee I must kill.

ISAAC When I am dead and closed in clay,
Who shall then be your son?

ABRAHAM Ah, Lord, that I should abide this day!

ISAAC Sir, who shall do the tasks I have done?

ABRAHAM Speak no such words, son, I thee pray.

ISAAC Shall ye me stay?

ABRAHAM That shall I, son:
Lie still! I smite!

ISAAC Sir, let me say.

ABRAHAM Now, my dear child, thou may not shun.

ISAAC The shining of your bright blade,
Makes me quake, my death to flee.

ABRAHAM Therefore face-down thou shall be laid,
Then when I strike thou shalt not see.

ISAAC What have I done, father, what have I said?

ABRAHAM Truly, nothing ill to me.

ISAAC Then slain thus guiltless is ill-paid.

ABRAHAM Now, good son, let such words be.

ISAAC I love you ay.

ABRAHAM So do I thee.

ISAAC Father!

ABRAHAM What, son?

ISAAC Let now be soon
For my mother's love.

ABRAHAM Let be, let be!
It would not help as thou dost mean;
But lie still till I come to thee.
I miss a little thing, I ween.
[*aside*]
He speaks so ruefully to me
I would these tears might not be seen.

All worldly joy that I might win
Would I give if he were unkind,
But no default I found in him;
For him in torture I would grind;
To slay him thus I think great sin,
So rueful words I with him find;
To part I feel such woe within
For he will never from my mind.

What shall I to his mother say?
For "Where is he?" comes quick from her;
If I tell her, "run away",
Swiftly answers she—"Nay, sir!"
And I am frightened her to slay;
I know not what I shall say to her.
He lies full still there, as he lay
Till I come there he dare not stir.

[GOD *appears above.*

GOD Angel, hie with all thy main!
To Abraham thou shalt be sent;
Say, Isaac shall not be slain;
Nor body burnt, nor his life spent.
This deed my servant shall refrain,
Go, put him out of his intent;
Bid him go home again,
I know well how he meant.

ANGEL Gladly, Lord, I am ready
Thy bidding shall be magnified;
I shall speed full hastily,
Thee to obey at evening tide;
Thy will, thy name to glorify,
Over all this world so wide;

And to thy servant now haste I,
    Good, true, Abraham, will I glide.

ABRAHAM But might I yet of weeping cease,
    Till I had done this sacrifice;
It must needs be despite his pleas,
    Though I carp thereof in this dull wise,
The more my sorrow it will increase;
    I quake to hear his cries;
I must rush on him my pain to ease,
    And slay him here right as he lies.

ANGEL Abraham! Abraham! [*Seizes him.*

ABRAHAM Who is there now?
    Alas let me go.

ANGEL Stand up, now, stand;
Thy good will I come to allow,
Therefore I bid thee hold thy hand.

ABRAHAM Say, who bad so? Any but thou?

ANGEL Yea, God; and sends this beast to thy offering [brand.

ABRAHAM But God spake lately to me how
To work this deed at his command.

ANGEL He has perceived thy meekness
    And thy goodwill also in this;
He would thou do thy son no distress,
    For granted to thee is his bliss.

ABRAHAM But know thou well that it is
    As thou hast said.

ANGEL I say thee yes.

ABRAHAM I thank thee, Lord, well of goodness,
    That all thus hast released me this.

To speak with thee have I no space,
    With my dear son till I have spoken.
My good son, thou shalt have grace,
    On thee now has my wrath not woken;
Rise up now, with thy comely face.

ISAAC Sir, shall I live?

ABRAHAM [*he kisses him*]
Yea, by this token
Son, thou hast escaped a full hard grace,
Thou should have been both burnt and [broken.

ISAAC But, father, shall I not be slain?

ABRAHAM No certain, son.

ISAAC Then I am glad;
Good sir, put up your sword again.

ABRAHAM Nay, hardly, but fear not my lad.

ISAAC Is all then well?

ABRAHAM Yea, son, certain.

ISAAC For fear, sir, I was almost mad.

I was never so afraid before,
As I have been on yonder hill,
But, by my faith, father, I swear
I will never more come there,
Unless it be against my will.

ABRAHAM Yea, come on with me, my own sweet son,
And homeward fast now let us be gone.

ISAAC By my faith, father, thereto I grant,
I had never so good will to go home,
And to speak with my dear mother.

ABRAHAM Ah! Lord of heaven I thank Thee,
For now may I lead home with me,
Isaac, my young son so free,
The gentlest child above all other.

[*Exeunt.*

THE FIFTH PLAY

Isaac

ISAAC ESAU
JACOB REBECCA

ISAAC Come here son and kiss me,
That I may sense the smell of thee;
The smell of my son is like
To a field with flowers or honey hive.
Where art thou, Esau, my son?

JACOB Here, father, and ask your benison.

ISAAC The blessing my father gave to me,
God of heaven and I give thee;
God thee with great plenty greet,
Of wine, of oil, and of wheat;
And grant thy children all
To worship thee, both great and small;
Whoso thee blesses, blessed be he;
Whoso thee curses, cursed be he.
Now hast thou my great blessing,
Love thee shall all thine offspring;
Go now whither thou hast to go.

JACOB Grant mercy, sir, I will do so.

[JACOB *retires.* ESAU *advances.*

ESAU Have, eat, father, of my hunting,
And give me then your blessing.

ISAAC Who is that?

ESAU I, your son
Esau, who brings you venison.

ISAAC Who was that was right now here,
And brought me the broth of a deer?

I ate well, and blessed him;
And he is blessed, in every limb.

ESAU Alas! I may weep and sob.

ISAAC Thou art beguiled through Jacob,
That is born thy very brother.

ESAU Have ye kept me no other
Blessing, but gave ye him each one?

ISAAC Such another have I none;
God grant that to thy lot may stand
The dew of heaven and fruit of land;
Other than this can I not say.

ESAU Now, alas, and welaway!
May I with that traitor meet,
I shall repay this bitter cheat;
My parents' grief should not away,
For if we meet I shall him slay.

[ESAU *retires.* REBECCA *advances.*

REBECCA Isaac, my own life would slip by,
If thus hated Jacob die.
I will send him to Aran,
There my brother dwells, Laban;
And there may he serve in peace
Till his brother's wrath will cease.
Why should I all in a day
Lose both my sons? Better nay.

ISAAC Thou sayest sooth, wife; call him hither,
And let us tell him where and whither
That he may Esau flee
Who vows such vengeance shall be.

[JACOB *advances.*

REBECCA Jacob, son! thy father and I
Would speak with thee; come, stand us by!
From the country must thou flee,
So that Esau slay not thee.

JACOB Whither should I go from here?

REBECCA To Mesopotamia;
With thine uncle Laban bide,
Who dwells Jordan's stream beside;
And there may thou with him live,
Until Esau, my son, forgive
And forget, and his rage be dead.

JACOB I will go, father, as is said.

ISAAC Yea, son, do as thy parents say;
Come kiss us both, and wend thy way.

JACOB Have good day, sir and dame!

[*He kisses* FATHER *and* MOTHER.

ISAAC God shield thee, son, from sin and shame!

REBECCA And give thee grace, good man to be,
And send me glad tidings of thee.

[JACOB *goes one way.* ISAAC *and* REBECCA *the other.*

THE SIXTH PLAY

Jacob

JACOB	JOSEPH
GOD	BENJAMIN
RACHEL	ESAU
LEAH	

JACOB Help me, Lord Adonai,
And hold me in the right way
To Mesopotamia;
For I came never till now here;
I came never to this country;
Lord of heaven, thou help me!
For I have gained along this street
Sore bones and aching feet.
The sun is down, what is best?
Here purpose I all night to rest;
Under my head this stone shall lie:
A night's rest take will I.

[GOD *appears above.*

GOD Jacob, Jacob, thy God I am;
Of thy forefather, Abraham,
And of thy father Isaac;
I shall thee bless for their sake.
This land that thou sleepest in,
I shall thee give, and thy kin;
I shall thy seed multiply,
As thick as powder on earth may lie
Thy generation shall spread wide,
From east to west on every side,
From the south unto the north;
All I say I shall bring forth;

And all the folk of thine offspring,
Shall be blessed with thy blessing.
Jacob, of terror take no heed!
I shall thee clothe, I shall thee feed.
Safe and sound shall be thy state;
I shall thee help early and late;
And all in comfort shall I bring thee
Home again to thy country.
I shall not fail, be thou bold,
But I shall do as I have told.

[JACOB *wakes.*

JACOB Ah! Lord! What may this mean?
What have I heard in sleep, and seen?
That from a ladder God leaned down
And spoke to me without a frown.
And where that ladder stood but late
Is but God's house and heaven's gate.
Lord how fearful is this stead!
Where I lay down my head,
In God's praise I raise this stone,
And oil will I put thereon.
Lord of heaven, hear me now,
Here to thee I make a vow.
If thou give me meat and food
With clothes withal to be endued,
And bring me home to kith and kin,
By the way that I walk in,
Without pain in any part,
I promise to thee with steadfast heart,
As thou art my Lord and God
I shall not leave thy ways untrod.
This stone I raise in sign today
I shall hold holy kirk for ay;
And of all that comes fresh to me
Righteously shall I give to thee.

[*Here* JACOB *leaves Aran for the country of his birth.*

God of heaven, my father dear,
That said to me with thy voice clear,

When I in Aran was dwelling,
My return should be compelling
To where I was both born and fed,
Lord, thou warned me in that stead,
As I went toward Aran
With my staff, and passed Jordan:
Again I come into my land,
With two hosts of men at hand.
Thou promised me, Lord, to bless me,
To multiply my seed as sand of sea;
Thou save me, Lord, through thy power
From Esau's vengeance this hour,
That he slay not, for former spite,
These mothers and children in his might.

[RACHEL *enters.*

RACHEL Our anguish, sir, is manifold,
From what our messenger has told
That Esau will you slay
With four hundred men more today.

JACOB Forsooth, Rachel, I have him sent
Full many a beast and present.

[LEAH *enters.*

Perchance our gifts he may yet take,
And right so shall his wrath slake.
Where are our things, are they past Jordan?

LEAH Go and look, sir, as ye can.

[JACOB *wrestles with* GOD.

GOD The day springs; now let me go.

JACOB Nay, nay, I will not so,
Save thou bless me ere thou part
Thee shall I stay with all my heart.

GOD In token that thou speakest with me
On thy thigh I shall touch thee,
That limp shalt thou evermore,
But thou shalt feel no sore;
What is thy name, thou me tell?

JACOB Jacob.

GOD Nay, but Israel;
Since thou to me such strength made known
All men on earth thy might must own.

JACOB What is thy name?

GOD Why ask thou so?
Wonderful, if thou would know.

JACOB Ah, bless me, Lord.

GOD I shall thee bless,
And be to thee full propitious,
And give thee my blessing for ay,
As Lord and he that all may.
I shall grace well thy going,
And ordain all thy doing:
When thou hast dread, think on me,
And thou shalt full well blessed be,
And look thou trust well what I say,
And fare thee well, now dawns the day.

JACOB Now have I a new name, Israel,
This place shall be called Fanuel,
For I have seen in this place,
God of heaven face to face.

RACHEL Jacob, lo, we have now word
That Esau's hosts at hand are heard.

[*Here* JACOB *divides his hosts into three parts.*

JACOB Rachel, with the last troop dwell,
For I would thou wert kept well;
Call Joseph and Benjamin,
And keep them close therein.

If it be so that Esau
Strike at us who go before,
Ye that are here the last
Ye may be saved if ye flee fast.

[JACOB *and* ESAU *meet and kiss,* JACOB *comes and kneels in prayer to* GOD, *raises himself and runs again to* ESAU *and embraces him.*

JACOB Lord, as thou promised, I pray thee,
That thou save my kin and me.

ESAU Welcome brother to kith and kin,
All wives and children thy host within.
How hast thou fared in that far land?
Tell tidings how things with thee stand.

JACOB My brother Esau, well,
If no malice in your men dwell.

[ESAU *speaks to his* SERVANTS.

ESAU Look now, fellows, hold your hands,
Ye see that he and I are friends,
And friendship here will we fulfil,
Since that it is God's holy will.

JACOB God grant it, brother, that it so is
That thou thy servant so would kiss.

ESAU Nay, Jacob, my dear brother,
Matters stand quite other;
Thou art my lord through destiny:
Go we together both thou and I,
To my father and his wife,
Who prize thee, brother, as their life.

[*They go out together.*

THE SEVENTH PLAY

Pharaoh

PHARAOH	2ND SOLDIER	GOD
1ST SOLDIER	MOSES	1ST BOY
		2ND BOY

PHARAOH Peace, on pain that no man pass,
But keep the course that I command,
And take good heed of him that has
Your health all wholly in his hand:
For King Pharaoh my father was,
And held the lordship of this land:
I am his heir and all surpass,
Ever in strength to stir or stand.

All Egypt is my own
To lead after my law:
I would my might were known
And held in fitting awe.
Full low he shall be thrown,
And flayed till he be raw,
If any grudge or groan,
Them shall I hang and draw.

But as your King I command peace,
To all the people of this empire.
Look no man thrust forth in the press,
But ye must do as I desire,
And of your words look that ye cease.
Pay heed to me, your sovereign sire,
That can your comfort most increase,
Submit to me your lives entire.

1ST SOLDIER My lord, if any were here,
That would not work your will,

If we might come them near,
    Full quick we should them kill.

PHARAOH Throughout my Kingdom would I ken,
    And give them thanks that would me tell,
If any were so cursed men
    That would my Kingdom fell.

2ND SOLDIER My lord, we have amongst us men
    Strong and powerful to rebel:
The Jews that dwell in Goshen
    Called the children of Israel.

They multiply full fast,
    And them we straight accuse
Of plotting in the past,
    Our leadership to lose.

PHARAOH Why, how have they such tricks begun?
Are they of might? Ye me amaze!

1ST SOLDIER Yea, lord, their numbers overrun
    As in the king, your father's days.
They came of Joseph, Jacob's son—
    He was a prince worthy of praise—
Rebellious deeds since have they done:
    That set your book of law ablaze.

They will confound you clean,
    Unless you make them cease.

PHARAOH What devil is that they mean
    That they so fast increase?

2ND SOLDIER How they increase full well we ken,
    As did our fathers understand:
They were but sixty and ten
    When they first came unto this land:
Since sojourning in Goshen
    Four hundred years, a crafty band:
Now are they numbered of mighty men
    More than three hundred thousand,

Counting no woman nor child,
    Nor cattle, a number vast.

PHARAOH How thus might we be beguiled?
But it shall not last:
For with cunning we shall them quell,
So that they shall not further spread.

1ST SOLDIER My lord, we have heard our fathers tell,
And learned clerks that were well-read,
There should a man amidst us dwell
That should undo and strike us dead.

PHARAOH Fie on him, to the devil of hell!
Such destiny will we not dread:

We shall make our midwives kill them
When any Hebrew babes are born,
The hopes of Hebrews, we shall spill them,
And that race shall feel forlorn.

For their parents hold I no awe,
Them to such bondage I shall bind,
To ditch and delve, and drudge and draw,
At all the basest tasks to grind:
So shall these lads hold to the law,
And keep their thralldom ay in mind.

2ND SOLDIER Such cunning shows no judgement raw,
We soon shall fewer Hebrews find.

PHARAOH Now help to hold them down,
No cruelty forsake.

1ST SOLDIER Ready, lord, true to thy crown,
In bondage them to break.

[*They go out.* MOSES *enters with a rod in his hand.*

MOSES Great God, that all this world began,
And grounded it in good degree,
Thou made me, Moses, unto man,
And later saved me from the sea:
King Pharaoh then had made a plan
No Hebrew man-child saved should be:
But I escaped despite his ban:
Thus has God shown his might to me.

Now am I set to keep
 Under this mountain side,
Bishop Jethro's sheep,
 Till better things betide.

Ah, Lord, great is thy might!
 What may to men that marvel mean?
Yonder I see the strangest sight,
 Such in the world was never seen:
A bush I see burning full bright,
 Yet still I see the leaves are green:
If this work by man has been
 I shall discover if I might.

GOD Moses, Moses!

[*Here* MOSES *hastens to a bramble bush, and* GOD *speaks to him.*

Moses, come not too near,
 In that stead stay where you dwell,
And hearken unto me here:
 Take heed what I thee tell.
Unlatch thy shoes for fear,
 Tread barefoot in this dell,
The place thou stands on there
 Forsooth, is hallowed well.

I am thy Lord, and for thy sake,
 I may thy life lengthen a space:
I am the God that erstwhile spake
 To learned elders of thy race:
To Abraham and Isaac,
 And Jacob also found my grace,
A mighty multitude they make,
 Whose seed has made a populace.

But now this king, Pharaoh,
 He hurts my folk so fast,
If that I suffer him so,
 Their seed should soon be past:
Them shall I not forgo,
 If their trust in me but last

Their bondage shall I overthrow,
  Therefore as prophet thou are cast,

To bear my message, keep in mind,
  To him that would my people harass:
Thou speak to him with words full kind,
  If that he let my people pass,
That to the wilderness their way they find,
  To worship me as I will ask.
If more my folk in bondage grind,
  Full soon his song shall be "alas".

MOSES Ah, Lord! Pardon me, by thy leave,
  That lineage loves me naught:
Gladly they would me grieve,
  Such message if I brought.
Good Lord, to another this entrust,
  That has more force to cause folk fear.

GOD Moses, perform this thing thou must;
  My bidding shall thou boldly bear:
If spitefully at thee they thrust,
  Of thy safety I shall take care.

MOSES Good Lord, me they will not trust
  For all the oaths that I can swear:

To announce such tidings new
  To folk of wicked will,
Without a token true,
  No good shall I fulfil.

GOD If that he will not understand
  This token true to thee is sent,
Before the king cast down thy wand,
  And it shall turn to a serpent:
Then take the tail again in hand—
  To lift it boldly be intent,
And with a rod again you stand,
  Such mastery for you is meant.

Then in thy bosom hide thy arm,
  Straight leprous shall be its touch,
Then whole again, no hurt nor harm:
  Lo, my tokens shall be such.

And if he will not suffer then
  My people for to pass in peace,
Plagues in vengeance, nine or ten,
  I shall send before I cease.

But the Hebrews, there in Goshen,
  Shall not be marked but find release:
As long as they my laws will ken
  Their comfort shall ever increase.

MOSES Ah, Lord, we ought to love thee well,
  That makes thy folk thus free:
I shall unto them tell
  As thou has told to me.
But to the king, Lord, when I come,
  If he ask what is thy name,
And I stand still, both deaf and dumb,
  How should I escape the blame?

GOD I tell thee thus, "*Ego sum qui sum,*"
  I am he that is the same:
If thou can neither muff nor mum,
  I shall shield thee from shame.

MOSES I understand full well this thing,
  I go, Lord, with all the might in me.

GOD Be bold in my blessing,
  Thy succour shall I be.

MOSES Ah, Lord of love, I shall declare,
  And straightway all this mystery tell:
To my friends now will I fare,
  The chosen children of Israel,
To bring them comfort in their care,
  In pressing danger where they dwell.

[MOSES *speaks to the* ISRAELITES.

Patient be ye still in prayer,
  And God your griefs will surely quell.

1ST BOY Ah, master Moses, dear!
  Our mirth is turned to mourning:
Held down harshly are we here
  As churls under the king.

2ND BOY We may mourn for evermore,
No man can bring us back to grace:
God may our people yet restore
And send us comfort in this case.

MOSES Brethren no more your dole deplore:
God's goodness will relieve our race,
From such woe which has gone before,
And put us in a pleasant place:
For I shall call upon the king,
And fast demand to make you free.

1ST BOY God grant you good going,
And evermore with you be.

[MOSES *goes to* PHARAOH.

MOSES King Pharaoh, be attent.

PHARAOH Why, boy, what tidings can you tell?

MOSES From God himself hither am I sent
To fetch the children of Israel:
To the wilderness he would they went.

PHARAOH Yea, go hence to the devil of hell!
I mind no matter he has meant,
In my displeasure shall thou dwell:
And, traitor, for thy sake,
In anguish they shall pine.

MOSES Then will God vengeance take
On thee, and all of thine.

PHARAOH On me? Fie on thee lad, out of my land!
Thinks thou thus our laws decay?
[*to the* SOLDIERS]
Say, whence is yon warlock with his wand
That thus would whisk our folk away?

1ST SOLDIER Yond is Moses, here at hand,
Against all Egypt has been ay,
He tried your father to withstand:
Now will he mar you if he may.

PHARAOH Fie on him! Nay, nay, that dance is done:
Lubber, thou learnt too late.

MOSES God bids thee not his will to shun,
And let me pass thy gate.

PHARAOH Bids God me? False lubberly lies?
What token told he? What is sent?

MOSES He said thou should despise
Both me and his commandment:
Therefore upon this wise,
My wand he bad, with thou present,
I should lay down, and thee advise
How it should turn into a serpent:
And in his holy name
Here I lay it down:
Lo, sir, here may thou see the same.

PHARAOH Ah, ha, dog! The devil thee drown!

MOSES He bad me take it by the tail,
Of his power to give proof plain:
Then he said, surely without fail,
It should turn to a wand again.
Lo, sir, behold!

PHARAOH Ill luck you assail!
Certain, this is a subtle swain!
But these boys shall abide in bale,
To them thy gadgets be no gain.
But worse, both morn and noon,
Shall they fare, for thy sake.

MOSES I pray God send us vengeance soon,
And on thee his wrath to wake.

1ST SOLDIER Alas, alas! This land is torn!
Our lives no longer can we mend:
Such mischief maimed us since morn
Which no medicine can amend.

PHARAOH Why cry ye so, lads? Who gives this scorn?

2ND SOLDIER Sir King, with care we must contend
More than knew man that e'er was born.

PHARAOH Tell on, quickly, and make an end.

1ST SOLDIER Sir, the waters for both man and beast
That lately were in flood,
Through Egypt land from west to east,
Are turned into red blood:

Full ugly and full ill is it,
That both fresh and fair was before.

PHARAOH Oh, ho! A wonder rare, I must admit,
No wizard worked such heretofore!

2ND SOLDIER More ill news, lord, I must submit,
That sows our land with troubles sore:
For toads and frogs may no man sit,
Their venom vexes us the more.

1ST SOLDIER Great gnats, sir, come both day and night,
Bite us full bitterly:
We suspect that comes this spite
Through Moses, our great enemy.

2ND SOLDIER My lord, unless this people leave,
No more shall mirth to us belong.

PHARAOH Go, say to him we will not grieve,
Save they the speedier go along.

1ST SOLDIER Moses, my lord you would relieve
By leading thy folk as you long,
So that at last we peace achieve.

MOSES Full well I know, these words are wrong:

But surely all that I have said
Full suddenly it shall be seen:
Men at such marvels shall have dread
And King Pharaoh cry and keen.

2ND SOLDIER Ah, lord, alas, for dole we die!
We dare look out from no door.

PHARAOH Now by the devil of hell, what ails you so to [cry?

1ST SOLDIER We fare worse than ever before:
Great hopping fleas over all this land [they fly,

Their bite leaves blisters big and sore,
And in every place our beasts dead lie.

2ND SOLDIER Horse, ox and ass,
They fall down dead, sir, suddenly.

PHARAOH Woe! lo, there is no man that has
Half as much harm as I.

1ST SOLDIER Yes, sir, poor folk have heavy woe,
To see their cattle thus out-cast.
The Jews in Goshen fare not so,
Their good luck seems sure to last.

PHARAOH Then shall we give them leave to go,
Until this peril be just passed
But ere too far has flit our foe,
In bondage bind them twice as fast.

2ND SOLDIER Moses, my Lord gives leave
That your people bid adieu.

MOSES More mischief still ye weave
Unless these tales be true.

1ST SOLDIER Ah, lord, of no more worth is life.

PHARAOH What, devil! Is grievance come again?

2ND SOLDIER Yea, sir, such powder now is rife,
That monstrous boils bide in its train:
It makes leprous man and wife,
And further hurt with hail and rain.
Sir, mountain vines fall in this strife,
Such frost and thunder has them slain.

PHARAOH Yea, but how do they in Goshen,
The Jews, can ye that say?

1ST SOLDIER Of all these cares nothing they ken,
Nothing of what may us dismay.

PHARAOH No? Out harrow! The devil! Sit they in [peace?
And we every day in doubt and dread?

2ND SOLDIER My lord, our cares will ever increase,
Till Moses away his folk has led:

Else are we lost, our hopes here cease,
Yet were it better that they sped.

PHARAOH That folk shall flit no more,
His madness shall I never dread.

1ST SOLDIER Then will it soon be war:
It were better that they sped.

2ND SOLDIER My lord, new harms have come to hand.

PHARAOH Yea, devil, will it no better be?

1ST SOLDIER Locusts are wasting all this land,
They leave no flower nor leaf on tree.

2ND SOLDIER Against that storm may no man stand:
And much more marvel it seems to me,
That these three days from strand to strand
Such mirk that no man can another see.

1ST SOLDIER Ah, my lord!

PHARAOH Huh!

2ND SOLDIER Great pestilence comes to do us shame:
It is like full long to last.

PHARAOH Pestilence, in the devil's name!
Then is our pride quite past.

1ST SOLDIER My lord, this care lasts long,
And will till Moses have his way:
Let him go, else work we wrong,
No shillyshallying helps today.

PHARAOH Then give them leave to go along:
Since such I needs must say:
Perchance we may their grief prolong
And mar them more through this delay.

2ND SOLDIER Moses, my lord says so:
Thou shall have passage plain.

MOSES Now have we leave to go,
My friends, now be ye fain:
Come forth, now shall ye wend
To a land of ease, I say.

1ST BOY But King Pharaoh, that false fiend,
Will us again betray:
He reckons soon our race to end,
His troops pursue in great array.

MOSES Be not abashed, God is our friend,
And all our foes will slay:
Therefore come on with me,
Have done and dread you nought.

2ND BOY That Lord, blessed might he be,
That us from bale has brought.

1ST BOY Such friendship saves us in this land:
Though dreadful perils me appal,
The red sea is here at hand,
We change again from free to thrall.

MOSES I shall make way there with my wand,
As God has said to save us all:
On either side the sea shall stand,
Till we be gone, right as a wall.

Leave none behind, with me keep near:
Lo try ye now your God to please.

[*Here they cross the sea.*

2ND BOY Oh, Lord! The way is clear:
Now wend we all with ease.

1ST SOLDIER King Pharaoh! This folk is gone.

PHARAOH Say, what annoyance new?

2ND SOLDIER These Hebrews are gone, lord, everyone.

PHARAOH How says thou that?

1ST SOLDIER Lord, that tale is true.

PHARAOH Woe! swiftly out, seize them again:
Full readily that rout shall rue,
We shall not cease till they be slain,
Them to the sea we shall pursue.

With charging chariots speed,
And fiercely follow me.

2ND SOLDIER Already, lord, gladly indeed
At your bidding to be.

1ST SOLDIER Lord, we be obedient to the crown,
For which our bodies well may bleed:
We shall not cease, but ding all down,
Till all be dead as is decreed.

PHARAOH Rejoice at Mohammed's renown,
He will be near us in our need:
Help! The ragged devil, we drown!
Now must we die for our ill deed.

[*The sea submerges them.*

MOSES Now are we free from all our woe,
And saved out of the sea:
Praise and love to God we owe,
As land we tread on safely.

1ST BOY Praise we that Lord of light,
And ever tell this marvel:
Drowned he has King Pharaoh's might,
Praised be that Lord Emmanuel.

MOSES Heaven, thou attend, I say, in sight,
And earth my words: hear what I tell.
As rain or dew the earth makes bright
And waters herbs and trees full well.

Give praise unto God's majesty,
His deeds are done, his ways are true,
Honoured be he in trinity,
To him be honour and virtue.
Amen.

[*Exeunt.*

THE EIGHTH PLAY

The Procession of the Prophets

MOSES SIBYL
DAVID DANIEL

MOSES All ye folk of Israel
Hearken to me! I will you tell
  Tidings wondrous good;
Ye all know how it befell
Wherefore Adam was damned to hell,
  He, and all his blood.

Therefore God has mind to raise
A prophet in these evil days,
  From our brethren's kin;
All shall believe what he may say
And walk after in his way,
  From hell he shall them win.

When his time begins to dawn,
No man should turn from him in scorn,
  But greet him with great trust;
And he that will not hear in awe,
He shall be held an outlaw,
  And from his folks be thrust.

Be ready that same prophet to meet,
Who shall come hereafter, full sweet,
  And many marvels show.
Man shall fall down at his feet,
Because all ills he can defeat,
  And our bliss bestow.

All that after truth will run
Shall he save, yea everyone
  Through him the truth shall see.

A prophet everywhere is found
Where proudly men his praises sound,
  Save in his own country.

Hearken all, both young and old!
God that all might may hold,
  Greets you by me;
His commandments are ten;
Behold, ye that are his men,
  Here ye may them see.

His commandments that I have brought,
Look that ye hold them nought
  For trifles, nor for fables;
For ye shall well understand
That God wrote them with his hand
  In these same tables.

Ye that these in heart will hold,
Unto heaven shall ye be called,
  The first to shun God's hate;
And ye that will not do so,
To hell's pains must ye go
  And bide a bitter fate.

Hear now, as ye hope for bliss;
The first commandment is this
  That I shall to you say;
Make no god of stick nor stone,
And trust in none but God alone,
  That made both night and day.

The second bids thou shalt not swear
For no reward nor snare,
  Falsely, in God's name;
If thou swearst unjustly,
Know thou well and wisely
  Thou deservest great blame.

The third is, that thou have in mind
The holy day, nor fail to find
  God's service in thy heart.
The fourth commandment don't neglect,

Mother and father hold in respect,
Rich or poor to play the part.

The fifth commands thou shalt forsake
Fornication, and a wife take,
And live in righteous state.
The sixth commands thou shalt not be
Manslayer for no kind of fee,
Nor for love nor for hate.

The seventh commands thee not to steal
Nor rob, nor wrongfully to deal,
Nor for more nor for less.
The eighth bids both old and young
That they be true of their tongue,
And bear no false witness.

The ninth bids thee, by thy life,
Thou desire not thy neighbour's wife,
Nor maiden that is his.
The tenth bids thee, in no case,
Covet thy neighbour's goods nor place;
Thou come thus not amiss.

I am the same man that God chose
The ten commandments of peace to disclose
On Mount Sinai;
This truth my speech here closes;
By name men call me Moses;
And have now all good day. [*Exit.*]

[DAVID *enters. He carries a harp.*

DAVID Hearken all that hear may,
And perceive well what I say,
All with righteousness.
Look ye put it not away,
But think thereon both night and day,
For it is truthfulness.

Jesse's son, ye know I am;
David is my right name,
And I bear a crown;
If ye me doubt, ye are to blame;

Of Israel, both wild and tame,
My rule spreads up and down.

As God of heaven has given me wit,
Shall I now sing you a song fit
For my minstrelsy;
Look ye put it into writing
Mar nor mock now my reciting,
For it is prophecy.

[*He plays the harp and sings.*

Mirth I make for all men,
With my harp and fingers ten,
And make them not dismayed;
God that Adam with his hand wrought
Shall send his son for our comfort,
He earth and heaven made.

He will come down from heaven's tower,
For to be man's saviour,
And what is lost to find;
For that I harp, and mirth make,
For on himself manhood will take,
Of my prophecy have mind.

In heaven shall he reign again
As gracious King with might and main,
In the highest seat;
There is neither king nor churl
Who may stain this princely pearl,
Nor hide him from his hate.

He shall be lord and king of all,
To his feet shall kings down fall
To offer graciously;
Blessed be that sweet flower,
That comes to be our saviour!
Joyful may we be.

Rich gifts they shall him bring,
And to him make offering,
Kneeling on their knee;
Well him befall that that lording,

And that dear darling,
    Might be alive to see.

Men may know him by his mark
Mirth and loving is his work,
    That shall he love most.
Light shall be born in that time dark,
To the unlearned and the clerk,
    Through the holy ghost.

Both emperor and king therefore,
Old and young, both rich and poor,
    Temper well your glee,
Until that king descends,
And our imprisonment ends,
    And makes us all free.

Thou show thy mercy, Lord, to us,
For till thou come, to hell we must,
    We have no other fate;
Lord, if it be thy will, then give
To us that blessed balm to live
    For thee whom we await.

Now have I sung my song to you;
Have it by heart lest you it rue,
    I warn with all my might;
He through his will that made us well,
Shield us from the pit of hell
    And grant us heaven's light. [*Exit.*]

[*Enter* SIBYL.

SIBYL Whoso will hear tidings glad,
Of him that all this world made,
    Hear attentively!
Sibyl sage is my name;
Unless ye hear ye are to blame,
    My word is prophecy.

All men through Adam's sin were slain,
And without ending put to pain,
    Through the falseness of the fiend;
A new king comes from heaven to fight

Against the fiend to win his right,
   So is his mercy gleaned.

All the world shall he judge,
For those who service do not grudge
   Much mirth he shall provide;
All shall see him face to face,
Rich and poor of every race,
   From him no man may hide;

But they shall in their flesh arise,
And all shall quake to realize
   The coming of that doom,
With his saints, full many a one,
He shall be seen in flesh and bone,
   That king that is to come.

All that shall stand him before,
All shall be both less and more,
   Of one age each one.
Angels shall quake and cease from mirth,
And fire shall burn the whole of earth,
   Yea, the world and all thereon.

Nothing shall on earth be known
But burnt it be and overthrown,
   All waters and the sea.
After shall both hill and dale
Come together, great and small,
   And all shall even be.

At his coming the trump shall blow,
That all men may his coming know;
   Full sorrowful shall be that blast;
There is no man that hears it,
But he shall quake out of his wit,
   Be he never so steadfast.

Then shall hell gape and grin,
That men may know their fate therein,
   Of that high justice;
The evil doers to hell must go;
And to heaven the others also,
   That have been righteous.

Therefore I warn every man,
Keep, as well as he can,
From sin and from misdeed,
My prophecy now have I told;
God you save both young and old,
And help you at your need. [*Exit.*]

[*Enter* DANIEL.

DANIEL God that made Adam and Eve,
While they lived well, he gave them leave
In paradise to dwell;
But when they had that apple ate,
They were damned, and soon beset
By the pains of hell,

To sorrow and suffering ever new;
Therefore will God our great griefs rue,
And his son down send
Onto earth, flesh to take,
That is all for our sake,
Our trespass to amend.

Flesh with flesh will be bought,
That he lose not what he has wrought
With his own hand;
Of a maiden shall he be born,
To save all that are forlorn,
Evermore without end. [*Exit.*]

THE NINTH PLAY

Caesar Augustus

EMPEROR
1ST COUNSELLOR
2ND COUNSELLOR
MESSENGER (LIGHTFOOT)
SIRINUS

EMPEROR Be still, bashirs, I command you,
That no man speak a word here now
But I myself alone;
And if ye do I make a vow,
This sword shall strike your head full low,
Therefore be still as stone.

And look ye grieve me not,
Or bitter will be your lot,
By Mohammed that I swear;
As ye know I reck not a jot
To slay you swiftly on the spot,
So sit ye stone-still there.

For all is in me that up may stand,
Castles, towers, towns in every land,
To me homage they bring;
No prince may my power withstand,
Everything bows unto my hand,
I want no earthly thing.

I am lord and sire over all,
All bow to me both great and small,
As lord of every land;
None is so comely on to call,
Whoso gainsays, ill shall befall,
I set thereto my hand.

For I am he that is mighty,
And all heathendom heeding me
Is ready at my will;

Both rich and poor, more and less,
At my liking for to redress,
Whether I save or kill.

Caesar Augustus I am called,
A fairer person to behold,
Is not of blood and bone;
Rich nor poor, young nor old,
Such another as I am told,
In all this world is none.

But one thing gives me heavy care,
I fear my land will soon misfare
For counsel loyal I lack;
My counsellors, of wisdom rare,
Give comfort to me in my care,
No wise words now hold back.

As I am man of most renown
I shall your counsel richly crown,
If help to me ye give.

1ST COUNSELLOR
Lord we would our lives lay down
To counsel you as none in town,
Full gladly while we live.

Your messenger I bid ye call
For anything that may befall,
Bid him go hastily,
Throughout your lands over all,
Among your folk both great and small
Your power and peace to cry.

For to command both young and old,
None is so hardy nor so bold
To hold that sway but thou;
And whoso does, in bondage hold,
And look thou pain them manifold.

EMPEROR
I shall, I make a vow;

Good counsel in these words I see.
It shall be done full hastily,
Without the least respite.

2ND COUNSELLOR
My lord, abide awhile, and why?
These words to you shall clarify.

EMPEROR
Then quickly tell me it.

2ND COUNSELLOR
Already, lord, without gainsay,
This have I heard for many a day,
Folk in the country tell;
A maid dwells in this land, they say
That shall bear a child to sway
Greater power than you can quell.

EMPEROR
Greater power? the devil? what may this be?
Out, harrow, full woe is me!
My wits fly from my head!
Ah, fire and devil! Whence came he,
That thus should wrest my power from me,
Before I see him dead?

For certainly my strength were shorn
If such a sneaking greenhorn
Should thus be my sovereign;
If I know when that boy is born,
Though the devil had it sworn,
That lad I would have slain.

1ST COUNSELLOR
Alas, my lord, grieve you not so,
But make your messenger forth go
After your cousin dear,
To speak with you a word or two,
The best device for death to show
And free you of your fear.

EMPEROR
As a wise knight all men him know.
Your counsel shall I not forgo.
Of wit art thou the well;
Praise on him all men bestow,
This lad shall not me overthrow
Were he the devil of hell.

Come, Lightfoot, lad, like a hare
With my message forth to fare,
To Sirinus, go quick.
Say sorrows strike I cannot bear,

Pray him to comfort me of care,
And heal him who is sick.

If thou come not again tonight,
Never come within my sight,
In no place in my land.

LIGHTFOOT Now certain, lord, I travel light,
Before the sun has reached his height
You shall grasp him by the hand.

EMPEROR Yea, boy, and as thou love me dear
Look that thou spy, both far and near,
Where thou come in each place;
If any rumours there appear,
Or any carping come to ear
Of that lad I shall disgrace.

LIGHTFOOT I am ready, lord, both up and down,
To seek and spy in every town
For talk of that young lad;
All such whisperings I shall drown,
And gladly crack the gossip's crown,
Wherever I am bad.

And therefore, lord, have now good day.

EMPEROR Mohammed guide thee on thy way.
That rules both wind and wave;
And especially I thee pray,
To speed thee as fast as thou may.
Yea, lord, no more I crave.

LIGHTFOOT Mohammed save Sirinus' kin!
[*to* SIRINUS]
Caesar, my lord and your cousin,
Greets you well by me.

SIRINUS Thou art welcome to me and mine;
Come near and tell me tidings thine,
Quickly, what they be.

LIGHTFOOT My lord prays you as you love him dear,
Before him soon you should appear,
To speak with him awhile.

SIRINUS Go greet him well, thou messenger,
Tell him I follow thee quite near,
Behind thee not a mile.

LIGHTFOOT [*to* CAESAR]
Already, lord, at your bidding,
Mohammed magnify my King,
And save thee by sea and sand.

EMPEROR Welcome, bashir, tell your tiding,
I would that hear before anything,
What heard thou in my land?

LIGHTFOOT I heard nothing, lord, but good;
Sirinus in all likelihood
Will be here this night.

EMPEROR I thank thee, by Mohammed's blood;
These tidings much amend my mood;
Go rest, thou worthy knight.

SIRINUS Mohammed unto thee I call,
He save thee, lord of great lords all,
Sitting in thy high degree.

EMPEROR Welcome, Sirinus, to this hall,
Beside myself here sit thou shall,
Quickly come up to me.

SIRINUS Lord, on your words I am intent.

EMPEROR Why, sir, after thee I sent
I shall at once recite;
Therefore show I you the extent
Of dangers which my land ferment.

SIRINUS How so, by Mohammed's might?

EMPEROR Sir, I am made to understand,
That a loose wench in this land,
Shall bear a child, I hear,
Who shall be crowned a king so grand,
That all shall bow unto his hand;
These tidings make me fear.
He shall command both young and old,

None be so hardy nor so bold
    To give service to me;
Then would my heart grow cold
If such a beggar bold
    My crown should take from me;

And therefore, sir, I would thee pray,
Give the best counsel that you may,
    To guide me as is best;
For if my hands on him I lay
When he be found I shall him slay,
    Either by east or west.

SIRINUS Lord, my advice is quickly said;
I counsel you, as I eat bread,
    What therefore best may be;
Go search in your land each homestead,
And bid that boy be brought back dead,
    By the first who may him see;

And also raise ye an outcry,
To put to flight that company
    Who give this king a crown;
Bid each man come separately
And bring to you a penny,
    That dwells in tower or town;

That this be done by the third day
Then may none of his friends say,
    But he has homage given.
If you do this your worship may
Live in joy for now and ay,
    Your foes to fealty driven.

EMPEROR As I might thrive, sir, I thank thee,
For these tidings that thou tell me,
    Thy counsel shall prevail;
Lord and sire of this country,
Without an end here make I thee,
    For thy good counsel.

My messenger, look thou be swift,
From town to town these rumours sift,
    And my firm will proclaim;

I pray thee, if thou rise by thrift,
I promise thee a precious gift,
  If thou come quick again.

Command the folk wholly each one,
Rich nor poor, forget thou none,
  To pay me homage truly,
And honour me as lord alone;
And slain be those who against me groan,
  This blade their bane shall be.

Both old and young bid know this thing,
That each man know me for his king,
  For dread I them dismay.
As token I am lord and king,
Bid each man a penny bring,
  And to me homage pay.

By my statutes who will not stand,
Fast they must flee out of my land,
  Bid them without mistake;
By Mohammed whom none withstand,
Thou shalt be made knight with my hand
  Speed fleetly for my sake?

LIGHTFOOT Already, lord, it shall be done;
But I know well I come not soon,
  And therefore be not wroth;
I swear here, sir, by sun and moon,
I can't return by afternoon,
  So count it not as sloth.

But have good day, now will I wend
For longer here I may not spend,
  But soon get on my way.

EMPEROR Mohammed his grace thee lend,
And bring thee to thy journey's end,
  With all the speed he may.

[*Exeunt.*

Notes to the Plays (Part One)

THE CREATION

The staging of *The Creation* demands four different levels: heaven; paradise; earth; hell. God's throne should be set well above the level on which the Angels stand. The Angels are grouped on either side of God's throne at the beginning of the play, Good and Bad interspersed. When after Lucifer's fall God creates Man, Adam should rise from near God's throne. The Cherubim then takes Adam and Eve to a slightly lower level, paradise, and later they are driven lower still, to middle-earth. The lowest level is hell-mouth which, provided the seating of the audience is suitably raked, can be played on the ground.

Existing records afford considerable guidance to the medieval manner of presentation; no two accounts indicate identical staging, but the diversity of evidence, since no one account is comprehensive in its directions, is of great value to the producer who wishes to realize the material he is handling. There are, for instance, two versions of The Fall of Man (1533 and 1565) which were performed by the Norwich Grocers. Their Account Book informs us that their pageant was 'a Howse of Waynscott paynted and buylded on a Cart with fowre whelys', painted cloths were hung about it, and it was drawn by four horses having 'headstallis of brode Inkle with knopps and tassells'. It had a square top with a large vane in the middle, another large vane at one end, and a great number of smaller ones all around. God was played in a wig and a mask (1565 Inventory 'a face and heare for ye Father'); the Serpent with a wig and crown (it; a new Heer, wt a crown for ye Serpent, 6d.) and 'a cote with hosen and a tayle steyned'; for the Angel 'An Angell's cote and overhoses of Apis

Skynns'; for Adam, wig, gloves, and 'a cote and hosen steyned'; for Eve, a wig, gloves and 'two cotes and a pair of hosen steyned'. The Tree displayed a wide variety of fruit and flowers: Apples and Figs, 4d.; Oranges, 10d.; 3 lbs. Dates, 1s.; 1 stone Almonds 3d.; Paid for coloured thread to bind the flowers, 2d. Dramatically, the most interesting property is 'a Rybbe colleryd Red'.

Payment to the actors of the Grocers' Play was as follows:

It., to Jeffrey Tybnam playeng the Father	16d.
It., to Mr. Leman's servant playing Adam	6d.
It., to Frances Fygot playing Eve	4d.
It., to Tho. Wolffe playing the Angelle	4d.
It., to Edmund Thurston playeng the Serpent	4d.

Records of the Coventry medieval guilds, although not referring specifically to *The Creation*, throw some light on the possible presentation of this play. Their pageants were strewn with rushes; in 1557 4d. was paid 'for kepyng of fyer at hell-mothe'; in 1567 'pd for makyng hell-mowth and cloth for hyt iiijs'; 1477, 'it. for mendyng the demons garment . . . it. for newe ledder to the same garment xxijd'; 1490, 'it. the devyls hede' (repairing the mask); 1494, 'it. paid to Wattis for dressyng of the devells hede viijd'; 1498, 'it. paid for peynttyng of the demones hede'; hair, 3 lbs. for the demon's coat and hose; suit for Angels –gold skins, wings for Angels; four diadems for Angels; 1578, 'it. payd for mendyng of two angelis crownes ijd'.

Eve would most probably have been played by a young apprentice, and such perhaps was 'Frances Fygot' who played the part in the Norwich Grocers' Play. All female parts were taken by men or boys. The Coventry Smiths' Company makes an entry for 1495, 'Ryngold's man Thomas that Playtt Pylatts wyff'; and in 1498, 'it. paid to Pylatts wyffe for his wages ijs'. The Coventry Weavers record for 1525, 'payd to Sodden for Ane (Anna in The Purification) xd'; and in 1450 under Fines, '(received) of Hew Heyns pleynge Anne for hys fyne vjd'. An exception to the practice of men playing women's parts is the Chester play of

The Assumption in which *all* parts were performed by 'the wives of the town'.

There is, however, an interesting difference in the sex of the Serpent in the various versions of the Fall of Man. In the *Ludus Coventriae*, the York, and Wakefield Plays the Serpent appears uniformly masculine. In the Chester Plays Satan describes his disguise:

> A manner of an Adder is in this place,
> that wynges like a byrd she hase,
> feete as an Adder, a maydens face;
> her kinde I will take.
>
> (*The Creation* 193–196)

The stage directions refer to Lucifer transforming himself to a Sphinx with feathered wings, a serpent below, a woman above. ('King Lear' IV, vi. 128–129.

> But to the girdle do the gods inherit,
> Beneath is all the fiends'.)

In the Cornish Plays Lucifer appears as 'a fyne serpen made with a virgyn face and yolowe heare upon her head'. Such a presentation is finely depicted on a misericord in Ely Cathedral. 'The snake in Paradise,' writes C. G. Jung in *The Psychology of the Unconscious*, 'is usually considered as feminine, as the seductive principle in woman, and is represented as feminine by the old artists, although properly the snake has a phallic meaning.'

The nakedness of Adam and Eve presents a problem to any producer, modern or medieval. The craft-guild that most frequently was given the responsibility for presenting *The Creation* was the Barkers or Tanners. It was the custom for Adam and Eve to be dressed in white leather skins. More practicable for modern performances are white woollen suits, made to a skin-fitting measure and dyed skin colour. The hose portion will require soles, as the Weavers of Coventry recorded in 1564, 'it. paid for solyng of Jesus hose jd'.

In the Wakefield *Creation* there are no directions for singing but, by analogy with the York Plays on this subject, the *Te Deum* would be sung shortly after the creation of the Angels (l. 30), and the *Sanctus* as God withdraws (l. 76) contrasting sharply with the discord that follows. There is no specific direction for song at the end of the play, although the Cherubim hints at it, 'Of sorrow may ye sing'. The earlier of the two Norwich versions of the Fall of Man ends:

EVA O wretches that we are, so ever we xall be inrollyd;
Therfor ower handes we may wrynge with most dullfull song.

And so thei xall syng walkyng together about the place, wryngyng ther handes.

Wythe dolorous sorowe, we may wayle and wepe
Both nyght and daye in sory, sythys full depe.

N.B. These last two lines set to musick twice over and again, for a chorus of four parts.

Whereas harmony characterizes scenes in heaven, each entry or exit from hell-mouth should be marked by the most strident cacophony. In medieval times the Cooks were famed for their hell-mouth effects, to which every available culinary article contributed.

At the heading of this play appear the words '*In dei nomine amen. Assit Principio, Sancta Maria, Meo. Wakefeld*'; in the margin 'Barkers', the guild that undertook production.

The manuscript breaks off after 267 lines. The twelve leaves which probably contained the temptation of Eve and the expulsion of Adam and Eve from paradise have been lost. The play here presented is completed by adapting the last 158 lines of the York Cowpers' Play.

The minimum number of speaking characters is listed. If the production of the whole cycle is being attempted, and staging facilities allow, it would be preferable to increase the number both of Good and Bad Angels. Apart from the Cherubim, the Archangels Michael and Gabriel, because of the part they play in the subsequent drama, should be included. The Archangel Michael, is depicted in the cycles as bearing a flaming sword.

In the *Ludus Coventriae* and the Chester *Creation* God

appears and commands Lucifer to fall. In this play (131) the Fall might be heralded by sound effects, and the Bad Angels topple down behind God's throne. If they fall down the various levels in full view of the audience, and there are only three Bad Angels to fall, the result might be an anticlimax. Immediately following the Fall it is dramatically important that two devils or more should be prepared to come scurrying out of hell-mouth to prove the swiftness of God's vengeance and the steep decline from angel to fiend. Lucifer and the Bad Angels have some 120 lines in which to transform themselves into devils.

Throughout Satan's speech (250–275), which includes the transition from the Wakefield to the York text, the devils should be clinging round hell-mouth listening gleefully to Satan's plot to corrupt man, and from their lower level watching the ensuing scene. The change from Satan to Serpent might best be accomplished through characteristic movement. The Serpent's suggestions to Eve are thick with sensuality, and his writhing and hissing reach a climax at Eve's biting of the apple, when he returns triumphant to his confederate devils. A stage direction in the Chester *Creation* (312) makes a point of the hissing: *Tunc recedet serpens, vocem serpentinam faciens.*

The creation of Adam and Eve calls for special attention in staging. If Adam has been lying supine, close to God's throne, he should not be noticed until God bids him rise (165). He certainly cannot make an entry, walking on from left or right. The Chester *Creation* has a direction 'Adam rises', and the Cornish plays show shrewd awareness of this practical problem: 'Meanwhile are got ready Adam and Eva aparlet in whytt lether in a place apoynted by the conveyour and not to be sene till they be called and thei kneel and ryse'. (O. Waterhouse, *Non Cycle Mystery Plays*, xxxiv.) The use of trapdoors for the creation of Adam and Eve is perhaps the most effective method. Failing this device, much may be concealed by the voluminous wings of the Angels. One such wing may also conceal Adam's rib (186).

In realistic terms there appears to be the necessity for at least two stage trees in paradise, one for the apple and one for the fig leaves. The Cornish play has a direction indicating that the fig leaves were handed to Adam and Eve, as it were, from the wings: 'fig leaves redy to cover ther members'. In the Coventry Accounts there is reference to two trees, one of which no doubt carried the fig leaves. But the medieval mind would not have been in the least deterred from using the same tree for both apples and fig leaves. The stained glass representation of the Garden of Eden in the York Minster East Window shows also a wide variety of fruit on the tree. The tree used by the Norwich Grocers was decorated with oranges, figs, almonds, dates, raisins, apples, and flowers bound on by coloured thread.

THE KILLING OF ABEL

This play, as at York, was presented by the Glovers' guild. *The Killing of Abel* following *The Creation* stresses the sharpness of Man's fall. Cain is the unredeemable blasphemer: he strikes his servant, slays his brother, curses God. In the York play he even strikes an angel. The Wakefield dramatist relishes his theme and brings the outrageous destructive vigour of his main character into striking contrast with the foregoing majesty and control of *The Creation.*

A minimum of three main levels is required: (1) the ground level on which Cain enters with, as A. C. Cawley points out, 'a plough team of eight animals, comprising four oxen and four horses'; (2) the hill on which the tithe-offering is made; (3) the upper level on which God appears and speaks.

Frequently in the mystery plays characters make their entry and exit on horseback, but the boldest producer, with the most sympathetic understanding of the concrete nature of medieval thought, might blench from a literal presentation of Cain's plough team. Whatever ingenuity he may have recourse to, pretence without some material representation would be alien to the medieval dramatic tradition.

After the tithe-offering Cain and Abel descend the hill and Abel is killed at the lower level. In medieval drama the pageant itself is frequently referred to as 'the hill' and the acting area on ground level as 'the green', 'the field', or 'the place'. When in the Chester Plays Cain leads Abel from the place of sacrifice, the text itself indicates where the killing will take place:

> Come forth, brother, with me to go
> Into the field a little here fro,
> I have a thing to say.
> (Chester Plays, II. *The Creation* 594–596.)

A similar movement from hill to field is required in this Wakefield play (294–302). Internal evidence sometimes reveals whether the pageants stood in fields or streets. Cain in the *Ludus Coventriae*, when cursed by God, laments his fate:

> In field and town, in street and stage,
> I may never make mirth more.
> (*Ludus Coventriae, Cain and Abel*, 187–188.)

'street and stage' are clearly juxtaposed as alternative acting areas.

The Boy is the type of pert youth who appears elsewhere in the Wakefield Plays, for instance, as Jack Garcio in *The First Shepherds' Play*. He is the forebear of Shakespeare's Moth and Launcelot Gobbo. Cain refers to him as 'pyke-harnes' which is usually glossed as 'a stealer of armour from the slain'. 'Pickbrain' is an alternative.

The Boy enters blowing a horn and then commands silence for his master. The same formula, considerably extended, is used for the entry of the main character in the Wakefield *Herod the Great*. The Boy in his master's name gains silence for his own speech, but encourages the spectators to welcome Cain with jeers and hisses. This interpretation is consistent with his relationship to Cain throughout. Cain complains (39) that he has both to hold the plough and drive the plough team, and when it comes to a fight (52) the Boy promises to give blow for blow. He soon proves too nimble for his master who, quickly puffed, calls a truce. Cain can only enlist the Boy's support (400) by promising him his release from serfdom.

The royal proclamation (411) announces that the king extends his pardon and protection to Cain and his Boy. Human and divine judgements are deliberately and ironically confused. God has protected Cain's life by threat of seven-fold punishment on his slayer (366); in the royal proclamation spectators are asked not only to love the first murderer and his Boy (427), but also to contribute to the collection they are making on their own behalf (430).

Abel enters (54) with a sheep which he intends offering as his tithe to God. The sheep as a stage property is also needed in this cycle in *Abraham, The Second Shepherds' Play,* and *John the Baptist.*

As a medieval ploughman Cain begrudges paying to the Church tithes which stay in the pockets of the priests (103). He cheats in his tithing by miscounting the sheaves as he selects from his stook of corn one in ten to offer to God. When he sets fire to his offering and tries to blow the kindled corn into a flame (267), smoke belches out and nearly chokes him.

'The words "over the wall" (290) may refer to the balustrade of the balcony on which God made his appearance in the craft-pageants.' (A. C. Cawley, *The Wakefield Pageants in the Towneley Cycle,* 93.)

Abel being killed with a cheek-bone (318) is unbiblical but well established in medieval tradition: *Cursor Mundi* 1073; *Ludus Coventriae* 'chavyl bon' or jaw-bone (149); the York Minster East Window; a Norwich Cathedral roof boss.

Goodybower Lane (360) was the site of the present Brook Street in Wakefield. In the adjoining field was the quarry from which the stone for the parish church, the rectory, and the Chantry Bridge Chapel was obtained.

NOAH

The story of Noah was an indispensable part of the medieval mystery cycle. Versions of it are found in all the extant cycles, including the Cornish Plays, and also in the Newcastle Shipwrights' Play. The Trinity Guild of Master Mariners and Pilots of Hull records in great detail the management of their Noah Play which was performed annually on Plough Monday, the first Monday after Epiphany.

The Flood prefigures the Last Judgement. In times of local or national stress—and such times were rarely absent from medieval life—these themes maintained their homiletic and dramatic appeal. The boisterous horse-play occasioned by Noah's wife in no way militates against the essential seriousness of the playwright's intention. The characterization of Noah's wife looks back to Eve, the first disobedient wife. This is even more explicit in the Newcastle Play where the Devil tempts her to strong drink, with which in turn she plies her husband, who responds

> What the devil, what drink is it!
> By my father's soul, I have near lost my wit!

Except in the *Ludus Coventriae* version of this play, Noah's wife is depicted as the stubborn, self-willed harridan, as adept at striking as at spinning with her distaff. The domination of such a character in the plays of the Wakefield Master gives rise to biographical speculation.

For staging, three main levels are required: heaven; the hill from which Noah first speaks and on which Noah's wife persists in spinning; and the Ark. Noah builds the Ark by himself, speaking at the same time, in full view of the spectators, with forty lines (249–288) in which to complete his task. This is just enough time for him to fit together prefabricated sections lying near at hand.

In medieval times the management of this problem of stage business varied considerably. In the York Shipwrights' Play Noah in eighteen lines complains that it has taken him a hundred years to build the Ark. Lincoln accounts show that three times as much was charged for housing the Noah pageant as for the others, and the Hull Trinity Guild accounts indicate that the Ark, a considerable structure, rigged with mast and sails, costing in 1522 £5. 8s. 4d., was set upon a framework on wheels. In these two latter cases the erection of prefabricated sections within a short space of time and by one person only would have been impossible. A ship on wheels must have been used in the Digby *Mary Magdalene,* a play most probably performed in the round, in which the ship calls at different stations or pageants. In the *Ludus Coventriae,* after Noah has received his instructions to build the Ark, he withdraws with his family during the fifty-six line interlude in which Lameth kills Cain. The interpolation of the Lameth-Cain interlude, an apparent irrelevance in this context, can only be justified in its allowing Noah and his family some short space of time in which to build the Ark and return with it, which they do on Lameth's exit, singing. The Ark in the Chester Deluge is presented to full view at the beginning of the play, before even God has told Noah to build it. The first stage direction in the 1600 version reads: 'The thirde pagent of Noyes flood and first in some heigh place or in the cloudes, yf it may be, God speaketh unto Noe standing without the Arke with all his family'. It is later in this play that the family mime the building of the Ark (*Tunc faciunt signa quasi laborarent cum diversis Instrumentis*). This is indication enough that the drama is no longer truly medieval. Biblically the three cabins (129) are set one above the other: 'A window shalt thou make to the ark, and in a cubit shalt thou finish it above; and the door of the ark shalt thou set in the side thereof; with lower, second, and third stories shalt thou make it'. (Genesis 6. 16.) A stained glass representation of such an ark, with Noah leaning out of the window 'above' welcoming the dove, is to be seen in the north aisle choir of Canterbury Cathedral. The reference to a trap door in the Hull Trinity House accounts (1525. Item for a band to the trape dore vd) suggests that there, too, the cabins were constructed one above the other.

The medieval ship was frequently crenellated: an example of such a Noah's Ark is to be found on one of the misericords in Ely Cathedral. The Chester Noah exhorts his wife and children to come aboard (97–98):

> Wife, in this castle we shall be kept,
> My children and thou I would in leapt.

'The hill' has hitherto in this cycle implied the lowest acting level on the pageant—Cain and Abel offer their tithes on 'the hill'—in which case the Ark might occupy a quite separate acting area. It is extremely doubtful whether Noah's wife would persistently refer to her position as 'upon this hill' if the three-storeyed Ark were towering above her on the pageant. It is more probable that the Ark, which is mobile, is located in another acting area. The fight certainly takes place on the hill (407).

The sending forth of the raven and the dove (507) might be managed by a suspension from above, as the Chester direction reads 'in some heigh place or in the cloudes'. There is however a particular stage direction in the Chester *Noah* which suggests how this may be done: 'Then shall Noah release a dove, and there shall be in the ship another dove carrying a branch of olive in its mouth, which it shall drop from the mast by means of a rope into Noah's hand'. (*Tunc emittet columbam et erit in nave alia columba ferens olivam in ore, quam dimittet ex malo per funem in manus Noe . . .*)

ABRAHAM AND ISAAC

Two leaves are missing in the manuscript after line 286. The version presented here concludes with fourteen lines (287–300) adapted from the Brome Abraham and Isaac Play.

Obedience is the theme of the plays that begin the cycle. Lucifer and Adam fall through disobedience; Noah and Abraham are blessed because of their obedience to God. Obedience to the deity in the sacrifice of an innocent child is also the theme of Euripides' *Iphigenia in Aulis*, in which Iphigenia, as Isaac, at first protests against her fate, but finally submits to the divine will. This archetypal pattern is best illustrated by the plays concerning Christ's Passion. The Chester *Sacrifice of Isaac* ends with the Expositor underlining, rather heavily, the play's significance:

This deed ye see done in this place,
In example of Jesus done it was,
That to win mankind to grace
Was sacrificed upon the rood.

By Abraham I bring to mind
The Father of heaven that did find
His Son's blood needed to unbind
  Us from the Devil, our foe.

By Isaac understand I may
Jesus that was obedient ay,
His Father's will to work alway,
  His death to undergo.
      (Chester, *Sacrifice of Isaac* 465–476.)

Three acting levels are required: heaven; the hill; the ground. To begin with Abraham speaks from the lowest level, and on this level he meets Isaac, and together with the ass and the two attendants they move towards the hill, and then leaving the ass and the two attendants at ground level Abraham and Isaac climb to the hill (145–148). The hill once again may be taken as the level of the pageant stage.

In the various versions of this play there are pointed references to the characters riding:

ABRAHAM Get hither our horses and let us go hence,
  Both I and Isaac and these two men.
(The Dublin *Abraham and Isaac* Play 128–129.)

'And Abraham rides towards Sara who says . . .'
(*Et equitat versus Saram dicit Sara.*)
(Stage direction following line 317,
Dublin Play.)

ISAAC Children, lead forth our Ass. . . .
(York. 109.)

'Melchisedech receiving the horse of Abraham very gladly . . .'
(Stage direction following line 96,
Chester, 1600 version.)

'Then Melchisedech shall ride up to Abraham. . . .'
(Stage direction following line 72,
Chester, 1592 version.)

We can assume that the animals were ridden on the ground ('upon this fair heath' Brome 407: 'Then hie thee that thou were on ground' God says as he despatches his angel to Abraham, Dublin 30). If this is so, the same station is used for hill and heaven and the riding is done in a circle to the point from which the characters started, or there are separate stations: one for heaven, one for the hill, and the dialogue between Abraham and Isaac preparatory to their journey takes place on 'the green'.

The main properties required are an altar on the hill on which Isaac is laid, a bundle of faggots, a flaming torch or the means of making fire on the altar, Abraham's sword, and the sheep for the sacrifice.

ISAAC AND JACOB

The two missing leaves of the manuscript which deprived us of the ending of *Abraham and Isaac* have also deprived us of the beginning of *Isaac*. *Jacob,* although categorised by A. W. Pollard as a fragment (*The Towneley Plays,* Introduction xxiii) and admittedly unusually short (142 lines), nevertheless appears complete in itself, beginning, as *Noah* and *Abraham and Isaac,* with the main character calling to God, and ending with the reconciliation of Jacob and Esau. The action of *Isaac* and *Jacob* is continuous and they may be regarded as one play [Professor Ten-Brink, *History of English Literature* (English Edition), vol. ii. p. 244]. Their style, thematic treatment, and dramatic art indicate earlier work than the other plays in the cycle. They represent the only medieval dramatic version of the story of Jacob and Esau in the vernacular. We may fill in the first part of *Isaac* (excluding the allegorical passages) and learn many details of early medieval staging from Karl Young's account of the late twelfth century Latin play of *Isaac and Rebecca:*

> At the opening of the first scene, as Isaac totters to his platform, a chorus sings some verses describing his decrepitude, fatigue and hunger. After he has lain down upon his bed, the choristers sing an 'allegory', in which

they somewhat darkly interpret Isaac's physical weaknesses as prefigurings of Christian realities. Then Isaac querulously demands that Esau be summoned. As the messengers depart, an allegory is sung explaining that Esau symbolizes the Jews, and Jacob the Christians. When Esau is brought before Isaac, the father asks for food, and straightway sends his son off to the hunt. After another allegory has been sung, the hunting expedition of Esau is represented in dumb-show. Meanwhile Rebecca proposes to Jacob a plan whereby he shall outwit Esau and obtain Isaac's blessing. The chorus then allegorizes the two kids which Jacob kills by way of deceiving his father. Prodded and aided by his mother, Jacob clothes himself in the skins of the goats, and in garments left at home by Esau. The choral allegory explains, among other things, that the garments left behind by Esau symbolize the decalogue abandoned by the Jews. In his disguise Jacob represents himself to his blind father as Esau, and offers him food. When Isaac expresses surprise at Esau's so speedy return from hunting, Jacob attributes it to God's help. With another allegory, hardly intelligible, the fragment ends.

The play clearly undertakes to represent the biblical story of Jacob and Esau with realistic thoroughness. The playing-space is set with three main 'mansions', or *tabernacula,* one for Jacob and Rebecca, and one each for Esau and Isaac. The mansions are provided with beds and such other furnishings as can be supplied. Kitchens are arranged for both Esau and Jacob. The stage equipment includes also a roe-buck, two kids, hairy coverings for the hands and neck of Jacob, a bow and arrows, and suitable Jewish hats and other garments for all. Whether or not all this realism was effected within the church building we cannot tell.

(Karl Young, *The Drama of the Medieval Church.* O.U.P. 1933, ii. 264–265.)

For *Jacob* many non-speaking parts are required. Jacob divides his host into three parts (115), and Esau makes his entry with a band of armed followers (122). In the course of the play Jacob journeys to Mesopotamia and back again to his own country. He would take his rest on the ground or on the pageant, and on waking he would be looking at 'God's house and heaven's gate' (41), erected on the pageant. (On the opposition of heaven to hell, see Leslie Hotson's *Shakespeare's Wooden O'*, Chapter IX.) Jacob's travelling, foot-sore 'along this street', suggests a linear rather than circular movement.

According to the text an Angel wrestles with Jacob (*luctetur angelus cum eo*), but it is God who says 'The day springs; now let me go'. The biblical version is as follows: 'And Jacob was left alone; and there wrestled a man with him until the breaking of the day'. (*Genesis* 32, v. 24.) Whatever spirit Jacob wrestles with must, as a ghost, glide away before dawn (108).

PHARAOH

In the manuscript *The Prophets* follows *Jacob,* and *Pharaoh* follows *The Prophets.* In the biblical order of events *Pharaoh* should precede *The Prophets,* and such is the order adopted here.

The Wakefield Dyers were responsible for the presentation of this play: 'Litsters Pagonn' (Dyers' Pageant) appears in the Manuscript margin. The play is almost identical with the York Hosiers' play. Miss Toulmin Smith sets out the parallel texts in her edition of *The York Mystery Plays* (O.U.P. 1885) and Marie C. Lyle and Grace Frank examine the interdependence of the two cycles (M. C. Lyle, *The Original Identity of the York and Towneley Cycles,* PMLA, xliv, 1929, 319–328; G. Frank, *On the Relation of the York and Towneley Plays,* PMLA, xliv, 1929, 313–319).

The cast of the York play includes two Counsellors who do not appear in the Wakefield *Pharaoh.* Their parts are almost identical with some of the speeches given to the Wakefield 1st. and 2nd. Soldiers. The reporting of the plagues is far better managed in the York version through four speakers than through the two of the Wakefield version. In a dramatic presentation of the Wakefield play it might be advisable to extend the number of Soldiers to four and to reallocate the Soldiers' parts, or to follow the York example and introduce two Counsellors who might appropriate some of the Soldiers' speeches. Left as it is, the Wakefield play demands that the two Soldiers rush on and off with news of fresh plagues with a relay-race rapidity that may too easily induce hilarity in the audience.

Both the Wakefield and York versions disregard the biblical tenth plague, the death of the first-born of Egypt, and replace it with the pestilence, the most terrible of afflictions in the Middle Ages. Pharaoh's words would be deeply felt:

> Pestilence, in the devil's name!
> Then is our pride quite past.

And, understandably, his decision to release the Israelites follows immediately. Even in the Middle Ages the Jews were frequently held responsible for the pestilence: 'in Mainz and other German-speaking towns (they) were burned in their hundreds or thousands by an infuriated mob in the belief that the plague was a malignant device of the Semitic race for the confusion of the Catholic creed' (H. A. L. Fisher, *A History of Europe*, 319). Furthermore, the massacre of the Jews at York in 1185 would not have been forgotten when the local medieval drama was written and performed.

The York play concludes very suddenly with the drowning of Pharaoh, his Egyptians, and his horses and chariots, at which the Hebrews burst into song '*Cantemus domino*, to God a song sing we'. The Wakefield version ends less precipitously but without reference to singing. A hymn of praise or a psalm of deliverance, Psalm 46 or Psalm 106 for example, might be a fitting conclusion to the play (*Exodus* 15, v. 1–21).

The staging of the Cornish play may give some guidance here. After God has ascended to heaven (1478), Pharaoh struts about on the pageant (*Hic pompabit rex pharo*

. . .). There is every possibility that Pharaoh 'pomps it' on the pageant, because in a later stage direction we learn that he descends (1584 *hic descendit pharo*) to the arena where Moses has been walking (1534 *Moyses ambulat in platea*). It is in 'the place' that Moses mounts his horse (1626 *ascendit super equum*) to lead the Israelites out of the land of Egypt. When Moses encounters the Red Sea he strikes at it (1674 *percutit mare*) and the following dialogue describes the dramatic action ensuing:

MOSES In the name of God, thou fair sea,
I strike thee with my rod;
Open wide a path for us,
That we may go to the land
Which is ordained for us perfectly,
By the Lord of heaven, really.

2ND SOLDIER As I say, Lord, to thee,
Moses far is gone
Into the sea, as it seems to me;
Forth quickly going,
The water striking wide
Every moment before him.

A SQUIRE All his people, they are
Following him every one;
And the sea on every side, to them
Standing like two walls.
They are kept within the enclosure,
And water will certainly never drown them.

(Edwin Norris' translation in his edition of *The Ancient Cornish Drama,* The Beginning of the World, 1675–1692.)

That the Red Sea is a very material stage property is emphasized by an item under Miscellaneous Entries in the Coventry Cappers' Company accounts (*Two Coventry Corpus Christi Plays,* Hardin Craig, 97), 'it. pd. for halfe a yard of rede sea vjd'.

THE PROCESSION OF THE PROPHETS

The Procession of the Prophets is an unfinished play, but it may be performed as complete in itself because of its unusual lineal structure: each prophet enters in succession, says his piece and departs. Daniel's 'Evermore without end' seems an admirable line on which to close the play, although in the completed text, no doubt, more prophecies would have followed. There are, for instance, twenty-six prophets, although mostly with only four lines apiece, in the *Ludus Coventriae Procession of the Prophets.* The York and Chester cycles contain no such play. In the *Ludus Coventriae* version the prophets, in the brief speeches allotted them, illustrate how their deeds and words have prefigured Christ's coming: King David reflects on the regal power of Christ; Jonas foretells the resurrection:

> I, Jonas, say that on the third morn
> From death he shall rise: this is a true tale,
> Figured in me which long before
> Lay three days buried in the whale.
> (*Ludus Coventriae, Procession of the Prophets*, 67–70.)

The essential difference between the two extant vernacular versions of this play is that whereas the *Ludus Coventriae* play is literally processional, the Wakefield play, both in the allocation of much longer speeches to the prophets and in the severe homiletic character of their harangues, looks back directly to the common origin, which was a sermon. 'This substantial homiletic piece, found among the spurious works attributed to St. Augustine, is entitled *Contra Judaeos, Paganos, et Arianos Sermo de Symbolo.* Although the Augustinian authorship is now discredited, the attribution to the great bishop persisted throughout the Middle Ages. The sermon appears to have been written during the fifth or sixth century. . . . It opens (Chapter XI in the modern edition) with a direct arraignment of the Jews for their perverse disbelief in the Messiahship of Christ. Since the Jews stubbornly demand evidence, the preacher grimly proposes to bring testimony from their own law. He first summons Isaiah, bidding him testify concerning Christ. . . . Similarly are summoned the prophets Jeremiah, Daniel, Moses, David, and Habakkuk. . . . With a tart reminder to the Jews that the testimony already adduced should be ample, the preacher adds utterances from the Gentiles, Virgil and Nebuchadnezzar, and finally a prophetic passage in hexameters from the Erythraean Sibyl. ['These prophetic verses are quoted and interpreted by St. Augustine in his *De Civitate Dei* (lib. xviii, cap. 23, Migne, P.L., xli, 579–581). Their appearance throughout the Middle Ages is frequent.'] (Karl Young, op. cit., ii. 125–132.)

In production of this play a remarkable fact emerges. Whereas the text appears devoid of dramatic incident and interplay of characters, if presented as a succession of short sermons delivered from a pulpit on a pageant around which throng the spectators, no play in the whole cycle is more fraught with dramatic tension. This is partly due to the variety within the play of character and homiletic material, but mainly to the astonishing power, though largely forgotten in our day, that a fiery sermon can exert on a mass of listeners. The achievements of Adolf Hitler and Billy Graham in this medium are recent reminders of such power.

Details of dress, make-up, and properties relating to the Latin plays on the same subject, originally performed on the feast of the Circumcision (1st January) at Laon and Rouen cathedrals, indicate that Moses is bearded, he carries his *tables* and a rod and is clad in a dalmatic or alb. David appears as a king; Sibyl, crowned and with hair streaming, has an expression of mad inspiration. Daniel, in a green tunic, has a youthful appearance and carries an ear of corn.

In the Wakefield play Moses would certainly carry his *tables,* which he would rest on the pulpit, referring to them as the text from which he preaches. David is crowned and carries a harp or lyre on which he accompanies himself as he sings (108–162). After Sibyl's spine-chilling forecasts, Daniel concludes with the comfort of the promised redemption.

CAESAR AUGUSTUS

The only Middle English text of a *Caesar Augustus* play is the one from the Wakefield cycle. The Chester *Annunciation* introduces the character of Octavian, before whom Sibyl is commanded to prophesy; but although, on his first appearance, Octavian conducts himself in the conventional manner of the medieval stage despot [he struts (*pompabit*), interlards his speech with French, and swears by Mohammed], on his second appearance, when Sibyl informs him that Jesus has been born, he loses his afflatus, and in humility worships the child.

The Wakefield *Caesar Augustus* is the tyrant throughout showing, as the Herod of the Coventry Pageant of the *Shearmen and Taylors*, particular pleasure in his own beauty (14). In performance the two Counsellors might be contrasted: the first quick and incisive, the second heavy and slow. Lightfoot is the nimble lad we have met as Garcio in *The Killing of Abel* and will meet again in *The First Shepherds' Play*. The staging requires two 'mansions' set apart, possibly on the same pageant: one for Caesar Augustus and one for Sirinus.

Part Two

THE TENTH PLAY

The Annunciation

GOD	MARY
GABRIEL	JOSEPH

GOD Since I have made all things of nought
And Adam with my hands have wrought,
Like to mine image, by my device,
And given him joy in paradise
To live therein as that I bad,
Until he did what I forbad;
And then I put him from that place,
But yet I mean to grant him grace,
And the oil of mercy for his gain,
And in time to ease his pain.
For he has suffered sin full sore,
For these five thousand years and more,
First on earth and then in hell;
But long therein he shall not dwell.
Beyond pain's power he shall be laid,
I will not lose what I have made.
I will make redemption,
As promised, in my person,
All with reason and with right
Both through mercy and through might.
With joy we shall be reconciled,
For he was wrongfully beguiled;
He shall out of prison pass
Because that he beguiled was
Through the serpent and his wife;
They made him touch the tree of life,
And eat the fruit that I forbad,
That doomed him to a life full sad.

Righteousness will we perform;
My son shall take on human form,
And reasons therefore shall be three,
A man, a maiden, and a tree:
Man for man, tree for tree,
Maiden for maiden; thus shall it be.
My son shall by a maid be born,
The fiend of hell to hold in scorn;
Without a spot, as sun through glass,
So pure a maid may none surpass.
Both God and man shall he be,
And both mother and maiden she.
To Abraham I once decreed
To save both him and all his seed;
And I intend that prophecy
Be here fulfilled by me;
For I am Lord and live anew,
My prophets shall be found most true.
As said Moses and Isaiah,
King David and Jeremiah,
Habakkuk and Daniel,
Sibyl sage, that spoke so well,
And mine other prophets all,
As they have said, it shall befall.
Rise up, Gabriel, and find

[GABRIEL *appears by* GOD.

A gentle maiden, meek and kind,
In Nazareth of Galilee,
Where she dwells in that city.
To that virgin and her spouse,
To a man of David's house,
Who as Joseph known is he,
And the maiden named Mary.
Angel must to Mary go,
For to Eve the fiend was foe;
He was hateful in my sight,
But thou art angel fair and bright;
And hail that maiden, as I plan,
As graciously as thou can.

On my behalf thou shall her greet,
I have her chosen, that maiden sweet,
She shall conceive my darling,
Through thy word and her hearing.
In her body will I come,
That to me is cleanly done;
She shall of her body bear
God and man, nor harm a hair;
Blessed shall she be, and ever so;
Bestir thee, Gabriel, and go.

[GABRIEL *goes to* MARY.

GABRIEL Hail, Mary, gracious!
Hail, maiden, and God's spouse!
  To thee I bow, devout;
Of all virgins thou art queen,
That ever was, or shall be seen,
  Without a doubt.

Hail, Mary, and well thou be!
My Lord of heaven is with thee,
  Without an end;
Hail, woman, most of grace!
Fear not nor feel disgrace,
  That I commend.

For thou hast found, without a doubt,
The grace of God that has gone out
  For Adam's plight.
This is the grace that gives thee bloom,
Thou shalt conceive within thy womb
  A child of might.

When he is come, that is thy son,
He shall take circumcision,
  Call him Jesus.
God's son men shall him call
Who comes to free the thrall
  Within us.

My lord shall also give to him
David's throne to sit therein,
  His lineage to show.

He shall be king of Jacob's kin,
And the crown eternal win,
  Lady, you must know.

MARY What is thy name?

GABRIEL Gabriel,
God's strength and his angel,
  That comes to thee.

MARY Wondrous words are in thy greeting,
But to bear God's gentle sweeting,
  How should it be?

I slept never by man's side,
But in maidhood would abide
  Unshaken.
Therefore, I know not how
This may be, because a vow
  I have taken.

Nevertheless, full well I know
God may work his will below
  Thy words fulfilling.
But, I know not the manner,
Therefore, teach me, thou messenger,
  God's way instilling.

GABRIEL Lady, this the secret hear of me;
The holy ghost shall come to thee,
  And in his virtue
Thee enshroud and so infuse,
Yet thou thy maidhood shall not lose,
  But ay be new.

The child that thou shalt bear, madame,
Shall God's son be called by name;
  And, Mary, understand,
Elizabeth, thy cousin, whom barren all believed,
A son in her old age she has conceived
  By her husband.

And this is, for who will know,
The sixth month since she conceived so,
  Whom barren all thought.

No word, lady, that I thee bring,
Is impossible to heaven's king,
    Who all has wrought.

MARY My lord's love will I not withstand,
I am his maiden at his hand,
    And in his fold.
Gabriel, I believe that God will bring
To pass with me each several thing
    As thou hast told.

GABRIEL Mary, gentle maid,
Too long now have I stayed,
    My leave of you I take.

MARY Fare to my friend,
Who did thee send,
    For mankind's sake.

[GABRIEL *retires;* JOSEPH *advances.*

JOSEPH Almighty God, what may this be!
Mary, my wife, amazes me,
    Herself she has forgot.
Her body is great, and she with child!
By me she never was defiled,
    Mine therefore is it not.

I am irked full sore with my life,
That ever I wed so young a wife,
    Repent I of that plan;
To me it was a doleful deed,
I might have known the wench had need
    To love a younger man.

I am old, indeed to say,
And passed the pleasures of love's play,
    Those games from me are gone.
Youth and age are poorly paired;
That know I well, since ill I fared,
    Some other she dotes on.

She is with child, I know not how;
Who could trust any woman now?
    No man of any good;

I know not what now I should do
Save go to her and ask her who
    Shall own the fatherhood.

JOSEPH Hail, Mary, and well ye be!
Why, but woman, what cheer with thee?

MARY The better, sir, for you.

JOSEPH So would I, woman, that ye were;
A mock now Mary you'll incur
    And your state sadly rue.

But one thing I must ask of thee,
This child's father, who is he?

MARY Sir, ye, and God of heaven.

JOSEPH Mine, Mary, leave be thy din;
Ye know, I have no part therein,
    Swear it, by those stars seven.

Wherefore link ye me thereto?
I had never with thee to do,
    How should it then be mine?
Whose is that child, so God thee speed?

MARY Sir, God's and yours, I say indeed.

JOSEPH   Spare those words of thine.

For none of mine it is, I know,
And I repent thou hast done so
    Ill deed as is seen;
And had thou thought thyself to kill,
Though full sore against my will,
    It better might have been.

MARY By God's will, Joseph, must it be,
For certainly save God and ye
    I know no other man;
Nor in flesh have been defiled.

JOSEPH How then art thou thus with child?
    Excuse that if ye can.

So God save me, I blame thee not
To weaken for a woman's lot;
    But to thee I must say this,

Well ye know, and so do I
That thy state cannot deny
    That thou hast done amiss.

MARY Yea, God he knows all my doing.

[MARY *retires a little.*

JOSEPH Woe! Now this is a wondrous thing,
    I can say nought thereto;
But in my heart I feel full sore,
And ever longer more and more;
    For dole what shall I do?

God's and mine she says it is;
I will not father it, she says amiss;
    With shame she is beset
To excuse her villainy to me.
With her I can no longer be,
    I rue that ever we met.

And how we met ye shall soon know:
Young children used to the temple go
    In learning's way to tread;
And so did she, till she grew more
Than other maidens wise of lore,
    Then to her the bishops said,

"Mary, it behoves thee to take
Some young man thy mate to make,
    As others have done before,
In the temple whom thou wilt name."
And she said, none, for still the same
    God of heaven she would adore.

She would none other for any saw;
They said she must, it was the law,
    She was of age thereto.
To the temple they gathered old and young,
All those from Judah's lineage sprung,
    To give the law its due.

They gave each man a white wand there,
And bad us in our hand it bear,
    To offer with good intent;
They offered their wands up at that tide,

But I was old and stood beside,
  I knew not what they meant.

They lacked one which came not nigh,
All had offered, they said, but I,
  For I ay withdrew me.
Forth with my wand they made me stand,
With bloom it flourished in my hand;
  Then said they all to me,

"Though thou be old, this marvel on thee
Shows God of heaven, thus ordains he,
  Thy wand shows clearly.
It flourishes so, without gainsay,
That to marry maid Mary is your way."
  A sorrier man then was I.

I was full sorry to be thus caught,
My age put marriage past my thought
  For us to share a tether;
Her youth would find my age no use,
But they would hear of no excuse,
  But wed us thus together.

When I all thus had wed her there,
We and my maidens home did fare,
  That kings' daughters were.
They all at silk worked everyone,
Mary wrought purple all alone,
  No other colour.

I left them in good peace, I thought,
And in the country where I wrought
  My craft with might and main,
I went to earn what we should need;
Of Mary I prayed them take good heed,
  Until I came again.

Nine months away from Mary mild,
When I came home she was with child;
  Alas, I said, for shame!
I asked those women who had that done,
They told me an angel had come,
  None other was to blame.

An angel spoke with Mary bright,
And no man else by day or night,
"Sir, thereof be ye bold."
They excused her thus readily,
To clear her of all folly,
And mock me that am old.

Should an angel this deed have wrought?
Such excuses help me nought,
Nor no cunning that they can;
A heavenly thing, forsooth, is he,
And she is earthly; this may not be;
It is some other man.

Her misdeed grieves me sore, in truth,
But yet such is the way of youth
So wantonly to sport.
Young women ever yearn to play
With youths and turn the old away,
Such is the world's report.

But Mary and I played never love's game,
Never together so closely we came,
Never so near.

As clean as uncut crystal she,
And shall be while I live, for me,
The law will have it so.
And then am I cause of her deed?
Of good counsel I am sore in need,
Alas, who recks my woe!

And if indeed it so befall
With God's son that she be withal,
Such grace is me denied;
I know well I am not he
Who should worthy deemed to be
That blessed body beside,

Nor yet to be in company;
To the wilderness then flee,
And there my fate deplore;
In future never with her deal,

But secretly from her shall steal,
    That meet shall we no more.

[JOSEPH *moves away from* MARY.

GABRIEL Be warned, Joseph, and change thy thought
Which to wandering thee has brought
    In the wilderness so wild;
Turn home to thy spouse again
Thy wife she is without a stain,
    Nor ever was defiled.

Tax not from earth the heavenly host,
She has conceived the holy ghost,
    And God's son she shall bear;
Therefore with her, in thy degree,
Meek and obedient, look thou be
    And of her take good care.

JOSEPH Ah, Lord, I love thee above all,
For so great boon as may befall
    That I should tend this stripling:
I that so ungracious were
To cast on her the slightest slur,
    Mary, my dear darling.

Repent I now what I have said
Against her matchless maidenhead,
    For she is pure in deed;
Therefore to her now will I go
And pray her be my friend not foe,
    And her forgiveness plead.

[JOSEPH *returns to* MARY.

Ah, Mary, wife, what cheer?

MARY The better, sir, that ye are here;
    Thus long where have ye been?

JOSEPH Fretting and walking up and down,
And troubled how to smooth thy frown
    Against my thoughts unclean.

But now I know and clearly see
My trespass against God and thee;
    Forgive me, I thee pray.

MARY Now all that ever ye said to me
God forgives as I do thee,
With all the might I may.

JOSEPH Blessed be, Mary, thy good will
In forgiving my words ill
When I did thee upbraid;
And blessed be he with such a wife;
Though dowerless, to share his life,
He may count himself well paid.

Lo, I am as light as a leaf!
He that can quench all grief
And every wrong amend,
Lend me grace, power, and might
My wife and her sweet son of light
To keep to my life's end.

[*They go off together.*

THE ELEVENTH PLAY

The Salutation of Elizabeth

MARY ELIZABETH

MARY My lord of heaven that sits on high,
And all things sees with his eye,
Save thee Elizabeth.

ELIZABETH Welcome, Mary, blessed bloom,
Joy I now that thou hast come
To me from Nazareth.

MARY How stands it with you, cousin mine?

ELIZABETH Daughter dear, I never pine,
Though I grow fast old.

MARY To speak with you has been my care,
For in age a child you'll bear,
Though barren you be called.

ELIZABETH Full long shall I the better be,
That I may speak my fill with thee,
My dear kinswoman;
To know how thy friends afar,
Fare in the land where now they are,
Thereof tell me thou can,
And how thou farest my dear darling.

MARY Well, dame, thank you for your asking,
You speak with purpose fair.

ELIZABETH And Joachim, thy father there,
And Anna, my niece, thy mother dear,
How stands it with him and with her?

MARY Dame, yet do they still have life,
Both Joachim and Anna his wife.

ELIZABETH Else were my heart full sore.

MARY Dame, God that does all,
Make good to befall,
And bless you therefore.

ELIZABETH Of all women be thou blest,
And the fruit that now doth rest
Within the womb of thee.
And this time may I bless
That my Lord's mother is
Come thus unto me.

For since that time full well I found
The trumpet voice of angel sound
Aringing in mine ear;
A wondrous thing comes with that word
The child makes joy, as any bird,
That I in body bear.

And now, Mary, be thou blest,
So steadfastly to rest
In the words of heaven's king.
Therefore all things shall known be now
That unto thee were pledged in vow
By the angel's greeting.

MARY *Magnificat anima mea dominum,*
My soul doth praise my Lord above,
My spirit sings with love,
For God my hopes renew.

For he has been seen again
And saved his servant without stain
And kept me maiden true.
Lo, what now shall me betide—
All nations on every side,
Blessed shall me call;
For he that is full of might,
Has raised me in his sight;
His name be blessed overall.

And his mercy is also
Upon mankind that meekly go
The Lord's way faring.

Mighty in arms is he;
He brings to low degree
  Proud men with high bearing.

Mighty men he hath put down;
But on those he set a crown,
  Meek men of heart.
The hungry with good things he filled,
But left the rich without a shield,
  Sadly to part.

Israel regards by law
His own son with great awe,
  By means of his mercy;
As before by name he told
Abraham, our father old,
  And seed of his body.

Elizabeth, mine aunt dear,
My leave I take of you here,
  For I have tarried long.

ELIZABETH If thou wilt go, then never fear,
Come kiss me daughter with good cheer,
  Before you go along
Farewell now, whom God hath wooed,
I pray thee be of comfort good,
  For thou art full of grace.
Greet well our kin of blood;
The Lord that thee with grace endued,
  Save all within this place.

[*They part.*

THE TWELFTH PLAY

The First Shepherds' Play

1ST SHEPHERD	JACK GARCIO
2ND SHEPHERD	ANGEL
3RD SHEPHERD	JESUS
	MARY

1ST SHEPHERD Lord, but they are well that hence have [passed,
For nought they feel them to downcast.
Here miseries dwell and long may they last,
Now in heart a happy spell, now in wet [now in blast
Now in care,
Now in comfort again,
Now is fair, now is rain,
Now in heart full fain,
And after despair.

Thus this world, as I say, fares on each [side,
For after our play cruel sorrows abide:
For he that most may as he sits in his pride,
When he makes his assay is cast quite [aside,
This is seen:
When richest is he,
Then comes poverty,
Horseman Jack Cope
Walks then, I mean.

Thanks be to God, hark ye what I mean,
For even or for odd great grief keeps me [lean:

As heavy as a sod I cry and I keen,
When I nap or I nod for care that has been,
And sorrow.
All my sheep are gone,
I am not left one,
All by plague undone:
Now beg I and borrow.

My hands may I wring and in misery [quake,
If no good will spring the country forsake:
Rent dues are coming full more than I [make,
I have almost nothing, to pay nor to take.
I may sing
With purse penniless,
What makes this heaviness,
Woe is me this distress!
And have no helping.

Thus set I my mind, now by St. Stephen,
By my wit to find what from me was riven:
For my sheep I have pined for odd for [even:
Now if fortune be kind God from his [heaven
Send grace.
To the fair will I hie,
To buy sheep, perdy,
And yet may I multiply,
For all this hard case.

2ND SHEPHERD Benedicite, benedicite, be us among,
And save all that I see, here in this throng,
He save you and me across and along,
Who hung on a tree, I tell you no wrong:
Christ save us
From all mischiefs,
From robbers and thieves,
From those men's griefs
That oft go against us.

Both boasters and braggers grant God over-
[throw,
That with their long daggers do us mighty
[woe.
These stabbers and stranglers with fierce
[knives that go
Such twisters and wranglers that bully and
[bellow,
Cause us quake.
Who seeks to complain,
Were better be slain:
Both plough and wain
Amends will not make.

He will prance as though proud as a lord
[that he were,
With his head in the cloud and curled all
[his hair:
He speaks out aloud, with grim looks that
[scare,
None would have allowed more gay in his
[gear
Than he glides.
I know not the better,
Nor which is the greater,
The lad or the master,
So stoutly he strides.

If he ask ought that he would we him pay,
Full dear is it bought if we say him nay:
By God that all wrought to thee now I say,
By his help be they brought to a better way
For their soul:
And send them good mending
With a short ending,
On thy word attending
When that thou call.

How, Gib, good morn, whither goes thou?
Thou goes over the corn, Gib, I say, how!

1ST SHEPHERD Who is that? John Horn, I make God a
[vow!

I say not in scorn, then, how fares thou?

2ND SHEPHERD Ha, hay!
Are ye in this town?

1ST SHEPHERD Yea, by my crown.

2ND SHEPHERD I thought by your gown
This was your array.

1ST SHEPHERD The same to a stitch. Still the old grudge [I nurse
That no shepherd is rich in this land, but [fares worse.

2ND SHEPHERD Poor men are in the ditch and empty their [purse:
This world is a bitch, but idle to curse,
Help is none here.

1ST SHEPHERD This from life I derive,
"A man may not wive
And also thrive,
All in a year."

2ND SHEPHERD First we must creep and afterwards go.

1ST SHEPHERD I go to buy sheep.

2ND SHEPHERD Nay not so:
What, dream ye or sleep? Where should [they go?
Here shall thou none keep.

1ST SHEPHERD Ah, good sir, ho!
Who am I?
Their pasture shall be
Whereso it please me,
Here shall thou them see.

2ND SHEPHERD Not so hardy!

Not one sheep's tail shall thou bring hither.

1ST SHEPHERD I shall bring, without fail, a hundred to-[gether.

2ND SHEPHERD What, does thou ail, long thou to go [whither?

1ST SHEPHERD They shall go, though, ye wail. Go now, [bell-wether!

2ND SHEPHERD I say, turn.

1ST SHEPHERD I say, turn, now again
I say skip over the plain.

2ND SHEPHERD Would you were never so fain,
Tup, I say, turn!

1ST SHEPHERD What, will thou not yet, I say, let the sheep [go?
Whop!

2ND SHEPHERD Abide yet.

1ST SHEPHERD Will ye but so?
Knave, hence I bid thee flit, 't were good [that thou do,
Or I shall thee hit on thy pate, lo,
Shall thou reel:
I say give the sheep space.

2ND SHEPHERD Sir, give over your grace,
Here comes Slow-pace
From the mill-wheel.

3RD SHEPHERD What a do, what a do is this you between?
A good day thou and thou.

1ST SHEPHERD Hark what I mean
You to say:
Of sheep bought I a store,
And drove them me before,
He says not one more
Shall pass by this way:

If witless did what he could this way shall [they go.

3RD SHEPHERD Yea, but tell me, good, where are your [sheep, lo?

2ND SHEPHERD Now, sir, by my hood, neither see I nor [know,
Not since I here stood.

3RD SHEPHERD God give you woe
And sorrow!
Ye fish without net,
Ye fight and ye fret,
Such fools never I met
By even or morrow.

It is wonder to wit, where wit should be [found;
Here are old knaves yet standing on this [ground,
These would by their wit make a ship be [drowned;
He were well quit who had sold for a [pound
Such two.
They fight and they flight,
Though senseless their spite;
No need them to smite
To cause such ado.

Sauce sooner ye need than sorrow I pray;
Like Moll may ye speed, that went by the [way—
Many sheep counted she, only one had she [ay—
To her count she took heed, while her [pitcher, I say,
Was broken.
"Oh, God," she said,
But one sheep instead,
And the milk pitcher sped,
And the pieces the token.

But since ye are bare of wisdom and lore,
Take heed how I fare and learn from me [more:
Ye need not to care save my words ye [ignore:
Hold ye my mare, throw this sack further- [more
On my back,

Whilst I with my hand,
Loose the sack's band:
Come nearby and stand
Both Gib and Jack.

Is not all shaken out and no jot left in?

1ST SHEPHERD Yea, there is no doubt.

3RD SHEPHERD Your wit is so thin.
When ye look well about ye gawp and ye [grin,
So goes your wit out even as it comes in:
Gather up,
And seek it again.

2ND SHEPHERD By our brawn and our brain,
He has told us full plain
Wisdom to sup.

JACK GARCIO Now God give you care, all fools to a man:
Saw I never none so fare but the fools of [Gotham.
Your parents had better beware, your sire [and your dam,
Had she brought forth a hare, a sheep, or [a lamb,
Had been well.
Of all the fools I can tell,
From heaven unto hell,
Ye three bear the bell:
God grant your sorrows swell.

1ST SHEPHERD Good friend, now tell me, how pasture our [sheep then?

JACK GARCIO In grass to the knee.

2ND SHEPHERD Fair befall thee! Amen!

JACK GARCIO If ye will ye may see, your beasts ye ken.

1ST SHEPHERD Sit we down all three and drink shall we [men.

3RD SHEPHERD What a turd!
I'd rather eat:

What, drink without meat?
A meal I entreat,
  And set up a board.

Then may we go dine our bellies to fill.

2ND SHEPHERD Let be thy whine.

3RD SHEPHERD Not for thee I will!
I am worthy the wine, and ready to swill:
No service of mine ye get, I fare ill
  At your manger.

1ST SHEPHERD Pack off to our meat,
Peace kept is sweet,
Better not bleat,
  Nor stand in danger:

Thou has ever been curst since we met [together.

3RD SHEPHERD Now in faith, if I durst, ye are even my [brother.

2ND SHEPHERD Sirs, let us mind first for one thing or other,
That these words be pursed, and let us [stuff fodder
  Within.
Lay forth all our store,
Lo, here! Brawn of a boar.

1ST SHEPHERD Set mustard before,
  Our meal now begin.

Here's a foot of a cow well sauced, I ween,
The shank of a sow that spiced has been,
Two blood-puddings, I vow, with liver be- [tween:
Let gladly, sirs, now, my brothers, be seen
  What more.
Both beef, and mutton
Of a ewe that was rotten,
Good meat for a glutton.
  Eat of this store.

2ND SHEPHERD I have in my bag no kale, but boiled and [roast,
Even an ox-tail that would not be lost:
Ha, Ha, good-hail! I stop for no cost,
A good pie or we fail: this is good for a [frost
In the morning:
Of two pigs the groin,
All a hare but the loin
No spoons we enjoin
Here at our feasting.

3RD SHEPHERD Here is to record the leg of a goose,
Basted for our board, pork or partridge to [choose,
A tart for a lord, how the gravy doth ooze.
A calf's liver stored with the verjuice:
Good sauce,
A restorative right
For a good appetite.

1ST SHEPHERD Is this a church rite
You make such discourse?
If ye could by your grammary reach us a [drink,
I should be more merry, bring me to the [brink.

2ND SHEPHERD Good ale is the ferry to slumber, I think,
If you deeply it bury, in thy pate it will [sink.

1ST SHEPHERD Ah, so:
This is balm of our bale,
Good wholesome ale.

3RD SHEPHERD Ye hold long the scale,
Now for my go.

2ND SHEPHERD Now curse those lips, but leave me some [part.

1ST SHEPHERD By God, he but sips, beguiled thou art:
Behold how he nips.

2ND SHEPHERD I cuss you so smart,
And me on my hips, death to thy heart,
Abate.
Be thou wine, be thou ale,
Until my breath fail,
I shall set thee asail:
God give me such state.

3RD SHEPHERD By my dam's soul, Alice, that was deeply [drunken.

1ST SHEPHERD Now as ever I have bliss, to the bottom it [is sunken.

2ND SHEPHERD Another bottle here is.

3RD SHEPHERD That is well spoken!
That must we kiss.

2ND SHEPHERD That had I forgotten.
But hark!

Whoso can best sing
Shall have the beginning.

[*They sing.*

1ST SHEPHERD Now pray at the parting,
I shall set you to work.

We have done our part and sung right well,
I drink for a start.

2ND SHEPHERD Stay, let the cup still.

1ST SHEPHERD God curse thy thirsty heart, thou drinks [with much zeal.

3RD SHEPHERD Thou has drunken a quart, therefore choke [thee the devil.

1ST SHEPHERD Thou raves:
For even a sow's share
There is drink to spare.

3RD SHEPHERD A blight on ye both I swear!
Ye be both knaves.

1ST SHEPHERD Nay! We be knaves all, thus think I it best,
So, sir, should ye call.

2ND SHEPHERD And so let it rest:
We will not brawl.

1ST SHEPHERD Then would I suggest
This meat we shall pack in a pannier chest.

3RD SHEPHERD Hear, sirs:
For our souls let us so,
On poor men bestow.

1ST SHEPHERD Gather up, lo, lo,
Ye hungry begging friars.

2ND SHEPHERD It draws near tonight, prepare we to rest:
All misty my sight, I think it the best.

3RD SHEPHERD For fear and for fright by a cross be we [blest,
Christ's cross keep us right, east and west,
In need.
Jesus onazorus
Cruciefixus,
Marcus, Andreus,
God be our speed.

[*They sleep. "Gloria in Excelsis" is sung in heaven.*

ANGEL Hearken, shepherds, awake! Give praises [ye shall.
He is born for your sake, Lord perpetual:
He has come to take and ransom you all,
Your sorrows to slake, King imperial,
Star of the east:
That child is born
At Bethlehem this morn,
Ye shall find him ere dawn
On each side a beast.

1ST SHEPHERD By God, our dear dominus! What was that [song?
It was full curious with short notes among:
I pray to God save us, now in this throng:
I am frightened, by Jesus, somewhat is [wrong:
Methought,

One screamed out aloud:
I suppose it was a cloud
In my ears it soughed,
By him that me bought!

2ND SHEPHERD Nay, that may not be, I tell you certain,
For he spake to us three, as he had been a [man:
When he lit up this lea, my heart to shake [began,
An angel was he that tell you I can,
No doubt.
Of a bairn he spake,
Whom to seek we now wake,
That star shines for his sake,
That yonder stands out.

3RD SHEPHERD It was a marvel to see so brightly it shone,
The sky I thought truly with lightning [strown,
But I saw with my eye, as I leaned on this [stone:
With sound fully merry, such heard I never [none,
I record.
As he said in a scream,
Or else that I dream
We should go to Bethlehem,
To worship that lord.

1ST SHEPHERD That same child is he of whom prophets [told,
Should make them free whom Adam had [sold.

2ND SHEPHERD Give heed unto me this is enrolled,
In the words of Isaiah, a prince most bold
Shall he be,
And king with crown,
Set on David's throne,
Such was never known
For us to see.

3RD SHEPHERD Also Isaiah says, our fathers us told,
That of Jesse's race a virgin that would
Bring forth by grace a flower so bold;
That virgin in this place may those words
[now uphold,
As ye see.
Trust it now we may,
He is born this day,
Exiet virga
De radice Jesse.

1ST SHEPHERD Of him spake more, sage Sibyl I mean,
And Nebuchadnezzar, to our faith unclean,
In the furnace there were three children
[seen,
The fourth stood before, who God's son
[must have been.

2ND SHEPHERD That figure
Was given by revelation,
That God would have a son;
This is a good lesson
For us to consider.

3RD SHEPHERD Of him did Jeremiah testify, and Moses
[also,
Where he saw him standing by a bush
[burning, lo!
When he came to espy if it were so,
Unburning was it truly when he stood close
[below.
A wonder
That was for all to see,
Her holy virginity
That undefiled should be;
On this I ponder,

And she should have a child, such was
[never seen.

2ND SHEPHERD Peace, man, thou art beguiled, thou shalt
[see him, I mean,

Of a maiden so mild no marvel so mighty
[has been;
Yea, and she undefiled, a virgin as clean
Is none.

1ST SHEPHERD Nothing is impossible,
Indeed, through God's will;
But God shall fulfil
What he would have done.

2ND SHEPHERD Habakkuk and Ely prophesied so,
Elizabeth and Zachary, and many more,
[you know,
And David as verily is witness thereto,
John the Baptist surely, and Daniel also.

3RD SHEPHERD So saying,
He is God's son alone,
Without him shall be none,
His seat and his throne
Shall ever be lasting.

1ST SHEPHERD Virgil in his poetry said in his verse,
Even thus by grammary, as I shall re-
[hearse;
"Iam nova progenies celo demittitur alto,
Iam rediet virgo, redeunt saturnia regna."

2ND SHEPHERD Alas! Turd! What speak ye, conjure ye or
[curse?
Give us no clergy, I count you with the
[friars
Who preach;
By the Latin you know
You have learnt your Cato.

1ST SHEPHERD Hark, sirs, ere you go,
I shall you teach.

From heaven he said his son he would
[send,
Through a virgin's maidenhead our ills to
[amend,
By her to be bred, thus make I an end;

And yet more may be read, God himself [shall bend
Unto us,
With peace and plenty,
With a great company,
True love and charity
Shall be among us.

3RD SHEPHERD And I hold it true for there should be,
When comes that King new, peace by land [and sea.

2ND SHEPHERD Now brothers, adieu! Give heed unto me:
I would that we knew of this song so free
Of the angel:
I heard by his sound,
From heaven he was bound.

1ST SHEPHERD It is truth ye have found,
As his words tell.

2ND SHEPHERD Now, by God that me bought, it was a [merry song:
I dare say that he brought four and [twenty to a long.

3RD SHEPHERD I would it were sought to sing us among.

1ST SHEPHERD In faith I trust nought, so many he strung
In a heap:
They were gentle and small,
And well toned withal.

3RD SHEPHERD Yea, but I know them all,
The tune I shall keep.

1ST SHEPHERD Sing not through your nose, let's see how [ye yelp.

3RD SHEPHERD My voice with my cold goes, save I have [help.

2ND SHEPHERD Ah, thy heart is in thy hose!

1ST SHEPHERD Now on pain of a skelp
This song ere ye dose.

3RD SHEPHERD Thou art an ill whelp
For anger!

2ND SHEPHERD Begin, if you please!

1ST SHEPHERD He will now take his ease.

3RD SHEPHERD God let us never cease:
List to my clangour.

[*They sing.*

1ST SHEPHERD Now end we our croon of the song at this [tide.

2ND SHEPHERD Thy snout who did prune, thy voice so to [hide?

3RD SHEPHERD Then let us go soon, I will not abide.

1ST SHEPHERD No light lends the moon, that have I [espied;
Nevertheless
Let us keep our behest.

2ND SHEPHERD That hold I best.

3RD SHEPHERD Then must we go east,
After my guess.

1ST SHEPHERD Would God that we might this young [babe see!

2ND SHEPHERD Many prophets that sight desired verily
To see that child bright.

3RD SHEPHERD If God would decree
To show us that mite, we could say truly,
We had seen
What many saints desired,
With prophets inspired,
When they him required
Yet dead long have been.

2ND SHEPHERD God grant us that grace.

3RD SHEPHERD God do so.

1ST SHEPHERD Abide sirs, a space, lo, yonder, lo!
It comes at a race, how yon star doth [glow.

2ND SHEPHERD It makes a great blaze, our way let us go,
Here he is!

[*They go to Bethlehem.*

3RD SHEPHERD Aye, this be the door.

1ST SHEPHERD Who shall go in before?

2ND SHEPHERD Ye are eldest by a score
It seems you for this.

[*They enter the stable.*

1ST SHEPHERD Hail, King I thee call! Hail, most of might!
Hail, the worthiest of all! Hail, duke! Hail [knight!
Of great and small thou art Lord by right:
Hail perpetual! Hail babe so bright!
Here I offer
I pray thee to take—
If thou would, for my sake,
Thou may game with this make,—
This little spruce coffer.

2ND SHEPHERD Hail, little tiny mop, rewarder of meed!
Hail, but one drop of grace at my need:
Hail, little milk-sop! Hail, David's seed!
Of our creed thou art top, hail, in good [heed!
This ball
That thou would receive,—
So little I grieve,
This with thee I leave,
To please thee withal.

3RD SHEPHERD Hail, maker of man, hail, sweeting!
Hail, as well as I can, pretty miting!
I bow to thee then in joy of this greeting:
Hail, Lord! in token I give at our meeting
This bottle—
It is an old by-word,
That a jest or bourd
May be had from a gourd,
Of two quarts or a pottle.

MARY He that all might may sway, our heaven's [King,
That is for to say, my son, my sweeting,
Reward you this day, as in seven he made [all spring:
He grant you for ay, his grace and his [blessing
Continuing:
He give you good grace,
Tell forth of this case,
He speed you apace,
And grant you good ending.

1ST SHEPHERD Farewell, fair Lord, with thy mother also.

2ND SHEPHERD We shall this record, wherever we go.

3RD SHEPHERD We must be restored, God grant it be so!

1ST SHEPHERD Amen, to that word, sing we thereto
On high:
Together in joy,
Our mirth now employ
To the praise of this boy
Sing we for ay.

[*They leave singing.*

THE THIRTEENTH PLAY

The Second Shepherds' Play

1ST SHEPHERD	MAK	ANGEL
2ND SHEPHERD	GILL, HIS WIFE	MARY
3RD SHEPHERD		JESUS

1ST SHEPHERD Lord, but this weather is cold, and I am [ill wrapped,
My hands in frost's hold, so long have I [napped;
My legs they fold, my fingers are chapped,
It is not as of old, for I am lapped
In sorrow.
In storms and tempest,
Now in the east, now in the west,
Woe to him who has no rest
Now or tomorrow.

But we simple shepherds that walk on the [moor,
Are soon by richer hands thrust out of [door;
No wonder as it stands, if we be poor,
For the tilth of our lands lies as fallow as [the floor,
As you know.
We are so lamed,
Overtaxed and maimed,
And cruelly tamed,
By our gentlemen foe.

Thus they rob us of our rest, may ill-luck [them harry!

These proud men are our pest they make
[the plough tarry.
What men say is for the best, we find it
[contrary:
Thus are ploughmen oppressed, no hope
[now to carry
Alive.
Thus hold they us under,
Thus bring us into blunder;
It were great wonder,
If ever we should thrive.

If one gets a modish sleeve or a brooch
[nowadays,
Take care if you him grieve or once cross
[his ways!
Dares no man bid him leave the power
[that he sways,
And yet may not believe one word that he
[says
The better
He grasps for his gain
In his bragging vein,
And boasts men maintain
Him, who are far greater.

There shall come a swain, a proud peacock
[you know,
He must borrow my wain, my plough also,
This for my gain I must grant ere he go.
Thus live we in pain, anger and woe;
By night and day
He craves what comes to his head,
And I give in great dread;
I were better be dead,
Than once say him nay.

It does me good as I walk thus on my own,
Of this world for to talk, and so make my
[moan.
To my sheep will I stalk and listen anon;

There abide on a balk or sit on a stone
    Full soon.
For believe you me,
True men, if they be,
We get more company
    Ere it be noon.

[2ND SHEPHERD *enters.*

2ND SHEPHERD *Benedicite dominus!* What may this mean?
The world faring thus, how oft have we [seen?
Lord, this weather works through us, and [the wind is so keen
And frost will undo us, fast blind I have [been,
    No lie.
Now in dry, now in wet,
Now in snow, now in sleet,
When my shoes freeze to my feet,
    It's not at all easy.

But as far as I ken or yet as I go,
We poor wedded men suffer much woe;
We have sorrow ever again, it falls often [so;
Old Capel, our hen, both to and fro
    She cackles;
But begin she to croak
To prod or to poke,
For our cock it is no joke
    For he is in shackles.

These men that are wed have not their [own will,
When full bitter they have sped their [tongue they keep still:
God knows they are led in a grim dance [full ill;
In bower and in bed, but speak not their [fill
    Nor chide.

My part have I found,
Learnt my lesson sound.
Woe to him who is bound
For he must abide.

But now late in our lives a marvel to me
That I think my heart rives such wonders
[to see.
Where that destiny drives it should so be;
Some men will have two wives, and some
[men three
In store.
Some are woe without any,
But so far as I see,
Woe is him that has many,
For he rues it sore.

But young men a-wooing, on God be your
[thought,
Be well warned of wedding, and think ere
[you're taught,
"Had I known" is a thing too lately you're
[taught;
Much bitter mourning has wedding home
[brought:
You achieve
With many a sharp shower,
What you may catch in an hour,
Which shall savour full sour,
A life-time to grieve.

As I've read Paul's Epistle, my helpmeet
[is here,
As sharp as a thistle, as tough as a spear;
She is browed like a bristle, with a sour
[looking cheer;
If she once wets her whistle she can sing
[full clear
Her paternoster.
As great as a whale withal,
She has a gallon of gall,

By him that died for us all
I would I had lost her.

1ST SHEPHERD Look over the hedgerow, are you deaf as [you stand?

2ND SHEPHERD The devil take you for so long have I [scanned.
Where saw you Daw go?

1ST SHEPHERD Here on the lea land.
I heard his pipe blow: he comes near at [hand
Hereby;
Stand still.

2ND SHEPHERD Why?

1ST SHEPHERD For he comes, say I.

2ND SHEPHERD He will beguile us with a lie
Unless we be spry.

[*Enter* 3RD SHEPHERD.

3RD SHEPHERD Christ's cross me speed and Saint Nicholas!
Thereof have I need; it is worse than it [was.
Who knows should take heed, and let the [world pass;
It is doomed as decreed and brittle as glass
And slithers.
This world fared never so:
As great marvels grow,
Move us from weal to woe,
The whole world withers.

Was never since Noah's flood such flood- [ings seen;
Winds and rains so rude and storms so [keen;
Some stumbled some stood in doubt, as I [ween;
Now God turn all to good, I say as I mean,
And ponder.

These floods they so drown,
Both in fields and in town,
And bear all things down,
And that is a wonder.

We that walk in the nights our cattle to [keep,
We see fearful sights when other men [sleep.
Now I think my eye lights on some rascals [that peep;
And to put all to rights I must give my [sheep
A turn.
But full ill have I meant,
And amend my intent,
I may lightly repent,
My toes if I spurn.

Ah, sir, God you save, and master mine!
A deep drink would I have and somewhat [to dine.

1ST SHEPHERD Christ's curse, you slave, you are a sluggish [swine!

2ND SHEPHERD What! Let the boy rave; sit down and dine.
We have had our fill
Ill luck be thy fate
Though the lad come late,
Yet he is in a state
To sup if he will.

Such servants as I who work till we sweat
Eat our bread quite dry and that makes [me fret;
We are often weak and weary when our [masters sleep yet;
Late home and dreary, in food and drink [we get
Less than our due.
Both our dame and our sire,

When we run in the mire
They dock us of our hire
And pay us late too.

But hear the truth master, for what I am [paid
I shall work no faster than a stubborn jade;
I shall be slacker and sport like a maid,
For never has my supper my stomach dis- [mayed
In fields,
Why should I weep?
With my staff can I leap;
Men say a bargain cheap
Poorly yields.

1ST SHEPHERD You were an ill lad to go a-wooing
With a master that had but little for [spending.

2ND SHEPHERD Peace, I say, lad, no more of jangling,
Or you will rue it sad, by heaven's king!
Hold your tongue!
Where are our sheep, boy, we've shorn?

3RD SHEPHERD Sir, this same day at morn
I left them in the corn,
When matins were rung.

They have pasture good they cannot go [wrong.

1ST SHEPHERD That is right, by the rood! These nights [are long,
Yet ere we went I would someone gave us [a song.

2ND SHEPHERD So I thought as I stood, our mirth to pro- [long.

3RD SHEPHERD I grant.

1ST SHEPHERD Let me sing the tenor free.

2ND SHEPHERD And I shall sing the trebel key.

3RD SHEPHERD Then the alto falls to me.
Let's see how we chant.

[SHEPHERDS *sing. Then* MAK *enters. He wears a short mantle over his gown.*

MAK Now Lord, in thy names seven that made [both moon and stars,
More than I can count in heaven, thy will [from bliss me bars;
My life is uneven with jangles and jars;
Now would God I were in heaven where [no bairn's tear mars
The still.

1ST SHEPHERD Who is it that pipes so poorly?

MAK Would God ye knew of me, surely!
Footing the moors so sorely,
Drudging against my will.

2ND SHEPHERD Mak, where hast thou been? Tell us thy [tidings.

3RD SHEPHERD If Mak come on the scene, look well to [your things.

[3RD SHEPHERD *takes away* MAK'S *mantle.*

MAK What! I be a yeoman true and one the [king's;
One who from no mean lord a mighty mes- [sage brings.
No lie.
Fie on you go hence
Out of my presence!
I must have reverence;
Why? Who am I?

1ST SHEPHERD Why are your quirks so quaint? Mak, [you do wrong.

2ND SHEPHERD Would you rather be a saint, Mak? Your [wish is so strong.

3RD SHEPHERD If the knave can paint to the devil might [he belong.

MAK I shall make complaint; beaten you'll be [ere long,
At a word,
And wracked without ruth.

1ST SHEPHERD But, Mak, is that truth?
Now take out that southern tooth,
And set in a turd.

2ND SHEPHERD Mak, the devil's in thee, a blow you'll be [getting.

3RD SHEPHERD Mak, know ye not me? Your blood I'll be [letting.

MAK God save you all three, now why are you [fretting?
You are a fair company.

1ST SHEPHERD What snare are you setting?

2ND SHEPHERD Why creep
You so late on your toes,
What will men suppose?
And thou hast an ill nose
For stealing of sheep.

MAK That I am true as steel no men debate,
But a sickness that I feel has brought me [to this state,
My belly lacks a meal and suffers ill fate.

3RD SHEPHERD Seldom lies the devil dead by the gate.

MAK Therefore
Full sore am I and ill,
If I stand stone still
I've ate not a needle
This month and more.

1ST SHEPHERD How fares thy wife, by my hood, how fares [she?

MAK Rolls around by the rood; by the fire she'll [be,
And a house full of brood, with the bottle [she's free,

Cares not for any good, whatever she may [see;
    But so
Eats as fast as she can,
And each year that comes to a man
Adds another to our clan;
    And some years two.

Now were I richer than the Pope of Rome
I would be eaten out of house and home.
So foul a wench, if close you come
You'll scarce believe; no worser one
    A man's peace stole.
Would you see what I would proffer;
I'd give all within my coffer
If tomorrow I might offer
    A prayer for her soul.

2ND SHEPHERD I have watched without nodding as none [in this shire;
I must sleep though it means taking less [for my hire.

3RD SHEPHERD I am cold and ill-clad and long for a fire.

1ST SHEPHERD I am worn out with walking and covered [in mire.
    Look to!

2ND SHEPHERD Nay, down I shall lie
For I must sleep soundly.

3RD SHEPHERD As good a man's son I
    As any of you.

But, Mak, come hither, and with us lie [down.

MAK Then your whisperings between you with [snores I would drown.
    Pay heed;
From my top to my toe,
Manus tuas commendo,
Pontio Pilato,
    Christ's cross me speed!

[*When the* SHEPHERDS *are asleep* MAK *rises.*

MAK It is time now to strike ere the iron grows [cold,
And craftily creep then into the fold,
And nimbly to work, but not be too bold,
For bitter the bargain, if all were told
At the ending;
My doubts may dispel,
But he needs good counsel
That would gladly fare well
With but little for spending.

Put about you a circle as round as the [moon,
Till I have done what I will, until it be [noon.
Lie you stone still as though in a swoon,
While I summon my skill some magic to [croon
Over you.
Above your heads I raise my hand.
Your sight is lost on sea and land!
But I must gain much more command
To get my due.

Lord, but they sleep hard, as you may well [hear;
Never yet was I shepherd, but of that I've [no fear,
If the flock be scared, then I shall nip near
Till one I've ensnared. Then will soon dis- [appear
Our sorrow.

[MAK *seizes a sheep.*

A fat sheep I dare say,
A good fleece I dare lay,
I'll requite when I may,
But this will I borrow.

[MAK *goes home.*

How Gill, are you in? Get us some light!

MAK'S WIFE Who makes such a din, this time of the [night?
I've sat down to spin; I hope now I might
Not rise for a pin. I'll curse in my spite
With no pause;
A housewife that has been
Fretted betwixt and between,
Has no work to be seen
For such small chores.

MAK Good wife, open this hatch; see you not [what I bring?

MAK'S WIFE I will let you draw the latch. Come in, my [sweeting.

MAK You care not a scratch for my long stand- [ing.

MAK'S WIFE Now your neck may catch a rope at a [hanging.

MAK Away!
I earn what I eat,
For in a fix can I get
More than they that toil and sweat
All the long day.

Thus it fell to my lot, Gill, you cannot [gainsay.

MAK'S WIFE It were a foul blot to be hanged, as you [may.

MAK I have escaped scot-free a far fiercer fray.

MAK'S WIFE But so long goes the pot to the water, men [say,
At last
Comes it home broken.

MAK Well know I the token,
But let it never be spoken,
But come and help fast.

I would he were slain, I want so to eat.
For more than a year I've dreamt of this [treat.

MAK'S WIFE They'll come ere he's slain, and hear the [sheep bleat,

MAK Then might I be ta'en; that gives me cold [feet!
Go bar
The outer door.

MAK'S WIFE Yes, Mak,
For if they pounce on your back. . . .

MAK Then might I get from the whole pack
A jolt and a jar.

MAK'S WIFE A fine jest have I spied, since you think of [none;
Here shall we hide him until they are gone,
In my cradle to abide, but let me alone,
And I shall lie beside in childbed, and [groan.

MAK Them warn
I shall that in the night
Was born a boy for our delight.

MAK'S WIFE Now bless I that day bright,
That ever I was born!

This is a cunning play and well cast;
What a woman may say can help at the [last.
None will gainsay; but get you back fast.

MAK If when they wake I'm away, there'll blow [a cold blast.
I will go sleep.

[MAK *returns to the* SHEPHERDS *and resumes his place.*

Yet sleeps the whole company
So I must tread carefully,
As though it had never been I
That stole their sheep.

1ST SHEPHERD *Resurrex a mortruis!* Hold hard my hand!
Judas carnas dominus! I scarcely can [stand.

My foot sleeps, by Jesus, my belly's a [brand;
My dream seemed to bring us quite near [to England.

2ND SHEPHERD Say ye!
Lord, but I slept well;
As fresh as an eel.
As light I do feel
As leaf on a tree.

3RD SHEPHERD Blessed all be within! My heart so quakes
To leap out of its skin such noise it makes.
Who makes all this din? My head sorely [aches.
I must stir from within for my fellows' [sakes.
We were four.
Saw you ought of Mak now?

1ST SHEPHERD We were up ere thou.

2ND SHEPHERD Man, I give God a vow,
He's still in the straw.

3RD SHEPHERD I dreamt he was wrapped in a wolf's skin.

1ST SHEPHERD Many such have entrapped now our poor [kin.

2ND SHEPHERD When long had we napped I dreamt of [Mak's sin,
A fat sheep he had trapped by stealth [with no din.

3RD SHEPHERD Be still!
Your dream proves you mad;
Your fancy's a fad.

1ST SHEPHERD God keep us from bad
If it be his will.

2ND SHEPHERD Rise, Mak, for shame! Thou liest right long.

MAK Now Christ's holy name be us among!
What is this? By Saint James, I can't get [along!

I trust I be the same. Ah! My neck has
[lain all wrong
In this hole.

[*They help him.*

Many thanks! Since yester-even,
Now by Saint Stephen,
A dream sent from heaven
Struck fear in my soul.

I dreamt Gill in her smock cried out full
[sad,
Gave birth at the first cock to a young lad,
To add to our flock; then be I never glad.
Of cares I've a stock more than ever I had.
Ah, my head!
Those moans of hunger pains,
The devil knock out their brains!
Woe to him whose brood complains
Of too little bread.

I must go home, by your leave, to Gill, as
[I thought.
First look up my sleeve that I've stolen
[nought:
I am loth you to grieve, or from you take
[ought.

[MAK *goes home.*

3RD SHEPHERD Go forth, ill-luck achieve! Now would I we
[sought
This morn
For the sheep in our care.

1ST SHEPHERD First I shall fare.
Let us meet.

2ND SHEPHERD Where?

3RD SHEPHERD At the crooked thorn.

[*The* SHEPHERDS *part.*

MAK Undo this door! Who is here? How long
[shall I stand?

MAK'S WIFE Who roars then out there? Be ye one or a [band?

MAK Ah, Gill, what cheer? It is I, Mak, your [husband.

MAK'S WIFE Ah, then never fear, the devil is at hand
With guile.
Lo, he strikes a harsh note,
As though held by the throat,
And cares never a groat
My work to beguile.

MAK Oh, the fuss that she makes when I stir [her repose.
She feigns all her aches and picks at her [toes.

MAK'S WIFE Why, who works, and who wakes, who [comes and who goes?
Who brews and who bakes? Who darns [all your hose?
And then
It is sad to behold,
Or e'er to be told,
How woeful the household
That wants a woman.

But how have you sped with the shep-[herds, Mak?

MAK The last word that they said when I turned [my back,
They would count each head of the sheep [in their pack.
Now have we no dread when they their [sheep lack,
Pardy;
But howe'er the game goes,
They'll be here, I suppose,
Our theft to disclose,
And cry out upon me.

Now do as you promised.

MAK'S WIFE To that I agree,
I'll swaddle him now, in his crib he will be;
A fine trick to twist on our poor shepherds [three.
To bed! Come assist. Tuck up!

MAK Let me.

MAK'S WIFE Behind.
Come Coll and his mate
To pry and to prate,
For help I'll cry straight
The sheep if they find.

Hark now for their call; on the breeze be [it blown.
Come make ready all and sing on thine [own;
Sing lullay you shall, for loud I must [groan,
And cry out by the wall on Mary and Joan
Full sore.
Sing lullay quite fast
When you hear them at last;
If my part is miscast,
Trust me no more.

3RD SHEPHERD Ah, Coll, good morn, why sleepest thou [not?

1ST SHEPHERD Alas that ever I was born! A sad grief we [have got.
Lost! A fat wether unshorn.

3RD SHEPHERD By God, a foul blot.

2ND SHEPHERD Who should give us this scorn? It won't be [forgot.

1ST SHEPHERD This he shall rue.
I have searched with my dogs
All Horbury shrogs,
And of fifteen hogs,
Found I but one ewe.

3RD SHEPHERD Now trust me, if ye will, by St. Thomas of [Kent,
Either Mak or Gill, had a hand in this [event.

1ST SHEPHERD Peace, man, be still! I saw when he went.
You slander him ill, you ought to repent
With good speed.

2ND SHEPHERD Now as ever I might thrive,
As I hope to keep alive,
Only Mak could contrive
To do that same deed.

3RD SHEPHERD Then off to his homestead, he brisk on our [feet.
I shall never eat bread till we've proved [this deceit.

1ST SHEPHERD Nor have drink in my head till with him I [meet.

2ND SHEPHERD I will rest in no stead till him I may greet,
My brother.
My promise I plight
Till I have him in sight,
Shall I ne'er sleep one night.
May I do no other.

[*They go to* MAK'*s house—singing within.*

3RD SHEPHERD Do ye hear how they croak? My lord will [now croon.

1ST SHEPHERD Ne'er heard I sing folk so clean out of [tune;
Call him.

2ND SHEPHERD Mak, may you choke! Undo your [door soon!

MAK Who is it that spoke, as if it were noon?
Who scoffed?
Who is that I say?

3RD SHEPHERD Good fellows, were it day!

MAK As far as ye may,
Speak soft,

Over a sick woman's head, who is not at [her ease,
I had rather be dead than she had a [disease.

[*The* SHEPHERDS *enter* MAK'S *home.*

MAK'S WIFE Be off from the bed, let me breathe, if you [please!
Each step that you tread from my nose to [my knees
Goes through me.

1ST SHEPHERD Tell us, Mak, if ye may,
How fare ye, say?

MAK But are ye in town today?
Now how fare ye?

Ye have run in the mire, and now are all [wet.
I shall make you a fire now we are met.
A nurse would I hire. Think ye on yet
My dream which entire has fulfilled its [threat
In due season.
I have bairns if ye knew,
Far more than a few,
But we must drink as we brew,
And that is but reason.

Would ye dined ere ye went? Ye sweat, as [I think.

2ND SHEPHERD Our feelings be vent not for meat nor for [drink.

MAK Is ought then ill meant?

3RD SHEPHERD Yea, in a wink,
A sheep lost we lament, borne off ere we [blink.

MAK Drink sirs.
Had I been there
Some had suffered full dear.

1ST SHEPHERD In that is our fear;
None of us errs.

2ND SHEPHERD Against you goes the grouse, Mak, thief [that ye be,
Either you or your spouse, and so say we.

MAK Nay, knit not your brows against my Gill [or me.
Come comb through our house, and then [ye may see
Who had her.
If any sheep I've got,
Alive or in the pot—
And Gill, my wife, rose not
Here since she laid her.

As I am true as steel, to God here I pray,
That this be the first meal that I shall eat [this day.

1ST SHEPHERD Mak, is such thy zeal! Then be advised, I [say:
He learns in time to steal that never could [say nay.

MAK'S WIFE I faint!
Out thieves from my home,
Ere I claw with my comb!

MAK If you marked but her foam,
You'd show some restraint.

MAK'S WIFE Out thieves from my cot, step you soft on [the floor.

MAK If ye knew her harsh lot, your hearts [would be sore.
Your behaviour's a blot, here to rant and [to roar:
Gill's plight ye've forgot. But I say no [more.

MAK'S WIFE Ah, my middle!
I pray to God so mild,
If ere I you beguiled,
That I should eat this child
That lies in this cradle.

MAK Peace, woman, for God's pain, and cry not [so:
Thou'lt burst thy brain and make me full [of woe.

2ND SHEPHERD I believe our sheep be slain, and that ye [know.

3RD SHEPHERD Our search has been in vain, now let us go.
He chatters
His way through our mesh.
Here's to be found no flesh,
Soft nor hard, salt nor flesh,
But two empty platters.

No creature but this, tame or wild,
As hope I for bliss, smelt so defiled.

MAK'S WIFE No, so God me bless, and give me joy of [my child!

1ST SHEPHERD We have aimed amiss; we be but beguiled.

2ND SHEPHERD Have done!
Sir, our Lady him save!
Be this a boy brave?

MAK'S WIFE Any lord might him have.
This child for his son.

When he wakes he smiles that joy is to see.

3RD SHEPHERD May now the world's wiles this bairn leave [be.
Who stood at the font that so soon were [ready?

MAK The first folk of these isles.

1ST SHEPHERD A lie now, hark ye!

MAK God give them thanks.
Parkin and Gibbon Waller, I say,

And gentle John Horn in grey.
He made such droll display
With his long shanks.

2ND SHEPHERD Mak, friends will we be, for we are all one.

MAK We? count not on me, for amends get I [none.
Farewell all three! And gladly begone.

[*They leave the cottage.*

3RD SHEPHERD Fair words there may be, but love there is [none
This year.

1ST SHEPHERD Gave ye the child anything?

2ND SHEPHERD Not I, ne'er a farthing.

3RD SHEPHERD I shall find an offering.
Wait for me here.

[*He returns to the cottage.*

3RD SHEPHERD Mak, by your leave, your son may I see?

MAK A mere mock I believe; his sleep you may [mar.

3RD SHEPHERD This child will not grieve, that little day [star.
Mak, by your leave, thy bairn never bar
From sixpence.

MAK Nay, go away, he sleeps.

3RD SHEPHERD I think he peeps.

MAK When he wakes he weeps;
I pray you go hence.

[*The other* SHEPHERDS *come back.*

3RD SHEPHERD Give me leave him to kiss, and once lift [him out.
What the devil is this? He has a long [snout!

1ST SHEPHERD He is marked amiss. Come, best meddle [nowt.

2ND SHEPHERD The ill-spun weft is ever foully turned out.
Quit talk!
He is like to our sheep.

3RD SHEPHERD How, Gib! May I peep?

1ST SHEPHERD Aye, cunning will creep
Where it may not walk.

2ND SHEPHERD A ruse to record, and craftily cast.
It was a fine fraud.

3RD SHEPHERD And prettily passed.
Let's burn this bawd and bind her fast.
This shrew with a cord will be hanged at [last.
So shalt thou.
Will you see how they swaddle
His four feet in the middle.
Saw I never in a cradle
A horned lad ere now.

MAK Peace, I say, what! Let be your blare!
I am he that him got, and yon woman him [bare.

1ST SHEPHERD Have you named him not, nor made him [your heir?

2ND SHEPHERD Now leave him to rot, and God give him [care,
I say.

MAK'S WIFE A pretty child is he
As sits on a woman's knee;
A dillydown dilly,
To make a man gay.

3RD SHEPHERD I know him by the ear mark; that is a good [token.

MAK I tell you sirs, hark! His nose here was broken.
Warned was I by a clerk what such spells [did betoken.

1ST SHEPHERD Do you hear the dog bark? Would fists [first had spoken!
Let be.

MAK'S WIFE He was witched by an elf;
I saw it myself:
When the clock struck twelve,
Misshapen was he.

2ND SHEPHERD Both be of ill-spun weft of twisted thread.
Since they uphold their theft, let's strike [them dead.

MAK If more I thieve, bereft may I be of my [head.

[MAK *kneels to the* SHEPHERDS.

At your mercy I am left.

1ST SHEPHERD Sirs, hear what's said.
For this trespass
We will neither curse nor chide,
No more deride,
Nor longer bide,
But toss him in a canvas.

[*They toss* MAK *in a canvas, after which* MAK *and his* WIFE *return home.*

1ST SHEPHERD Lord, but I am sore; to leave now were [best.
In faith I may no more, therefore must I [rest.

2ND SHEPHERD As a sheep of seven score pound he [weighed on my chest,
Now to sleep out of door I'd count myself [blest.

3RD SHEPHERD Then, I pray,
Lie down on this green.

1ST SHEPHERD Brisk have these thieves been.

3RD SHEPHERD Never split your spleen
For them, I say.

[*They sleep. The* ANGEL *sings "Gloria in Excelsis" then speaks.*

ANGEL Rise, shepherds, attend! For now is he born
Who shall fetch from the fiend what from [Adam was torn.
That warlock to end, this night is he born.
God is made your friend; now at this [morn—
Leave your flocks:
To Bethlehem go see
Where he lies so free,
A child in crib poorly,
Between ass and ox.

1ST SHEPHERD This was a sweet sound as ever yet I [heard;
To tell would astound where we this [averred.

2ND SHEPHERD That God's son be unbound from heaven, [spoke he word;
And lightning then crowned the woods as [they stirred
In their fear.

3RD SHEPHERD He came us to warn,
In Bethlehem will be born
A babe.

1ST SHEPHERD Be we drawn
By yon star there.

2ND SHEPHERD Say, what was his song? Heard ye not how [it went?
Three shorts and a long.

3RD SHEPHERD The very accent.
With no crochet wrong, and no breath [misspent.

1ST SHEPHERD For to sing us among as he merciful meant,
I can.

2ND SHEPHERD Let's see how ye croon.
Can ye bark at the moon?

3RD SHEPHERD Hold your tongues full soon!

1ST SHEPHERD Or sing after, man.

[*He sings.*

2ND SHEPHERD To Bethlehem he bad that we should go:
And sure we be mad to tarry so.

3RD SHEPHERD Be merry and not sad, our mirth may [overflow:
To be forever glad is the reward we shall [know
And choose.

1ST SHEPHERD Then let us hither hie,
Though we be wet and weary,
To that child and that lady;
We have no time to lose.

2ND SHEPHERD We find by the prophecy—let be your din—
Of Isaiah and David, and more of their kin,
They prophesied by clergy that in a virgin
Should God come to lie, to atone for our [sin,
And abate it.
Our folk freed from woe,
Isaiah said so.
For a maid comes to show
A child that is naked.

3RD SHEPHERD Full glad may we be and abide that day,
That sweet sight to see who all power may [sway.
Lord so bless me, for now and for ay,
Might I kneel on my knee some word for [to say
To that child.
But the angel said
In a crib was he laid;
He was poorly arrayed,
Both meek and mild.

1ST SHEPHERD Patriarchs have been, and prophets have [sworn

They desired to have seen this child that is [born,
Past hope now to glean the gold of this [corn.
To see him we mean now ere it be morn,
As a token.

When I see him and feel,
Then know I full well
It is as true as steel
What prophets have spoken.

To so poor as we are that he would appear
First, and to us declare by his messenger.

2ND SHEPHERD Go we now, let us fare, the place is us near.

3RD SHEPHERD I am glad to go there; set off in good cheer
To that mite mild.
Lord, if thy will be,
We are unlearned, all three,
Grant us thy gracious glee
To comfort thy child.

1ST SHEPHERD Hail, comely and clean! Hail, young child!
Hail, maker, as I mean, of maiden so mild!
Thou hast crushed in his spleen, the war- [lock so wild;
That false traitor has been beyond doubt [beguiled.
Lo, he merry is.
Lo, he laughs, my sweeting,
A welcome meeting;
Take my promised greeting:
Have a bob of cherries.

2ND SHEPHERD Hail, sovereign saviour, for thou hast us [sought!
Hail, joyous food and flower, that all things [hast wrought!
Hail, full of favour, that made all of [nought.
Hail, I kneel and I cower. A bird have I [brought,

Bairn that ye are.
Hail, little tiny mop,
Of our creed thou art top,
At your mass I shall stop,
Little day star.

3RD SHEPHERD Hail, darling dear, full of godhead!
I pray thee be near when that I have need.
Hail, sweet is thy cheer! My heart would [bleed
To see thee sit here in so poor a stead
With no pennies.
Hail, hold forth thy hand small;
I bring thee but a ball:
Have thou and play withall,
And go to the tennis.

MARY The father of heaven, God omnipotent,
Made all in days seven, his son has he sent.
My name has he given, his light has me [lent.
Conceived I him even through his might [as he meant,
And now is he born.
May he keep you from woe!
I shall pray him do so.
Tell of him as you go;
Have mind on this morn.

1ST SHEPHERD Farewell, lady, so fair to behold,
With child on thy knee!

2ND SHEPHERD But he lies full cold.
Lord, well is me, now back to our fold.

3RD SHEPHERD In truth already it seems to be told
Full oft.

1ST SHEPHERD What grace we have found.

2ND SHEPHERD Come, now are we unbound.

3RD SHEPHERD Let's make a glad sound,
And sing it not soft.

[*The* SHEPHERDS *leave singing.*

THE FOURTEENTH PLAY

The Offering of the Magi

HEROD	1ST DOCTOR OF LAW
MESSENGER	2ND DOCTOR OF LAW
1ST KING: GASPAR	ANGEL
2ND KING: MELCHIOR	MARY
3RD KING: BALTHASAR	JESUS

HEROD Peace, I bid, both far and near,
Let none speak when I appear:
Who moves his lips while I am here,
I say, shall die.
Of all this world both far and near,
The lord am I.

Lord am I of every land,
Of tower and town, of sea and sand:
Against me dares no man stand,
That prizes life:
All earthly things bow to my hand,
Both man and wife.

Man and wife, pay heed my vow,
Who in this world are living now,
To Mohammed and me shall bow,
Both old and young:
Homage to us must all allow,
Both purse and tongue.

For anything it shall be so;
Lord of all wherever I go,
Who gainsays shall be laid low,
Whereso he dwell;
The fiend, if he were my foe,
I should him fell.

I kill all traitors to my crown,
And destroy those dogs in field and town,
Who trust not in Mohammed's renown,
  Our god so sweet;
Those false fellows I shall strike down
  Under my feet.

Under my feet they shall ill fare,
Those lads who dare my laws forswear;
My might is measured everywhere
  By such a pack;
Clean and shapely, hide and hair,
  Without a lack.

My mighty power may no man gauge,
If any cause me rant and rage,
Dinged to death will be his wage,
  And lasting woe:
His blood will flow my wrath to assuage,
  Before I go.

And therefore will I send and see
In all this land, full hastily,
To look if any dwelling be
  In tower or town,
That will not hold wholly to me,
  And Mohammed's renown.

If any be found under my sway,
With bitter pain I shall them slay.
[*to the* MESSENGER]
My messenger, speed on thy way
  Through this country,
In all this land, by night and day,
  I command thee.

And truly look thou subtly spy,—
In every corner thou come by,—
Who scorns Mohammed the mighty,
  Our god so free.
And look thou bring them hastily
  Hither unto me.

And fast I shall them strip to flay,
Those lads that will our law gainsay:
Therefore, boy, now I thee pray
Speed my cause.

MESSENGER It shall be done, lord, if I may,
Without a pause.

And sure, if any I may find,
I shall not leave them there behind.

HEROD No, but boldly thou them bind
And with thee lead:
Mohammed that wields water and wind,
Thee spur and speed!

MESSENGER All peace, lordings, and hold you still
Till I have said what I will:
Take good heed unto my skill,
What news I bring:
This command quickly fulfil
From Herod, the King.

He commands you everyone,
To have no king but him alone,
And other gods ye worship none
But Mohammed so free:
But if ye do ye be undone,
Thus told he me.

[*Then enters the* 1ST KING *riding: he looks at the star and says,*

1ST KING Lord, from whom this light is lent,
And unto me this sight has sent,
I pray to thee, with good intent,
From shame me stay,
That from harm's path I be bent,
And so wild a way.

Also I pray thee specially,
Thou grant me grace of company,
That some fellowship be nigh,
Of good avail:

Then as I fare, to live or die,
I shall not fail.

Until to that land I have been,
To find out what this star might mean,
That has led me by its sheen
From my country:
Go I now my meed to glean,
The truth to see.

[*Then enters the* 2ND KING *riding.*

2ND KING Ah, Lord, that is without an end!
From where could such strange light descend,
Whose bright bidding made me bend
Out of my land,
And pointed me which way to wend,
Till still it stand?

Sure, I saw never none so bright:
I shall ne'er rest by day nor night,
Until I learn whence comes this light,
And from what place:
He that it sent unto my sight
Grant me that grace!

1ST KING Ah, sir, whither are ye away?
Tell me, good sir, I you pray.

2ND KING Certainly, the truth to say,
None knows but I:
Yon star has patterned out my way
From Araby.

For I am king of that country,
And Melchior there men call me.

1ST KING And King, sir, was I wont to be,
Of Tarsus fame,
Both of town and city,
Gaspar is my name.
The light of yon star saw I thither.

2ND KING That Lord be loved that sent me hither!
For it will surely show us whither,
That we shall wend:

We ought to love him both together,
    That such to us would send.

[*Then enters the* 3RD KING *riding.*

3RD KING Ah, Lord! In land what may this mean?
So strange a sight was never seen,
A star shining with so great sheen,
    Saw I never none:
Its light is spread throughout this scene
    By him alone.

What it may mean, that know I nought:
But yonder are two, methinks, in thought,
I thank him that them here has brought
    Thus unto me:
I shall assay if they know ought
    What it may be.

Lordings, I give you greetings dear,
I pray you tell me with good cheer
Whither ye wend, be it far or near,
    And where that ye have been:
And of this star, that shines thus clear,
    What it may mean.

1ST KING Sir, I tell you certainly,
From Tarsus yon star sought have I.

2ND KING To see yon light from Araby,
    Was my intent.

3RD KING Now heartily to him thanks be,
    That it has sent.

1ST KING Sir, what land counts you no stranger?

3RD KING This light has led me from Saba:
And my name is Balthasar,
    The truth to tell.

2ND KING And two kings, sir, we are,
    There where we dwell.

3RD KING Now, sirs, since we are gathered here,
I counsel that we ride together,

Until we know, in what manner,
For good or ill,
That it may mean, this star so clear
That shines there still.

1ST KING Ah, lordings, behold the light
Of yonder star, with beams so bright!
Saw I never such a sight
In any land;
A star thus about midnight,
A blazing brand!

1ST KING It gives more light itself alone
Than any sun that ever shone,
Or moon, borrowed from that burning zone
Of light so clean:
A stranger sight was never known
What e'er it mean.

2ND KING Behold, lordings, see its speed,
Its nearness to the earth, give heed:
It is a token clear indeed
Of great portent:
A marvel, we are all agreed,
From high is sent.

For such a star was never seen,
As wide in world as we have been,
Its blazing beams, shining full sheen,
From it are sent.
Marvel I what it may mean
In my intent.

3RD KING Certain, sirs, the truth to say,
I shall unfold now if I may,
What it may mean so bright a ray,
Shining on us:
It has been said since many a day
It should be thus.

Yon star betokens, well know I,
The birth of a prince, sirs, surely,
As proved well in prophecy
That it so be:

Or else the laws of astronomy
    Deceive me.

1ST KING Certain, Balaam speaks of this thing,
That from Jacob a star shall spring
That shall overcome kaiser and king,
    Without a strife:
Him shall all folk be obeying
    That cherish life.

Now know I well this is the same,
Who every home as his may claim,
All bow to him who bear a name
    In each country;
All unbelievers are to blame,
    Who e'er they be.

2ND KING Certain, lordings, full well know I,
Fulfilled is now the prophecy:
That prince shall overcome on high
    Kaiser and king,
This star bears witness, surely,
    Of his coming.

3RD KING Now is fulfilled here in this land
What Balaam said, I understand;
Now is he born that sea and sand
    Shall wield at will:
Such means this star, that blazing brand,
    This to fulfil.

1ST KING Lordings, go we now all three
To worship straight that child so free,
In token that he King shall be
    Of everything:
This gold now will I bear with me,
    As my offering.

2ND KING Go we fast, sirs, I you pray,
To worship him if that we may:
I bring incense, the truth to say,
    As I intend
By token his godhead to convey,
    Without an end.

3RD KING Sirs, counsel I as ye have said:
Haste we quickly to that stead
To worship him, as our great head,
With our offering:
In token that he shall be dead,
This myrrh I bring.

1ST KING Where is that king of Jews' land,
That shall be lord of sea and sand,
And folk shall bow unto his hand
Both great and small?
Here no longer let us lingering stand,
But go we all.

2ND KING We shall not rest, even nor morn,
Until we come where he is born.

3RD KING Surely we be not forlorn,
If that star guide us:
Then press onward, I ye warn,
Let none outride us.

[*The* KINGS *retire:* HEROD *and his* MESSENGER *advance.*

MESSENGER Mohammed that is most mighty,
My lord, sir Herod, thee save and see!

HEROD Where hast thou been so long from me,
Vile stinking lad?

MESSENGER Lord, as your herald, through this land,
As ye me bad.

HEROD Thou liest, loafer, the devil thee hang!
Why has thou dwelt away so long?

MESSENGER Lord, ye chide me all too wrong.

HEROD What tidings? say!

MESSENGER Some ill with good is mixed among.

HEROD How? I thee pray.
Tell me now fast how thou has fared,
And thy reward shall not be spared.

MESSENGER As I searched, one road I shared,
Lord, on the way,

With three kings, who a babe they declared
    They sought that day.

HEROD They sought a babe? For what thing?
What tidings of him did they bring?

MESSENGER Why, lord, they said he should be king
    Of town and tower:
Therefore they went with their offering,
    Him to honour.

HEROD King! The devil! But of what empire?
Of what land should that lad be sire?
My tortures shall that traitor tire:
    Sore shall he rue!

MESSENGER Lord, by a star as bright as fire
    This king they knew:
It led them out of their country.

HEROD Woe, fie! Fie! Devils on them all three!
He shall never master me,
    That new born lad.
Those whose trust in a star may be
    I hold them mad.

Those great louts know not what they say:
They've split my head, that dare I lay:
No such tidings for many a day
    Caused me more rue:
For woe my wit is all away:
    What shall I do?

Why, what the devil is in their mind?
What wisdom in the stars they find?
Such news makes me in grief to grind:
    And of this thing
The very truth shall I unwind,
    Of this new king.

King? What the devil! Who else but I!
Woe, fie on devils! Fie, fie!
This that boy shall dear abuy!
    To death downright!

Shall he be king thus hastily?
    Who the devil made him knight?

Alas, for shame! This is a scorn!
Find they no reason, night nor morn,
Why should that wretch that late is born
    Be most of main?
Nay, if the devil of hell had sworn,
    He shall again.

Alas, alas, for grief and care!
I never supped of sorrow's fare:
If this be truth, then I despair,
    I am undone:
My counsellors must now prepare
    My fate to shun.

But first yet will I send and see
The answer of those lubbers three.
Messenger, straight hasten thee,
    Be brief and bold:
Go bid those kings come speak with me,
    Of whom you told.

Say a message I have for them still.

MESSENGER It shall be done, lord, at your will,
Your bidding shall I soon fulfil
    In this country.

HEROD Mohammed thee shield from every ill,
    As he is mighty.

MESSENGER Mohammed you save, sir Kings all three,
I have a message for you privily,
From Herod, king of this country,
    Who is our chief:
And lo, sirs, if ye trust not me,
    Here is my brief.

1ST KING Welcome be thou heartily!
His will thou tell us fully.

MESSENGER Certain, sir, that know not I
    But thus he said to me.

That ye should come full hastily
To him all three.

For needful news, he told me so.

2ND KING Messenger, ahead thou go,
And tell thy lord we gladness show
His will to do:
Both I and my fellows two
Will follow you.

MESSENGER Mohammed guard my lord so dear.

HEROD Welcome be thou, messenger!
How has thou fared since thou was here?
Thou quickly say.

MESSENGER Lord, I have travelled far and near
Without a stay.

And done your bidding sir, truly:
Three kings with me brought have I,
From Saba, Tarsus, Araby,
Thee have they sought.

HEROD And thy repayment shall be high,
For what is wrought:

[*The* KINGS *dismount and greet* HEROD.

For certainly you cure my ill.
Welcome, sirs, renowned in skill.

3RD KING Lord, thy bidding to fulfil
We came with speed.

HEROD Much thanks for your goodwill
To meet my need.

For certain, I coveted greatly
To speak with you, and hear reply:
Tell me, I pray you specially
Above anything,
What token saw ye in the sky
Of this new king?

1ST KING We saw his star rise in the east,
That shall be king of man and beast,

Therefore, lord, we have not ceased,
    Since that we knew,
With our gifts, both most and least,
    To hear his due.

2ND KING Lord, when shone that star as dawn,
Thereby we knew that child was born.

HEROD Out, alas, I am forlorn
    For ever more!
I would my flesh be rent and torn
    For sorrows sore.

Alas, alas, I am full of woe!
Sir Kings, sit down, and rest you so.
From scripture, sirs, what do ye know?
[*to the* DOCTORS]
    Quickly speak:
What tidings therefrom flows
    Speedily seek.

These kings make me understand,
That born is newly in this land
A king that shall rule sea and sand:
    They tell me so:
And therefore, sirs, I you command
    To your books go.

And sharply look for anything
Concerning ought of such a king.

1ST DOCTOR It shall be done at your bidding,
    We shall report
Right soon and tidings bring
    If we find ought.

2ND DOCTOR Soon shall I know, lord, if I may,
What our written law does say.

HEROD Therefore, masters, I you pray,
    Yourselves bestir.

1ST DOCTOR Come forth, let us assay
    With our books to confer.

2ND DOCTOR Certain, sir, lo, here find I
Well written in a prophecy.

How that prophet Isaiah,
   That never beguiled,
Tells that a maiden of her body
   Shall bear a child.

1ST DOCTOR And also, sir, to you I tell
The most marvellous that e'er befell,
Her maidhood still with her shall dwell,
   And take no scorn:
That child be called "Emmanuel"
   When he is born.

2ND DOCTOR Lord, this truth I verify,
So doth Isaiah prophesy.

HEROD Out, alas, for dole I die,
   Long ere my day!
Shall he have more power than I?
   Ah, welaway!

Alas, alas, I am forlorn!
I would my flesh be rent and torn:
But look again, if ye may warn
   For love of me:
And tell me where that boy is born:
   Make haste and see.

1ST DOCTOR Already, lord, right as you bad.

HEROD Have done in haste or I go mad:
And it were better for that lad
   To grieve me nought:
That bairn's blood shall make me glad,
   By him that me has bought.

2ND DOCTOR Micah, the prophet, without gainsay,
Writes, as I shall tell you, if I may:
In Bethlehem of Judea, yea,
   Now bear in mind,
Shall spring a duke, I say:
   Now thus we find.

1ST DOCTOR Sir, thus we find in prophecy:
Therefore we tell you surely,

In Bethlehem, most certainly,
  Born is that king.

HEROD The devil hang you high to dry,
  Such news you bring!

And certainly ye lie! It cannot be!

2ND DOCTOR Lord, we witness to it truly:
Here the truth yourself may see,
  If ye can read.

HEROD Ah, welaway! full woe is me!
  The devil you speed!

1ST DOCTOR Lord, it is truth, all that we say,
Read it in our law, we pray.

HEROD Go hence, harlots, in twenty devils' way,
  If ye would survive!
Mighty Mohammed, as well he may,
  Let you never thrive!

Alas, why wear I a crown?
Or am called of great renown?
I am the foulest born in town
  Of any man:
And foulest scamp both up and down,
  That no good can.

Alas, that ever I should be knight,
Or held a man of such great might,
If a lad should rob me of my right,
  So young a foe.
Sooner death I would invite
  Ere this were so.

Ye noble kings, be kind and hear!
Ye have safe conduct, never fear:
But again to me appear
  Before ye go:
I shall prove your friend sincere
  If ye do so.

If it be truth, this new tiding,
Some homage would I pay that king,

Therefore I pray you that ye bring
    Me tidings soon

1ST KING Already, lord, at your bidding
    It shall be done

[*The* KINGS *mount their horses.*

2ND KING Alas, in world how have we sped!
Where is the light that has us led?
Some cloud about that star has spread
    And hidden away:
In sad straits we are stead:
    What may we say?

3RD KING Woe work on Herod, cursed wight!
Woe to that tyrant day and night!
For through him have we lost that sight,
    And through his guile,
That shone to us with beams so bright
    For that short while.

[*Here the* KINGS *dismount.*

1ST KING Lordings, let us pray all three
To that Lord, whose nativity
That star betokened we did see,
    As was his will:
Pray we specially that he
    Would show it to us still.

[*Here all three* KINGS *kneel down.*

2ND KING Thou child, whose might no tongue may tell,
As thou art Lord of heaven and hell,
Thy noble star, Emmanuel,
    Send for our prayer:
That we may know by firth and fell
    Which way to fare.

3RD KING Ah, to that child be ever honour,
That our grief has stemmed this hour,
And lent us light as our succour
    Our fears to free:
We love thee, Lord of town and tower,
    Wholly, all three.

[*Here they all rise up.*

We ought to love him above everything,
That thus has sent us our asking:
Behold, yon star aloft is staying,
Sirs, surely:
Of this child shall we have knowing,
Speedily.

2ND KING Lordings dear, dread need we nought,
Our great travel to an end is brought:
Yond is the place that we have sought
From far country:
Yond is the child that all has wrought,
Behold and see!

3RD KING Let us make offering, all three,
Unto this child most mighty,
And worship him with gifts freely
That we have brought:
Our balm of bale ay will he be,
Well have we sought.

1ST KING Hail to thee, maker of everything!
That balm of our bale may bring!
In token that thou art our King,
And shall be ay,
Receive this gold as my offering,
Prince, I thee pray.

2ND KING Hail, conqueror of king and knight!
That formed fish and fowl in flight!
For thou art God's son, most of might,
And all ruling,
I bring thee incense, as is right,
As my offering.

3RD KING Hail, King by kind, cowering on my knee!
Hail, one-fold God in persons three!
In token that thou dead shall be,
Without gainsay,
For thy grave this myrrh of me
Receive, I pray.

MARY Sir kings, be comfort you between,
And marvel not what it may mean:
This child, that from me born has been,
All strife may win:
I am his mother, and maiden clean
Without a sin.

Therefore, lordings, where so ye fare,
Boldly tell ye everywhere
How I this blessed child did bear,
That best shall be:
Yet kept my maidhood, clean and fair,
Through his glory.

And truly, sirs, how may ye know
Such other Lord is none below:
Both man and beast shall worship show
In town and field:
My blessing, sirs, take as ye go,
With comfort shield.

1ST KING Ah, lordings dear! The truth to say,
That star did not our wits betray:
We love this Lord, that shall last ay
Without an end:
He is our comfort, night and day,
Where'er we wend.

2ND KING Lordings, we have travelled long,
With little rest our road along:
To make us for our journey strong
As we go home,
Sleep we a spell, nor count it wrong
Before we roam.

For in great stress have we been stead.
Lo, here is a litter ready spread.

3RD KING I love my Lord! We have well sped,
To rest herein:
Lordings, since we shall go to bed,
Ye shall begin.

ANGEL Sir courteous kings, of me take heed,
And turn in time, ill-fate to flee:

God himself bad me thus speed
 As faithful friend to warn all three
How Herod's fears on malice feed,
 He means your murderer to be:
To be so from his fury freed,
 Another way God will guide ye
 Into your own country:
And if ye ask him any boon,
God shall grant it to you soon,
 Your comfort will he be.

1ST KING Awake, awake, lordings dear!
We must dwell no longer here:
An angel spake close to my ear,
 And bad us all,
We should not go, for mortal fear,
 Home by Herod's hall.

2ND KING Almighty God in trinity,
With heart entirely thank I thee,
That thine angel sent to us three,
 Such words to say:
Our false foe swiftly for to flee,
 That would us slay.

3RD KING We must love him great and small,
The comely King of mankind all:
It grieves me we apart must fall
 In such a way:
For we gladly came at the star's call
 From afar to obey.

[*The* KINGS *mount.*

1ST KING We must part, sirs, without delay,
And each fare on his several way:
This will me lead, the truth to say,
 To my country:
Therefore, lordings, now have good day!
 God with you be!

2ND KING Now I must pass by sea and sand:
This is the gate, I understand,

That will lead me unto my land
    The right way:
May God of heaven your guardian stand,
    And have good day!

3RD KING This is the way that I must wend:
Now God to us his succour send,
And he that is without an end
And ay shall be,
Save us from falseness of the fiend,
    Lord, almighty.

[*The* KINGS *go their several ways.*

THE FIFTEENTH PLAY

The Flight into Egypt

ANGEL JOSEPH MARY

ANGEL Awake, Joseph, and take good heed!
Arise and sleep no more!
If thou wilt save thyself indeed
Fast flee to foreign shore.
I am an angel at your need
Sent to shield you as decreed
And save from evils sore.
If not hence soon thou speed
For pity thou wilt plead
And mourn thy fate the more.

JOSEPH God on his throne!
What wondrous deed
Yields so sweet tone?

ANGEL No, Joseph, it is I,
An angel sent to thee.

JOSEPH Alas! I pray thee why?
What is thy will with me?

ANGEL Fast from here now hie,
And take with thee Mary,
And also her child so free;
For Herod deems must die
All boys born, surely,
But yet of age that be
Not two.

JOSEPH Alas, full woe is me!
What shall we do?

ANGEL To Egypt shall thou fare
With all the speed you may;
And Joseph, bide you there
Till otherwise I say.

JOSEPH This is a sad affair
For a man so old to bear,
To feel such fear to stay.
My bones are bruised and bare,
Unfit to fare. Would it were
My life's last day
Come to an end.
I know not which is the way;
How shall we wend?

ANGEL Thereof have thou no dread;
Go forth and cease thy din;
The Lord, where thou wilt tread,
Will guide thy steps from sin.

JOSEPH God guard us where we're led
Or we shall be ill sped
Before we can begin;
Therefore my wits are fled,
I that am almost dead,
In age how should I win
My way.
I am full bare and thin,
My strength—decay

Now fails my strength, I fear,
And sight that I should see,
Mary, my darling dear,
I am full woe for thee!

MARY Sweet Joseph now, what cheer?
To see you shed a tear
It truly troubles me.

JOSEPH Our cares are coming near
If we dwell longer here;
Therefore we have to flee
Unseen.

MARY Alas! How may this be?
Whatever may this mean?

JOSEPH It means of sorrows a blight.

MARY Ah, Joseph dear, how so?

JOSEPH As I dreamt in the night
As I turned to and fro,
An angel full of light
As on bough is blossom bright
Warned me of our woe:
How Herod in his spite
All boys born would affright
With death: he would also,
That fiend,
Thy son's life in his might
Most shamefully end.

MARY My son? Alas, my care!
Who may my sorrows still?
Ill may false Herod fare.
My son why should he kill?
Alas! Let's seek a lair,
This bairn I bore to snare
What worldly wretch had will?
His heart should feel the tear
Which he will have to bear
That never yet did ill.
Nor't thought.

JOSEPH Now Mary dear, be still;
This helps us nought.
It is not well to weep
When weeping is in vain;
Our cares we still must keep,
And this makes more our pain.

MARY The sorrows that I reap
That my sweet son asleep,
Is sought for to be slain.
Should I to Herod creep

I'd show my hatred deep.
Sweet Joseph speak words plain
To me.

JOSEPH Swift swaddle your son again,
And his death flee.

MARY His death would I not see
For all the world to win;
Alas, full woe were me,
Our bane should so begin;
My sweet child on my knee,
To slay him were pity,
And a foul heinous sin.
Dear Joseph, what say ye?

JOSEPH To Egypt wend shall we;
Therefore let be thy din
And cry.

MARY The way how shall we win?

JOSEPH Full well know I.

As quickly as we may
Now haste we out of here;
There is nought else to say
But quick pack up our gear.
For fear of future fray
Let us wend hence away
While danger lurks so near.

MARY Great God, as he well may,
That made both night and day
Shield us, we have great fear
To roam.
My child how should I bear
So far from home.

Alas I am full woe!
Our plight's beyond my skill

JOSEPH God knows I may say so,
That burden bear I still;
For barely can I go

And lead from land such two;
No wonder I feel ill
And face now such a foe.
Will no death lay me low?
My life I like it ill.
Now hear,
He that all hurts may heal,
Keep me from care.

So riled a wretch as I,
In world was never man;
Household and husbandry,
Man's bane since he began;
That bargain dear I buy.
Young men beware, say I:
My wedding makes me wan.
Take hold thy bridle, Mary,
Look to that lad lively,
With all the care you can;
And may
He that this world began,
Show us the way.

MARY Alas, full woe is me!
None is so sad as I!
My heart will break in three,
My son to see him die.

JOSEPH Ah, Mary love, let be,
And nothing dread for thee.
In haste hence let us hie;
To save thy lad so free,
Fast forth now let us flee,
Dear wife—
To meet his enemy
It were to lose our life.

And that will I not hear.
Away then we must be,
My heart would be full drear
You two apart to see.
To Egypt let us fare;

This pack till I come there
Thou leave me to carry.
Therefore have thou no care
My help I shall not spare
Thou wilt find no fault in me,
I say.
God bless this company,
And have now all good day!

[*They go out.*

THE SIXTEENTH PLAY

Herod the Great

MESSENGER	1ST COUNSELLOR
HEROD	2ND COUNSELLOR
1ST SOLDIER	1ST WOMAN
2ND SOLDIER	2ND WOMAN
3RD SOLDIER	3RD WOMAN
	CHILDREN

MESSENGER Mohammed of mighty renown, make for you [mirth!
Both of borough and town, by fell and by [firth,
Both king with crown, and barons of birth;
Rumours up and down tell of peace on earth
That shall come.
Give ear and attend
What our words portend;
Lest ill be your end,
Listen, but be dumb.

Herod, the good King, by Mohammed's re- [nown,
In Jewry and Jourmonting, sternly with [crown,
All life that is living in tower and in town,
With grace gives you greeting, commands [you bow down
At his bidding;
Love him with loyalty,
Dread him that is doughty!
He charges you be ready
To run at his ruling.

What man dare unfold a grievance or pain,
His grief shall be told, knight, squire, or
[swain;
Be he never so bold, buys he that bargain
Twelve thousandfold, when his hopes in vain
Are dashed.
Herod in his hurry,
Is heavy with worry,
For a babe, in this flurry,
Has him abashed.

A king they him call, and that we deny;
How should it so fall great marvel have I;
Therefore over all shall I make a cry,
That ye'd better not brawl nor gossip nor lie
This tide;
Carp of no king
But Herod, that lording,
Or beware of a whipping
Your heads for to hide.

He is king of kings whom all must adore
Chief lord of lordings, chief leader of law,
Knights waft on his wings to the heights they
[may soar,
Great dukes he down flings, in his great awe,
Makes humble.
Tuscany and Turkey,
All India and Italy,
Syria and Sicily,
At his feet tumble.

From paradise to Padua to Mount Flascon;
From Egypt to Mantua into Kemp Town;
From Saraceny to Susa to Greece it may
[abound;
Both Normandy and Norway bow to his
[crown;
How spread
His fame no tongue can tell,
From heaven to hell,

Of him none speak so well
    As his cousin Mohammed.

He is the worthiest of all boys that are born;
Free men are his thrall and in his rage torn;
Begin he to brawl men must suffer his scorn;
Obey must we all or straight be forlorn
    And moan.
Drop down on your knees
All that him sees,
If him you displease,
    He will break every bone.

Here he comes now, I cry, of that lord I [spake;
Fast before will I hie, me swiftly betake
To welcome him worshipfully, his mirth for [to make,
As he is most worthy, and kneel for his sake
    So low;
Down demurely to fall,
Most royal prince to call;
Hail, the worthiest of all!
    My service to show.

[HEROD *enters with* COUNSELLORS *and* SOLDIERS.

Hail, lovely lord, anew; thy laws most firm [are laid;
I have done what I could do, and peace [these people prayed;
And much more thereto, openly displayed;
But rumours rush through their mind till is [made
    A vain boast.
They carp of a king,
They cease not such chattering.

HEROD But I shall tame their talking,
    Though some of them roast.

Leave, loafers, your din, to all be it known!
Till I have gone in make not a moan,

For if I begin I shall break every bone,
Till carcass from skin lie scattered and
[strown,
By my decree!
Cease all this wonder,
And make you no blunder,
Lest I rip you in sunder,
Be ye foolhardy.

Peace both young and old, at my bidding I
[have said,
For princely power I hold to have you alive
[or dead;
Who that is so bold I shall brain him
[through the head;
Speak not before I have told what I wish in
[this stead;
Ye know not
How you I shall grieve;
Stir not till ye have leave,
If ye do I shall cleave
You small as meat in pot.

My mirth is turned to pain, my meekness
[into ire,
This boy burns my brain, within I feel a fire,
If I see this young swain, I shall give him
[his hire;
Unless my will I gain, I were a simple sire
Upon throne.
Had I that lad in hand,
As I am king in land
I should with this steel brand
Break every bone.

My name spreads far and near the dough-
[tiest, men me call,
That ever ran with spear, a lord and king
[royal;
What joy for me to hear, a lad will seize my
[stall!

If I this crown may bear that boy shall pay
[for all.
Stronger
My anger, what devil me ails,
To torment me with tales,
That by God's dear nails,
I'll stand it no longer!

What the devil! How I blast for anger and
[spleen!
I fear those kings have passed that here with
[me have been;
They promised me full fast before now to be
[seen,
Or else I should have cast another sleight,
[I mean.
I tell you,
A boy they said they sought,
With offering that they brought;
It moves my heart right nought
To break his neck in two.

But if they passed me by, by Mohammed
[in heaven,
Then in haste shall I set all at six and seven,
Think ye a king as I will suffer them even
To have any mastery but what to me is
[given?
Nay, friend.
The devil me hang and draw,
If once that boy I saw
And then let slip my law
Before his life I rend.

These perils foretold increase if they be gone;
If so ye hear it told I pray tell me anon,
For if they be so bold by God that sits on
[throne,
Tortures untold they shall suffer each one,
For ire.
Such pains heard never man tell,
Both furious and fell

That Lucifer in hell,
Their bones shall break entire.

1ST SOLDIER Lord, think not ill if I tell you how they are [passed;
My tongue lies not truly: since they came [here last,
Another road hereby they tread and that full [fast.

HEROD Why and have they passed me by? Woe! [Out! The devil them blast!
Woe! Fie!
Fie on the devil! Where may I abide?
But fight in my fury and at these cheats [chide!
Thieves, I say, ye should full better have [spied
And told when they went by.
Knights I trusted most! Nay, wretches and [thieves!
I could yield up my ghost, so sore my heart [grieves.

2ND SOLDIER Be not abashed, I dare boast these are no [great mischiefs;
You may play yet the host.

3RD SOLDIER Why give us these griefs
Without cause?
Thus should ye not chide us,
Ungainly deride us,
And not abide us,
Without better pause.

HEROD Lazy lubbers and liars! Loafers each one!
Traitors to my fears! Knaves, but knights [none!
Had ye been worth your ears, hence had [they not run;
Come those kings near my spears, I'll break [every bone;
First vengeance

Shall I see on their bones;
If ye cluster like crones
I shall strike you with stones,
Such addled attendants.

I know not where to sit for anger and spleen;
My crown I've not quit, as clearly is seen;
Fie! Devil! Now how is it? None comes in [between.
I have no cause to flit, but be king as I mean
For ever.
To safeguard my part,
I tell you my heart,
I shall make them start,
Or else trust me never.

1ST SOLDIER Sir, they went suddenly, before any knew,
Else had met us, trust me, in a meeting to [rue.

2ND SOLDIER So bold nor so hardy, to counter our crew,
Was none of that company; none saw my fist
But feared.

3RD SOLDIER They dared not abide,
But ran home to hide;
Might I them have spied,
Elsewhere had they steered.

What could we more do to save your hon- [our?

1ST SOLDIER We were ready thereto, and shall be each [hour.

HEROD Now since it is so, ye shall have favour;
Whither ye will, go, by town and by tower,
Go hence!

[SOLDIERS *withdraw.*

I have tidings to tell
To my privy council;
Clerks, bear ye the bell,
Burn for me incense.

One spoke in my ear, a wonderful talking,
Said a maiden should bear another to be
[king;
Sirs, I pray you find where, in all writing,
In Virgil, in Homer, in each other thing
But legend;

[*They look at their books.*

In Boethius, in tales;
Where church work prevails,
Mass scarcely avails,
So elsewhere attend.

I pray you tell truly, now what ye find.

1ST COUNSELLOR Truly, sir, prophecy, it is not blind;
Isaiah writes plainly, he shall be so kind,
That a maiden meekly, most pure of mind,
Shall him bear;
"Virgo concipiet,
Natumque pariet."
Emmanuel is yet
His name to declare.

2ND COUNSELLOR "God is with us," that is for to say.
And others say thus, trust me ye may:
"From Bethlehem a gracious lord shall hold
[sway,
That of Jewry spacious King shall be ay,
Lord mighty;
And him shall honour
Both king and emperor."

HEROD Why, and should I to him cower?
Your lies I take lightly.

Fie the devil thee speed and me, hear my
[moan!
This has thou done indeed to make me grieve
[and groan;
And thou, knave, thy meed shall have, by
[cock's bone!

Ye know not half your creed! Out thieves
[from my throne!
Fie, knaves!
Fie, dotty polls, with your books!
Go cast them in the brooks!
With your wiles and sly looks
Whereat my wit raves!

Heard I never quirk so quaint that a knave
[so slight
Should come like a saint and rob me of my
[right;
Nay without restraint, I shall kill him down-
[right;
Woe! For fury I faint; now strive I to fight
The stronger;
My guts will burst out
If I hang not this lout;
If my vengeance he flout,
I may live no longer.

Should a cub in cave but of one year of age,
Thus make me to rave.

1ST COUNSELLOR
Sir, cease this outrage!
Away let ye wave all such language,
Your worship to save; is he ought but a page
Of a year?
We two shall between
Plot in our spleen,
That if ye do as I mean,
He shall die on a spear.

2ND COUNSELLOR
For fear that he reign, do as is said;
Through Bethlehem proclaim, and each
[other stead,
That knights must ordain, and ding down
[dead
All boys to their bane that be two, and dread
No more.
This child may ye kill,
Thus at your own will.

HEROD These noble words fill
Me with joy evermore.

If I live in this land a long life as I hope,
By this shall I stand to make thee Pope.
How my heart may expand, surprising its [scope!
For this news at your hand, you shall not [long grope
Without gain;
Pence, shillings, and pounds,
Great castles and grounds.
Booty beyond bounds
Be yours to retain.

Now will I proceed and take vengeance;
The flower of knighthood call to allegiance;
Bashir, I thee bid it may advance.

MESSENGER Lord, I shall me speed and bring, perchance,
To thy sight.

[HEROD *retires.* KNIGHTS *advance.*

Hark knights, I you bring
Here new tiding;
Unto Herod King.
Haste with all your might!

In all the haste that ye may in armour [full bright,
In your best array to seem a gay sight.

1ST SOLDIER What should we say?

2ND SOLDIER This is not all right.

3RD SOLDIER Sirs, without a delay I fear that we fight.

MESSENGER I pray you,
As fast as ye may,
Come to him this day.

1ST SOLDIER What, in our best array?

MESSENGER Yea, sirs, I say you.

2ND SOLDIER Somewhat is in hand, whatever it mean.

3RD SOLDIER Tarry not for to stand before we have been.

[HEROD *advances.*

MESSENGER Herod, king of this land, well be ye seen!
Your knights to command, in armour full [sheen,
At your will.

1ST SOLDIER Hail, doughtiest of all!
We have come at your call,
So trust to us all
Your wish to fulfil.

HEROD Welcome, lords, in bliss, both great and [small!
The cause now is this, that I sent for you all;
A lad, a knave, born is that should be king [royal;
Unless I kill him and his I burst, I guess, my [gall;
Therefore, sirs,
Vengeance shall ye take,
All for that lad's sake,
And honour shall it make
For you evermore, sirs.

To Bethlehem take your way, and all the [coast about,
All male children ye slay, and, lords, ye shall [be stout,
That be but two this day, and leave of all [that rout
No child me to dismay that lies in swaddling [clout,
I warn you.
Spare no one's blood,
Let all run in flood,
The mothers ye thud,
If mad of mood they scorn you.

Hence! Now go your way, make haste, I [implore.

2ND SOLDIER I fear there'll be a fray, but I will go before.

3RD SOLDIER Ah, think, sirs, I say, I shall hunt like a boar.

1ST SOLDIER Let me make assay, I shall kill by the score;
Herod all hail!
We shall for your sake
This massacre make.

HEROD If my vengeance ye take
Seek favour without fail.

[HEROD *withdraws.*

2ND SOLDIER Play our parts now by rote, and handle them [well.

3RD SOLDIER I shall pay them on the coat, begin I to revel.

[1ST WOMAN *and* CHILD *advance.*

1ST SOLDIER Hark, fellows, ye dote, do the work of the [devil;
I hold here a groat, she views me as evil,
And would part;
[*to the* WOMAN]
Dame, think it not ill,
Thy knave if I kill.

1ST WOMAN What thief! Against my will?
Lord, save his sweet heart.

1ST SOLDIER Abide, now, abide, no farther he goes.

1ST WOMAN Peace, thief! Shall I chide and make here a [noise?

1ST SOLDIER I shall rob thee of pride: Kill we these boys!

1ST WOMAN Ill thee betide; keep well thy nose,
False thief!
Have then at thy hood.

1ST SOLDIER How whore! What hardihood!

[*Kills the* CHILD.

1ST WOMAN Out, alas my child should
Bleed, for grief.
Alas for shame and sin! Alas that I was born!

My weeping must begin to see my child for-
[lorn?
My comfort and my kin, my son thus cruelly
[torn!
Vengeance for this sin, I cry, both even and
[morn.

2ND SOLDIER Well done!

[2ND WOMAN *and* CHILD *advance.*

Come hither hag, and why?
That lad of thine shall die.

2ND WOMAN Mercy, lord, I cry!
It is mine own dear son.

2ND SOLDIER No mercy receive you for your moans,
[Maud!

2ND WOMAN Then thy scalp shall I cleave! Do you wish
[to be clawed?
Leave, I bid thee leave!

2ND SOLDIER Peace, bid I, bawd!

2ND WOMAN Fie, fie, for reprieve! Fie, full of fraud!
No man!
Have at thy tabard,
A guy for a guard!
Now shall it go hard!
I curse as I can!

[*He kills the* CHILD.

Out! Murder! Man, I say, cruel traitor and
[thief!
Out! Alas! And welaway! My boy's life was
[so brief!
My love, my blood, my play, that gave man
[no grief!
Alas, alas, this day! Break heart beyond be-
[lief
In sunder!
Vengeance I cry and call,
On Herod and his knights all!

Vengeance, Lord, upon them fall,
That wicked men may wonder!

3RD SOLDIER This is well wrought gear that ever may be;

[3RD WOMAN *and* CHILD *advance.*

Come ye hither here! Ye need not to flee!

3RD WOMAN Will ye harm no hair of my child or me?

3RD SOLDIER He shall die, I thee swear, his heart blood [shall thou see.

3RD WOMAN God forbid!
Thief! Thou sheds my child's blood!

[*He kills the* BOY.

Of my body the bud!
Alas my heart is all in flood,
To see my child thus bleed.

By God, thou shall abuy this deed that thou [has done.

3RD SOLDIER Hag, nought reck I, by moon and sun.

3RD WOMAN Have at thee, say I! Take thee there a foin!
Out on thee I cry! Have at thy groin
Another!
This keep I in store.

3RD SOLDIER Peace now, no more!

3RD WOMAN I cry and I roar,
Out on thee, man's murderer!

Alas! My babe, mine innocent! Begot of my [flesh! For sorrow
That God grievously sent, who of my bales [would borrow?
Thy body is sadly rent; I cry both even and [morrow,
Vengeance for thy blood thus spent! Out! I [cry, and harrow!

1ST SOLDIER Go quickly!
Get out of this place!

And, trotts, leave no trace,
Or by cock's bone's apace
    I shall shift you slickly.

[*The* MOTHERS *retire.*

Let them go and rot, they fear to abide.

2ND SOLDIER Let us run foot hot, now would I we hide,
And tell of this lot, that these boys have died.

3RD SOLDIER You can quit this spot, that do I decide;
    Go forth now,
Tell thou Herod our tale!
For all our avail,
I tell you without fail,
    He reward will allow.

1ST SOLDIER I am best of you all and ever have been;
The devil have my soul, but I be first seen;
It fits me to call him my lord as I mean.

2ND SOLDIER What need now to brawl? Be not so keen
    In this anger;
I shall say thou did best.
[*Aside*]
Save myself, as I guessed.

1ST SOLDIER Now that is most honest.

3RD SOLDIER Go, tarry no longer.

[*They approach* HEROD.

1ST SOLDIER Hail Herod, our king, full glad may ye be!
Good tidings we bring, hark now unto me;
We have roved in our riding throughout [Jewry:
And know ye one thing, that murdered have [we
    Many thousands.

2ND SOLDIER I held them full hot
And paid them on the dot;
Their dames now cannot
    Ever bind them in bands.

3RD SOLDIER Had ye seen how I fared, when I came [among them!
There was none that I spared, but laid on [and dang them.
When they were so scared began I to bang [them
I stood and I stared, no pity to hang them
Had I.

HEROD By Mohammed's renown,
That spreads up and down,
As I swear this crown
Ye shall have a lady,

For each one a maid to wed at his will.

1ST SOLDIER So long have ye said, but unpaid is the bill!

2ND SOLDIER And I was never flayed, for good nor for ill.

3RD SOLDIER Ye can count it well-paid our wish to fulfil,
It strikes me,
With treasure untold,
Before us to unfold,
Both silver and gold
To give us great plenty.

HEROD As I am king crowned I think it but right!
There goes none on ground as ye by this [light;
A hundred thousand pound is good wage for [a knight,
Of pennies good and round to enjoy day and [night
Such store;
And ye knights of ours
Shall have castles and towers,
Both for you and yours,
For now and evermore.

1ST SOLDIER Was never none born by down nor by dale,
Before us, be it sworn, that could so prevail.

2ND SOLDIER We have castles and corn, of much gold to [avail.

3RD SOLDIER It will never be worn without any tail;
All hail!
Hail lord! Hail king!
Forth are we faring!

HEROD Now Mohammed you bring
To his faith without fail.

Now in peace may I stand, through Mo-
[hammed's renown!
And give of my land that belongs to my
[crown;
And bring to my hand both fortress and
[town;
Marks for each a thousand, shortly paid
[down,
Shall ye hold.
I shall give for your gain,
My word was not vain,
Watch when I come again,
Then to beg be ye bold.

[HEROD *dismisses the* SOLDIERS.

I set by no good now my heart is at ease,
That I shed so much blood, I reign as I
[please!
For to see this flood from the feet to the
[knees
Moves nothing my mood, I laugh that I
[wheeze;
As down,
So light is my soul,
That all of sugar is my gall;
I may now do withal
What I wish with my crown.

I was cast into care so fearful afraid,
Now I need not despair for low is he laid
As these knights declare who so have him
[flayed;
Else great wonder, where that so many
[strayed

In the way,
That one should escape
Without hurt this scrape;
Too many mothers gape
Childless, their wrongs to abate.

A hundred thousand, I know, and forty are [slain,
And four thousand; also passed is my pain;
Such murder and woe shall never be again.
Had I but one blow at that poor swain
So young,
It should have been seen
What my vengeance had been
And the spate of my spleen
Told by many a tongue.

Thus knaves shall I teach example to take,
In their wits that screech, such masters to [make;
In vain ye may preach and in babel out [break!
Saved by no sovereign's speech your necks [shall I shake
In sunder;
No king on to call
But on Herod the royal,
Else many a thrall
Shall pay for that blunder.

For if I hear it spoken when I come again,
Your brains shall be broken, so pay heed to [pain;
The sleeping shall be woken, it shall be so [plain;
Now by this token my nose may disdain
Such a stench.
Sirs, this is my counsel,
Be not too cruel,
But adieu—to the devil!
I know no more French!

[*Exit* HEROD *followed by his* MESSENGER.

THE SEVENTEENTH PLAY

The Purification of Mary

SYMEON	JOSEPH
1ST ANGEL	MARY
2ND ANGEL	JESUS

SYMEON Mighty God, that us to aid
Heaven and earth and all has made;
Bring us to bliss that never shall fade,
As thou well may;
And think on me that am unwell—
Lo, I so limp and hobble,
Sadly my years begin to tell—
Now help, Lord, Adonai!

But yet I marvel, both even and morn,
Of elders long before me born,
If they be safe or quite forlorn,
Where they may be;
Abel, Noah, and Abraham,
David, Daniel, and Balaam,
And many more by name,
In their degree.

I thank thee, Lord, with good intent,
For all the guidance thou has sent,
That thus long time my life has lent,
Now many a year;
For all are past now but only I;
I thank thee, Lord God almighty!
For none is old as I, truly,
Now living here.

For I am old Symeon;
So old in life know I none,

That is made of flesh and bone,
    On middle-earth today.
No wonder if my woes I tell;
Fever and flux keep me unwell;
So thin my arms and legs as well,
    And all my beard is grey.

My eyes are worn both dim and blind;
My breath is short, and I want wind;
Thus has age destroyed my kind,
    And me bereft of all;
But shortly must I wend away;
What time and when, I cannot say,
For it has gone full many a day
    Since death began to call.

There is no task that I may work,
But scarcely crawl I to the kirk;
When I come home I feel such irk
    That further may I nought;
But sit me down with grunts and groans,
And lie and rest my weary bones,
And yawn all night amidst my moans,
    Till I to sleep be brought.

But, nevertheless, the truth to say,
If I may neither night nor day
For age neither stir nor play,
    Nor make no cheer,
Yet if I be never so old,
I mind full well what prophets told,
That now are dead and laid full cold,
    Gone since many a year.

They said that God, full of might,
Should send his son from heaven bright,
In a maiden for to alight,
    Come of David's kin;
Flesh and blood in her to take,
And become man for our sake,
Our redemption for to make,
    That lost has been through sin.

Lord, grant us thy promised grace aright,
Send me thy word both day and night,
Grant me that grace of heaven's light,
And let me never die,
Until such grace to me thou send,
That I may touch him as my friend,
Who shall come our ills to amend,
And see him with my eye.

1ST ANGEL Thou, Symeon, dread thou nought!
My Lord, that thou has long besought,
For thou has righteous been,
Thine asking has he granted thee,
Without death in life to be,
Till thou thy Christ has seen.

2ND ANGEL Then Symeon, hearken a space!
I bring thee tidings of solace;
Therefore, rise up and go
To the temple; there shall he be
God's son before thee,
Whom thou yearned for so.

SYMEON Praised be my Lord in will and thought,
That forgets his servant nought,
When that he sees time!
Well is me I shall not die
Till I have seen him with my eye,
That child sublime.

Praised be my Lord in heaven above,
That by his angel showed such love,
And warned me of his coming!
Therefore will I with intent
Put on me my vestment,
In worship of that king.

He shall be welcome unto me;
That Lord shall make us all free,
Of all mankind the king;
For with his blood he shall us save
Both from hell and from the grave,
That were slain through sin.

[*The bells ring out.*

Ah, dear God! what may this be?
Our bells ring so solemnly,
For whomsoever it is;
I cannot understand this ringing,
Unless my Lord God be bringing
Our saviour and our bliss.

This noise gives my old heart cheer,
I shall never rest if I stay here,
Though I must go alone.
Now blessed am I, I dare avow,
For such noise heard I never ere now;
Our bells ring on their own.

[JOSEPH *with two doves, and* MARY *with her baby advance.*

JOSEPH Mary, it begins to pass,
Forty days since that thou was
Delivered of thy son;
To the temple I say we draw,
To cleanse thee and fulfil the law,
Our elders' wont be done.

Therefore Mary, maid and friend,
Take thy child and let us wend
Unto the temple;
And we shall with us bring
These turtles two as our offering,
The law will we fulfil.

MARY Joseph, that will I with a cheerful heart,
That the law in every part
Be fulfilled in me.
Lord, that all things may,
Give us grace to do this day
What is pleasing unto thee!

[*The* ANGELS *sing.*

1ST ANGEL Thou, Symeon, righteous and true,
Thou has desired both old and new,
To have a sight of Christ Jesu,

As prophecy has told!
Oft has thou prayed to have a sight
Of him that did in maid alight;
Here is that child of so great might,
Now that thou would, behold!

2ND ANGEL Thou has desired it most of all.

[*Incomplete*]

THE EIGHTEENTH PLAY

The Play of the Doctors

1ST DOCTOR	JESUS
2ND DOCTOR	MARY
3RD DOCTOR	JOSEPH

[*The beginning of this play is missing.*]

2ND DOCTOR That a maiden a bairn should bear;
And his name thus did they tell,
From the time that he born were,
He shall be called Emmanuel;

Counsellor and God of Strength,
And Wonderful also
Shall he be called, of breadth and length,
As far as man may go.

3RD DOCTOR Masters, your reasons are right good,
And wonderful to name,
Yet find I more by Habakkuk;
Sirs, listen while I quote the same.

Bliss of our bale shall be the fruit
Hereafterward some day;
A wand shall spring from Jesse's root,—
The certain truth, thus did he say,—

And from that wand shall spring a flower,
That shall rise to a great height:
Thereof shall come full sweet odour,
And thereupon shall rest and light

The holy ghost, full of such might;
The ghost of wisdom and of wit,
Shall build his nest with power and right,
And in it breed and sit.

1ST DOCTOR But when, think ye, this prophecy
Shall be fulfilled in deed,
That here is told so openly,
As we in scriptures read?

2ND DOCTOR A great marvel it is decreed,
For us to hear such mastery;
A maid to bear a child, indeed,
Without man's seed is mystery.

3RD DOCTOR The holy ghost shall in her light,
And keep her maidenhead full clean;
Whoso may bide to see that sight,
They need not dread, I ween.

1ST DOCTOR Of all these prophets wise of lore
That knew the prophecy, more and less,
Was none that told the time before,
When he should come to us in peace?

2ND DOCTOR Whether he be come or not,
No knowledge have we for certain;
But he shall come, that doubt we not;
The prophets have preached it full plain.

3RD DOCTOR Prophets foretelling this event
Owe thanks to God that is on high,
Who gave them knowledge of his intent,
His will to tell and glorify.

[JESUS *enters.*

JESUS Masters, love be to you sent,
And comfort all this company!

1ST DOCTOR Son, hence away I would thou went,
For other things in hand have we.

2ND DOCTOR Son, whoever thrust thee near,
They were not wise, thus tell I thee;
For we have other tales to hear,
Than playing now with bairns to be.

3RD DOCTOR Son, if thou list ought to learn to live by [Moses' law,
Come, we shall not spurn thee, but hear and [then withdraw.

For in some mind it may thee bring
    To hear our sayings read in rows.

JESUS — To learn of you need I nothing,
    Your deeds and sayings, know I those.

1ST DOCTOR — Hark to yon bairn and his bragging!
    He thinks he kens more than he knows;
Now, son, thou art but a fledgeling,
    Not clergy knowing how law goes.

JESUS — I know as well as ye how that your law was [wrought.

2ND DOCTOR — Come sit, son, we shall see, for certain seems [it nought.

3RD DOCTOR — It were wonder if any wight
    Unto our reasons right should reach;
And thou says thou has in sight
    Our laws truly to tell and teach.

JESUS — The holy ghost did in me alight,
    And anoint me like a leech,
And gave to me both power and might
    The kingdom of heaven to preach.

2ND DOCTOR — Whence ever this bairn may be
    Who tells these tidings new?

JESUS — Certain, sirs, I was ere ye,
    And shall be after you.

1ST DOCTOR — Son, thy sayings soothe and heal,
    And thy wit is a wondrous thing;
But, nevertheless, full well I feel
    That it may fail in working;
For David deems of such to deal,
    And thus he says of children young:

"Ex ore infantium et lactentium, perfecisti [laudem."

Out of their mouths, said David well,
    Our Lord has brought forth praising.

Nevertheless, son, stint thou should yet,
    Here for to speak at large;

For where masters are met,
    Children's words must not take charge.

For certain if thou would never so fain
    Give all thou could to learn the law,
Thou art neither of might nor main
    To know as clerk without a flaw.

JESUS Sirs, I tell you for certain,
    That truth alone shall be my saw;
And power have I full and plain,
    That ye my speaking hold in awe.

1ST DOCTOR Masters, what may this mean?
    Marvel, methinks, do I
Wherever this bairn has been,
    That speaks thus knowingly.

2ND DOCTOR In world as wide as ever we went,
    Found we none such ever before;
Certain, I think this bairn be sent
    From heaven to heal our sore.

JESUS Sirs, I shall prove with you present,
    All the saws I said before.

3RD DOCTOR How say you the first commandment
    And the greatest in Moses' law?

JESUS Sirs, since ye sit in a row,
    And to your books you can give heed,
Let us see, sirs, if it is so,
    How correctly you can read.

1ST DOCTOR I read that this is the first bidding
    That Moses in us did instil;
Honour thy God above everything,
    With all thy wit and all thy will;
And all thy heart to him shall cling,
    Early and late, both loud and still.

JESUS Ye need no other books to bring,
    But strive first this to fulfil.

The second may men prove,
    And clergy know thereby;

Your neighbours shall ye love
  Right as yourself truly.

This commanded Moses to all men,
  In his commandments clear;
On these two biddings, shall ye ken,
  Hang all the laws we need to hear.

Whoso fulfils these two, then
  With might and main, holding them [dear,
He fulfils truly all ten,
  Which follow altogether.

Then we should God honour
  With all our might and main,
And love well every neighbour,
  Right as ourself certain.

1ST DOCTOR Now, son, since thou has told us two,
  Which are the eight, can thou ought [say?

JESUS The third bids, whereso ye go,
  That ye shall hallow the holy day;
From bodily work ye take your rest;
  Your household, too, look they do so,
Both wife, child, servant, and beast.
  The fourth is then, in weal and woe,

Thy father and mother, thou shall honour,
  Not only with thy reverence,
But in their need thou them succour,
  And keep ay good obedience.

The fifth bids thee no man slay,
  Nor harm him never in word nor deed,
Nor suffer him in woe to stay,
  If thou may help him in his need.

The sixth bids thee thy wife to take
  But none other lawfully;
Lust of lechery thou flee and fast forsake,
  And fear God whereso thou be.

The seventh bids thee be no thief,
    Nor nothing win through treachery;
Usury and simony will bring you grief,
    But conscience clear keep truly.

The eighth bids thee be true in deed,
    And no false witness look thou bear;
Lie not for friend, it is decreed,
    Lest thy soul's weal thou might impair.

The ninth bids thee not desire
    Thy neighbour's wife nor his women,
But as holy kirk would thee inspire,
    Set thy purpose right therein.

The tenth bids thee for nothing
    Thy neighbour's goods to yearn for;
His house, his rent, nor his having,
    And the Christian faith hold evermore.

Thus in tables, shall ye ken,
    Our Lord to Moses wrote;
These are the commandments ten,
    For true men to take note.

2ND DOCTOR Behold, our laws how he displays,
    And learnt he never on book to read!
Full subtle saws, methinks, he says,
    And also true, if we take heed.

3RD DOCTOR Yet let him forth on his ways,
    For if he stay, well we may dread
The people will full soon him praise
    Well more than us for all our deed.

1ST DOCTOR Nay, nay, then work we wrong!
    Such speaking we deplore;
As he came, go along,
    And move us now no more.

[JOSEPH *and* MARY *enter.*

MARY Ah, dear Joseph! How ill have we sped!
    No comfort in our loss find we;
My heart is heavy as any lead,
    Until my comely son I see.

Now have we sought in every stead,
Both up and down, for these days three;
But whether he be quick or dead
Yet know we not, so woe is me!

JOSEPH Sorrow had never man more!
But mourning, Mary, may not amend;
Let us go on before,
Till God some succour send.

About the temple if he be ought,
That would I know ere it be night.

MARY For certain I see what we have sought!
In world was never so seemly a sight;
Lo, where he sits, see ye him nought
Among yon masters of so great might?

JOSEPH Bless God who us hither brought.
In land now lives there none so light.

MARY Now, dear Joseph, for all our sake,
Go forth and fetch your son and mine;
Now far is it past day-break,
And homeward we must start in time.

JOSEPH With men of might I never spake,
Such bidding I must needs decline;
I cannot with them meddle or make,
They are so gay in their furs fine.

MARY To them you must your errand say,
Sure to that no dread you feel!
They will take heed to you alway,
Because of age, I know it well.

JOSEPH When I get there what shall I say?
For I know not how I should deal,
But thou would have me shamed for ay,
For I can neither crook nor kneel.

MARY Go we together, I hold it best,
To yon men dressed so fine indeed;
And if I see, as I have rest,
That ye will not, then I must need.

JOSEPH Go thou and tell thy tale first,
  Thy son to see will take good heed;
Wend forth, Mary, and do thy best,
  I come behind, as God me speed.

MARY Ah, dear son, Jesus!
  Since we love thee alone,
Why does thou this to us,
  Thus to make us moan?
Thy father and I between us two,
  Son, for thy love, have fared but ill,
We have thee sought both to and fro,
  Weeping sorely as parents will.

JESUS Wherefore, mother, should ye seek me so?
  My life, you know how I must fill,
My father's works for weal or woe,
  Thus am I sent for to fulfil.

MARY These sayings on them I dwell,
  And truly understand,
I shall think on them well,
  And what follows take in hand.

JOSEPH Now truly, son, the sight of thee
  Has comforted us of all our care;
Come forth now with thy mother and me!
  At Nazareth I would we were.

JESUS Believe then, ye lordings free!
  For with my friends now will I fare.

1ST DOCTOR Son, whereso thou shall abide or be,
  God make thee good man evermore.

2ND DOCTOR No wonder if thou, wife,
  At his finding be fain;
He shall, if he have life,
  Prove a worthy swain.

3RD DOCTOR Son, look thou mind, for good or ill,
  The matters that we have named but [now;
And if thou like to abide here still,
  And with us dwell, welcome art thou.

JESUS Grammercy, sirs, for your good will!
No longer must I bide with you,
My friends' wish will I fulfil,
And to their bidding meekly bow.

MARY Full well is me this tide,
Now may we make good cheer.

JOSEPH No longer will we bide;
Now farewell all folk here.

[MARY, JOSEPH *and* JESUS *go off together*.

Notes to the Plays (Part Two)

THE ANNUNCIATION

The action of the play is located in three different places: heaven, the house of Joseph and Mary, and the wilderness. Gabriel descends from heaven's tower to greet Mary. When they part (154) Gabriel retires beneath heaven's tower and Mary withdraws to her mansion opposite. The manuscript does not identify the Angel who addresses Joseph (326) with Gabriel, but such an identification is adopted here as a staging convenience. Joseph's first words refer to Mary's pregnancy (158), and if she is going to appear pregnant she will need to prepare herself in her mansion before her dialogue with Joseph begins. All medieval texts on this theme stress Mary's physical appearance and the stress would have been as apparent in medieval drama. A direction in the thirteenth-century play of The Prophets performed in Laon cathedral, refers to Elizabeth as 'dressed as a woman and pregnant'. It is highly probable that such a detail found in a cathedral production would have been carried over to the more secular management of the mystery plays.

God, having dispatched Gabriel, looks on during the subsequent action (77–154). His concern in Mary's conception is depicted in The Annunciation by the Master of the *Heures de Rohan* (fifteenth century), in which as the angel kneels to Mary, who is seated, God looks down and sends his blessing from above. The centre panel of the Altarpiece of *Aix-en-Provence, Église de la Madeleine,* represents the Annunciation as taking place within a church with Mary kneeling at a lectern and Gabriel fully robed and winged kneeling facing her. God and his angels look down from the triforium casting beams of golden light upon the Virgin. A regular feature of paintings of the Annunciation is a flowering plant, sometimes held by the angel, sometimes in a vase, as for instance it occurs in The Annunciation of the Master of St. Sebastian, in which Gabriel appears suspended between heaven and earth.

Karl Young describes the early treatment of this theme in medieval churches:

> At Salisbury and at Bayeux, when the deacon read the gospel in Matins on Wednesday of Ember Days in December, he held a branch of palm in his hand, as an angelic symbol. At Parma, in the Mass, artificial figures of the Angel Gabriel and Mary were used at the pulpit where the gospel was read. The figure of Gabriel was lowered from an opening in the roof. . . . From Tournai we have a full description of this ceremony as arranged there by Pierre Cotrel in the sixteenth century (a ceremony established at Tournai as early as 1231). This was performed on Ember Wednesday in December. During Matins two boys are to be costumed as Mary and the angel, and after the seventh lesson they are to mount their respective curtained platforms. At the beginning of Mass, which follows Matins, the curtains of Mary's 'sedes' are opened, showing her in a kneeling posture. Gabriel is not disclosed until the singing of the *Gloria in excelsis*. When the deacon sings the gospel, Mary and Gabriel themselves utter the words assigned to them in the text. In singing the words *Ave, gratia plena,* Gabriel bows to Mary thrice. At the words *Spiritus Sanctus superveniet in te,* the image of a dove is made to descend to a position before the platform of Mary, and there it remains until after the *Agnus Dei,* when it is drawn aloft again. After the *Ite, missa est,* Mary and Gabriel leave their platforms, and with lights preceding them, go to the vesting-room.
>
> (op. cit., ii. 245, 246.)

The Holy Ghost appears as a speaking character in the *Ludus Coventriae* play of *The Parliament of Heaven*. The stage direction at the moment of conception reads: 'Here the holy ghost descends with three beams to our lady, the son of the godhead next with three beams to the holy ghost, the father godly with three beams to the son. And so enter all three to her bosom . . .' The liturgical plays, the cycle plays, and pictorial representations of the Annunciation, in which frequently are depicted the three beams that occasion the divine conception, stress the material interpretation given to this theme in the Middle Ages. No doubt somewhere in the accounts for the properties of the *Ludus Coventriae* play was to be found an item concerning nine beams, three for the Holy Ghost, three for the Son, and three for God. This medieval approach to the subject is reinforced by records of performances in the churches at Besançon and Padua. 'At Besançon the part of Mary was taken by a young girl ten or twelve years of age; and in the gallery from which the dove descended was stationed an elderly man to represent God (1452). . . . In an "ordo" of the fourteenth century from the cathedral of Padua . . . at Gabriel's words *Spiritus Sanctus superveniet in te*, a dove is let down over Mary, and as she says *Ecce ancilla Domini*, she receives it under her cloak, thus symbolizing her conception.' (Karl Young, op. cit., ii. 246, 248, 250.)

Mary's vow of chastity (117/118) and the manner of her marriage with Joseph derive from non-biblical sources and are fully dramatized in the *Ludus Coventriae*, in which the three maidens (270) that attend on Mary are given names, and they defend Mary's innocence against Joseph's accusations. In the Chester play of *The Annunciation* Joseph lists the tools of his trade that he carries with him:

> With this axe that I bear,
> This gimlet and this auger,
> Axe, hammer, together
> I have won my meat.
>
> (Chester Plays, *The Annunciation*, 409–412.)

The play is an obvious occasion for the introduction of music. There are no directions for music in the Wakefield Annunciation, but the York, Chester and Coventry Annunciation plays include references to the *Ave Maria* and the *Magnificat*. The *Magnificat* is, however, contained in the following play in the Wakefield Cycle, *The Salutation of Elizabeth.* A hymn of praise might be sung by the angels before God speaks at the beginning of the play; the angels might also sing the *Ave Maria* as Gabriel descends from Heaven to Mary (76), or the example in the *Ludus Coventriae Conception of Mary* might be followed: 'here the Angel descends, the heaven singing *Exultet celum laudibus resultet terra gaudiis Archangelorum gloria sacra canunt solemnia*'. The York *Annunciation* includes Gabriel singing *Ne timeas Maria* following his salutation of the Virgin. This Wakefield play might end with the angel choir singing *Angelus ad Virginem.*

THE SALUTATION

This is the shortest, simplest and most harmonious play in the Cycle. There is no problem of staging: the two characters meet, speak, and part on the same pageant or stage. *The Visit to Elizabeth* in the *Ludus Coventriae,* on the other hand, represents Mary and Joseph travelling fifty-two miles (*et sic transient circa placeam*) to meet Elizabeth. And in this *Ludus Coventriae* play the *Magnificat* is spoken alternately by Mary and Elizabeth, each taking two lines at a time, Mary the Latin and Elizabeth the English equivalent. Mary concludes this section on a didactic note:

> This psalm of prophecy said between us two,
> In heaven it is written with angel's hand,
> Ever to be sung and also to be said
> Every day among us at evensong.

(*Ludus Coventriae, The Visit to Elizabeth,* 105–108.)

In the Wakefield play the *Magnificat* is spoken by Mary alone. If these words are delivered slowly against an angel-choir singing the *Magnificat,* perhaps in Latin, some of the antiphonal character of the *Ludus Coventriae Magnificat* may be recreated, and the significance of the scene itself will be enriched and deepened. A suggestion for the music at the beginning and the end of the play comes also from the *Ludus Coventriae:*

With Ave we began, and Ave is our conclusion,
Ave regina celorum to our lady we sing.
(*Ludus Coventriae, Epilogue of Contemplacio to The Visit to Elizabeth,* 35/36.)

THE FIRST SHEPHERDS' PLAY

At the beginning of the play it is necessary for the initial speeches of the First and Second Shepherd, which are addressed to the audience, to be delivered from two distinct acting areas. At the end of his first speech the First Shepherd moves off 'to the fair' (42) and he comes near to where the Second Shepherd has been speaking after forty lines (82). In its simplest form the play can be performed with only two stations or main acting areas: the one for the entry of the Second Shepherd, the main dialogue of the three Shepherds, the feasting, and the appearance of the Angel; the other for heaven—the lodging of the heavenly choir—and beneath heaven the mansion which later reveals the Holy Family, and it is in front of this mansion that the First Shepherd opens the play. On the other hand a multiple stage might make production even more flexible, whereby journeys could be made from station to station, incorporating the ground between as part of the acting area—the Third Shepherd enters riding a mare (164). Some support is given to this presentation of the Shepherds' plays by references to lea, valley, and hill as stage areas (Wakefield 316, York 51, Coventry Shearmen and Taylors' 214, 218). Different levels for the Shepherds' action are stressed in the Chester version:

THIRD SHEPHERD Hankin, hold up thy hand and have [me,
That I were on high there by thee.
(Chester, *Adoration of the Shepherds,* 93–94.)

When in this play the Shepherds reach the manger, they hesitate before the door (454), arguing who shall go in first. It is probable then that there is either a door or a curtain representing a door which, when opened, reveals the Holy Family. A Chartres stained glass representation of the Nativity is framed in a curtained setting, and in the earlier liturgical form of the play as performed at Rouen in the thirteenth century, when the Shepherds come to Bethlehem they approach the altar, beyond which is set the crib, on either side clergy as midwives, and when the curtain over the crib is drawn aside, the artificial figures of the Virgin Mary and the child are revealed.

The actual orientation of heaven's tower and Mary's mansion to the east of the pageant or acting area, perhaps another vestige of the liturgical drama, is strongly suggested in plays on this theme. Reference occurs in this Wakefield play (438) to the Shepherds moving towards the east, and the following from York, when the Shepherds look towards the angel choir:

Lo! Hud! behold unto the east!
A wondrous sight there shall you see
Up in the sky.
(York, *The Angels and Shepherds*, 46–48.)

The heritage of liturgical drama may also account for the laconic parts in this play allotted to Mary and Joseph. As artificial plastic figures they traditionally left the main part of the drama to be conducted by the Shepherds and Midwives. In the mystery plays on this theme Joseph says very little or nothing at all, as in this Wakefield play; indeed it is debatable whether he should even appear. Medieval iconography frequently omits him from this scene, and when he does appear he is often depicted as either bored or asleep, as in the Chartres example. The First Shepherd's description of Joseph in the Chester play might interest the make-up artist:

Whatever this old man that here is,
Take heed his head is hoar,
His beard like bush of briers,
With a pound of hair about his mouth and more.
(Chester, *Adoration of the Shepherds*, 507–510.)

It is traditional in this scene for the Holy Family to be revealed only when the Shepherds arrive at Bethlehem and are ready to present their gifts.

The part of Jack Garcio may well be absorbed into that of the Third Shepherd. It is obviously unsatisfactory as it stands. His abuse of the First and Second Shepherds is in the same tone as that administered by the Third Shepherd. Like the Third Shepherd in the following play, Jack Garcio appears to be the youngest and responsible to the others for finding pasture for the sheep. The main difficulty in giving Jack Garcio's lines to the Third Shepherd lies in the following section of his part:

> Of all the fools I can tell,
> From heaven unto hell,
> Ye three bear the bell. (185–187.)

Either the last line is changed to 'Ye two bear the bell', or the Third Shepherd, as the jester of the group, thrusts a coxcomb with a bell into one of the other Shepherds' hands (the Chester First Shepherd offers the baby Jesus a bell). It is barely plausible that the jest may be of the kind Feste in *Twelfth Night* makes at the expense of Sir Toby Belch and Sir Andrew Aguecheek: 'Did you never see the picture of "we three"?'

The persistence of satire, at times little more than tomfoolery, at times trenchant social criticism, in the Shepherds' plays of the mystery cycles, relates them to the ceremonies of the Boy Bishop, the Feast of Fools, and the pagan Kalends, all festivities falling in the same Christmas season. Accepted order is reversed, revered tradition is discarded, and the young mock their elders and betters. This last point is admirably illustrated by the Garcio of the Chester play wrestling with, and throwing, each of the three Shepherds in turn. In the Wakefield play the hallowed *Gloria in excelsis* is hilariously muffed (430), the lordly fare of the aristocrats is lumped with the blood-puddings of the peasants (217), and Latin, the language of religion, is hooted at (390) or reduced to gibberish (292).

The folk-lore which informs these mid-winter festivities is clearly pre-Christian. In a time of desperate need great plenty appears. The First Shepherd, having lost all, imagines that he has regained a hundred sheep (110). The groans of poverty and oppression give way to orgiastic delight in the Shepherds' gargantuan feast. The sky which one moment is gloomy and foreboding (434) is the next ablaze with light (452). Such details suggest that a spring festival has been moved back to mid-winter, and although the rebirth themes associated with spring are everywhere apparent, the original performances of the liturgical Shepherds' plays in the mid-winter season is amply evinced by the repeated references to the cold weather. The Wakefield Cycle was performed on *Corpus Christi* Day or, in the late sixteenth century, during Whitsun week, but in both of the Shepherds' plays we hear of the suffering caused by a bitter winter. The cold itself is turned to exquisite dramatic purpose in the Coventry Pageant of the *Shearmen and Taylors:*

MARY Ah! Joseph, husband, my child grows cold,
And we have no fire to warm him with.

JOSEPH Now in my arms I shall him fold,
King of kings by field and frith;
He might have had better, if truth were told,
Than the breathing of beasts to warm him [with.
(287–292.)

In one of the Six Scenes From the Life of Christ in the Psalter of Robert, Baron de Lisle (before 1339), we see the Shepherds well wrapped up and one of them wearing mittens.

The section of the play (341–403) which contains the Shepherds' learned references to the prophets and even the First Shepherd's quotation from Virgil, might in production be omitted, especially if *The Procession of the Prophets* has already been performed. The passage, however, is of particular interest in illustrating the 'type and antitype' which medieval dramatist and artist were equally fond of juxtaposing. There is, for instance, a stained glass window at Canterbury cathedral, down the centre of which are scenes from the life of Christ, while either side are 'types' from the Old Testament, which illustrate or prefigure these scenes. In this play the story of the burning bush is a 'type' to the 'antitype' of the Virgin birth (360–367). This association is most vividly depicted in Nicholas Froment's The Virgin in the Burning Bush—The Vision of Moses (1476), in Saint-Sauveur Cathedral, Aix-en-Provence.

The Angels in heaven sing the *Gloria in excelsis* (295) and the Shepherds give their discordant version of it (431). The season and the play call for song. After feeding and drinking the Shepherds sing (266), and they sing again at the very end of the play (502). No song is extant in the Wakefield text, but the Pageant of the *Shearmen and Taylors* of Coventry presents us with the following Shepherds' songs, appropriate to the above occasions:

As I rode out this other night,
Of three jolly shepherds I saw a sight,
And all about their fold a star shone bright;
  They sang terli terlow;
  So merrily the shepherds their pipes did blow.

and

Down from heaven, from heaven so high
Of angels there came a great company,
With mirth and joy and great solemnity,
  They sang terli terlow;
  So merrily the shepherds their pipes did blow.

THE SECOND SHEPHERDS' PLAY

Two mansions are required, one for Mary and the child, and one for Mak's home. Above Mary's mansion is heaven from where the Angel speaks to the Shepherds (638). In the original text (649) the Second Shepherd suggests to us the direction from which the Angel appeared: 'he spak upward'. The part of the stage or pageant between the two mansions can be used for the rest of the action, although it may be preferable, and indeed more true to the original production, to use the ground space in front of the pageant. Daw, the Third Shepherd, comes over the lea land (111), the Shepherds sleep out of door (632) on the 'green'

(634), and their journey to Bethlehem is more convincing if they have in fact farther to travel and another level to climb. The tossing of Mak in a canvas or blanket—a popular medieval method of accelerating childbirth—is more conveniently and safely carried out on ground level. The curtains around the mansions conceal the actors within until the action of the play is transferred to the mansions. On the occasions when Mak returns home (295 and 404), although a curtain representing a door might divide Mak from his wife, to enjoy the dialogue fully, the audience should be able to see both characters simultaneously. The meeting of the three Shepherds at the Crooked Thorn, if staged below the level of the pageant, might lend greater dramatic effect to their threatening move towards Mak's house (475).

Reference is made to the pranked-up dress of the swaggering retainers. Their 'modish sleeve' (28) displayed their livery, and as some nobleman's henchmen they oppressed the peasantry. On his first entry Mak pretends to wield such authority (201), but his short cloak, beneath which he might have concealed his 'pickings', is wrenched from his shoulders by the Third Shepherd (200); and after he has already stolen the sheep Mak ostentatiously invites the three Shepherds to examine his capacious sleeves to make sure that he is innocent of any theft (396).

In his endeavour to impress the three Shepherds with his superiority Mak apes the speech of the south, but they know him too well to be taken in (216). His Latin likewise is false (267), and shortly after having called a doubtful blessing on the sleepers in the name of Pontius Pilate, he proceeds to cast over them a magic spell which will enable him to steal their sheep with impunity. The First Shepherd's Latin (350–351) is no more accurate than Mak's, but at least without pious affectation.

Daw, the Third Shepherd's name, is a diminutive for David, but more probably has here the connotation of 'fool'. In which case it corresponds to 'Slow-pace', the Third Shepherd in *The First Shepherds' Play*. John Horn and Gibbon (Gib), asserted by Mak as the godparents of his child, are also the names of the First and Second Shepherd in the earlier play.

The Shepherds' painful attempts to reproduce in song the Angel's *Gloria* extend intermittently from l. 665 to l. 674. The Second Shepherd's threatening 'let be your din' brings such an attempt to an end. The two Shepherds' songs from the Coventry Pageant of the *Shearmen and Taylors* might be used here: the first, 'As I rode out', as the part song (189), the second, 'Down from heaven, from heaven so high', in conclusion.

THE OFFERING OF THE MAGI

The structure and staging of this play is, in many ways, similar to that of *The Second Shepherds' Play*. The liturgical plays of the Magi were very much more popular than those of the Shepherds, and the latter may have derived many of their characteristics from the former. That the Magi should be three in number, and by analogy the Shepherds also, is probably due to the number of gifts ascribed to them in the Bible (*Matthew* 2. 11). The symbolism of these gifts becomes a feature also of *The Second Shepherds' Play:* the bird representing, as the dove in the Annunciation and the Baptism, the Holy Ghost; the tennis ball, the orb, the symbol of royalty; the bob of cherries, the mid-winter miracle, the symbol of death and resurrection. The Magi in medieval iconography, like the Shepherds in the plays, are depicted as one old, one middle-aged, and one young (*L'Art Religieux du XIIIe Siecle en France* by Emile Male, 228–230). The tradition that the 'wise men' were kings arose during the sixth century, if not before, and the names they bear in this play were assigned to them during the twelfth century. The tradition of representing one of the Magi as a Moor may go back to the early Middle Ages. 'According to the information available from Besançon it appears that before the singing of the gospel three of the clergy costume themselves with crowns and differently coloured regal garments. They are accompanied by attendants carrying gifts in gold vases, and by other clerics bearing silver staffs, lighted candles, and thuribles. The attendants are dressed as Persians, and one of them is blacked to represent a Moor.' (Karl Young, op. cit., ii. 41.)

In this Wakefield play the Magi enter on horseback and conduct their initial soliloquies and subsequent dialogue from the saddle (85–258). They dismount for their meeting with Herod and again for the adoration. They ride away, as they came, in different directions, the Second King referring to the gate through which he must pass (632). It is possible that the original staging of this play took place in an area resembling an amphitheatre with two mansions placed opposite each other on the raised part of the circumference. This would allow for the separate mounted entries of the Kings, for their continuing their journey following the star round the amphitheatre while the main attention of the audience is given to Herod, and for their resting in the litter (590) placed either in another mansion on the circumference of the amphitheatre or, as the bed in *The Castle of Perseverance*, in the very centre. This use of the litter is unique in the English versions of this play, although a stone carving at Chartres shows the three Kings in one bed, while beyond a partitioning door a servant holds their three horses by the bridle.

The Magi plays from other Cycles, with the exception of York, suggest presentation in the round. The Kings are mounted, and in *Ludus Coventriae* Herod himself enters on horseback and asks the audience to excuse him while he retires to his chamber to dress more splendidly. In the Coventry Pageant of the *Shearmen and Taylors* the three Kings ride towards each other on horseback and speak in the street together (539, 570, 582), and later in the play 'Herod rages in the pageant and in the street also'. The *Ludus Coventriae* Magi ride towards Herod over 'street and stone' (137), they dismount and kneel before Herod, and on their way towards Bethlehem lie down on a bank beneath the bright star, and it is on 'this hill' (291) that the Angel warns them of the danger of returning to Herod's court. The Chester Magi leave their horses while they climb a hill to pray (48), and there the star appears to them. The stage direction following line 112 in this

Chester version stresses the arena form of presentation (*Descendunt et circumamblant bis et tunc ad Equos*).

The star in liturgical drama was frequently drawn by a string over the Magi's heads. At Rouen two stars were used, one over the action which occurred at the main altar, and one over the altar in the nave where the Kings present their gifts. The Magi in the Coventry Pageant see a child in the star (588), and the Chester Magi see in the star the Virgin carrying the child, a plastic representation apparently, for the stage direction following line 89 suggests that the Angel carried the star (*Tunc Reges iterum genua flectunt, et Angelus Stellam portans dicat*).

The opposition of Herod's mansion to the manger is paralleled in *The Second Shepherds' Play* by the opposition of Mak's house to the manger. The Shepherds and Kings treat the space between as neutral territory, but it is clear that Herod's hall and Mak's house, where is found 'the horned lad', have close affinities with hell.

THE FLIGHT INTO EGYPT

In the Wakefield and York cycles *The Flight into Egypt* stands as a separate play; in the *Ludus Coventriae* and Chester cycles and in the Coventry Pageant of the *Shearmen and Taylors* it is absorbed into the larger structure of *The Massacre of the Innocents*. The York and Wakefield versions resemble each other in many ways, but whereas in the York play a humorous situation is developed out of Joseph's predicament at being faced with yet another hazardous long journey—he complains with some bitterness that he does not even know the way to Egypt—the Wakefield playwright develops a more sympathetic and harmonious relationship between Joseph and Mary. The lyricism of the shorter line and the ambitious rhyme scheme contribute to this effect.

The acting area used by Joseph and Mary can be the same for the sequence of plays from *The Second Shepherds'* to *Herod the Great*. Their manger is visited by both Shepherds and Kings, and the ass that has warmed Jesus at his nativity now bears his mother to Egypt. The ass is a feature introduced into all the other cycle plays on this theme and, mostly, with specific reference to riding (York, 199, *Ludus Coventriae,* 83, Chester 273). E. K. Chambers, quoting the Ducange Glossary, and Karl Young, referring to a thirteenth-century service-book of Padua cathedral, show how, in liturgical representations of the Flight into Egypt, Mary, seated on the ass would be led through the church. The association of this ceremony with those of the Boy Bishop and the Feast of Fools recalls the buffoonery of Herod's part in the preceding play *The Adoration of the Magi,* and in the following play, *Herod the Great.*

In the Chester play of *The Slaying of the Innocents,* the Angel appears to Joseph, warns him of Herod's plans and accompanies the holy family to Egypt, singing as they go. The stage direction suggests that, if possible, as the Angel sings, idols and statues should come crashing down:

ANGEL For Mohammeds, both one and all,
That men of Egypt gods do call,
At your coming down shall fall,
When I begin to sing.

(*Tunc ibunt, et Angelus cantabit 'Ecce dominus super nubem levem, et ingredietur Egiptum, et movebuntur simulacra Egipti a facie Domini Exercituum', et si fieri poterit, cadet aliqua statua sive imago.*)

The same Angel appears after Herod's death in this play to lead Mary and Joseph back to Judah, again offering to sing:

ANGEL Forsooth I will not from you go
But ever help you from your foe.
And I will make a melody,
And sing here in your company.
A word was said in prophecy
A thousand years ago.

(*Ex Egipto vocavi filium meum, ut Salvum faciet populum meum.*)

(Chester *Slaying of the Innocents,* 491–496.)

The performance of the Wakefield *Flight into Egypt* might be enhanced by the angel-choir making such a melody.

HEROD THE GREAT

Two main acting areas are required, one for Herod's court and one for the killing of the children. Herod is traditionally seated on a high throne. In his raging he may descend, as indicated by the stage direction in the Coventry Pageant of the *Shearmen and Taylors* (Herod rages in the pageant and in the street also), but in general the plays stress the proud height at which Herod sits. In the *Ludus Coventriae* Herod greets the soldiers returning from their killing of the children:

Well have ye wrought,
My foe is sought,
To death is he brought;
Now come up to me.

(*Ludus Coventriae, The Massacre of the Innocents,* 125–128.)

The staging of the Wakefield play necessitates that the killing should take place well away from Herod's court. Internal evidence from the Coventry Pageant suggests that it took place in the street or in the arena area. The avenging mothers are at some disadvantage in striking at the mounted soldiers:

3RD WOMAN Sit he never so high in saddle,
But I shall his brain-pan addle,
And here with my pot-ladle
With him will I fight.

(Coventry Pageant of the *Shearmen and Taylors,* 862–865.)

A similar area may have been used for the Wakefield play, but there is no indication that the Soldiers are mounted, indeed they are much more assailable: the Women strike at hood, tabard, and groin (339, 357, 382).

Such references to tabard and hood are interesting pointers to costume. Herod's soldiers, the sort of retainers, about whom the Shepherds are so bitter, wear on their tabards Herod's coat-of-arms. Cowards that they are, they would also wear helmets for the fray:

2ND WOMAN Their basinets be big and broad;
Beat on now! let's see!
(Chester, *Slaying of the Innocents*, 319–320.)

The killing of the children in their mothers' arms is most effectively done with short knives rather than with spears, the method suggested by the First Counsellor (252). The *Ludus Coventriae* Women probably carried dolls with readily detachable heads:

1ST WOMAN Long lulling have I lorn,
Alas, why was my bairn born,
With swiping sword now is he shorn,
The head right from the neck . . .
(*Ludus Coventriae, The Massacre of the Innocents*, 89–92).

The Women's defence rests in boots and distaff (Chester) and the pot-ladle (Coventry). The Wakefield Women attack with no less venom and might add to the above weapons their bodkins (337) and their nails (353).

In the Chester *Slaughter of the Innocents*, Herod's Son, himself a victim of the massacre, is described as dressed in gold 'painted wondrous gay'. The Goldsmiths presented this pageant and they would certainly have made Herod a truly resplendent sight. His headwear, since he claims kinship with Mohammed, might well be a large crown fitting over a turban. It is apparent from the following account taken from the Coventry Smiths' Company records that Herod's headpiece was the most vulnerable of stage articles:

'1477, it. to a peynter for peyntyng the fauchon and Herods face xd. It. for assadyn, silver papur and gold paper, gold foyle and green foyle ij s j d, it. for redd wax ij d, it. payd to Thomas Suker for makyng the crests xxij d; 1478, it. for assaden for the harnes x d; 1480, expense for a slop for Herod (inter alia), pd for peyntyng and dressyng Heruds stuf ij d; 1487, it. for mendyng of

Arrodes crast xij d; 1489, it. paid for a gowen to Arrode vij s iiij d, it. paid for peyntyng and steynyng ther-off vjs iiij d, it. payd for Arroddes garment peynttyng that he went a prossasyon in xx d; 1490, a fawchon, a septur, and a creste for Heroude repaired; 1494, it. payd for iij platis to Heroddis crest of iron vj d, it. payd for a paper of aresdyke xij d, it. payd to Hatfield for dressyng of Herods creste xiiij d: 1499, it. payd to John Hatfielde for colours and gold foyle and sylver foyle for the crest and for the fawchem (inter alia); 1501, it. for vj yards satten iij quarters xvj s x d, it. for v yardus of blowe bokeram ij s xj d, it. pd for makyng of Herodus gone xv d; 1516, it payd to a peynter for peyntyng and mendyng of Herodes heed iiij d; 1547, pd to John Croo for mendyng of Herrods hed and a myter and other thyngs ij s; 1554, payd to John Hewet payntter for dressyng of Erod hed and the faychon ij s.'

(Hardin Craig, *Two Coventry Corpus Christi Plays*, 86.)

Apart from the headdress it will be seen that the falchion, a broad curved sword, calls for constant attention. This is obviously much used by the tyrant upon his menials. He might also use his sceptre which could be made of flexible material, similar to those inflated bladders originally used in the thirteenth-century celebrations of Innocents' Day in the cathedral at Padua:

'At Padua, it appears, in the absence of a decorous play of the Magi, Herod takes a lawless part in the concluding parts of Matins itself. After the eighth lesson he and his chaplain come from the sacristy, clad in untidy tunics, and carrying wooden spears. Before he mounts the platform, Herod angrily hurls his spear towards the chorus, and then proceeds, *cum tanto furore*, to read the ninth lesson. Meanwhile his attendants dash about the choir belabouring bishop, canons and choristers with an inflated bladder. At the conclusion of his reading, Herod joins in these antics *cum supradicto furore*—presumably whilst the chorus is attempting to sing the last responsory.'

(Karl Young, op. cit., ii. 100.)

The regularity with which all the tyrants of the mystery plays, on making their first entry, call for silence indicates that they were invariably greeted with a storm of jeers and cat-calls. But, like the devils, Herod could be both ridiculous and terrifying. His mansion is adjacent to hell-mouth; in the Chester version he sees the fiends swarming out of hell to seize him:

I bequeath here in this place
My soul to be with Satan.
(Chester, *The Slaying of the Innocents*, 429–430.)

The entry of Death in the *Ludus Coventriae* play (167) at the moment of Herod's triumphant feasting is superb drama. As the minstrels blow 'a merry fit' death strikes Herod and the Devil receives him exultantly:

All ours, all ours, this castle is mine.

Herod's castle is opposed to heaven's tower. Although the Wakefield Herod remains triumphant at the end, fanfares of trumpets heralding his coming and going would be appropriate throughout. This cowardly, ignorant, mean and malicious monster makes a characteristic final exit holding a nosegay to his face as he inveighs against the stench of the multitude.

The Soldiers ape the bragging cowardly conduct of their master and add a touch of their own gallows' humour (331). Their parts are grotesque but never farcical. The response of the Women to the killing of their children should be deeply felt, and this would be impossible if the Soldiers were played farcically. To dispel any suspicion of the farcical element the Women might make their entry singing the Coventry Carol:

Lully, lullay, thou little tiny child,
By by, lully lullay, thou little tiny child,
  By by, lully lullay!

O sisters two,
How may we do
  For to preserve this day

This poor youngling
For whom we do sing
  By by, lully lullay?

Herod, the king,
In his raging,
  Charged he hath this day
His men of might
In his own sight
  All young children to slay,—

That woe is me;
Poor child for thee,
  And ever mourn and may
For thy parting
Neither say nor sing,
  By by, lully lullay.

THE PURIFICATION OF MARY AND THE PLAY OF THE DOCTORS

Two leaves of the manuscript are missing between the end of *The Purification of Mary* and the beginning of *The Play of the Doctors.* The *Ludus Coventriae* and the Coventry Pageant of the Weavers preserve complete plays of *The Purification of Mary,* and *The Play of the Doctors* is included in the York Cycle and the Coventry *Pageant of the Weavers;* the York version from line 73 until the end is a very close parallel of the Wakefield play.

Part Three

THE NINETEENTH PLAY

John the Baptist

JOHN	2ND ANGEL
1ST ANGEL	JESUS

JOHN God, that made both more and less,
Heaven and earth, at his own will,
And marked man to his likeness,
As one who would his wish fulfil,
Upon the earth he sent lightness,
Both sun and moon to shine there still,
He save you all from sinfulness,
And keep you clean from every ill.

Among prophets then am I one
That God has sent to teach his law,
And man to amend, that wrong has done,
Both with example and with saw.
My name, forsooth, is baptized John;
My father's faith contained a flaw
For which the angel thereupon
Dumb, till my birth, kept him in awe.

Elizabeth my mother was,
Aunt unto Mary, maiden mild;
And as the sun shines through the glass,
Within her womb so did her child.
The Jews yet ask me as I pass
If I be Christ; they are beguiled,
Jesus shall amend man's trespass,
Whose faith through frailty is defiled.

I am sent but a messenger
From him who may all sins amend;
I go before, such words to bear,

As a forerunner to my friend.
His law to teach, his way to fare,
To all mankind that may offend.
Of buffets full bitter his share,
Before he brings all things to end.

These Jews shall hang him on a cross,
He grieves so for man's unbelief,
That of his life he suffers loss,
As he were traitor or a thief,
Dying, to cleanse us of our dross,
And save us from our own mischief;
Thus gladly away his life will toss,
And rise again for our relief.

In water clear then baptize I
The people living on this coast;
But he shall do more mightily,
And baptize in the holy ghost;
And with the blood of his body
Wash our sins both least and most,
Therefore, it fits, both ye and me
Against the fiend to join God's host.

I am not worthy to unloose
The least thong that ties up his shoe,
But God almighty us may use
On earth indeed his will to do.
I thank thee, Lord, that did diffuse
Among mankind thy seed; it grew.
Now every day earth doth produce
For each man food as is his due.

We are, Lord, duty bound to thee,
To love thee here both day and night.
For thou hast sent thy son so free
To save man's soul from perilous plight.
Through Adam's sin and Eve's folly,
Our parents fell through the fiend's might;
But, Lord, on man now have pity,
And bless thy bairns in heaven so bright.

[*Enter two* ANGELS, JESUS *follows at a distance.*

1ST ANGEL John the Baptist hearken to me!
The father of heaven he greets thee well,
For true and trusty finds he thee,
Doing thy devoir where thou dost dwell;
Welcome his will in this decree,
Since thou standst firm though faced with hell,
Baptized by thee Christ Jesus be
In Jordan's river, man's care to quell.

JOHN Ah! Dear God! What may this be?
I heard a voice but nought I saw.

1ST ANGEL John, it is I that spake to thee;
To do this deed stand not in awe.

JOHN Should I abide till he come to me?
That should not be, I thee implore;
I shall go meet that Lord so free,
Fall at his feet him to adore.

2ND ANGEL Nay, John, that is not well fitting;
His father's will thou needs must work.

1ST ANGEL John, be thou here abiding,
But when he comes feel thou no irk.

JOHN This tells my understanding
That children should be brought to kirk,
In every land for baptizing;
This law to keep man must not shirk.

2ND ANGEL John, this place it is pleasing,
And is called the river Jordan;
Here is no kirk, nor no building
But where the father will ordain,
It is God's will and his bidding.

JOHN By this, forsooth, it seems clear then
This work shall be to his liking;
And so please the Lord should all men.

Since I must needs his wish fulfil
He shall be welcome unto me;
I yield me wholly to his will,
Wheresoever I abide or be.
I am his servant, to be still

Messenger to that Lord free;
Whether he will cure or kill
I shall not grudge in no degree.

JESUS John, God's servant and prophet,
My father, that to thee is dear,
Has sent me to thee, well thou wit,
To be baptized in water clear;
To reprieve man's fall, as is writ,
The law I will fulfil right here;
My father's ordinance, thus is it,
And thus my will is, never fear.

I come to thee baptism to take,
To whom my father has me sent,
With oil and cream that thou shalt make
Unto that worthy sacrament.
And therefore, John, it not forsake,
But come to me in this present,
No further shall myself betake
Till I have done his commandment.

JOHN Ah, Lord! I love thee for thy coming!
I am ready to do his will,
In word in work in every thing,
Whatsoever I must fulfil;
This beauteous Lord himself to bring
To his own servant humble still
A knight to baptize his Lord King,
This task may be beyond my skill.

And if I were worthy
For to fulfil this sacrament,
I have no cunning, surely,
To do it for thee as is meant;
And therefore, Lord, I ask mercy;
Hold me excused if I dissent;
I dare not touch this blessed body,
My heart will never to it assent.

JESUS Of thy cunning, John, dread thou nought,
My father himself he will thee teach;
He that all this world has wrought,

He sent thee plainly for to preach;
He knows man's heart, his deed, his thought;
He knows how far man's might may reach,
Therefore hither have I sought;
My father's wish none may impeach.

Behold he sends his angels two,
In token I am both God and man;
Give me baptism before I go,
And dip me in river Jordan.
Since he will thus, I would know who
Durst him gainsay? John, come on then,
And baptize me for friend or foe,
And do it, John, right as thou can.

1ST ANGEL Obedience, John, do not disdain,
And be not grudging in no thing,
Gladly you ought to count it gain
For to fulfil my Lord's bidding.
Early and late, with might and main,
Therefore to thee this word I bring,
My Lord has given thee power plain,
And dread thee nought of thy cunning.

2ND ANGEL He sends thee here his own dear child,
Thou welcome him with right good cheer,
Born of a maiden meek and mild,
That he may now to thee appear;
With sin was never his mother defiled,
There was never man who came her near,
In word nor work she was never wild,
Therefore her son thou baptize here.

1ST ANGEL This reason for you I will draw
Why that he comes thus unto thee;
He comes now to fulfil the law,
From peerless principality;
And therefore, John, hold thee in awe,
Fail no function in no degree—
To baptize him that thou here saw
For wit thou well this same is he.

JOHN I am not worthy to do this deed;
Yet I shall meet God's great demand;
But yet, dear Lord, look on my need,
As act I must at thy command.
I tremble and I quake for dread!
I dare not touch thee with my hand,
But to my gain I will give heed;
Abide, my Lord, and by me stand.

[*He baptizes* JESUS.

I baptize thee, Jesus, on high,
In the name of thy father free,
In nomine patris et filii,
Since he wills that it so be,
Et spiritus altissimi,
And of the holy ghost on high;
I ask thee, Lord, of thy mercy,
Hereafter that thou would bless me.

Here I thee anoint also
With oil and cream, with this intent,
That men may know, where so they go,
This is a worthy sacrament.
There are six others, no more so,
The which thyself to earth hath sent,
And in true token here below,
The first on thee now is it spent.

Thou guide me Lord if I go wrong;
My will is bent to do but well;
My part I fear I may prolong,
If I did right I should down kneel.
Bless me before thou go along,
So that I may thy friendship feel;
I have desired this sight so long,
Now death would come as no ordeal.

JESUS This beast, John, thou bear with thee,
It is a beast full blessed;

[*Here he gives him the lamb of God.*

John, I give this lamb to thee,
None such among the rest;

To keep thee from adversity,
So guard it as the best;
By this beast known shalt thou be,
That thou art John Baptist.

JOHN For I have seen the lamb of God
Who washes away the sin of this world,
And touched him, for even or odd,
My heart before was ever hard.
To show me truth's way lay untrod
An angel had me almost marred,
But he that rules all with his rod
He bless me when I draw homeward.

JESUS I grant thee, John, for thy travail,
Ay lasting joy in bliss to abide;
And to all those that trust this tale,
And saw me not yet glorified.
I shall bring comfort to their bale,
And send them succour from every side;
My father and I may them avail,
Men and women that leave their pride.

But, John, go thou forth and preach
Against the folk that do amiss;
And to the people the truth thou teach;
To righteousness turn those remiss,
And as far as thy wit may reach
Bid them be there to bide my bliss;
For at doomsday I shall impeach
All who scorn thee nor trust not this.

Bid them leave sin, for I it hate;
For it I must die on a tree,
By prophecy I know my fate;
Indeed my mother that sight must see,
That sorrow shall her joys abate
For I was born of her body.
Farewell, John, I go my gait;
I bless thee with the trinity.

[JESUS *withdraws slowly. The two* ANGELS *precede him.*

JOHN

Almighty God in persons three,
All in one substance ay engrossed,
I thank thee, Lord, in majesty,
Father, son, and holy ghost!
From heaven thou sent thy son so free,
To Mary mild, unto this coast,
And now thou sends him unto me.
For to be baptized in this host.

Farewell! The favour that none shall forget!
Farewell! Flower more fresh than flower de [luce!
Farewell! Steersman for them so beset
In storms, by sickness and distress!
Thy mother wed but was maiden yet;
Farewell! Pearl of price peerless!
Farewell! The loveliest that on earth was set!
Thy mother is of hell empress.

Farewell! Blessed both blood and bone!
Farewell! The seemliest that ever was seen!
To thee, Jesu, I make my moan;
Farewell! Comely, of body so clean!
Farewell! Gracious Lord so close to God's [throne,
Much grace through thee we now may glean;
Leave us thy living way on loan,
Mending our ways more than we mean.

I will go preach both to more and less,
As I am charged most surely;
Sirs, forsake your wickedness,
Pride, envy, sloth, wrath and lechery.
Hear God's service as ye guess,
Please God with praying, thus say I;
Beware when death comes with distress,
So that ye die not suddenly.

Death spares none that life has borne,
Therefore think on what I say;
Beseech your God both even and morn
You for to save from sin that day.

Think how in baptism ye are sworn
To be God's servant, without a nay;
Let never his love from you be lorn,
God bring you to his bliss for ay.

[*Goes out.*

THE TWENTIETH PLAY

Lazarus

JESUS	THOMAS
PETER	MARTHA
JOHN	MARY
	LAZARUS

JESUS Come now, brethren, and go with me;
We will pass forth unto Judea;
To Bethany will we wend,
To visit Lazarus our friend.
Gladly would I with him speak
For he is sick that we should seek.

PETER I counsel ye not thither go,
Where the Jews hold you for their foe;
I counsel ye near not that stead,
For if ye do then ye be dead.

JOHN Master, trust thou not one Jew,
Since many a day now thou them knew,
And last time that we were there,
We kept our lives in dreadful care.

THOMAS When we were last in that country
This other day, both thou and we,
We thought thou there should have been slain;
Will thou now go thither again?

JESUS Hearken, brethren, this counsel keep;
Lazarus our friend has fallen asleep;
The way to him now will we take,
To stir that knight and bid him wake.

PETER Sir, methinks it were the best
To let him sleep and take his rest;

And watch that no man come him near,
If he sleep he will mend his cheer.

JESUS I tell you truly without fail,
No watching may to him avail,
No sleep may stand him in good stead,
I tell you surely, he is dead;
Therefore I say to you at last
Leave this speech and go we fast.

THOMAS Sir, whatsoever ye bid us do
Willingly we assent thereto;
I hope to God ye shall not find
None of us shall lag behind;
For any peril that may befall,
Wend we with our master all.

[*They go to* MARTHA's *house*.

MARTHA Help me, Lord, my rest is fled!
Lazarus, my brother, now is dead,
That was to thee beloved and dear;
He had not died had thou been here.

JESUS Martha, Martha, peace to your pain,
Thy brother shall rise and live again.

MARTHA Lord, I know that he shall rise
And come before the good justice;
For at the dreadful day of doom
There must ye keep him when he come,
To look what doom ye will him give;
Then must he rise, then must he live.

JESUS I warn you, both man and wife,
I am the rising, and I am the life;
And whoso truly trusts in me,
That I was ever and ay shall be,
One thing I shall him give,
Though he be dead yet shall he live,
Say thou, woman, trust thou this?

MARTHA Yea, forsooth, my Lord of bliss,
Else were I worthy to be chid,
For from thee no truth is hid.

JESUS Go tell thy sister, Magdalene,
That I come ye may be fain.

MARTHA Sister, leave this sorrowful band,
Our Lord comes close by here at hand,
And his apostles with him also.

MARY Ah, for God's love let me go!
Blessed be he that sends me grace,
That I may see thee in this place.
Lord, much sorrow may men see
Befall my sister here and me;
We are as heavy as any lead,
For our brother that thus is dead.
Had thou been here and him first seen,
Dead forsooth had he not been.

JESUS Hither to you now we fare,
To bring you comfort for your care,
But look no faintness nor no sloth
Bring you from the steadfast truth,
Then shall I grant you both my aid,
Lo, where have ye his body laid?

MARTHA Lord, if it be thy will,
I doubt by this he savours ill,
For it is now the fourth day gone
Since he was laid under yon stone.

JESUS I told thee right now as thou stood
That thy truth should ay be good,
And if thou may that fulfil
All shall be done right as thou will.

[JESUS *prays to the Father.*

Father, I pray thee that thou raise
Lazarus that was thine,
And bring him out of hell's fierce blaze
That he no more need pine.

When I thee pray thou says always
Thy will is such as mine,
Therefore we shall increase his days
If thou to me incline.

Come forth, Lazarus, and stand us by,
In earth shall thou no longer lie;
Take and loose him foot and hand,
And from his throat take the band,
To one side that napkin throw,
And all that gear and let him go.

LAZARUS Lord, that all things made of nought,
All praise be to thee,
That such wonder here has wrought,
Greater may none be.
When I was dead hell's gate I sought,
And thou, almighty,
Raised me up and thence me brought,
Behold and ye may see.

There is none so bold decreed,
Nor none so proud to greet,
Nor none so doughty in his deed,
Nor none for daïs more meet,
Nor king, nor knight, nor bondman freed,
Death's destiny could defeat,
Nor flesh where he was wont to feed,
But it shall be worms' meat.

Your death is worm's cook,
Your mirror here ye look,
And let me be your book,
    Example take from me;
Though charms for death ye took,
    Such shall ye all be.

Each one in such array, death shall him sud-
[denly smite,
And close him in cold clay, whether he be king
[or knight
For all his garments gay that were a seemly sight,
His flesh shall fall away, as for many in this
[plight.

    On them a worm delights
    To gnaw at these gay knights,
    At their lungs and at their lights,

Their hearts eaten asunder;
These masters held the heights,
Thus shall they be brought under.

Under the earth ye shall thus full of care then [couch;
The roof of your hall your naked nose shall [touch;
Neither great nor small to you will kneel nor [crouch;
A sheet shall be your pall, toads for jewels will [vouch;
The slime of toads shall smear,
The fiends fill you with fear,
Your flesh that fair was here
Thus ruefully shall rot;
Instead of a gay collar
Such bands shall bind your throat.

Your cheer that was so red, your looks the lily [like,
Then shall be wan as lead and stink as dog in [dyke;
And worms be in you bred as bees breed in a [hive,
The eyes out of your head shall spotted toads [thus rive;
To pick you are pressed
Many a loathsome beast,
Thus they shall make a feast
Of your flesh and of your blood.
Your sorrows then are least
When greatest seems your good.

Your goods ye shall forsake though ye be never [so loth,
And nothing with you take but such a winding [cloth;
Your wife's sorrow shall slake, also your chil- [dren's both,
Your memory all shall forsake though ye be never [so wroth;

They mind you as nothing
That may be to your helping,
Neither in mass singing
    Nor even with alms deed;
Therefore in your leaving,
    Be wise and take good heed.

Take heed then how you deal while ye still have [life,
To frail friends never appeal, trust not child nor [wife,
Executors do but steal; and for your goods will [strive;
Where lies your soul's weal may no man there [them shrive.

To shrive no man them may,
After your ending day,
    Your soul for to glad;
Your executors will swear nay,
And say ye owed more than ye had.

Amend thee, man, whilst thou may,
    Let never no mirth undo thy mind;
Think thou on that dreadful day
    When God shall judge all mankind.
Think thou fares as doth the wind;
    This world is wasted clean away;
Man, have this in thy mind,
    And amend thee whilst that thou may.

Amend thee, man, whilst thou art here,
    Lest thou abide a bitter fate;
When thou art dead and laid on bier,
    Wit thou well thou art too late;
For if all thy goods however great
    Were given for thee after thy day,
In heaven it would not mend thy state,
    Therefore amend thee whilst thou may.

Though thou be right royal in rent,
    As is the steed standing in stall,
In thy heart know and think
    That they are God's goods all.

He might have made thee poor and small
    As he that begs from day to day;
But a true account give thou shall,
    Therefore amend thee whilst thou may.

And if I might with you dwell
    To tell you what I mean,
A long tale could I tell
    What I have heard and seen,
Of many a great marvel,
    Of many a sight unclean,
In the halls of hell,
    There where I have been.

Been have I in woe,
    Therefore fear ye may show;
Whilst ye live do so,
    If ye will dwell with him
That can make you thus go,
    And heal you joint and limb.
He is a Lord of grace,
Bethink you in this case,
    And pray him full of might,
He keep you in this place
    And have you in his sight.

[*All withdraw.*

THE TWENTY-FIRST PLAY

The Conspiracy

PILATE	JUDAS	ANDREW
CAIAPHAS	ST. JOHN	SIMEON
ANNAS	PETER	PHILIP
1ST SOLDIER	PATERFAMILIAS	THADEUS
2ND SOLDIER	JESUS	MALCUS
		GOD

PILATE Peace, curs, I command, uncouth churls [I call you;
I say stop and stand, or foul might befall [you.
Not this burnished brand, now when I [behold you,
I warn you withstand, or else the devil [scold you
To moans.
All men hold me in awe,
As leader of law;
Wise men, heed every saw
Lest I break all your bones.

Ye know well what I mean, what great [king has come to town,
So comely clad and clean, a ruler of great [renown;
In sight if I were seen, Mohammed's my [grandson,
My name Pilate has been, was never king [with crown
More worthy;
My wisdom and my wit,
In seat here as I sit,

Was never more like it,
    My deeds to descry.

For I am he that may make or mar a
    [man;
Myself if I it say as men of court now can;
Support a man today, tomorrow against
    [him plan,
On both parts thus I play, and, feigning,
    [fight in the van
    Of right;
But all false indictors,
Courtmongers and jurors,
And all these false outriders,
    Are welcome to my sight.

More need had I never of such servants
    [now, I say you,
If I did well consider the truth I must dis-
    [please you,
And therefore come I hither; so peace
    [therefore I pray you;
There is a lazy lubber, I would not should
    [dismay you,
    About;
As prophet is he praised,
And a great rout has raised,
But if my bans be blazed,
    His death is due, no doubt.

Preaches to the people here, that false
    [fellow Jesus,
That if he live a year our law shall fall
    [with us;
And yet I stand in fear, so wide his works
    [and virtuous,
No fault in him is clear, that many come
    [to tell us;
    But sleight
Against him shall be sought,
That all this woe has wrought;

A bitter bargain shall be bought,
In vengeance for our right.

That fellow says that three should ever [dwell in one godhead,
That ever was and shall be, a truth for [men to heed;
He says of a maiden born was he, that [never took man's seed,
And that himself shall die on tree, and [man's soul out of prison lead;
Let him alone,
If this be true indeed,
His power shall spread with speed,
And overcome our own.

CAIAPHAS Sir Pilate, prince of princes, prize,
Proved in power without a peer,
And lords that our words legalize,
To the law now must we adhere,
And in our works we must be wise,
For else we lose our wealth, I fear,
Therefore say now what you advise
For hideous harms that we have here,

Touching that traitor strong,
That brings us this belief,
For if thus he goes along,
It will be to our grief.

ANNAS Sir, our folk are so afraid,
His lies our laws outweigh;
Amendment must be made,
That he wend not away.

PILATE Now certain, sirs, this was well said,
And I assent, right as ye say,
Some privy point to be purveyed,
To mar his might if that we may;

And therefore, sirs, in this present,
Which point most we may praise,
Let all be in assent,
Let's see what each man says.

CAIAPHAS Sir, before I said must not be borne
His subtleties and sleights so sore;
He turns our folk both even and morn,
And ay makes marvels more and more.

ANNAS Sir, if he escape it were great scorn;
So kill him quickly we implore,
For if our laws are thus outworn,
Men would our foolishness deplore.

PILATE For certain, sirs, ye speak right well.
And wittily, say I;
But yet some fault in him now tell
Wherefore that he should die;
And therefore, sirs, think ye not so?
For what thing we should him slay?

CAIAPHAS Sir, I can reckon you a row
Of thousand wonders, more some say,
Of many maimed men we well know,
Who sound in limb he sent away,
Our law he would have laid full low,
From us he tempts our folk to stray.

ANNAS Lord, deaf and dumb in our presence
Delivers he, by down and dale;
Whatever hurt or harm they sense,
Full hastily he makes them hale.
When for such work he needeth pence
Of each man's wealth he may avail,
But unto us he gives offence,
For all men trust well in his tale.

PILATE Yea, devil! And does he thus
As ye well bear witness?
Such fault falls to us,
By our rule for to redress.

CAIAPHAS And also, sir, I have heard say,
Another annoyance comes us near,
He will not keep our sabbath day,
That holy should be held ay here,
But forbids men far and near
To work as we demand.

PILATE By Mohammed's blood so dear,
He shall cower at my command.

The devil will he be there?
I have so great a hating.

ANNAS Nay, nay, well more is there;
He calls himself heaven's king,
And says that he is so mighty
To teach the righteous where to tread.

PILATE By Mohammed's blood, that shall he [abuy
With bitter bales ere I eat bread!

1ST SOLDIER Lord, Lazarus of Bethany
That lay stinking in one stead,
Quick he raised up bodily
The fourth day after he was dead.

2ND SOLDIER And for that he him raised,
That had lain dead so long a space,
The people him profusely praised
Over all in every place.

ANNAS Amongst the folk he has the name
That he is God's son and none else,
And himself says the same,
That his father in heaven dwells;
That he shall rule both wild and tame;
In all such matters he excels.

PILATE This is the devil's game!
Would any trust such tales he tells?

CAIAPHAS Yes, lord, have here my hand,
And each man holds him as his brother;
Such quaint tricks doth he understand,
Lord, ye never knew such another.

PILATE Why, and knows he not that I have
Bold men to be his bane?
I command both knight and knave
Cease not till that lad be slain.

1ST SOLDIER
Sir Pilate, calm you now your care,
But soothe your heart and mend your [mood;
For if that sneak-thief learn our snare,
And leave his tricks, he were as good;
For in our temple we will not spare
To take this madcap as we should.

PILATE
In our temple? The devil! What did he [there?
That shall he abuy, by Mohammed's [blood!

2ND SOLDIER
Lord, we knew not your will;
With wrong ye us scold;
Had ye told us to kill,
We should have been more bold.

PILATE
The devil, he hang you high to dry!
Know ye not what our laws say?
Go, bring him hither hastily.
So that he wend not thus away.

CAIAPHAS
Sir Pilate, be not too hasty.
But suffer to pass our sabbath day;
In the meantime to seek and spy
More of his marvels, if men may.

ANNAS
Yea, sir, and when his feast is done
Then shall his knacks be known.

PILATE
With you, sirs, I am one
For to abide as ye have shown.

[*Then* JUDAS *enters.*

JUDAS
Masters, mirth be to this gang,
And grace this noble company!

CAIAPHAS
Go back again from whence thou sprang
With sorrow; who sent after thee?

JUDAS
Sirs, if I hindered your harangue,
At your own bidding will I be.

PILATE
Go hence, harlot, high might thou hang!
Whence, in the devil's name, had we [thee?

JUDAS Good sir, I mean not you to grieve;
My venture then might not avail.

ANNAS Look, lad, thou should ask leave
To come amid such counsel.

JUDAS Sir, all your counsel well I ken;
Ye mean my master for to take.

ANNAS Ah ha! Here is one of his men.
That thus unwitting makes us wake.

PILATE Lay hands on him, and hurl him then
Among you for his master's sake;
For we have matters more than ten,
More troublesome far to undertake.

CAIAPHAS Set on him buffets sad,
His master to disgrace,
And teach ye such a lad
Better to know his place.

JUDAS Sir, my presence may both please and pay
To all the lords that gather here.

PILATE Out! Go hence in the devil's way!
We have no leisure time, I fear.

JUDAS The prophet that doth your power dis-
[may
With wondrous works where he draws
[near,
If ye will crush him as ye say,
His sale to you I will make clear.

PILATE Ah, sir, hark! What say you?
Let's see, and show thy skill.

JUDAS Sir, a bargain, I pray you
Buy it if ye will.

ANNAS What is thy name? Tell quick, no lie,
That we may know if you do wrong.

JUDAS Judas Iscariot, called am I,
That with the prophet have dwelled long.

PILATE
Sir, thou art a welcome ally!
Your purpose here now we would know.

JUDAS
Nought else but if ye will him buy;
Now tell me truly ere I go.

CAIAPHAS
Yes, friend, in faith will we,
Naught else; but heartily say
How that bargain may be,
And prompt we shall thee pay.

ANNAS
Judas, for to hold thee hale,
And for to ward off foul defame,
Look that thou vouchsafe this sale;
Then may thou be without a blame.

JUDAS
Sir, of my grief give ye no heed,
If once you bring him here to shame;
Following him I found no meed,
He certainly shall find the same.

CAIAPHAS
Sir Pilate, hear your fill,
Listen and lose nought,
Then may ye do your will
On him that ye have bought.

ANNAS
Yea, and then may we be bold
From all the folk to hold him free;
But keep him hard within our hold.
Right as one of your company.

PILATE
Now Judas, since he shall be sold,
How prize thou him? That say to me.

JUDAS
For thirty pennies truly told,
Or else may not that bargain be.
So much he made me lose
Maliciously and ill;
Therefore ye may now choose,
To buy or let be still.

ANNAS
Made he thee lose? I pray thee, why?
Tell us now promptly ere thou pass.

JUDAS
I shall straight tell without a lie,
Every word right as it was.

In Simon's house with him sat I
With other company that he has;
A woman came that fellow nigh,
Calling him "Lord", saying "alas!"

She wept that she had wrought
Always such sin and vice,
And an ointment she brought,
That precious was of price.

With tears she washed him in his seat,
And then dried him with her hair;
This ointment her dole to defeat,
Upon his head she put it there,
That it ran all about his feet;
It was a wonderful affair,
The house was full of odour sweet;
Then to speak might I not spare,

For certainly I had not seen
No ointment half as fine;
Thereat I split my spleen
To waste what was so fine.
I said it was worthy to sell
For three hundred pence as a present,
Which parted between us were well;
But would ye see what there I meant?
The tenth part, truly to tell,
To keep by me was my intent;
For of the treasure that to us fell,
The tenth part ever with me went;

And if three hundred be right told,
The tenth part is just thirty;
Right so he shall be sold;
Say if ye will him buy.

PILATE

Now certain, sir, thou sayst right well,
Since he tricked you with such a sleight,
Repay your wrong, your hurt now heal,
And for his fury have no fright.

ANNAS Sir, as you ask so shall we deal,
Here shall thou have what is your right;
But look that we no falsehood feel.

JUDAS Sir, my promise here I plight.
What I have spoken in my spite
I shall fulfil in deed,
And well more with my might,
In time when I see need.

PILATE Judas, of speaking thou must spare,
And chatter never, night nor day;
What we know make no man aware,
For fear of a far fiercer fray.

CAIAPHAS Meet us no more then, take good care;
We are well pleased, take there thy pay.

[*Giving him money.*

JUDAS He made me lose what was my share;
Now are we even for once and ay.

ANNAS This promise will not fail,
Thereof we may be glad;
Now were the best counsel,
In haste that we him had.

PILATE We shall him have, and so hie ye,
Full hastily here in this hall.
Sir knights that are of deeds doughty,
Stay never in stead nor stall,
But look ye bring him hastily,
That fellow false whate'er befall.

1ST SOLDIER Sir, be not abashed thereby,
For as ye bid, work shall we all.

[*All retire, then* JESUS *and his* DISCIPLES *advance.*

ST. JOHN The Passover, Sir, where will ye eat?
Tell us that we may dress your meat.

JESUS Go forth, John and Peter, to yon city;
When ye come there ye shall then see
Straightway in the street a man
Bearing water in a can;

The house he goes to greet,
Follow that ye may him meet;
The lord of that house ye shall find,
A simple man both meek and kind,
To him ye shall speak and say
That I come here by the way;
Say, I pray him, if his will be,
A little while to ease me,
That I and my disciples all
Might rest awhile within his hall,
Our Passover we may eat there.

PETER Lord, we shall hasten in our care,
Till that we come to that city;
Your Passover shall ordered be.

[*Then* JOHN *and* PETER *go to the city and meet a man.*

Sir, our master, the prophet,
Comes behind in the street;
A large room would he have, if you [please,
To eat and drink therein with ease.

PATERFAMILIAS Sirs, he is welcome unto me,
And so is all his company;
With all my heart and all my will
Is he welcome to stay his fill.
Lo, a chamber lies close here,
Wherein to keep your feasting cheer,
With rushes strewn, although well swept;
You shall see it neatly kept.

[*Then* JOHN *and* PETER *prepare the table.* JESUS *enters.*

JOHN Sir, your meat is ready with good cheer,
Will ye wash and sit down here?

JESUS Hand me the water, be content
To take the grace that God has sent;
Come forth each one with another,
If I be master I will be brother.

[*They eat together and* JUDAS *thrusts his hand into* JESUS' *dish.*

Judas, by this what mean you?

JUDAS Nothing, Lord, but to eat with you.

JESUS Eat on, brothers, I you pray,
For one of you shall me betray.

PETER Lord, whoever that be may,
Lord, I shall never thee betray.
Say, dear master, is it I?

JESUS Not thou, Peter, certainly.

JOHN Master, can I be he then?

JESUS Nay, not thou John, of all men.

ANDREW Master, is it I, that shrew?

JESUS Not thou, forsooth, Andrew.

SIMON Master, then can it be I?

JESUS Nay, not Simon, surely.

PHILIP Is it then I should do that deed?

JESUS Nay Philip, thou hast no need.

THADEUS Should I, Thadeus, betray thee?

JAMES Or we two James?

JESUS Nay, none of you is he;
But he that eats from my own dish,
My body's betrayal is his wish.

JUDAS What then, think ye me to name?

JESUS Thou sayst true, thou bearst the blame;
Each one of you shall this night
Forsake me, and well he might.

JOHN Now God forbid and take good heed
That never should we do that deed.

PETER If all, master, forsake thee,
Shall I never from thee flee.

JESUS Peter, thrice shalt thou deny me so,
And forsake me ere cock crow,
Take up this cloth, I go with you,
For we have other things to do.

[*Here he washes the* DISCIPLES' *feet.*

Sit all down here at your ease
I wash your feet upon my knees.

[*And taking water in a bowl he comes to* PETER.

PETER Lord, should thou kneel and wash my [feet?
My service, Lord, would be more meet.

JESUS Ye know not yet why I do so,
Peter, hereafter thou shalt know.

PETER Nay, master, now I thee implore
That thou wash our feet no more.

JESUS Unless I wash thee thou must miss
Part of me in heaven's bliss.

PETER Nay, Lord, before I that forgo,
Wash head, hands and feet also.

JESUS Ye are clean, but not all;
That shall be seen when time shall fall;
Who shall be washed as I mean,
He dare not wash his feet clean;
And forsooth clean are ye,
But not all as ye should be.
I shall tell you take good heed
Why that I have done this deed;
Ye call me master and Lord by name;
Ye say full well for so I am;
As doth your Lord and master kneel
To wash your feet, so ye must deal.
Now know ye well what I have done;
Example have I given you;
Look ye do the like, each one;
Each other's feet may ye wash too.

For he that servant is
In truth, I tell you,
Not more than his lord he is,
To whom service is due.

Before this night be gone,
Alone will ye leave me;
For in this night each one
From me away shall flee;

The shepherd when he is smitten,
The sheep shall flee away,
Be scattered wide and bitten;
Thus do the prophets say.

PETER Lord, if that I should die,
Forsake thee shall I nought.

JESUS Forsooth, Peter, to thee say I,
In so great dread thou shalt be brought

That ere the cock can have crowed twice,
Thrice shalt thou me deny.

PETER Never shall I, Lord, for no price;
Rather shall I with thee die.

JESUS Now look your heart be grieved nought,
Neither in dread nor woe;
But trust in God who hath you wrought,
And trust in me also;

In my father's house, indeed,
Is many a meet homestead
That hereafter as their meed
Men shall have when they are dead.

And here may I no longer bide
But I shall go before,
That your going I may guide
And bring you to that shore;

I shall come to you again,
And take you to me;
That wherever I remain,
Ye shall with me be.

I am the way, the path of truth,
The life that ever shall be;
And to my father comes none, forsooth,
Except they come through me.

I will not leave you all helpless,
As men without a friend,
As fatherless and motherless,
Though from you I must wend;

I shall come once to you again;
This world shall me not see,
But ye shall see me well certain,
And living shall I be.

And ye shall live in heaven;
Then shall ye know all this,
That I am in my father even,
And my father in me is.

And I in you, and ye in me,
And each man like thereto,
My commandment that keeps truly
And after it will do.

Now have ye heard what I have said;
I go and come again;
Be pleased this news to spread;
Your joy is not in vain.

For to my father I wend;
For more than I is he;
I let you know, as faithful friend,
Before that it shall be.

That ye may trust when it is done;
For indeed I may not now
Say certain things to anyone
Nor break that silence vow.

For the prince of this world comes herein,
But no power has he in me,
But as that all the world within
May both hear and see.

My love is to my father due,
Since he me hither sent,
And all things that I do
After his commandment.

Rise ye up each one,
And wend we on our way,
The path we may not shun,
To Olivet to pray.

Peter, James, and thou, John,
Rise up and follow me!

[*They go to Olivet.*

My time now comes anon;
Abide still here, ye three.

Pray here while ye have breath,
From the tempter God you save;
My soul is heavy unto death
To go down to the grave.

[*Then he shall pray, saying:*

Father, let this great pain be still,
And pass away from me;
But, father, not that my will,
But thine fulfilled may be.

[*He turns to the* DISCIPLES.

Simon, I say, sleepst thou?
Awake, I tell you all!
Satan assails you now
Into despair to fall.

But I shall pray my father too
That he may keep you clear
My spirit is depressed thereto,
My flesh is sick for fear.

[*He prays again.*

Father, thy son I was,
Of thee I ask this boon;
If this pain may not pass,
Father, at thy will soon.

[*He returns to the* DISCIPLES.

Ye sleep, brothers, still, I see,
It is for sorrow that ye do so;
Ye have so long wept for me
That ye are dazed and lapped in woe.

[*The third time he prays.*

Dear father, thou hear my will!
This passion thou put from me away;
And if my life I must needs spill,
I shall fulfil thy will today;

Therefore this bitter passion
If I may not put by,
My doom in humble fashion
I meet, for comfort sure is nigh.

GOD My comfort, son, I shall thee tell,
And give therefore the reason;
As Lucifer, for sin that fell,
Betrayed Eve with his false treason,
And Adam weakened to Eve's will;
The wicked spirit asked a boon
Which has irked mankind full ill;
These were the words he uttered soon:

All that came of Adam's stock
With the fiend should find their fate,
With him to dwell, a mirthless flock,
In pain that never shall abate.

Until a child might be born
Of a maiden whom none surpass,
As pure as petal in the morn,
As clean as silver or shining glass:
But soon when death dimmed that child's [sight
Himself he raised on the third day,
And entered heaven through his own [might.
To do this none but God may.

Since thou art man, and needs must die,
And as others go to hell;
But that were wrong without a lie.
That God's son there should dwell—
In pain with that unruly rout;
Ponder well, it must be plain,
When one is ransomed all shall out,
And saved be from their pain.

[JESUS *returns to pray; the* DISCIPLES *sleep.*

JESUS

Sleep ye now and take your rest!
My time is near at hand;
And I am near the traitor's nest,
Betrayed into the sinners' band.

PILATE

Peace! I command you curs remain
And stand as still as any stone!
In dungeon deep he shall find pain,
If any move or make a moan;

For I am governor of the law;
My name it is Pilate!
You I may happily hang or draw,
I stand in such estate,

To do what so I will,
And therefore peace I bid you all!
And look ye hold you still,
And with no beggars brawl.
Till we have done our deed,
Who so makes noise or cry,
His neck I shall make bleed,
With this I bear on high.

[*Showing his sword.*

For this traitor let us make,
That would destroy our law,
Judas, thou may it not forsake,
But my word keep in awe.

Think what thou hast done,
That hath thy master sold;

Time now this bargain were begun;
Thou hast thy money in thy hold.

JUDAS
Name ye knights to come with me,
Richly arrayed, sturdy and stout;
Then my pledge fulfilled shall be,
If such fellows be about.

PILATE
Whereby, Judas, should we him know,
If we work wisely, not amiss?
Some know him not for friend or foe.

JUDAS
Lay hands on him that I shall kiss.

PILATE
Have done, sir knights, make known your [strength,
And nimbly strike when you see need;
Seek over all both breadth and length!
Spare ye not but spur with speed!

We have sought him less and more,
His lodging could not learn;
Malcus, thou shalt go before,
And bear with thee a lantern.

MALCUS
Sir, this journey I undertake
With all my might and main,
If I should, for Mohammed's sake,
Here in this place be slain,
Christ that prophet for to take,
It shall be for our gain.
Our weapons look ye ready make,
To seize this strutting swain
This night.
Go we now on our way,
Our power for to sway;
Take what lanterns that we may,
And look they be alight.

2ND SOLDIER
Sir Pilate, prince peerless of all,
Made from most mighty men's mould,
We are ever more ready to come at thy [call,
And bow to thy bidding as bachelors [bold.

But that prince of apostles hold we in [scorn,
Men call him Christ, come down from [David's kin,
His life full soon shall be forlorn,
And easy victory we shall win,
And soon!
For, as ever I eat bread
Ere I stir from this stead,
I would strike off his head;
Lord, I ask that boon.

1ST SOLDIER That boon grant to our need,
And vengeance on him soon shall fall;
For we shall snare him with all speed;
God's son himself he shall not call.
We shall give him his true meed;
By Mohammed, god of all,
Such three knights boldly might succeed
To bind the devil as our thrall,
Indeed;
For a thousand were too few,
Prophets and apostles too,
Such before these two hands slew,
And bravely made them bleed.

PILATE Now courteous kaisers of Cain's kin,
Most gentle Jews that I may find,
My comfort from care may ye soon win,
That prophet if ye bring and bind.

But go ye hence speedily, spare not I im- [plore;
My friendship, my furtherance, shall still [with you be;
And Mohammed most mighty be gra- [cious evermore!
Come you safe and sound with that beg- [gar to me!
What place
Wherever ye wend,
Noble knights, your friend,

Sir Lucifer, the fiend,
May cheer you in the chase.

[*All retire,* JESUS *and his* DISCIPLES *advance.*

JESUS
Rise up, Peter, and go with me,
And follow me without a strife
Judas wakes, and sleeps not he;
He comes to betray me of my life.

Woe be to him that works such wrong!
He were better far his life forsake;
But come forth, Peter, you bide too long.
Lo, where they come that will me take!

JUDAS
Rest well, master, Jesus free!
That thou wouldst kiss me once, I pray;
I have come to succour thee;
Thou art espied, make no delay.

JESUS
Judas, thy part is overplayed!
Thinkst thou not I know thy will?
With kissing hast thou me betrayed:
That sometime shalt thou rue full ill.
[*to the* KNIGHTS]
Whom seek ye, sirs, by name?

2ND SOLDIER
We seek Jesus the Nazarene.

JESUS
I have not hid myself in shame;
Lo, I am here, the same ye mean;
Whom would ye with these weapons [maim?

1ST SOLDIER
To tell thee truth and not to lie,
We seek Jesus the Nazarene.

JESUS
I told you once that it was I.

MALCUS
Dare no man on him lay a hand?
I shall catch him if I may;
A flattering fool whom none withstand,
But now has come thy ending day.

PETER
I would be dead within short space
Ere I should see this sight!

[*Strikes* MALCUS.

Go, groan unto Sir Caiaphas,
And bid him do thee right!

MALCUS Alas, the time that I was born!
That ever I took breath!
My right ear I have forlorn!
Help, alas, I bleed to death!

JESUS Thou man, that moans thy hurt so sore,
Come hither, let me thy wound see;
Take thy ear that be off shore;
In nomine patris whole thou be!

MALCUS Now am I whole, healed is my ear,
My hurt is never the worse;
Therefore, fellows, draw me near!
Who spares him may the devil curse!

JESUS Therefore, Peter, I tell thee this,
In my book it must be written:
Put up thy sword nor do amiss,
For he that smites, he shall be smitten.

Ye knights that now are coming here,
Thus assembled in a rout,
As if a band of thieves ye fear,
With weapons circle me about;

Methinks, forsooth, ye do full ill
Thus for to seek me in the night:
But work on me your evil will,
Let not my fellows share my plight.

2ND SOLDIER Lead him forth fast by the gate!
Hanged be he that spares him ought!

[JESUS *is led to* PILATE.

1ST SOLDIER How think ye, sir Pilate,
About this wretch that we have brought?

PILATE Is he the self same prophet, say,
That has caused us this care?
It has been told now many a day,
His works all men declare.
It gave us a great woe

That Lazarus thou raised to life;
On sea men saw thee stalking go;
The maimed you heal both man and wife.
Thy deeds pass Caesar's by,
Or sir Herod, our King.

2ND SOLDIER Let's doom him fast to die,
And stop now for nothing.

1ST SOLDIER Since he against our law has spoke,
Let us hang him high up here.

PILATE I will not grant so swift a stroke,
A wiser course I shall make clear.

MALCUS A wiser course? The devil! How so?
And strengthen our grievance the more?
Should he in freedom thus forth go,
He would destroy our law.
Would ye all assent to me,
This bargain shall be quickly done;
Dead by night-time should he be,
For such a course votes everyone.

PILATE Peace, harlots, the devil you speed!
Would you thus privily murder a man?

MALCUS If every man to that agreed,
Let's hear spoken a better plan.

PILATE To Caiaphas' hall look fast ye work,
And thither right he shall be led;
He has the rule of holy kirk,
To doom him downright quick or dead;

For he has wrought against our law,
Sir Caiaphas has most craft thereon.

2ND SOLDIER Your order, sir, we hold in awe;
Come forth, good sirs, let us be gone.

MALCUS [*to* JESUS]
Step forth, thou art in our hand!
Thinkest thou ay to stand still?
Nay, lurking lubber, laws of the land
Shall fail, but we shall have our will;

Out of my hands shalt thou not pass
For all the craft thou can;
Till thou come to Sir Caiaphas,
Save thee shall no man.

[*All withdraw.*

THE TWENTY-SECOND PLAY

The Buffeting

1ST TORTURER	ANNAS
2ND TORTURER	JESUS
CAIAPHAS	FROWARD

1ST TORTURER Go forth there, ho! And trot on apace!
To Annas will we go and sir Caiaphas;
Know thou well of them two thou getst [not grace,
But everlasting woe for thy wilful trespass
So great.
Thy fate is to fare
Far worse in cruel care;
Thou hast been everywhere
False and fickle to the state.

2ND TORTURER It is a marvel to me thus to be going;
We have had for thee such a sharp sting- [ing;
But at last shall we be eased of our hearts' [longing;
By thee shall two or three heads be worth [the hanging;
No wonder!
Such mischief can thou make
Force the people forsake
Our laws, and thine take;
Thus art thou brought in blunder.

1ST TORTURER Gainsay this thou mayn't, if thou be true;
Some men hold thee a saint, and that shalt [thou rue;
Fair words can thou paint, and lay down [laws new.

2ND TORTURER Now be ye attaint, for we will pursue
This matter.
Many words hast thou said,
Many men hast misled,
As good had thou instead
Left off thy clatter.

1ST TORTURER Better to sit still than rise up and fall;
Thou has long had thy will and made
[many a brawl;
At the last would thou kill and ruin us all,
If we did never ill.

2ND TORTURER I trust not, he shall
Endure it:
For if other men abuse him,
We shall accuse him,
Himself shall not excuse him;
To you I assure it,

With my allegiance.

1ST TORTURER He would sleep in a twink,
By the cast of his countenance, I say as I
[think.

2ND TORTURER He has done us grievance, therefore shall
[he drink;
And come to much mischance; we sweat
[till we stink,
For walking,
That scarce may I more.

1ST TORTURER Peace, here is the door!
I shall walk in before,
And tell of his talking.

[*They come to* CAIAPHAS *and* ANNAS.

Hail, sirs, as ye sit, on those worthy
[thrones!
Why ask ye not yet how fared have your
[crones?

2ND TORTURER Sir, bitterly we admit all weary are our
[bones;

Our quest we did not quit, though with [great groans
We tarried.

CAIAPHAS Say, were ye put in dread?
Were ye ought misled?
In such a strait, ye said?
Sirs, which of you miscarried?

ANNAS Say, were ye ought in doubt for lack of [light
As ye there watched out?

1ST TORTURER Sir, as I am true knight,
Since as babe I learnt to shout, had I [never such a night;
My eyes were kept throughout watching [right
Since morn,
But yet it was well spent,
This traitor to present
To you, sir, as we meant,
Who gave so great scorn.

CAIAPHAS Can ye him now impeach? Fled his men [for fear?

2ND TORTURER He has been used to preach for full [many a year;
And to the people teach a new law.

1ST TORTURER Sirs, hear!
So far as his wit may reach many lend an [ear;
When we took him,
In a garden we him found,
My sword I swung around,
His disciples to confound,
And soon they forsook him.

2ND TORTURER Sir, he said he could destroy too our tem- [ple so gay,
And once more build anew on the third [day.

CAIAPHAS How might that be true? It took much to [array,
The masons I knew that built it, I say,
So wise,
That hewed every stone.

1ST TORTURER Good sir, let him alone;
He lies for the whetstone,
I give him the prize.

2ND TORTURER The halt runs, the blind sees, through his [false wiles;
Thus gets he many fees of them he be- [guiles.

1ST TORTURER Dead men he raised with ease; folk come [from many miles;
And ever through his sorceries our Sabbath [day defiles
Evermore, sir.

2ND TORTURER This is his wont and custom,
To heal the deaf and dumb,
Wheresoever he come;
I told you before, sir.

1ST TORTURER Men call him prophet, king, and God's [son, the same;
Down gladly would he bring our laws to [ill fame.

2ND TORTURER Yet is there another thing that I heard [him declaim;
He sets not a flea's wing, by sir Caesar's [great name;
He says thus;
Sir, this same is he
That excused with his subtlety
A woman in adultery;
Full well may ye trust us.

1ST TORTURER Sir Lazarus he could raise, back his breath [he gave,
When he had lain four days dead in his [grave,

All men him praise, both master and [knave,
Such his witchcraft ways.

2ND TORTURER If us he brave
Much longer,
Curse him we can,
For turning many a man;
Since the time he began,
Our hate is the stronger.

1ST TORTURER He will not believe it though he be culpa- [ble;
Men call him a prophet, a lord most nota- [ble,
Sir Caiaphas, by my wit, he should be [damnable,
But would ye two, as ye sit, make it firm [and stable
Together;
For ye two held in awe,
May defend all our law;
To you therefore we draw,
And bring this wretch hither.

2ND TORTURER Sir, I can tell you before, as might I be [married,
If he reign any more our laws be mis- [carried.

1ST TORTURER Sir, his works we deplore, his power should [be parried;
We may not ignore where he has long [tarried
And walked.
His cheer is misbegotten
There is something forgotten,
I shall thrust out what's rotten,
Before we have talked.

CAIAPHAS Now fair you befall for your talking!
For certain I myself shall make an exam- [ining.

Hearest thou, harlot, of all? For care mayst
[thou sing!

[*to* JESUS]

How durst thou thee call either emperor
[or king?

I defy thee!
What the devil dost thou hear?
That claim will cause thee fear;
Come whisper in my ear,
Or I shall decry thee.

An ill hour wast thou born! Hark! Says he
[nought still?
Thou shalt before morn be glad to say thy
[fill.
This is a great scorn your tricks to fulfil;
Wolf's-head I thee warn we have thee at
[will
Vile traitor!
Thou might say something with ease,
It might our rage appease,
Et omnis qui tacet
Hic consentire videtur.

Speak but one word, now in the devil's
[name!
Was thy sire abroad when he met with
[thy dame?
What neither booted nor spurred and a
[lord of some fame!
Speak on for a turd, the devil give thee
[shame,
Sir Sibree!
Indeed, if thou wert King,
Yet might thou be riding;
Fie on thee, foundling!
Thou livest but by bribery.

Lad, I am a prelate, a lord of degree,
I sit in great state as thou may see,
Knights may on me wait of divers degree;

Thy pride shall abate, thou shalt kneel on
[thy knee
In my presence;
As ever sing I mass,
Whoso keeps the law has
By profession a mass
More than his land's rents.

The devil give thee shame that ever I knew
[thee!
Neither blind nor lame will none pursue
[thee;
Therefore I shall thee name that ever shall
[rue thee,
King Coppin in our game, thus shall I in-
[due thee,
Impostor.
Say, to speak art thou afeared?
I will not be thus fleered,
Alack! The devil's dirt in thy beard,
Vile false traitor!

Whatso thy quirks betoken, yet still thou
[might say, mum;
Great words hast thou spoken, then wast
[thou not dumb;
Be it whole word or broken, come, out
[with some,
Lest my rage be awoken, or thy death the
[outcome
Of all.
Either thou hast no wit,
Or stopped your ears to it;
Why but hear you not yet,
So I cry and bawl?

ANNAS Ah, sir be not ill-paid, though he answer
[not;
He is inwardly afraid, his reason may rot.

CAIAPHAS But the words he has said make me fear
[a plot.

ANNAS At his trial none will him aid.

CAIAPHAS That shall not be forgot.

ANNAS May this ease you.

CAIAPHAS Now foul might him befall!

ANNAS Sir, ye are vexed at all,
And peradventure he shall
Hereafter please you.
By law we may though examine him first.

CAIAPHAS Unless I give him a blow, my heart will [burst.

ANNAS Abide till ye his purpose know.

CAIAPHAS But thrust out I durst
Both his eyes in a row.

ANNAS Sir, be not athirst
For vengeance.
But let me oppose him.

CAIAPHAS Yea, with death to depose him.

ANNAS Sir, we may not dispose him,
But be damned for mischance.

CAIAPHAS He deserves to be dead, a king himself [called;
Out! Let me strike off his head!

ANNAS No! Be ye forestalled;
Sir, heed what is said, be not so galled.

CAIAPHAS Shall I never eat bread till he be installed
In the stocks.

ANNAS Sir, speak soft and still;
Let us do as the law will.

CAIAPHAS Nay, I myself shall him kill,
And murder with knocks.

ANNAS Sir, think ye that ye are a man of holy [kirk,
Ye should be our teacher meekness to [work.

CAIAPHAS Yea, but he sticks like a burr on my heart
[it to irk.

ANNAS Softly to go is farthest to stir, our laws are
[not murk,
I mean;
Your words are rambusteous,
Et hoc nos volumus
Quod de jure possumus:
What comes will be seen.

It is best that we treat him with fairness.

CAIAPHAS But, nay!

ANNAS And so we might get him some word for to
[say.

CAIAPHAS Alack! Let me beat him!

ANNAS Come, sir, away!
For if thus ye meet him, he speaks not this
[day;
But hear:
If he cease and abide,
I shall take him aside
And inquire of his pride,
How he brings folk cheer.

CAIAPHAS He has robbed over long with all his false
[lies,
And done us great wrong, sir Caesar he
[defies;
To hang him I long before I arise.

ANNAS Sir, the law is so strong, his fate he can
[no wise
Avert.
But first would I hear
What he would answer;
Except his crimes be clear
How can we do him hurt?

And therefore examining first will I make,
Since he calls himself a king.

CAIAPHAS Save he that forsake,
I shall give him a wring that his neck shall [break.

ANNAS Sir, ye may not him ding, no word yet he [spake,
That I know.
Hark, fellow, stand there!
[*to* JESUS]
Hast thou never a care?
I marvel that thou dare
Thyself endanger so.

But I shall do as the law will if the people [abuse thee;
Say, did thou do this ill? Can thou ought [excuse thee?
Why standest thou so still, when men thus [accuse thee?
For to hang on a hill hark how they use [thee
To damn.
Say, the God of heaven's son art thou,
As thou art wont to avow?

JESUS So thou sayest even now,
And right so I am;

For after this shalt thou see when that I [come down
From heaven shining brightly in the clouds [that form my gown.

CAIAPHAS Ah, ill might the feet be that brought thee [to town!
To die thou art worthy! Say, thief, where [is thy crown?

ANNAS Abide sir,
Let us lawfully redress.

CAIAPHAS We need no witness,
If thus he express;
Why should I not chide, sir?

ANNAS Was there never man so wicked but he
[might amend.
When it comes to the prick it is better to
[bend.

CAIAPHAS Nay, sir, but I shall him stick even with
[my own hand:
For if he rob and stay quick we are at an
[end,
And damned!
Therefore while I have breath,
Let me put him to death.

ANNAS *Sed nobis non licet*
Interficere quemquam.

Sir ye know better than I, we should slay
[no man.

CAIAPHAS His deeds I defy, curse his works we can
And that he shall abuy.

ANNAS Nay, but by another plan,
And do it lawfully.

CAIAPHAS As how?

ANNAS Tell you I can.

CAIAPHAS Let's see.

ANNAS Sir, take heed of my saws;
Men of temporal laws
They may judge such a cause,
But so may not we.

CAIAPHAS My heart is full cold, yet I almost melt;
For the tales that are told, I burst out of
[my belt,
It scarcely can hold my body, if ye it felt;
Yet would I give my gold yon traitor to
[pelt
For ever.

ANNAS Sir, do as ye said to me.

CAIAPHAS What if he overthrew me?
Sir Annas, if ye undo me
Forgive I you never.

ANNAS Sir, ye are a prelate.

CAIAPHAS So may I well seem,
Myself if I say it.

ANNAS It does not beseem
Such men of estate so fierce to have been;
But send him to Pilate in temporal law [supreme
Is he;
He may best greet him,
Rebuff and ill-treat him;
You need not to beat him
Therefore, sir, let be.

CAIAPHAS Fie on him, beware! I am out of my gate;
Say why stands he so far.

ANNAS Sir, he came but late.

CAIAPHAS No, but I have knights that dare rap him [on the pate.

ANNAS Ye need but to scare, be calm and abate,
Good sir.
Why spend you your spite?
What need you to fight?
If yon man you smite,
You are irregular.

CAIAPHAS He that first made me clerk and taught me [of prayer
To browse in books dark, the devil give [him care!

ANNAS Ah, good sir, hark! Such words might ye [spare.

CAIAPHAS Else had I left my mark on yon noisome [nightmare,
Perdy!
But ere he go I would

This were done for my good,
That some knights knock his hood
With knocks two or three.

For since he has trespassed and broken [our law,
Let us make him aghast and set him in [awe.

ANNAS Sir, as ye have asked, so I you assure.
Come make ready fast, ye knights now [draw
Your armament;
And that king to you take,
And with knocks make him wake.

CAIAPHAS Yea, sirs, and for my sake
Give him good payment.

For if I joined your ring as I would that [I might,
I should vow by the king that once before [midnight
I should make his head sing where that I [hit right.

1ST TORTURER Sir, fear you nothing, nor at him take af- [fright
Today,
For we shall so rock him
And with buffets knock him.

CAIAPHAS Then look that ye lock him
That he run not away.

Bide for no benefit if that lad be fled.

2ND TORTURER Sir, on us be it, but we'll clout well his [head.

CAIAPHAS If ye beat as ye boast it would soon ding [him dead.

1ST TORTURER See, see ye and sit, how our blows have [sped.
Hold fast,

But ere we do this thing,
Bless us, lord, with thy ring.

CAIAPHAS Now they shall have blessing
Who best buffets cast.

2ND TORTURER Go we now to our trade with this fond fool.

1ST TORTURER He shall learn how is played a new play [for Yule.
And find himself flayed. Froward, a stool
Go fetch us!

FROWARD Ye jade! Let me overrule;
Let him rough it.
For the woe that he shall see
Let him kneel on his knee.

2ND TORTURER And so shall he for me;
Go fetch us a light buffet.

FROWARD Why must he sit soft who made such mis- [chance
That has vexed us so oft?

1ST TORTURER Sir, at this prank we prance;
If he stood up aloft, we must hop and [dance
As cocks in a croft.

FROWARD Now a vengeance
Come on him!
Good skill do ye show,
As I by my blow;
Take this, bear it, so!
Soon all fall upon him.

2ND TORTURER Come, sir, and sit down, must ye be [prayed?
Like a lord of renown; your seat is arrayed.

1ST TORTURER We shall prove on his crown the words he [has said.

2ND TORTURER There is none in this town, I trust, be ill- [paid
For his sorrow,
But the father that him got.

1ST TORTURER Now truly I know not
But his kin have forgot
His body to borrow.

2ND TORTURER I would we got onward.

1ST TORTURER But his eyes must be hid.

2ND TORTURER But if they be well sparred we lost what [we did;
Step forth thou, Froward!

FROWARD Now what would you bid?

1ST TORTURER Thou art ever in the rearward.

FROWARD Must none be chid
But me?
My ill luck I bewail.

2ND TORTURER Thou must get us a veil.

FROWARD It is ever the old tale.

1ST TORTURER Ill luck light on thee!
Well had thou thy name for thou wast [ever curst.

FROWARD Sir, I might say the same to you if I durst;
Yet my hire may I claim, no penny I [pursed;
I have had great shame, hunger and thirst,
In your service.

1ST TORTURER Not one word so bold!

FROWARD Why, it is true that I told!
The proof I still hold.

2ND TORTURER At the church porch tell this.

FROWARD Here a veil have I found, I trust it will last.

1ST TORTURER Good son, hand it round, it is just what I [asked.

FROWARD How should it be bound?

2ND TORTURER About his head cast.

1ST TORTURER Yea, and when it is well wound, knit a [knot fast,
As I said.

FROWARD Is it well?

2ND TORTURER Yea, knave.

FROWARD What, think ye that I rave?
Christ's curse might he have
That last bound his head!

1ST TORTURER Now since he is blindfold I must begin,
And thus was I counselled the mastery to [win.

2ND TORTURER Nay, wrong hast thou told thus should [thou come in!

FROWARD I stand and behold, ye touch not the skin,
I feel.

1ST TORTURER How will thou I do?

2ND TORTURER In this manner too!

FROWARD Yea, ye give him his due,
There starts up a weal.

1ST TORTURER Thus we him bereave of all his fond tales.

2ND TORTURER Thy fist fails to grieve or else thy heart [fails.

FROWARD I can my hand upheave and upset the [scales.

1ST TORTURER God forbid then ye leave but set in your [nails
As you thrust.
Sit up and prophesy.

FROWARD But tell us no lie.

2ND TORTURER Who smote thee last?

1ST TORTURER Was it I?

FROWARD He knows not, I trust.

1ST TORTURER Fast to Sir Caiaphas go we together.

2ND TORTURER Rise up with ill grace so come thou hither.

FROWARD It seems by his pace he grudges to go [thither.

1ST TORTURER We have given him a glaze that, ye may [consider,
Will keep.

2ND TORTURER Sir, for his great boast,
He looks more like a ghost.

FROWARD In faith, sir, we had almost
Knocked him to sleep.

CAIAPHAS Now since he is well beat, pass through [the gate,
And tell of this cheat to sir Pilate;
He sits in the judge's seat among men of [state,
Make haste I entreat.

1ST TORTURER Come forth, old crate,
Look alive!
We shall lead thee a trot.

2ND TORTURER Lift thy feet mayst thou not,

FROWARD Then no task I have got
But come after and drive.

CAIAPHAS Alas, now take I heed!

ANNAS Why mourn ye so?

CAIAPHAS In fear I proceed, in wonder and woe,
Lest Pilate for meed, let Jesus go;
But had I slain him indeed with my hands [at a blow,
At once,
All then had been quit;
But gifts many men admit,
If he dare him acquit,
The devil have his bones!

Sir Annas, thou art to blame, for had ye [not been,

I had made him full tame, yea struck him [I mean,
To the heart so to maim, with this dagger [so keen.

ANNAS Sir, feel you no shame to use words so [unclean
To men?

CAIAPHAS I will not stay in this stead,
But spy how they him led,
And pursue till he is dead.
Farewell! We go, then.

THE TWENTY-THIRD PLAY

The Scourging

PILATE	JESUS
1ST TORTURER	JOHN
2ND TORTURER	MARY
3RD TORTURER	MARY MAGDALENE
1ST COUNSELLOR	MARY JACOBI
2ND COUNSELLOR	SIMON

PILATE

Peace at my bidding, be tame as ye are [told!
Look none be so hardy to speak word but I,
Or by Mohammed most mighty, my force [shall unfold,
With this brand that I bear ye shall bitterly [abuy.
Say, know ye not I am Pilate, peerless to [behold?
Most doughty in deeds of all dukes of [Jewry;
At beguiling in battles I am the most bold,
Therefore my name is not, surely,
Amiss.
I am full of subtlety,
Falsehood, guile, and treachery;
Therefore I am named by clergy
As *mali actoris*.

For like as on both sides of iron the ham- [mer makes it plane,
So do I that have here the law in my [keeping,
The right side to succour certain I am full [fain,

If I may get thereby advantage or winning;
Then to the false part I turn me again,
For I see the bribes I'm offered are sur-
[prising;
Thus every man should fear I cause him
[pain,
And all faint-hearted fellows be me
[obeying,
Truly.
All false indictors,
Inquesters and jurors,
All such outriders
Are welcome to me.

Now this prophet, that has preached and
[published so plain
Christian law, Christ they call him in our
[country;
But our princes full proudly this night have
[him ta'en,
Full soon to be damned he shall be hurled
[before me;
I shall seem him to favour as friend, most
[certain,
And show him fair countenance and words
[of vanity,
But ere this very night on cross shall he be
[slain,
Thus against him in my heart I bear great
[enmity
Full sore.
Ye men that use back-bitings,
And seethe with slanderings,
Ye are my dear darlings,
And Mohammed's for evermore.

For nothing in this world does me more
[grieve
Than to hear of Christ and of his new laws;
To know he were God's son my heart
[would crack and cleave,

Though he be true in deed and word, that
[thought me awes;
Therefore shall he suffer of me much
[mischief,
And every disciple that unto him draws;
For above any solace it lightens my grief
Christian blood to be shedding, that Jewry
[adores,
I avow.
My knights now so strong,
Will their strength show ere long,
If they tarry they do wrong;
Lo, where they come now!

1ST TORTURER I have run till I sweat from sir Herod our
[King
With this man that will let our laws come
[to nothing;
Our mercy must be forfeit, of care may he
[sing:
He is doomed by sir Pilate to get an ill
[ending
And sore;
The great works he has wrought
Shall serve him as nought,
But they be dearly bought
Believe me no more.

But make room in this pass and lest there
[be strife,
Your noise ye now cease, both man and
[wife;
To sir Pilate on daïs this man will we
[drive,
His death gives us peace, so we rob him
[of life
This day;
Go draw him forward!
Why stand ye so backward?
Come on, sir, hitherward,
As fast as ye may!

2ND TORTURER Go, pull him apace while we are going;
I shall spit in his face though it be fair [shining;
Of us three getst thou no grace, thou art [so annoying,
The more thy disgrace our mirth is in- [creasing,
No lack.
Fellows, with a quick cast,
With this band that will last
Let us bind him fast,
Both hands behind his back.

3RD TORTURER I shall lead thee a dance unto sir Pilate's [hall;
Thou fell on ill chance to come among us [all.
Sir Pilate, with your chieftains, to you we [cry and call
That ye make some ordinance for this [wretched thrall,
With skill;
This man we have led
On cross ye kill him dead.

PILATE What! Without more said?
That is not my will;

But ye, wisest of law, attend as ye stand;
This man without awe which ye lead in a [band,
In word or deed I saw no wrong to [reprimand,
Why here ye should him draw or bear [falsely in hand
With ill.
Ye say he turns our people,
Ye call him false and fickle.
To see his life-blood trickle
With shame should you fill.

Of all causes ye have shown which ye put [on him;

Herod, true as any stone, could find no
[fault in him;
Nothing was known that signified a sin;
Why should I then be prone further to pry
[therein?
Therefore
This is my counsel,
I will not with him meddle;
Let him go where he will
For now and evermore.

1ST COUNSELLOR Sir, I tell thee one thing, and not amiss,
He calls himself a king when none he is
Thus down would he bring our laws by
[this,
With his false lying, we cannot dismiss
This rebel.

PILATE Hark, fellow, come near!
Thou knowest I have power
To excuse or damn thee here,
And house thee ay in hell.

JESUS Such power hast thou nought to work thy
[will thus with me,
But from my father that is brought, one-
[fold God in persons three.

PILATE Certain, it comes well into my thought, at
[this time as well know ye,
A thief that any felony has wrought, him
[let we escape or go free
Away;
Therefore ye let him pass.

1ST TORTURER Nay, nay, but Barabbas!
And Jesus in this case
To death ye damn this day.

PILATE Sirs, look ye take good heed, strip his dress
[without ado,
His body make ye bleed, and beat him
[black and blue.

2ND TORTURER This man, as might I speed, that brought
[us bane anew,
Now "judicare" comes in the creed, that
[lesson he shall rue,
And his cause.
Bind him to this pillar.

3RD TORTURER Why standest thou so far?

1ST TORTURER To beat his body bare,
Without a pause.

2ND TORTURER Now fall I the first to flap on his hide.

3RD TORTURER My heart would near burst till his body I
[chide.

1ST TORTURER A glad swipe, if I durst, would I lend thee
[this tide.

2ND TORTURER No, I am athirst to see the blood down
[glide
So quick.

3RD TORTURER Have at!

1ST TORTURER Take thou that!

2ND TORTURER I shall knock thee flat,
So strong is my trick.

3RD TORTURER Where now serves thy prophecy, thou tell
[us in this case,
And all thy works of great mastery thou
[showed in divers place?

1ST TORTURER Thy apostles full readily ran swiftly from
[the race,
Thou art here in our custody without a
[hope of grace
Or escape.

2ND TORTURER Go, thrash him!

3RD TORTURER And slash him!

1ST TORTURER Nay, I myself should smash him
But for Sir Pilate.

Sirs, at the feast of Architreclyn this
[prophet had a place,
There turned he water into wine, that day
[he had such grace,
That made to him some men incline, and
[others sought his face;
The sea he lived by as a sign it let him
[walk thereon apace
At will;
The elements were seen,
The winds that are so keen
And the firmament I mean,
His bidding to fulfil.

2ND TORTURER A leper came full fast to this man that
[here stands,
And prayed him in all haste from bale to
[loose his bands,
His trouble was not waste though he came
[from far lands;
This prophet to him passed and healed him
[with his hands,
Full glad.
The son of the centurion,
For whom his father made great moan,
Of the palsy he healed anon,
For that much praise he had.

3RD TORTURER Sirs, as he came from Jericho, a blind man
[sat by the way;
To this wretch amid the rout thus crying
[did he say,
"Thou son of David ere thou go of blind-
[ness heal thou me this day."
There was he healed of all his woe, such
[wonders can he work alway
At will;
He raises men from death to life,
And casts out devils that stir up strife;
He soothes the sickness that is rife,
He heals them all of ill.

1ST TORTURER For all these deeds of great loving, four
[things have I found, certainly
For which he is worthy to hang: one is our
[king that he would be;
Our Sabbath day finds him working, not
[resting to heal the sick, truly;
He says our temple he shall down bring,
[and in three days build it on high
All whole again;
Sir Pilate, as ye sit,
Look wisely to your wit,
Damn Jesus ere ye flit,
On cross to suffer pain.

PILATE Thou man that suffers all this ill, why will
[thou us no mercy cry?
Humble thy heart and thy high will whilst
[that we have mastery!
In such great works show us thy skill; men
[call thee king, thou tell us why;
Wherefore the Jews seek thee to kill, the
[cause I would know certainly,
Inform me.
Say what is thy name,
Feel thou no shame?
They put on thee great blame,
Else might thou escape from me.

2ND TORTURER Sir Pilate, prince peerless, hear what is
[said,
That he escape not harmless but ye doom
[him dead:
He calls himself king in every place, thus
[has he misled
Our people for a space, and might our laws
[down tread
In all.
Sir, your knights count it loss
Save to the people you him toss
To hang him high upon a cross,
For that they cry and call.

PILATE Now, sure this is a wondrous thing that ye
[would bring to nought
Him that is your liege lording; in faith,
[this was far sought;
But say, why be ye not obeying him whom
[all has wrought?

3RD TORTURER Sir Caesar is our chief lording, sitting in his
[Roman court
So bold.
Pilate, do after us,
And damn to death Jesus,
Or to sir Caesar we'll shift us,
And make thy friendship cold.

PILATE Now that I am blameless of this blood shall
[ye see;
Both my hands expressly washed now shall
[be;
This blood is dear bought, I guess, that ye
[spill so free.

1ST TORTURER We pray it fall endless on us and our
[company
For ever.

PILATE Now your desire I give you all
Away you may him haul,
On cross to put that thrall,
His life there to sever.

1ST TORTURER Come on! Trip on thy toes, without any
[feigning;
Fulsome lying arose from thy false talking.

2ND TORTURER Much praise be to those that thus have
[brought a king
From sir Pilate and other foes thus into our
[ring
Without delay.
Sirs, he calls himself king,
So a crown is the thing.

3RD TORTURER I swear by everything
I shall make one this day.

1ST TORTURER Lo! here a crown of thorn to burn his brain [within,
Put on his head with scorn and spear it [through the skin.

2ND TORTURER Hail King! Where wast thou born, such [worship for to win?
We kneel night and morn our service to [begin,
That be thou bold;
Now by Mohammed's blood!
No meat will do me good
Till he be hanged on rood,
And his bones be cold.

1ST TORTURER Sirs, we may be fain for I have found a [tree,
I tell you for certain it is of great beauty,
On which he shall suffer pain, fastened by [nails three,
There shall he nothing gain thereon till [dead he be,
Surely, say I.
Go bring him hence.

2ND TORTURER Then heave our gear thence.

3RD TORTURER I would spend all my pence
To see him hang high.

1ST TORTURER This cross up thou take though it break [every bone,
Without grudging betake thee through the [town on thy own;
Mary, thy mother, I know will make great mourning and moan,
But for thy false deeds' sake shalt thou be [slain alone,
No nay;
The people of Bedlem,
And gentles of Jerusalem,
All the commoners of this realm,
Shall wonder on this day.

[JOHN *and the* HOLY WOMEN *appear in another part.*

JOHN THE APOSTLE
Alas! For my master most of might,
That yester-even with lantern bright
Before Caiaphas was brought;
Both Peter and I saw that sight,
And after we fled away in fright,
When the cruel Jews him caught;
At morn among them was said false wit-
[ness should be sought,
Who might condemn him dead that no
[wrong had wrought.

Alas! For his mother that this must know,
My mother and her sister also,
Sat together sighing sore;
They knew nothing of all this woe,
Therefore to tell them will I go,
Since I may mend no more.
If he should die thus soon and they not
[know before,
They may me then impugn; I will go fast
[therefore.

[*Goes to the* WOMEN.

God save you, sisters together!
Dear lady, if thy will were,
I must tell tidings plain.

MARY
Welcome, John, my cousin dear!
How fares my son since thou wast here?
What peace to ease my pain?

JOHN
Ah, dear lady, with your leave the truth
[must still remain,
At God's will never grieve.

MARY
Why, John, is my son slain?

JOHN
Nay, lady, I said not so,
But bear in mind he told us two
And them that with us were,
How he in pain from us should go,

And again should come to us so
 To amend our signing sore;
Avails it not instead for you to weep [therefore.

MARY MAGDALENE Alas! This day for dread! Good John, name [this no more!

Speak privily I thee pray,
I fear if she be told this fray,
 That she will run and rave.

JOHN The truth behoves I needs must say,
He is doomed to death this day,
 No sorrow may him save.

MARY JACOBI Good John, tell unto us two what thou of [her will crave,
And We will gladly go and help what thou [wouldst have.

JOHN Sisters, your mourning may not this amend;
If once ye would before his end,
 Speak with my master free,
Then must ye rise and with me wend
To find him who has been your friend,
 Beyond this same city;
With me if ye draw near, come fast and [follow me.

MARY Ah, help me, sisters dear! That I my son [may see.

MARY MAGDALENE Lady, we would ease your pain,
Heartily, with might and main,
 Your comfort to compose.

MARY Go, John, before and ascertain.

JOHN Lo, where he comes to us again
 And round him flock his foes!
Weeping is in vain, no tear may give him [now repose.

MARY Alas, for my son dear, that me as mother [chose!

[*They meet* JESUS.

Alas dear son for care, I see thy body [bleed;
My life for thee I'd spare or for thy pardon [plead,
This cross on my shoulder bear to help thee [in thy need,
Though it bring me deep despair, whither [they will thee lead.

JESUS This cross is large in length and rough to [hold withal;
If thou put to thy strength, to the earth [thou must down fall.

MARY Ah, dear son, thou let me help thee in this [case!

[*And he shall incline the cross to his* MOTHER.

JESUS Lo, mother, I tell it thee, thou might not [for one pace.

MARY I pray thee, dear son, it may so be, to man [thou givest thy grace,
On thyself thou have pity, and now thy [foes outface.

JESUS Mother, there is no other way but death [upon the tree,
And from death rise on the third day, thus [prophets say of me;
Man's soul that I loved ay, I shall redeem [surely,
Unto bliss of heaven for ay, I shall bring [it to me.

MARY MAGDALENE It is to all a sorrowful sight Jesus with [these Jews to see,
Here set in such a painful plight, my wail- [ing will I not let be.

MARY JACOBI This lord that is of might, did never ill [truly,

These Jews they do not right if condemned
[to die is he.

MARY MAGDALENE Alas! What shall we say! Jesus our so dear
[chief,
To death these Jews this day lead him in
[unbelief.

MARY JACOBI He was full true I say, though they damn
[him as a thief,
Mankind he loved alway; my heart will
[crack for grief.

JESUS Ye daughters of Jerusalem, I bid you weep
[no more for me,
But for yourselves and your children, be-
[hold I tell you surely,
With pains this realm shall teem in days
[hereafter for to be;
Your mirth to misery shall stream in every
[place of this city.

Children, blessed be they indeed, women
[that no children bear,
And the breasts that gave no suck, so heavy
[their heart with care;
The mountains high and these great hills
[shall fall upon them there,
For my blood that guiltless spills will bring
[my foes despair.

2ND TORTURER Walk on, and leave thy vain carping, it
[will not save thee from thy death,
Whether these women cry or sing, for sav-
[ing thee they waste their breath.

3RD TORTURER Say why do we hang thus here about,
And hear these harlots scream and shout?
Will no man change their cheer?

1ST TORTURER Get home and howl whore, with that clout!
Or, by the Lord I'll lay about,
Thou shalt abuy it dear.

MARY MAGDALENE
This deed shall vengeance call on you all [together.

2ND TORTURER
Go, hurry hence withal, or bide a beating [here!

3RD TORTURER
Let all this bickering be, since our toils are [before;
This traitor and this tree I would we were [fain there.

2ND TORTURER
No further can he fetch this cross that [gives him care,
But yonder comes a wretch shall help him [it to bear.

[*Enter* SIMON *of Cyrene*.

Thereof shall we soon make assay.
Hark, good man, whither lies thy way?
Thy striding shows no sloth.

SIMON
Sirs, I have a great journey
That must be done this same day,
Or harm comes, by my troth.

3RD TORTURER
Thou may with little pain ease him and [thyself both.

SIMON
Good sirs, I gladly would remain, but to [tarry I am loth.

1ST TORTURER
Nay, nay! Thou shalt full soon be sped;
Lo here's a lad that must be led
For his ill deeds to die,
And he is bruised and long has bled,
Such are our straits as I have said;
So, sir, do not deny,
That thou wilt take this tree to bear to [Calvary.

SIMON
Good sirs, that may not be, for full great [haste have I,
Though I would grant your boon.

2ND TORTURER
In faith, thou shalt not go so soon
For nought that thou can say

This may not be eschewn,
And this churl dead by noon,
And now is near midday;
Help therefore in our need and make no [more delay.

SIMON I pray you do your deed and let me go my [way;
And I shall come full soon again,
To help this man with might and main,
At your own will.

2ND TORTURER Once gone thou comest not again!
Nay, fellow, thou shalt be fain,
Our bidding to fulfil;
Or by Mohammed's renown thou shalt [find it ill.

1ST TORTURER Quick, ding this dastard down, if stubborn [he be still.

SIMON Indeed it were unwisely wrought,
To beat me save I trespassed ought
Either in word or deed.

2ND TORTURER Upon thy back it shall be brought,
Bear it whether thou will or nought!
The devil! Whom should we heed?
Take it therefore, on thy life, and bear it [with good speed.

SIMON Now here avails no strife, to bear it then I [need;
And therefore, sirs, I lend my aid;
As ye have said, I am well paid,
This man his pain to spare.

3RD TORTURER Ah, ha! Now are we right arrayed,
But look our gear be ready laid,
For work when we come there.

1ST TORTURER I warrant all ready, of our tools there's no [loss.
Now sir Simon truly, bear before us the [cross.

By Mohammed, our heaven's king,
I would that we were in that stead
Where on the cross we might him bring
Step on before, let him be led
  Apace.
Come on, thou!

2ND TORTURER Step forth, thou!

3RD TORTURER I come fast now,
  And follow in the chase.

[*The procession goes off.*

THE TWENTY-FOURTH PLAY

The Hanging of Judas

JUDAS Alas, alas, and welaway!
Accursed caitiff I have been ay;
I slew my father, and after lay
With my mother;
And later, falsely, did betray
My own master.

My father's name was Reuben, right;
Sibaria my mother bright;
He knew her once upon a night
In fleshly wise,
In her sleep she saw a sight
Beyond surmise.

She thought there lay her side within
A loathly lump of fleshly sin,
Of the which destruction should begin
Of all Jewry;
That cursed clot of Cain's kin,
Forsooth was I.

Dread of that sight made her awake,
And all her body did tremble and quake;
She thought her heart would well-nigh break—
No wonder was—
The first word my mother spake
Was alas, alas!

Alas, alas! She cried full fast,
With weeping she was deep downcast:
My father stirred himself at last,
And asked her why;
She told him how she was aghast,
No word of lie.

My father bad "let be thy woe!
My counsel is, if it be so,
A child begotten betwixt us two,
  Daughter or son,
Let it never on earth once go,
  But be undone.

"Better it is undone to be
Than it should slay both thee and me,
For in a while then shall we see,
  And know forsooth
Whether that dream was vanity
  Or held some truth."

The time was come that I was born,
And from my mother's body torn;
Alas that I had been forlorn
  Within her side!
For there then sprang a cursed thorn
  That spread full wide.

For I was born without a grace,
They me named and called Judas;
The father of the child ay has
  Great pity;
He would not suffer before his face
  My death to see.

My death to see then might be nought;
A basket small he bad be wrought;
A-bed within there I was brought
  And bound full fast;
And then the deep salt sea they sought,
  And in me cast.

The waves rose, the wind blew;
That I was cursed full well they knew;
The storm me on an island threw,
  In that cot;
And from that land my name I drew,
  Judas Iscariot.

There, as wrecked in sand I lay,
The queen came passing by that way,

With her maidens to sport and play;
    And privily
A child she found in such array,
    Most strangely.

Nevertheless she was well paid,
And gently on her lap me laid;
She me kissed and with me played,
    For I was fair;
"A child God has me sent" she said,
    "To be my heir."

She had me nursed, and all was done
To foster me as her own son,
And told the king that she had gone
    All year with child;
And with fair words his ear she won,
    And him beguiled.

Then the king had made a feast
For all the land, right of the best,
For begotten was a guest
    A sweet small thing,
When he was dead and brought to rest,
    That might be king.

Soon afterwards, within years two,
In the land it befel so,
The queen herself with child did go;
    A son she bore;
No fairer child from top to toe
    Was seen before.

[*Incomplete*]

THE TWENTY-FIFTH PLAY

The Crucifixion

PILATE	JESUS
1ST TORTURER	MARY
2ND TORTURER	JOHN
3RD TORTURER	LONGEUS
4TH TORTURER	JOSEPH OF ARIMATHEA
	NICODEMUS

PILATE Peace I bid you one and all!
Stand as still as stone in wall,
Whilst ye are present in my sight;
That none of you chatter nor call;
Then I shall be to you a blight,
I warn each one both great and small,
With this brand burnished so bright,
Therefore in peace look ye be all.

What! Peace in the devil's name!
Ye dastards and dolts, I mean!
Or the gallows shall make you tame,
Thieves and cut-purses keen!
Will ye not peace when I bid you?
By Mohammed's blood, my spleen
Will split, save I devise for you,
Such pains as never were seen,
    Soon to be shown!
Be ye so bold beggars, I warn you,
Full boldly shall I beat you,
To hell the devil shall draw you,
    Body, back, and bone.

I am a lord, magnificent in might,
Prince of all Jewry, sir Pilate, by right,
Next to King Herod, greatest of all;

Bow at my bidding both great and small,
 Or else be destroyed;
Therefore steer your tongues, I warn you [all,
 That I be not annoyed.

1ST TORTURER All peace, all peace, among you all!
And hearken now what shall befall
 To this false fellow here;
That with his dark devices,
As none but God suffices
 Among us to appear.
He calls himself a prophet,
Says the sick he can make fit,
 And bring comfort to all lands;
But ere long it shall be plain
Whether he heals his own pain,
 Or escapes out of our hands.

Was not this a wondrous thing,
That he durst call himself a king,
 And make so great a lie?
But by Mohammed, whilst I live,
Such proud words shall I never forgive,
 Till he be hanged on high.

2ND TORTURER His pride, fie, we set at nought,
But each man now cast in his thought,
 That of nothing we be scant,
For I shall try, if that I may,
By the order of knighthood, today
 To cause his heart to pant.

3RD TORTURER And so shall I with all my might,
Abate his pride this very night,
 And amend his creed;
He let on he could do no ill,
But he can surely, when he will,
 Do a full foul deed.

4TH TORTURER Yea, fellows, yea, as I have rest!
Now is time as I have guessed
 To bring this thief to death;

Look that we have what we should need,
To fasten this fellow firm, give heed.

1ST TORTURER Thou speakst with noble breath!

Lo, here I have the bands,
If need be to bind his hands,
This thong, I trust, will last.

2ND TORTURER And this one for the other side,
That shall abate his pride,
So be it first drawn fast.

3RD TORTURER Lo, here's a hammer and nails also,
For to fasten down our foe
To this tree, soon now.

4TH TORTURER Ye are wise to take this heed
Of those things that we shall need,
And so for them allow.

1ST TORTURER Now dare I say hardly
Shall he with his idolatry
Find it serve him well.

2ND TORTURER Since Pilate sent him to us again
Have done quick and make it plain
At what tortures we excel.

3RD TORTURER Now are we at the Mount of Calvary;
Have done fellows and let's now see
That we no sport may lack.

4TH TORTURER Yea, for as proud as he may appear,
Yet he would have changed his cheer,
If he had had the rack.

1ST TORTURER In faith, sir, since ye call yourself a king,
You must prove a worthy thing
That wends thus to the war;
You must joust in tournament;
Unless ye sit fast ye may repent,
By me thrust down before.

2ND TORTURER If thou be God's son, as thou tell,
Thou can surely keep thee well?
Else a mystery most complete.

And if thou can we will not own
What thou hast said, but make our moan
When thou sittst in yon seat.

3RD TORTURER Thank us when thy steed thou straddle
For we shall set thee in thy saddle,
Fear no fall, be thou bold.
I promise no lance will shift thee,
Unless thou sit well thou had better let be
The tales that thou hast told.

4TH TORTURER Stand near, fellows, and let us see
How we can horse our king so free,
By any chance;
Stand thou yonder on that side,
And we shall see how he can ride,
And how well wield a lance.

1ST TORTURER Sir, come hither and have done,
Your palfrey would it were begun,
He is ready, I can tell.
That ye be bound on be not wroth,
To mount you unfirm we are loth,
Lest ever ye down fell.

2ND TORTURER Knit thou a knot with all thy strength,
Out to draw this arm in length,
Till it come to the bore.

3RD TORTURER Thou madest man, by this light!
It lacks to each man's sight,
Half a span and more.

4TH TORTURER Yet draw out this arm and fix it fast,
With this rope that well will last,
And each man lay hand to.

1ST TORTURER Yea, and bind thou fast that band;
We shall go to that other hand
And look what we can do.

2ND TORTURER Drive a nail right here throughout,
And then we need us nothing doubt
That home it comes to rest.

3RD TORTURER That shall I do, as might I thrive!
For to clench and for to drive,
Of all I am the best.
So let it stay for it is well.

4TH TORTURER As have I bliss, the truth you tell!
Move it no man might.

1ST TORTURER Hold down his knees.

2ND TORTURER That shall I do,
Your nurse no better help gave you;
Pull his legs down tight.

3RD TORTURER Draw out his limbs much further yet.

4TH TORTURER That was well drawn and cost much [sweat;
Fair befall him that pulled so!
For to have brought him to the mark
Unlettered churl nor clerk
More skill could show.

1ST TORTURER Hold it now fast therefore,
And one of you take the bore,
And then it may not fail.

2ND TORTURER That shall I do with good heed,
As ever hope I well to speed,
And cause him bitter bale.

3RD TORTURER So that is well, it stood the test,
But now let's see who does the best
With any sleight of hand.

4TH TORTURER Go we now to the other end;
Your hands, fellows, look you lend
To pull well at this band.

1ST TORTURER I tell thee fellows, by this weather,
That we draw now altogether,
And look how it will fare.

2ND TORTURER Let's now see, and leave your din!
His sinews now to snap within;
For nothing let us spare.

3RD TORTURER Nay, fellows, this is no game!
All of us pull not the same,
Some slacking have I spied.

4TH TORTURER Yea, for as I hope for bliss,
Some tug while some twitch this,
Not straining at our side.

1ST TORTURER It is better, as I hope,
Each by himself to draw this rope,
And then may we see
Who it was that erstwhile
Thought his fellows to beguile,
In this company.

2ND TORTURER Since thou wilt have it so, here's for me!
Draw I not hard, as thou might see?

3RD TORTURER Thou drew right well;
Have here for me half a foot!

4TH TORTURER Why, man! Not an inch more you put!
It budged not, I can tell.
But have from me here what I may!

1ST TORTURER Well drawn, son, by this day!
In thy work there's a spark!

2ND TORTURER Yet again, while thy hand is in,
Pull thereat like an engine.

3RD TORTURER Yea, and bring it to the mark.

4TH TORTURER Pull, pull!

1ST TORTURER Have now!

2ND TORTURER Let's see!

3RD TORTURER Ah, ha!

4TH TORTURER Heave, ho!

1ST TORTURER Now we have not far.

2ND TORTURER Hold still, I implore!

3RD TORTURER So fellows! Now look alive,
Which of you now best can drive,
And I shall take the bore.

4TH TORTURER Now to try my turn let me;
Best farrier I hope to be
For to clench it right.
Do rouse him up now when we may,
For I hope he and his palfrey
Shall not part this night.

1ST TORTURER Come hither, fellows, and lend hand!
And make this tree to stand
Aloft with all your might.

2ND TORTURER Yet let us work awhile,
And none the other beguile,
Till it stand to its height.

3RD TORTURER Fellows, your hands now you lend,
For to raise this tree on end,
And let's see who is last.

4TH TORTURER It is best to do as he says;
Set we the tree in the mortice,
And there will it stand fast.

1ST TORTURER Up with the timber.

2ND TORTURER Ah, it holds!
For him that all this world upholds
Thrust from thee with thy hand!

3RD TORTURER Hold even amongst us all.

4TH TORTURER Yea, and let it in the mortice fall,
For then will it best stand.

1ST TORTURER Go we to it and be we strong,
And raise it, be it never so long,
Since firmly we have done.

2ND TORTURER Up with the timber fast on end!

3RD TORTURER Fellows, your full force now lend!

4TH TORTURER So sir, gape against the sun!

1ST TORTURER Now fellow, wear thy crown!

2ND TORTURER Trust thou this timber will fall down?

3RD TORTURER Yet help that it were fast.

4TH TORTURER Shake him well and let us lift.

1ST TORTURER Full short shall be his shrift.

2ND TORTURER Ah, it stands up like a mast.

JESUS I pray you people that pass me by,
That lead your life so pleasantly,
Heave up your hearts on high!
Behold if ever ye saw body
Buffeted and beaten bloody,
Or thus dolefully to die;
In world no wretch as I
That suffered half so sore,
In mind and mood I sigh
For sorrow comes me nigh,
And comfort comes no more.

My folk, what have I done to thee,
That thou all thus shall torment me
That for thy sin I suffer?
How have I grieved thee? answer me,
That thou thus nails me to a tree,
And all for thine error;
Where shalt thou seek succour?
This mistake how shalt thou mend?
When that thou thy saviour
Drives to this dishonour,
His feet and hands to rend!

All creatures have a home to rest
Beasts and birds, all have their nest,
When they are woe-begone;
But God's son that should be best,
Has not whereon his head to rest,
But on his shoulder bone.
To whom now may I make my moan?
When they thus martyr me,
And guiltless make me groan,
And beat me, blood and bone,
That should my brothers be.

What kindness further could I do?
Have I not done what I ought to,

Made thee in my likeness?
Robbed of all rest that is man's due,
Thus mocked by all men who me view!
Such is thy wickedness.
I have shown you kindness, unkindly ye [requite;
See thus thy wickedness! Behold your deep [despite!

To guiltless death ye me consign,
Not, man, for my sins, but for thine,
Thus rent on rood am I,
I would not lose that treasure fine,
That I marked and made for mine,
Thus Adam's blood I buy,

That sunken was in sin,
Within no earthly good,
But with my flesh and blood
That loth was to win.

My brothers that I came to buy,
Have hanged me here thus hideously,
And friends find I few;
Thus have they done most dreadfully,
Spat at me most spitefully,
And heaved me up to view.
Father in heaven I pray to you,
Forgive them thou this guilt,
Grant but this boon:
They know not what they do,
Nor whose blood they have spilt.

1ST TORTURER Yes, what we do full well we know.

2ND TORTURER We pay back fully what we owe.

3RD TORTURER Now the plague take his corpse, say I.
Thinks he that we should care or cry,
What the devil, that he should ail?

4TH TORTURER He would hold us here all day,
Of his death to make delay,
I tell you, without fail.

1ST TORTURER Lift up this tree among us all.

2ND TORTURER Yea, and let it in the mortice fall,
And that should give him a jar.

3RD TORTURER Yea, this should rend him limb from limb.

4TH TORTURER Breaking every joint within,
He may not our sport mar.

[MARY *advances.*

MARY Alas! For care I cry, and stagger in my [need!
Why hangst thou, son, so high? My ills [begin to breed.
All blemished is thy beauty, I see thy body [bleed!
In world, son, had we never such ill fate [decreed.

My flesh that I have fed,
In life lovingly led,
Full straitly art thou stead
Among thy foemen fell;
Such sorrow for to see,
My dearest child on thee,
Is more pain to me
Than any tongue can tell.

Alas, thy holy head
Without rest is revealed;
Thy face, with blood now red,
Was fair as flower in field;
Who may not stand in dread
To see her bairn thus bled,
Beaten blue as lead,
And have no limb to wield!

Fastened by hands and feet
With nails that his flesh eat,
With wounds his foes him greet,
Alas, my child for care!
Thy flesh is open wide
I see on either side

Tears of blood down glide
  Over all thy body bare.
Alas that I should bide
To see my son thus fare!

[JOHN *advances.*

JOHN Alas, for woe, my lady dear!
Quite changed now is thy cheer,
To see this prince without a peer
  Thus lapped all in woe;
He was thy child, thy fairest one,
Thy hope, thy joy, thy lovely son,
That high on tree thus hangs alone
  Beaten by many a blow;
Alas!
  Him, many of us know
  No master could surpass.
But lady, since it is his will
The prophecy to fulfil,
That mankind should know their ill,
  For them he suffers pain;
He with his death shall ransom make,
As before the prophets spake,
Thy sorrow therefore thou forsake,
  Weeping may nothing gain;
He now in sorrow takes our stain,
That we live clean tomorrow.

MARY Alas! Thine eyes as crystal clear, that shone [as sun in sight,
That lent thy countenance such cheer, lost [they have their light,
And faded fast I fear, all dim and dark as [night!
In pain hast thou no peer, none suffered [such a plight.

Sweet son, tell me thy thought,
What wonders hast thou wrought
To be in pain thus brought
  Thy span of life to end?

Ah, son, think on my woe!
Wilt thou thus from me go?
On earth no man I know
Who may my mirth amend.

JOHN Comely lady, kind and true, gladly would
[I comfort thee;
My master spoke these words unto all
[within his company,
That he should suffer so sore pain and die
[upon a tree,
And then to life rise up again the third day
[should it be
Full right!
Therefore, my lady sweet,
Thy weeping is not meet!
Our dole he shall defeat
In his risen might.

MARY My sorrow it is so sad, no solace may me
[save,
My mourning makes me mad, no hope of
[help I have;
Such woe I never had, I fear that I may
[rave,
Nought now may make me glad till I be
[in my grave.

To death my dear is driven,
His robe is rent and riven,
That him by me was given,
And fashioned by my hands;
These Jews with him have striven, their
[evil he withstands.

Alas, my lamb so mild, why wilt thou
[leave me so?
Among these wolves so wild, that work
[thee all this woe?
From shame who may thee shield, if
[friends thus from thee go,

Alas, my comely child, why wilt thou leave
[me so?

Maidens, make your moan!
And weep ye wives, each one,
With me who grieve alone
For the babe that was born best!
My heart is stiff as stone that breaks not
[in my breast.

JOHN Ah, lady, well know I, thy heart is full of
[care
When thou thus openly seest thy child
[thus fare;
Love drives him forcibly, himself he will
[not spare,
To redeem all faithfully, us who have
[sinned our share
And more,
My dear lady, truly, your mourning cease,
[therefore.

MARY Alas! May ever be my song, whilst I my
[life may lead;
Methinks now that I live too long, to see
[my bairn thus bleed.
The Jews have done to him great wrong,
[but why did they this deed?
Lo, so high they have him hung, with
[shameless spite and speed:
Why so
Is he his foes among? His friends are few
[below.
I see this fair flower from me go; what
[shall become of me?
Thou art so wrapped in woe and spread
[out on this tree
So high.
I grieve, but none may know, the pain
[seen in thine eye.

JOHN Dear lady, well were me
If I might comfort thee;

For the sorrow that I see
Shears my heart asunder;
When that I see my master hang
In pain both bitter and strong,
Was never wretch with wrong
Wrought to so great wonder.

MARY Alas, death thy delay is long! Why art
[thou hid from me?
Who made thee to my child belong to en-
[shroud him on the tree;
Now wickedly thou workst all wrong, the
[more shall I chide thee,
My life thou need no more prolong but
[make me with him free
To abide;
Sore sighing is my song, for his wounds
[gape wide.

Ah, death, what hast thou done? With
[thee would I were soon,
Since of children I had but one, the best
[under sun and moon;
Friends few had I won, that makes me
[weep and swoon
Full sore.
Good Lord, grant me my boon, and let me
[live no more!
Gabriel, so good, that one time did me
[greet,
And then I understood thy words that
[were so sweet;
But now they change my mood, that
[promised grace replete,
To bear of my body and blood a child
[our bale to defeat
Through right;
Now hangs he here on rood. Is this the
[promised sight?

All that thou of bliss promised me in that
[stead,

From mirth has fared amiss, yet trust I
[what thou said;
Thy counsel now in this, how should my
[life be led,
When from me gone is he that was my
[head,
So soon?
My death now come it is. Dear Son, grant
[mercy's boon!

JESUS My mother mild, change thou thy cheer!
Cease with sorrow thy soul to sear,
It weighs my heart with heavy care;
The sorrow is sharp I suffer here,
That pain thee pierces, mother dear.
My martyrdom none share.
To do my father's will I dare
From bonds to loose mankind;
His son will he not spare,
To save them that despair
That in the fiend's grasp grind.

The first cause, mother, of my coming
Was for mankind's miscarrying,
To save their souls I sought;
Mother make now no more mourning,
Since mankind through my dying
May thus to bliss be brought.
Woman weep thou right nought!
Take there John unto thy child!
Mankind must needs be bought,
And thou cast, cousin, in thy thought;
John, lo there thy mother mild!

Blue and bloody sorely beset,
Wickedly whipped till with blood I sweat,
Mankind, for thy misdeed!
Would thou for me thy lust regret
When thy heart is sadly set,
Since thus for thee I bleed?
Such life, forsooth, I lead,
That scarcely may I more;

This suffer I for thy need,
For thy grace I do this deed;
Now thirst I wonder sore.

1ST TORTURER Nought but hold thy peace!
Thou shall have drink to give thee ease,
Myself shall be thy slave;
Have here a draught to cool thy heat,
I doubt if you will find it sweet,
I give but what you crave.

2ND TORTURER So sir, say now all your will!
For if your tongue you had kept still
Ye had not here been led.

3RD TORTURER Thou would of all the Jews be King,
But now, I trust, rue everything,
All that thou hast said.

4TH TORTURER He has boasted of great prophecies,
That he should make our temple,
Clean to the earth down fall;
And yet he said he should it raise
As once it stood, within three days!
He lies, that know we all;

And for his lies, in our great hate
We will divide his clothing straight,
Unless he works his art.

1ST TORTURER Yea, as I hope my fortunes mend,
Soon will we this mantle rend,
And each man take his part.

2ND TORTURER How would thou we share his clothes?

3RD TORTURER If his garment this way goes,
In sections it is spoiled;
But let my word be law,
And each of us lots draw,
Then none of us is foiled.

How so befalls now will I draw!
This is mine by common law,
That may none gainsay.
Now since it may no better be,

Bargain thou for it with me,
  My groats may make you gay.

2ND TORTURER How fellows, see ye not yon scrawl?
Written in that time withal
  When our lots we drew.

3RD TORTURER Indeed, there is no man alive,
But for Pilate, as might I thrive,
  That dare write in our view.

4TH TORTURER Go we fast and let us look
What is written in yon book,
  Whatever it may mean.

1ST TORTURER Ah, the more I look thereon,
The less I think upon;
  All is not worth a bean.

2ND TORTURER Yes, forsooth, methinks I see
Languages written thereon three,
  Hebrew and Latin.
And Greek, methinks is written thereon,
Full hard it is to expound upon.

3RD TORTURER Say on, by Appolyon!

4TH TORTURER Yea, as I am a knight most true,
I am better at Latin than you
  Of this company;
I will go without delay
And tell you what it has to say;
  Listen, sirs, carefully.

Yonder is written "Jesus of Nazareth
He is King of Jews" it saith.

1ST TORTURER Ah, that is written wrong.

2ND TORTURER He names himself, but none him own.

3RD TORTURER Go we to Pilate and make our moan;
  Have done, and dwell not long.

[*They approach* PILATE.

Pilate, yond are lies upon that label,
Thereon is written nought but fable;

Of Jews he is not King!
Himself says so, but none is he;
It is therefore written falsely,
A much mistaken thing.

PILATE Boys, I say, what tell ye me?
As it is written so shall it be,
For certain;
Quod scriptum scripsi,
Such I decree,
Which fellow fears not to complain?

4TH TORTURER Since that he is a man of law, he must [needs have his will;
I trust he had not written that saw with- [out some proper skill.

1ST TORTURER Yea, let it hang above his head,
It shall avail him little dead,
Nor ought that he can write.

2ND TORTURER Now ill the day that he was born.

3RD TORTURER His life and hope both are forlorn,
His death will slake our spite.

If thou be Christ as men thee call,
Come down among us all,
And endure not this dismay.

4TH TORTURER Yea, and help thyself that we may see,
And all of us shall trust in thee,
Whatsoever thou say.

1ST TORTURER He calls himself a god of might,
I would gladly see that sleight
Performed for such a deed.
Lazarus, from the grave he raised,
To help himself he is too dazed
Now in his great need.

JESUS Eloi, Eloi, lamasabacthany!
My God, my God, wherefore and why
Hast thou forsaken me?

2ND TORTURER How, hear ye not as well as I,
How he did on Eloi cry?
For his ill teaching?

3RD TORTURER Yea, there is no god in this country
Shall deliver him from our company
For all his preaching.

4TH TORTURER I warrant it is time almost
That he shall soon yield up the ghost,
For torture takes its toll.

JESUS My flesh no more this pain withstands!
Father of heaven, into thy hands
I commend my soul!

1ST TORTURER Let one prick him with a spear,
If he flinch not, never fear,
Then is his life quite past.

2ND TORTURER This blind knight may that best do.

LONGEUS Force not on me what I should rue.

3RD TORTURER No, but thrust up fast.

LONGEUS Ah, Lord, what may this be?
Blind was I quite, now may I see;
God's son, hear me, Jesu!
Forgive what I most sorely rue
Lord, men made me play this part
That I struck thee to the heart;
Thou hangst on high I see
And die to fulfil the prophecy.

4TH TORTURER Go we hence and leave him here,
For plainly now it doth appear
He feels no more pain;
Through neither god nor man,
Do whatever good they can,
Gets he his life again.

[*Exeunt* TORTURERS. JOSEPH OF ARIMATHEA *and* NICODEMUS *advance.*

JOSEPH Alas, alas, and welaway!
That ever I should live this day,

To see my master dead;
So fiercely has his flesh been rent,
With so bitter torment,
Through what the Jews have said.

Nicodemus, we have need
That to sir Pilate we might speed,
His body for to crave;
I will make haste with all my might,
For his body to ask that knight,
To grant it but a grave.

[*They go to* PILATE.

NICODEMUS Joseph, I will wend with thee
To do all that is in me,
For that body to pray;
For our good will and our travail
I hope that it may us avail
Hereafterward some day.

JOSEPH Sir Pilate, God thee save!
Grant me what I crave,
If that it be thy will.

PILATE Welcome, Joseph, might thou be!
Whatso thou asks I grant it thee,
If it I may fulfil.

JOSEPH For my long service I thee pray
Grant me the body—say me not nay—
Of Jesu, dead on rood.

PILATE I grant well if dead he be,
Good leave shalt thou have of me,
Do with him what thou thinkest good.

JOSEPH Grammercy, sir, for your good grace,
So freely granted in this place;
Go we on before:

[*They return to Calvary.*

Nicodemus come forthwith,
For I myself shall be the smith
The nails out for to draw.

NICODEMUS

Joseph I am ready here
To go with thee with full good cheer,
To help with all my might;
Pull forth the nails on either side,
And I shall hold him here beside;
Ah, Lord, such is thy plight!

JOSEPH

Help now, fellow, with all thy might,
Till he be bound and dressed aright,
And lay him in this bier;
Bear we him forth unto the kirk
To the tomb that has been my work
Since full many a year.

NICODEMUS

It shall be so without a nay.
He that died on Good Friday
And crownéd was with thorn,
Save you all that now here be!
That Lord that died for thee
And rose on paschal morn.

Notes to the Plays (Part Three)

JOHN THE BAPTIST

John throughout plays on an acting area distinct from the Angels, and here Jesus joins him. It is feasible that this is the arena area below the pageant, on which most probably the Angels are ensconced in heaven's tower. The Second Angel refers pointedly to the area where the baptism will take place as being without a building of any sort (91), and when the First Angel speaks John hears but does not see him (73).

An alternative presentation suggested by the York and *Ludus Coventriae* plays might take place on the pageant with provision for the heavens to open and for the Holy Spirit to descend while God speaks from above (*Ludus Coventriae,* stage direction following 91, *Spiritus sanctus hic descendat super ipsum et deus pater celestis dicet in celo*). The York direction is contained in the words of the Second Angel to John (63–68):

But in his baptism, John, take tent,
  The heavens shall be open seen,
The holy ghost shall down be sent
  To see in sight,
The father's voice with great talent
  Be heard full right. . . .

Pictorial representations of the baptism frequently depict God leaning through a cloud, holding in his hand the dove of the Holy Ghost above Jesus' head. The York *Transfiguration* suggests the use of lowering machinery for clouds and characters (stage direction following 168, *Hic descendunt nubes, Pater in nube*). In the York version, following the baptism, the two Angels sing (stage direction following 154, *Tunc cantabunt duo angeli 'Veni creator spiritus'*).

Tradition has John thinly clad, possibly half-naked, bearded, and bearing a staff. In this play he carries oil and cream as well with which to anoint Jesus. Jesus carries, or at least should have easy access to, the lamb which he hands to John after the baptism (210).

Of particular interest is line 197 referring to the sacraments of the Roman Church ('There are six others, no more so'). In the manuscript six, represented in Roman numerals, has the 'v' erased, and the whole stanza has been crossed through and in the margin, in what must be a post-Reformation hand, are the words 'correctyd & not playd'.

LAZARUS

Two acting areas are required, one for the dialogue between Jesus and his disciples (1–38) and one for Martha's house. Lazarus' tomb, with what appears to be a stone over the top, should be placed a little way from the house. Both the Chester play and the *Ludus Coventriae* indicate that Lazarus is buried in clay, but most versions agree that a heavy stone rests on top. The play is clearly a prefiguration of the resurrection. It can be simply staged on a pageant using one mansion.

At his resurrection we see Lazarus completely bandaged and Jesus, having raised him, directly orders his bands to be loosed from foot, hand and throat. Each of the Cycle plays on this theme emphasizes the dreadful stink of corrupted flesh which all fear at the opening of the tomb, and this is reflected too in medieval art. 'The Raising of Lazarus' by Gerard de Saint-Jean of the Dutch School, painted in the second half of the fifteenth century, shows, among the many bystanders looking on as Lazarus sits up in his tomb, one holding his nose and grimacing painfully, and another with his cloak pressed to his nose and mouth.

The structure of the play presents a staging problem. It proceeds in normal dialogue up to the raising of Lazarus, but following this event no other character but Lazarus speaks, and he indulges in a long homiletic harangue on the terrors of carnal corruption. The difficulty of the situation is aggravated by Jesus being among the other characters who, with the audience, are exhorted to heed the sermon. It may be more satisfactory if Lazarus and Jesus take deliberate and ceremonial leave of each other at line 110, allowing Lazarus to continue his blood-chilling account of mortality after Jesus has withdrawn.

In the manuscript *Lazarus* appears after *The Judgement*, and although as a play it is complete in itself, its structure is so unusual and its verse forms so extraordinarily divergent that it is manifestly the result of much revision. It is, however, included in this edition within the main body of the Mystery Cycle because of its importance as a prefiguration play, and because of the terrifying power of its homily which, as Professor Owst has observed, bears such close resemblance to a sermon preached by the Dominican, John Bromyard. This power is most apparent when the verse form approximates to that used by the Wakefield Master (125–173).

THE CONSPIRACY

The action of this play covers both the conspiracy against Jesus and his capture, and within this framework contains *The Entry into Jerusalem*, *The Last Supper*, and *The Agony and Betrayal*, each of which is represented by a separate play in the York Cycle. The play is therefore composite and a great number of different acting areas are required; moreover it would be particularly difficult to use the same acting area for different groups of actors because each area has its marked characteristic: Pilate's hall; the room of the Last Supper; Mount Olivet; God in heaven (528); the Garden of Gethsemane. There are altogether seven different localities in the play, and there is also a stress on the movement of groups of actors: Jesus and his disciples meet (313), John and Peter are dispatched to the city, and they are later followed there by Jesus and the other disciples, all of whom sit down to the Last

Supper. This scene alone requires considerable acting space. Allowance must be made for the table and benches, and sufficient space left for Jesus to move round the table washing the disciples' feet. Here are obvious reasons why in production this area should be used exclusively for this scene. But the movement of groups continues: Jesus goes with his three disciples to Mount Olivet. When Jesus reaches the Mount he leaves his disciples at a lower level and climbs up to pray, and it is from an even higher level that God speaks (528–555). This arrangement of levels immediately suggests the disciples at the foot of the pageant, Jesus standing or kneeling in prayer on the pageant itself, and God speaking from heaven, the castle-like structure erected on the pageant.

If the Last Supper and the Mount Olivet scenes point to distinct acting areas, it is also apparent that Pilate in his three scenes is to be located in his own acting area, although his soldiers pass freely from his hall to the Garden of Gethsemane and back again. The soldiers at the end of the play lead Jesus to the hall of Sir Caiaphas (740, 754), and the next play, *The Buffeting,* begins as this has left off with the soldiers, who are now called Torturers, dragging their victim towards the unscrupulous priest.

Practical staging considerations suggest that Pilate's hall, Caiaphas' hall, the scene of the Last Supper, and Mount Olivet are located on different scaffolds or pageants, and that it is in 'the place', 'green', or arena that the first dialogue between Jesus and his disciples is conducted and also the scene in the Garden of Gethsemane. A similar arrangement of the playing area is indicated in the *Ludus Coventriae,* in which Annas, Caiaphas and Pilate each have separate scaffolds. The interior of the house in which the Last Supper takes place can be, probably through the use of a curtain, quickly concealed or revealed ('and þan xal þe place þer cryst is in xal sodenly unclose rownd Abowtyn shewyng cryst syttyng at þe table and his dyscypulys eche in ere degre . . .' *Ludus Coventriae,* Passion Play I, stage direction following 669). The same contrivance for concealing or revealing an interior scene is used for the oratory erected in the very middle of 'the place' ('here þe buschopys with here clerkys and þe pharaseus mett in þe myd place and þer xal be a lytil oratory with stolys and cusshonys cleynly be-seyn lych as it were a cownsel hous . . .'; '. . . and in þe mene tyme þe cownsel hous beforn-seyd xal sodenly onclose shewyng þe buschopys prestys and jewgys syttyng in here Astat lyche as it were A convocacyone.' (*Ludus Coventriae*, Passion Play I, stage directions following 124 and 397.) In *The Conspiracy* of the Wakefield Cycle scenes are similarly concealed and revealed thus enabling action to pass swiftly from, say, Pilate's hall to the Last Supper. At (559) where the action turns from Mount Olivet to Pilate's hall, there is no need for the drawing of a curtain to conceal Jesus and the three disciples; when Pilate is sending out his soldiers to apprehend Jesus, there is a tableau on Mount Olivet of Jesus praying and below him his three disciples sleeping, and this tableau is held until the action returns to Mount Olivet on (652).

The medieval dress worn by the actors in the mystery cycles is exemplified by the references to costume in the following stage directions from the *Ludus Coventriae:*

> 'Here xal annas shewyn hym-self in his stage be-seyn after a busshop of þe hoold lawe in a skarlet gowne and over þat a blew tabbard furryd with whyte and a mytere on his hed after þe hoold lawe. ij doctorys stondyng by hym in furryd hodys and on be-forn hem with his staff of A-stat and eche of hem on here hedys a furryd cappe with a gret knop in þe crowne and on stondyng be-forn as a sarazyn þe wich xal be his masangere . . .'
>
> (*The Passion Play* I, following John the Baptist's Prologue.)

> 'here goth þe masangere forth and in þe mene tyme cayphas shewyth him-self in his skafhald Arayd lych to Annas savyng his tabbard xal be red furryd with white ij doctorys with hym arayd with pellys aftyr þe old gyse and furryd cappys on here hedys . . .'
>
> (*The Passion Play* I, following (44).)

'here jhesus with his dyscipulis goth in-to þe place and þer xal come in A x personys weyl be-seen in white Arneys and breganderys (body armour) and some dysgysed in odyr garmentys with swerdys gleyvys (spears) and other straunge wepone as cressettys with feyr and lanternys and torchis lyth. . . .'

(*The Passion Play* I, following 972.)

Annas and Caiaphas of the Wakefield Cycle would also be dressed as medieval bishops. The last extract referring to the lighted torches corresponds to a similar stage effect in the Wakefield play (599, 611, 612). Medieval iconographic representations of the capture of Jesus almost invariably depict weapons and lanterns or torches held aloft.

Apart from these torches and a variety of weapons, essential properties are also the thirty silver pennies, perhaps most conveniently contained in a glove, as in the *Ludus Coventriae Conspiracy* (625, 626), and also the bowl and towel for the washing of feet, Pilate's sword (575), Peter's sword (681), and the cord with which Jesus is bound and by which he is dragged away at the end of the play. Pilate, who, like the other tyrants in the Cycle, is given to laying about him in his frequent fits of fury, might be allotted, as in the Coventry *Corpus Christi* Plays, a club and balls, stuffed with wool and covered with leather (Hardin Craig, *Two Coventry Corpus Christi Plays*, p. 96).

THE BUFFETING

The action of this play is continuous with the last, and indeed this is so of the whole Passion sequence of plays. One play flows directly into another. At the end of *The Conspiracy* the action is swept from Pilate's hall to Caiaphas' hall where *The Buffeting* takes place. At the end of *The Buffeting* the action returns to Pilate's hall, and the dialogue appears deliberately included to cover these journeys. For instance in *The Buffeting* the Torturers drive Jesus for forty-five lines, bitterly complaining of the distance they have to cover to Caiaphas' hall (40–41), and their return journey to Pilate's hall is covered at the beginning of *The Scourging* by Pilate's fifty-two line prologue.

The medieval practice of having completely different casts for each play, while serving admirably for a production staged on pageants moving from station to station through a city, might be less satisfactory for performances given in a single area, employing 'the place' and a series of fixed pageants set in a circle or semi-circle on the periphery of 'the place'. Continuity of action, which is strongly suggested here by the sequence of the Passion plays, is surely strengthened by continuity of actors.

In *The Buffeting* the references to the Torturers leading Jesus from Pilate's to Caiaphas' hall suggest movement in 'the place'. Such stage movement is explicit in the *Ludus Coventriae* direction, 'here þei ledyn jhesu A-bowt þe place tyl þei come to þe halle' (*Passion Play* II, following 244). When the procession reaches Caiaphas' hall the two priests are seated on thrones (46). Acting as false witnesses the Torturers stand on the pageant by the priests' thrones and, when given the word, they drag Jesus back into 'the place' just below the pageant, so that the priests may enjoy the ensuing action (337) and, making a ring round Jesus (325), administer the buffeting. Following this, not needing to mount the pageant, they lead Jesus to its edge (415) and receive their orders from Caiaphas to take their victim to Pilate (425). It is for Pilate's hall, too, that Annas and Caiaphas leave at the end of the play.

The Torturers play with Jesus the game of Hot Cockles. They sit him on a foot-stool or 'light buffet' (351), an obvious pun; Froward begins to blindfold him but leaves the final touch, and consequently 'Christ's curse', to the Second Torturer. The bandage is taken off by Froward on (412) 'But tell us no lie', which coincides with the culmination of the Torturers' brutality. Their weapons for the buffeting may well have been leather casings, stuffed with wool, set on wooden handles.

Caiaphas is infuriated that Jesus stands beyond the range of his blows (299) but he has access to other weapons that will reach. He carries a dagger in his belt (281, 444) and it is only the strongest persuasion from Annas that prevents him using it. Both he and Annas wear on their fingers bishops' rings. Caiaphas will not bless the torturers with his ring (340) until he has discovered which of them delivers the harshest blows.

Jesus' description of how he shall return to earth (253, 254) may be interpreted as a stage direction relevant to both *The Ascension* and *The Judgement*. A wooden miniature in the museum at Chartres shows Jesus attached to a blue cloud which can be raised or lowered.

THE SCOURGING

All the other English mystery cycles contain at this stage the scene of *Christ's Trial Before Herod.* There are signs that at one time such a play had its place in the Wakefield Cycle also: the First Torturer makes his entry with the words 'I have run till I sweat from sir Herod our king' (53), and Pilate himself says 'Herod, true as any stone, could find no fault in him' (99). In the manuscript, however, there is no obvious omission between *The Buffeting* and *The Scourging,* and if such a Herod play did exist, then on some subsequent revision of the Cycle it was deliberately omitted. As mentioned before in reference to the previous play, the dramatic action from *The Buffeting* to *The Scourging* may be treated as continuous.

The Torturers' initial dialogue extends over thirty lines (53–82) before they reach Pilate's hall. Their path probably lies through 'the place', where they have to ask for room to be made for them to pass (62) before they can confront Pilate sitting on his dais (82, 184). On the pageant level Jesus is bound to a pillar (130) and beaten, the Torturers making, as they did in *The Buffeting,* a ring round their victim (227). When Jesus is unbound he is thrust again into 'the place' where he moves slowly and painfully with the cross over his shoulder.

The scene between John and the Marys may be played on a pageant or in another part of 'the place'. The meeting between this group and Jesus' procession is best staged in 'the place', from where both groups move towards that most important pageant which is to represent Calvary.

A bowl, water and towel will be required for the washing of Pilate's hands (216). An even more refined touch is introduced in the York *Judgement of Jesus* (443), when Pilate's Beadle says 'Will ye wash while the water is hot?' Other cycles specify that a white garment is put on Jesus after the buffeting and a purple one after the scourging, but no such indication exists in the Wakefield Cycle. The cross itself is the major property of the whole cycle. It is required to be strong enough and large enough to support the body of a man, and yet not too heavy for a man to carry, or at least drag, with some ease. The scourges themselves may be made of long strips of felt set on short wooden stocks.

Maximum dramatic effect might be gained from the Torturers' persuasion of Simon of Cyrene to take up the cross, if they adopt an unwonted politeness in their preliminary overtures to him (361–390) which explodes into violence and compulsion (391). The force of

As ye have said, I am well paid,
  This man his pain to spare. (401–402.)

is brought home when Simon, having shouldered the cross, looks for the first time into Jesus' face.

THE HANGING OF JUDAS

This play, which is incomplete, appears at the very end of the manuscript and is written in a sixteenth-century hand. It is a poem rather than a drama, and even in its complete form it seems probable that the monologue would have been sustained throughout. Classical, biblical, and romantic elements meet together in what must be one of the strangest fragments in the Mystery Cycles. Judas looks into his past for, as it were, a psychological justification of his actions, and he sees there not only the 'Oedipus complex' but Oedipus himself.

The more usual interpretation of this theme as, for instance, in the York Cycle and the *Ludus Coventriae*, is centred on the action which stems from Judas' remorse at his betrayal of Christ, his return to the high priests, offering back the money and pleading for Jesus' release, and their contemptuous rejection. The biblical conclusion comes in the *Ludus Coventriae* stage direction (*Passion Play* II, following 236) 'þan judas castyth down þe mony and goth and hangyth hymself.'

THE CRUCIFIXION

The play begins with a prologue spoken by Pilate in his own pageant. The procession to Calvary, as at the end of *The Scourging*, continues on its way. By approximately line forty-seven the procession establishes itself on or near the pageant which is to represent Mount Calvary. The nailing of Jesus to the cross calls for considerable space, and it might be advisable to group the majority of the onlookers, while this action is taking place, at the foot of the pageant. Indeed it would be extremely difficult and even dangerous for any other action to be taking place on the pageant until the cross is raised (232).

It is evident that Pilate is located initially in an entirely different area from Calvary, because each time there is communication between him and a group from Calvary a journey appears necessary (544 and 619–620). It appears that Pilate crosses from his pageant and places the superscription on the cross while the torturers are haggling over Jesus' clothing (498–515). How Pilate manages to place what he has written on the cross above Christ's head is a staging problem on which the Wakefield text is completely unhelpful. In the Chester *Christ's Passion* (stage direction following l. 600), Pilate orders a soldier to fix the superscription before the cross is raised, a device not easily transferred to the Wakefield play. The *Ludus Coventriae*, however, faces the staging difficulty squarely and deals with it in a way that may be of help to the producer of the Wakefield text:

'here xal pylat Askyn penne and inke and A tabyl xal be take hym wretyn Afore hic est jhesus nazarenus rex judeorum. and he xal make hym to wryte and þan gon

up on A leddere and settyn þe tabyl abovyn crystys hed. . . .'
(*Ludus Coventriae, Passion Play* II, following l. 853.)

The Torturers who cross from Calvary to Pilate's pageant (545) in a violently querulous mood are quelled by Pilate's own aggression and return (560–562) to their vicious taunting of Jesus.

All the cycles include Longeus being cured of his blindness. The detail of the miracle, obscure in the Wakefield play, is explicit elsewhere. Longeus, his spear-hand guided, thrusts at Jesus' heart. The blood falls from the wound onto Longeus' hands which he puts to his eyes and is so healed of his affliction.

Joseph of Arimathea and Nicodemus, witnesses of the crucifixion, approach the cross when the Torturers withdraw (612). They go together from Calvary to Pilate's pageant at the end of or during Nicodemus' speech (625–630). On their return to Calvary they take Jesus down from the cross, Joseph using long pincers to extract the nails (648). In this they may be glad of assistance from Simon of Cyrene and John the Evangelist. The detail of the deposition is most graphically described in the *Ludus Coventriae, Passion Play* II, stage directions following l. 1131 and l. 1139:

> 'an joseph doth set up þe lederys and nychodemus comyth to help hym.'
> 'here joseph and nychodemus takyn cryst of þe cros on on o ledyr and þe tother on An-other leddyr and qwan is had down joseph leyth hym in oure ladys lappe. . . .'

Joseph and Nicodemus carry Jesus out of the acting area. The burial is not enacted in full view of the audience. Indeed, if at some stage the action and the actors of this cycle were continuous, the playwright seems here to have shown as much concern for resting his main character, after what is in effect a most severe physical ordeal, as Shakespeare in relaxing the burden on his tragic protagonist in the fourth act. Jesus does not appear in *The Talents,* the play following *The Crucifixion.* On the other hand any producer of this cycle must concern himself with placing the intervals in relationship to the development of the drama. The end of *The Crucifixion* is a possible choice. The Cornish Plays which extended over three days, brought their second day to an end with *The Crucifixion.*

The blessing of Jesus on ye ever,
And that always I pray.
Go ye all on the side of home,
The Play is ended;
And come early
To-morrow, I pray you,
To see how Christ rose
Out of the tomb, bright and gentle.
(*The Ancient Cornish Drama*, Volume 1, p. 477, translated by Edwin Norris.)

The complicated business of nailing Jesus to the cross might be managed as follows: Jesus lies down on the cross with the First, Second, and Third Torturers at his right hand and the Fourth Torturer at his left hand (118); the Second and Third Torturers tie a cord to his right hand, which they stretch out along the cross and nail down (134); the First Torturer goes to help the Fourth Torturer with the left hand at (129); at (140) the Second Torturer goes to the knees and the Third Torturer goes to help the Second Torturer with stretching out the knees at (143); the Fourth Torturer leaves the left hand and goes to Jesus' feet at (143); the Third Torturer hammers the nail into the feet at (157), after which all pull at the left hand, which the Fourth Torturer hammers down (202).

The four of them raise the cross vertically between (202) and (215) and on (224), with it still vertical, lift it towards the mortice and place it in (225). On (230) they shake the cross, lift it out of the mortice slightly and let it fall back into position. By (232) it should be firmly established and, if necessary, wedged. The horseplay of (308) can be mere pretence of lifting, shaking, and letting the cross fall once more.

Jesus is supported on the cross by the ropes round his arms and feet. A small ledge should support his feet, and wooden pegs in the cross between thumb and finger help to distribute the strain. If some nails are already half sunk into the cross, the Torturers at the appropriate time can give a very much more realistic impression of zestful hammering.

Part Four

THE TWENTY-SIXTH PLAY

The Talents

PILATE	2ND TORTURER (SPELL PAIN)
1ST TORTURER	3RD TORTURER
	COUNSELLOR

PILATE *Cernite qui statis quod mire sim probitatis,*
Hec cognoscatis vos cedam ni taceatis,
Cuncti discatis quasi sistam vir deitatis
Et maiestatis michi fando ne neceatis,
Hoc modo mando;
Neve loquaces,
Sive dicaces,
Poscite paces,
Dum fero fando.

Stint, I say! Men give place, *quia sum* [*dominus dominorum!*
He that dares me outface *rapietur lux* [*ocvlorum;*
Therefore give ye me space *ne tendam vim* [*brachiorum,*
And then get ye no grace, *contestor Iura* [*polorum,*
Caveatis;
Rule I in Jewry,
Maxime pure,
Town *quoque rure,*
Me paveatis.

Stemate regali, King Atus begat me of Pila;
Tramite legali, I am ordained to reign in [Judah,
Nomine vulgari, Pontius Pilate who holds [you in awe,

Qui bene vult fari should call me founder
[of all law.
Iudeorum
Iura guberno,
Please me and say so,
Omnia firmo
Sorte deorum.

Mighty lord of all, *me Caesar magnificavit;*
Down on your knees ye fall, great God *me*
[*sanctificavit,*
Me to obey over all, *regi reliquo quasi*
[David,
Hanged high be the thrall *hoc iussum qui*
[*reprobavit,*
I swear now;
And be your head
Bare in this stead,
Lest my sword turn red;
Beware now!

Atrox armipotens I grant men peace by
[my good grace,
Atrox armipotens, most mighty called in
[every place,
Vir quasi cunctipotens, I grant men peace
[by my good grace,
Tota refert huic gens, that none is worthier
[in the face,
Quin eciam bona mens, truth and right my
[true laws trace,
Silete!
In generali,
Sic speciali,
Yet again bid I
Iura tenete.

Look that no boy be boisterous, no blast
[here to blow,
But truly to my talking hear my harangue;
If here be any boy that will not our law
[follow,

By mighty Mohammed, high shall he
[hang;
South, north, east and west,
In all this world in breadth and length,
Is none so doughty as I, the best,
On foot or horse who strikes with strength.

Therefore I say,
Look ye incline to my liking,
Or a clout ye will get for your grieving,
Diligently comply to my pleasing,
As prince most mighty me pay.

Say nought, by this sword;
For who stirs or any din makes
The ash of my anger he rakes,
If as sovereign me he not takes
And as his own lord.

He is master of his night's rest that naps
[not at noontide!
Boy, lay me down softly and wrap me well
[from cold;
Look that no lads annoy me with crying
[nor crooning,
Nor in my sight none grieve me so bold.
If there be any boys that make any cry,
Or else that will not obey me,
They were better be hanged up high,
Than in my sight once move me.

1ST TORTURER Look to! For now come I,
The most curst in this country;
Full fast in haste here run have I,
Hither to this town;
To this town now come have I
From the mount of Calvary:
There Christ hung, and that full high,
I swear here by my crown.

At Calvary when he hanged was,
I spued and spat right in his face,

When that it shone as any glass
So seemly to my sight;
But yet for all that fair thing
I laughed at him in hating,
Robbed him of his clothing,
To me it was but right.

And when his clothes were off together,
Lord, we so laughed, and made good [cheer,
And crowned that churl with a briar,
As he had been a king;
And yet I did full properly,
I clapped his corpse by and by,
I thought I did full curiously
In faith him for to hang.

But to Mohammed I make a vow,
Hither have I brought his clothing now,
To try the truth before you,
Even this same night;
Of me and of my fellows two
To whom these garments ought to go;
But sir Pilate must cast lot too,
I tell you by this light.

For whosoever may get these clothes,
Need reck never where he goes,
To him good fortune flows,
If so that he them wear.

But now, good fellows of renown,
Because the devil comes to town,
Let us rumour up and down,
Of our most gracious gear.

2ND TORTURER Make way, before I knock you down!
For I must meet my mates in town,
And I shall clout him on the crown
That dares stand in my way;
By leaps and bounds I needs must flit,
As though I now had lost my wit;

My breeches I had almost shit,
So great was my delay.

But, by Mohammed! Now am I here!
The most accursed, that dare I swear,
That ye shall find anywhere,
Spell pain my name, a knight
That was at Calvary this same day,
Where the King of Jews lay,
And there I taught him a new play,
Truly I thought it right.

The play we lately had in town,
That he should lay his head low down,
And straight I bobbed him on the crown,
That game methought was good.
When we had played with him our fill,
Then led we him unto a hill,
And there we wrought with him our will,
And hung him on a rood.

No more now of this talking,
But the cause of my coming,
As token meet for promising
This coat I would I had;
For if I might this coat entreat,
Then my joy would be complete,
I would even fast from drink and meat,
In faith as I were mad.

3RD TORTURER Out, alas! how do ye crones,
Haste have I made to break my bones!
I have burst both my bollock stones,
So fast I hurried hither;
Nothing gives me such relief
As murder a cut-purse or hang a thief;
If here be any that cause me grief
I shall thrash them altogether;

For I swear in any sin
I am the worst of all my kin,
That is from this town unto Lynn,
Here my two fellows, lo!

Now have we three come in
A new game for to begin,
This same coat for to win,
    Before we further go.

Now to sir Pilate, I guess, that we go be-
[fore,
And give him the cause why hither we
[gad;
But this gown that is here, I tell you there-
[fore,
By mighty Mohammed I would not he
[had.

1ST TORTURER I assent to those words by Mohammed's
[renown!
Let us go to sir Pilate and tell him no fable;
But, sirs, on my oath, he gets not this
[gown;
Among us three we count it profitable;
    Spell pain what sayst thou?

2ND TORTURER Your cunning counsel I assent to now.

1ST TORTURER Then will I straightway in this place,
Speak to Pilate, if he allow,
For I am seemly and fair of face;
And we shall profit, that I vow.

3RD TORTURER Sir, tell me, by my loyalty,
Where that prince, sir Pilate, is?

COUNSELLOR Sir, as might I thrive, I tell thee,
He lies here in the devil's service.

1ST TORTURER With that prince—foul him befall—
Must we have to do.

COUNSELLOR I shall go to him and call,
What ye would say to him, look to.

My lord, my lord!

PILATE What boy, let once suffice!
Call no more, thou hast called twice.

COUNSELLOR My lord!

PILATE What mite of grievance moves me in my [mind?

COUNSELLOR I, lord, your counsellor, come to entreat [you go.

PILATE Are there any traitors, or plots of any kind?

COUNSELLOR Nay, lord, none that I know.

PILATE Annoy us no more with this noise;
You careless curs, who bad you call me?
By your mad mothers you are but boys,
That ye shall abuy, else foul befall me.
I shall not die in your debt!
Come sir, I bid that up thou take me,
And in my seat me softly set.

Now shall we know and that right now,
If that be true what thou did say;
If lies be told, pay for it shalt thou,
For meddling in matters of law today.

COUNSELLOR Nay sir, not so, without delay,
The cause of my calling is of that boy bold,
For it is said forsooth now this same day,
That he should die in doleful pain;
For certain
Then may your cares grow cold
If guiltless he be slain.

PILATE Fair and softly, sir, and say not too much;
Seem to be sorry, then truth shows the [less,
The law look thou study, show deference [to such,
Lest I grieve thee greatly with buffets [express;
False fellow, in faith I shall slay thee!
Thy reasons so reckless thou had better [redress,
Or meddle no more with these matters, I [pray thee.

COUNSELLOR Why should I not mention what I have [you taught?
Though ye be prince Pilate without [any peer,
Were it not for my wisdom, your wits [come to nought;
As is seen expressly and plainly right here,
Else be ye misled.

PILATE Why, boy, but has thou said?

COUNSELLOR Yea, lord.

PILATE Therefore, the devil thee speed, thou [churl, thou thing!
Tales of such fellows are laughed at [abroad!
The behaviour ye know not that belongs to [a king.

1ST TORTURER Mohammed most mighty, make glad your [reign,
Sir Pilate, peerless prince, all your days,
And save you sir, sitting, so seemly a [sovereign!
We have come to your hall along hazard- [ous ways,
But this must be said:
Ye know whom he doomed this day upon [dais,
We fear not his doing for now is he dead.

PILATE Ye are welcome indeed, right worthy ye [are;
If that traitor be dead, that deed makes [for my gain.

2ND TORTURER We have done for that dotard, no more [shall he mar;
We prayed you, sir Pilate, to put him to [pain,
And we thought it well wrought.

PILATE Leave sirs, from such words look ye refrain;
For the part I played name ye it nought.

3RD TORTURER Make mirth of that meddler as much as [we may,
And love more our lives for loss of that lad;
But, sir Pilate peerless, one point I thee [pray;
Have ye hope in your heart that harness [he had
To hold that was his?

PILATE That belongs unto me, by my faith! Art [thou mad?
I meant in no manner you men to have this.

1ST TORTURER Move thee not, master, though more he [may ask,
Nor part from our pilfering however he [plead.

PILATE Start not so aback nor be so aghast;
This gown as a gift I would you decreed;
It may make profit for you.

2ND TORTURER Wherefore this flattery? You have made [known your need,
But it falls first to us four before you.

PILATE My needs are no man's business but mine.

3RD TORTURER Yea, lord, let us tear it in shreds.

PILATE Now to that I agree, take thou this, and [thou that,
And this shall be thine,
And by warrant of law this is left still.

1ST TORTURER Oh, lording! We do this all wrong,
In good time I took it, if we follow thy will,
The fairest parts to thee, the foulest [to us belong.

PILATE And thou art paid for thy part full truly I [trust.

1ST TORTURER It is shame for to see, I am left but a [shred.

2ND TORTURER That the whole of this harness be yours is [unjust,
If I am left but a scrap with scarcely a [thread,
So tattered and torn.

3RD TORTURER By mighty Mohammed, of our faith [the head,
If he escape with this coat it would [give us great scorn.

PILATE Now since ye fret so at this, take it to you
With all my spite and that of Moham- [med's renown!

1ST TORTURER Dread ye not doubtless, for so will we do;
Grieve ye not greatly, ye get not this [gown,
But in four as it falls.

2ND TORTURER For a falchion to cut it despite Pilate's [frown!

3RD TORTURER Lo, one is here for whoever calls.
It is sharp to cut with, shear if thou may.

2ND TORTURER Even in the middle to mark the mas- [tery for me.

1ST TORTURER Most seemly it is for certain the seam to [assay.

2ND TORTURER I have sought all this side and none can I [see,
Great or small.

PILATE Bashirs, abide you, I bid you let be!
I command not to cut it, but keep it [whole all.

1ST TORTURER Now are we bound, because ye bad, to do [as ye tell?

PILATE Out! Harlots! Go hang you, for whole [shall it be.

3RD TORTURER Grieve you not greatly, he meant it but [well.

PILATE Had I thought that he spoke then in [scorn of me,
Swift had I struck then to kill him.

2ND TORTURER That would grieve him, my lord, on [my loyalty,
Therefore grant him your grace.

PILATE No grievance I will him.

1ST TORTURER Grammercy thy goodness!

PILATE But grieve me no more, look to!
Full dear is it bought
In faith, if ye do.

1ST TORTURER Shall I then save it?

PILATE Yea, so say I, but to draw lots is best,
And lo, who gets the long cut shall win.

3RD TORTURER We agree to your saying and put it to test;
Let one now assay, but who shall begin?

PILATE Ye follow after, the first falls to me.

2ND TORTURER Nay, dread you not doubtless, for that do [ye nought
O, he seeks to deceive us that plainly we [see.

3RD TORTURER Good fellows, give ear, I have here brought
Three fine dice along.

1ST TORTURER That is of all games the best, by him that [me bought,
For at dicing he does us no wrong.

PILATE And I am glad of that game; one assay, [who shall begin?

1ST TORTURER First shall ye, and then after we all.
Have the dice and have done,
And leave all your din,
For whoso throws most this garment may [call
His own and the dice.

PILATE I assent to your saying, assay now I shall,
As I would at one throw win all in a [trice.

[PILATE *throws.*

2ND TORTURER Ah! Ha! How now! Here are a heap.

PILATE Have mind then among you how many [there are.

3RD TORTURER Thirteen among three, that score ye may [keep.

PILATE Then shall I win or many men mar.

1ST TORTURER Truly, lord so may it befall;
But grieve you not greatly, your joy I may [jar,
If fortune attend me, have here for all!

[*He throws.*

PILATE And I have seen as great a knight of his [promise failed.
I count but eight for all your groans.

1ST TORTURER Eight? by his arms, that is all! Whatever [me ailed!
I was falsely beguiled with these bitched [bones;
There cursed they be!

2ND TORTURER He gets not the garment who these dice [disowns,
I fain would this fortune might fall unto [me.

PILATE An ill affair, in faith, if thou won.

2ND TORTURER No, but stand out of my way.

[*He throws.*

3RD TORTURER By Mohammed's bones, this is ill done!
Seven is but the second, the sooth for to [say.

2ND TORTURER Woe, fie! That is short.

3RD TORTURER Go shoot at thy hood! Now I should be [first,
If I have luck for this gown, and goes all [good;
Bitched bones be as I bid ye or be [curst!

[*He throws.*

Fellows, as I forecast here have I fifteen!
As ye know I am worthy this gown for to [win.

PILATE What, whistle ye and the moon waning! [Where have ye been?
Thou shalt abuy that throw, have done [your din!

3RD TORTURER Here be men in this throng,
Loyal to our law, not scared of their skin,
And witness they may if I wrought any [wrong.

1ST TORTURER Thou wrought no deceit, forsooth, that we [know,
Therefore thou art worthy and gained the [gown at thy own will.

PILATE Yea, but I play not the game with a puff [or a blow;
I reck not nor reason if right be his skill,
I grudge it him nought.

3RD TORTURER Have good day, sir, and grieve you not ill,
For if it were double full dear is it bought.

PILATE Sir, since thou hast won this gown, wilt [thou vouchsafe, say,
To give of thy goodness this garment to [me?

3RD TORTURER Sir, this shall ye not have, I say thee nay.

PILATE Thou shalt repent with no delay,
Fie, what art thou free?
Accursed then remain!

3RD TORTURER For your threats go through me,
Were there such three
I'd give them you truly.

[*Gives the garment to* PILATE.

PILATE Now, grammercy, again!
Many thanks, and have mind of a pay-
[ment.

1ST TORTURER But I had not left it so lightly if play my
[way went.

PILATE No, but he is faithful and free, as truly I
[meant,
And more if I may,
If of me he have need,
To him shall I heed.

3RD TORTURER I vouchsafe it be so, the sooth for to say.

1ST TORTURER Now these dice are unworthy for the loss
[of this good,
Here I forswear heartily, by Mohammed's
[blood;
For I was never so happy in mind or in
[mood,
To win with such subtlety my very life's
[food,
As ye ken;
These dicers and these drabbers,
These boozers and these brawlers,
And all purse-cutters,
Be well warned of these men.

2ND TORTURER Fie, fie, on these dice, may the devil them
[take!
Unwitty, unwise, to set all on a stake;
As may fortune devise to mar or to make;
Men she can make rise, or downhill them
[take;
The rich
She turns upside-down,
The poor gain a crown,

Most chief in renown
  She casts in the ditch.

By her means she makes dicers to sell,
As they play at their stakes, their corn and [their cattle;
Then with cries and with crakes they are [ready for battle,
His oven then bakes no simnel
  As it used.
But farewell, thrift!
Is there none other shift
But a sweet lady's gift?
  These dicers are confused.

3RD TORTURER What comes of dicing I pray you hark [after,
But loss of goods in playing and often [men's slaughter!
Thus sorrow is at parting, if at meeting [there be laughter;
Better leave such vain thing and serve [God hereafter,
  For heaven's bliss;
That Lord is most mighty,
And gentlest of Jewry,
We hold him as holy;
  How think ye of this?

PILATE Well worthy all three, most doughty in-[deed!
Of all scholars I know, most cunning ye be,
Your sayings of subtlety, your laws kept [dutifully;
I grant you full power and friendship [freely,
  I say;
Dieu vous garde, monseigneurs!
Mohammed most mighty in castles and [towers
He keep you, lordings, and all yours,
  And have all good day.

THE TWENTY-SEVENTH PLAY

The Deliverance of Souls

JESUS	MOSES
ADAM	RIBALD
EVE	BEELZEBUB
SYMEON	DAVID
JOHN THE BAPTIST	SATAN
	ISAIAH

JESUS

My father me from bliss did send
To earth for mankind's sake,
Adam's misdeed to amend,
My death I needs must take.

I dwelt there thirty years and two
And something more, the truth to say:
In anguish, pain, and bitter woe,
I died on cross this day.

Therefore to hell now will I go,
To challenge what is mine;
Adam and Eve and more to show,
That there no longer need they pine.

The fiend beguiled them with a lie,
Through fraud of earthly food,
Redeemed I have them truly,
By the shedding of my blood.

And now I will that place restore,
Which the fiend fell from for sin;
Some token will I send before,
With mirth they may their games begin.

A light I would they saw,
To know that soon I come;

My body in death's maw
  Lies till this be done.

ADAM My brothers, hearken to me here!
  More hope of health never we had;
Four thousand and six hundred year
  Have suffered we this darkness sad;
See signs of solace now appear,
  A glorious gleam to make us glad,
Whereby I hope that help is near,
  That soon shall slake our sorrows sad.

EVE Adam, my husband kind,
  This means solace certain;
Such light did we find
  In paradise full plain.

ISAIAH Adam, through thy sin
  Here were we put to dwell,
This wicked place within;
  The name of it is hell;
Pain's wheel ay shall spin
  For those wicked and fell,
To love that Lord begin,
  Whose life for us would sell.

[*And all shall sing "The Saviour of the World", the first verse.*

Adam, thou well understand
I am Isaiah, as God me sent.
I spake of folk in a dark land,
And said a light should them be lent;
This light now comes at Christ's command,
Which he to us has hither sent,
Thus my point is proved in hand,
As prophet preached I this event.

SYMEON So might I marvels more reveal,
For in the temple I saw him stand,
And grew in grace with him to deal,
And clasped him homely with my hand;
I said, Lord, let thy servant loyal
Pass in peace to life's far strand;

Thy salvation now I feel,
No longer long to live in land.

This light thou hast purveyed
For them that live in need;
What I before of thee have said
I see it is fulfilled indeed.

JOHN THE BAPTIST My crying voice did recommend
The ways of Christ for men to scan;
I baptized him as my dear friend
In water of river Jordan;
The holy ghost did then descend
As white as dove's down on me then;
The father's voice, our mirth to amend,
Was made for me like as a man;

"Yond is my son," he said,
"Who pleases me full well."
His light is on us laid,
He comes our cares to quell.

MOSES Now this same night great news have I,
To me, Moses, he showed his might,
And to another prophet truly,
Where on a hill we stood at height;
As white as snow was his body,
His face was like the sun so bright,
No man on earth was so mighty
Who dared look against that light;

And that same light here see I now
Shining on us, certain,
Whereby truly I avow
That we shall soon pass from this pain.

RIBALD Since first that hell was made, and I was put [therein,
Such sorrow never I had, nor heard I such a [din;
My joys begin to fade, my wit waxes thin,
No longer be we glad, these souls we cannot [win.

How Beelzebub! Bind these boys, such har-
[row was never heard in hell!

BEELZEBUB Out Ribald! Thou roars, what is betid? Can
[thou ought tell?

RIBALD Why, hearest thou not this ugly noise?
These lubbers that in limbo dwell,
They make meaning of many joys,
And mirth makes them to swell.

BEELZEBUB Mirth? Nay, nay! That point is past,
More hope of health shall they never have.

RIBALD They cry on Christ full fast,
And says he shall them save.

BEELZEBUB Yea, though he do not, I shall,
For they are sparred in special space;
Whilst I am prince and principal,
They shall never pass out of this place.
Call up Astaroth and Anabal,
To give us counsel in this case;
Bell, Berith, and Belial,
These men their mastery to outface.

Say to sir Satan, our sire,
And bid him stir also
Sir Lucifer's ire.

RIBALD All ready lord I go.

JESUS *Attollite portas, principes, vestras et elevamini*
[portae aeternales, et introibit rex gloriae.

RIBALD Out, harrow, out! What devil is he
That calls him king over us all?
Hark Beelzebub, with me,
For hideously I heard him call.

BEELZEBUB Go, spar the gates, ill might thou be!
And set the watches on the wall;
If once that wretch we see
Fight we till we fall.

And if he more call or cry,
To make us more debate,

Lay on him lustily,
    And drive him from the gate.

DANIEL Nay, with him may ye not fight,
    For he is king and conqueror,
And of so great a might
    Doughty in deeds and dour;
From him comes all this light
    That shines now in this bower;
He is full fierce in fight,
    Worthy to win honour.

BEELZEBUB Honour! Hearest, thou harlot, for what deed?
    All earthly men to me are thrall;
That lad that thou calls Lord, indeed,
    Had never harbour, house, nor hall.

How, sir Satan, come thou near
    And hearken to this cursed rout!

SATAN The devil, what is this I hear!
    What ails thee so to shout?
And me, if I come near,
    Thy brainpan shall I clout!

BEELZEBUB Help bar the gate up here,
    We are besieged about.

SATAN Besieged about! Why, who durst be so bold
    For fear to give us such a fray?

BEELZEBUB It is the Jew that Judas sold
    That died on cross this other day.

SATAN How! In time that tale was told,
    That traitor treats us ill each way;
He shall be here full hard in hold,
    But look he pass not, I thee pray.

BEELZEBUB Pass, nay, nay, he will not void
    From hence without a war;
Nor pause till is destroyed
    All hell in this uproar.

SATAN Fie, fellows! Thereof shall he fail,
    For all his fame I him defy;

I know his tricks from top to tail,
    He gloats on gauds and glory.
Thereby he brought forth from our bale
    The loathed Lazarus of Bethany,
But to the Jews I gave counsel
    That they should cause him die;

I entered there into Judas,
    That fortune to fulfil,
Therefore his hire he has,
    Always to live here still.

RIBALD Sir Satan, since we hear thee say
    Thou and the Jews came to assent,
And knew that Lazarus he won away
    That in our care was surely sent,
Hopest thou the least him mar thou may
    To mend the malice that he has meant?
For if he rob us of our prey
    We will chide ye ere he went.

SATAN Be not at all dismayed
    But boldly seek renown,
Call cunning to your aid,
    And ding that dastard down.

JESUS *Attollite portas, principes, vestras et elevamini*
    [portae aeternales, et introibit rex gloriae.

RIBALD Out, harrow! What harlot is he
    That says such kingdom lies ahead?

DAVID That may thou in psalter see,
    For of this prince thus ere I said;

I said that he should break
    Your bars and bonds by name,
On your works vengeance take;
    Now shalt thou see the same.

JESUS Princes of hell open your gate,
    And let my folk forth go;
The prince of peace comes in his state
    Whether ye will or no.

RIBALD What art thou that speakest so?

JESUS A king of bliss called Jesus.

RIBALD Yea, hence fast I guess thou go,
And meddle thou not with us.

BEELZEBUB Our gates I trust will last,
Though strongly he assail;
If but our bars hold fast
They surely shall prevail.

JESUS This place shall be no longer barred;
Open up, and let my people pass.

RIBALD Out harrow, our mirth is marred,
And burst are all our bonds of brass!

BEELZEBUB Harrow! Our gates begin to quake!
In sunder, I see them go,
All hell I fear to shreds will shake.
Alas, I wail with woe!

RIBALD Limbo is lost, alas!
Sir Satan see our loss;
This work is worse than ever it was.

SATAN Yea, hanged be thou on a cross!

Thieves, I bad ye show renown,
If he made mastery more,
To ding that dastard down,
And beset him sad and sore.

BEELZEBUB Beset him sore, that is soon said!
Come thou thyself and serve him so;
This bitter battle we may dread,
To more than us he would bring woe.

SATAN Fie, fellow, wherefore have ye fled?
Be bold to bandy blow for blow.
Give me my gear, time now I sped,
Myself shall to that gelding go.

Now, thou hell-breaker, abide,
For all thy champion's cheer!
And tell me at this tide
What mastery makest thou here?

JESUS I make no mastery but for mine,
I will them save, whom held hast thou;
Thou hast no power to make them pine,
In my prison I did allow
Them to sojourn, nought as thine,
But thy curst cunning knows just how.

SATAN Where hast thou been that thy design
Was not to come near them ere now?

JESUS Now is the time certain
My father ordained therefore,
That they should pass from pain,
In bliss to dwell for evermore.

SATAN Thy father knew I well by sight,
Carpentry he traded in;
Mary, thy mother, named aright,
The utmost end of all thy kin;
Say who made thee wield such might?

JESUS Thou wicked fiend, let be thy din!
My father lives in heaven's light,
And bides in endless bliss therein.

I am his only son, his promise to fulfil,
To confound thee I come, to sunder at my will.

SATAN God's son! Nay, then might thou be glad,
For nothing need thou crave;
But thou hast lived ay like a lad,
In sorrow, as a simple knave.

JESUS Ah, that was for the love I had
For man's soul, it for to save,
And thee to make amazed and mad,
And ruefully at these tidings rave.

My godhead was not shown
Save to that mother mine,
Whence never was it known
To thee nor none of thine.

SATAN How now? Would this were told in town;
Thou says God is thy sire;

I shall prove by my renown
    Thou moves astray as man in mire.
To break thy bidding these full soon
    Had wrought most readily my desire;
From paradise thou put them down,
    In hell here to have their hire;

And thou thyself by day and night,
    Among men taught full long,
To follow reason and the right
    But here thou workest all wrong.

JESUS I work no wrong nor I teach it,
    If I my men from woe will win;
My prophets plainly preach it,
    All this business I begin;
Of hell they said I would breach it,
    When that I should enter in,
To save my servants from that pit
    Where damnéd souls sit for their sin.

And each true prophet's tale
    Shall be fulfilled in me;
Redeemed now from their bale,
    In bliss now shall they be.

SATAN Now since thou please to pass the laws,
    And boast ye be above all sin,
For those that thou as witness draws
    Full plain against thee shall begin;
As Solomon said in his saws,
    Who that once comes hell within
Never shall escape its claws,
    Therefore, fellow, let be thy din.

Job thy servant also
    In his time did tell
That neither friend nor foe
    Shall find release from hell.

JESUS He said full sooth, that shalt thou see,
    In hell shall be no more release,
But of that place then meant he
    Where sinful care shall ay increase,

In that bale ay shalt thou be,
Where sundry sorrows never cease,
And my folk that were most free
Shall pass unto the place of peace;

For they were here with my will,
And so they shall forth wend;
Thou shalt thyself full fill
The cup of sorrow without end.

SATAN Wilt thou then make me all forgo?
Methinks thou art indeed unkind;
Nay, I pray thee do not so;
Bethink thee better in thy mind;
Or else then let me with thee go,
I pray thee leave me not behind!

JESUS Nay, traitor, thou shalt live in woe,
And to a stake I shall thee bind.

SATAN Now hear I how thou meanst among
Us all with malice to meddle;
But since thou says it shall be long,
Yet some let always with us dwell.

JESUS Yes, know thou well, else were great wrong;
Thou shalt have Cain that slew Abel,
And all that hastes themselves to hang,
As did Judas and Achitophel;

And Dathan and Abaron, and all of their [assent,
Cursed tyrants every one, that me and mine [torment.

And all that will not heed my law,
That I have left in land as new,
That they may hold my name in awe,
And all my sacraments pursue.

My death, my rising, hold in awe,
Who believes them not they are untrue;
Under my doom I shall them draw,
And judge them worse than any Jew.

And they that list to hear my law and live [thereby,
Shall never have harm here, but wealth as [is worthy.

SATAN Have here my hand, I am well paid,
This points to profit I avow.
If this be true that thou hast said,
We shall have more than we have now.
These laws that late thou hast down laid,
I shall them teach not to allow;
If they believe they are betrayed,
I quickly shall them trick somehow.

I shall walk east, I shall walk west,
And work them fiercely, never fear.

JESUS Nay fiend, fast in arrest,
Thou stay, nor shall thou flit from here.

SATAN Fast? Fie! That were a wicked treason!
Fellow, I thee fiercely hit.

JESUS Devil, I command thee down
Into thy seat where thou shalt sit.

SATAN Alas, for dole and care!
I sink into hell pit!

RIBALD Sir Satan, so said I ere,
Now shalt thou have a fit.

JESUS Come now forth, my children all,
Forgiven now what was amiss;
With me now go ye shall
To joy and endless bliss.

ADAM Lord, thou art full strong in might,
So meek to come in this manner,
To help us all the fiend to fight,
When we had paid that forfeit dear;
Here have we dwelt without a light
Four thousand and six hundred year;
Now see we by this solemn sight
What means thy mercy to us here.

EVE Lord, we are worthy more torments to taste;
But now, Lord, thy mercy will not lay us
[waste.

JOHN Lord, I love thee inwardly,
Who me would make thy messenger,
Thy coming on earth to cry,
And teach thy faith both far and near;
Since before thee I was to die,
To bring them tidings that be here,
How they should have God's help from high,
Now see I all those points appear.

MOSES David, thy prophet true,
Oft-times told unto us,
Of thy coming he knew,
And said it should be thus.

DAVID As I said ere yet say I so,
"*Ne derelinquas, domine,*
Animam meam in inferno;"
"Leave never my soul, Lord, after thee,
In deep hell where the damned shall go;
Suffer thou never thy saints to see
The sorrow of such as live in woe,
Ay full of fear, and may not flee."

MOSES Make mirth both more and less,
And love our Lord we may,
That has brought us from bitterness
In bliss to abide for ay.

ISAIAH Therefore now let us sing
In love of Lord Jesus;
Unto his bliss he will us bring,
Te deum laudamus.

[*They process out of hell-mouth.*

THE TWENTY-EIGHTH PLAY

The Resurrection

PILATE	4TH SOLDIER
CAIAPHAS	1ST ANGEL
CENTURION	2ND ANGEL
ANNAS	JESUS
1ST SOLDIER	MARY MAGDALENE
2ND SOLDIER	MARY JACOBI
3RD SOLDIER	MARY SALOME

[*Enter* PILATE, ANNAS, CAIAPHAS, *and* SOLDIERS.

PILATE

Peace, I warn you, if you have wit!
And stand aside or else go sit,
For here are men that go not yet,
And lords of so great might;
We think to abide and not to flit,
I tell you all in sight.

Spare your speech, ye bondmen bold,
And cease your cry till I have told
How my fame I shall unfold
Here in this place;
Who dares my due withhold,
Hanged high be his bones apace.

Know ye not that I am Pilate,
That sat as Justice but of late,
At Calvary where I was at
This day at morn?
I am he of so great state,
Who saw that lad all torn.

Now since that loathed lubber is dead,
A great joy round me has spread,

Therefore I would in every stead
  All should take heed,
Lest any fellows his ways should tread,
  Or dare follow his lead.

For if I knew it, cruelly
His life is lost and that shortly,
That he were better hung full high
  On gallows tree;
Therefore ye prelates should espy
  If any such be.

As I am man of might the most,
If there be any that blow such boast,
In keenest torments shall he roast
  For evermore;
The devil to hell shall harry his ghost,
  But I say no more.

CAIAPHAS Sir, ye need be nothing adread,
The centurion in that stead,
Guards as he has said
  To see that none offend;
We left him there as man most wise,
If any ribalds dare to rise,
To seize them for the next assize,
  And then to make an end.

[*The* CENTURION *enters on horseback.*

CENTURION Ah, blessed Lord Adonai,
What may this marvel signify
That here was shown so openly
  Unto our sight
When did the righteous Jesus die
  In our despite.

All heaven seemed to swoon,
Then ceased to shine both sun and moon,
And dead men also rose up soon,
  Out of their grave;
Stones lay splintered and strewn
  From wall and architrave.

There was seen many a fearful sight,
Our princes indeed, did nothing right,
And so I said to stop their spite;
  As it is true,
That he was most of might,
  The son of God, Jesu.

Fowls in the air and fish in flood,
That day changed their mood,
When that he was rent on rood,
  Lord Adonai;
Full well they understood
  That he was slain that day.
Therefore right as I mean to them fast will [I ride,
And straight from them all glean what [they will say this tide
  Of this affray;
I will no longer bide,
  But fast ride on my way.

God save you, sirs, on every side!
Worship and wealth in world so wide!

PILATE Centurion, welcome this tide,
  Our comely knight!

CENTURION God grant you grace well for to guide,
  And rule you right.

PILATE Centurion, welcome, draw near at hand!
Tell tidings now for which we long,
For ye have gone throughout our land,
  Ye know all still.

CENTURION Sir, I fear me ye have done great wrong
  And wondrous ill.

CAIAPHAS Wondrous ill? I pray thee why?
Declare that to this company.

CENTURION So shall I, sir, full surely,
  With all my main;
A righteous man is he, say I,
  That ye have slain.

PILATE Centurion, thy wit is raw;
Ye are a great man of our law,
And should we any witness draw,
Us to excuse,
Ye should not now withdraw
And us refuse.

CENTURION To maintain truth is well worthy;
I said when I saw him die,
That it was God's son almighty,
That hung there,
So say I still and abide thereby,
Now and for ever.

ANNAS Yea, sir, such reasons may ye rue,
Thou should not name this thing anew
But thou know some tokens true,
Unto us tell.

CENTURION Such sights of wonder never ye knew
As then befell.

CAIAPHAS We pray thee, tell us, of what thing?

CENTURION The elements did themselves down fling,
And in a manner made great mourning,
With strident breath;
They knew by countenance that their king
Was done to death.

The sun for woe waxed all wan,
The moon and stars ceased shining on
The earth that trembled thereupon
As though it spake;
Stones that never stirred, anon
In sunder burst and brake.

And dead men rose up bodily, both great [and small.

PILATE Centurion, beware withal!
The scholars the eclipse it call
Such sudden sight;
That sun and moon a season shall
Lack of their light.

CAIAPHAS Sir, if dead men rise up bodily,
That may be done through sorcery,
Therefore we nothing set thereby,
And nothing grieve.

CENTURION Sir, that saw I truly,
What I shall evermore believe.

Not that for each deed ye did work,
Not only that the sun grew murk,
But how the veil rent in the kirk,
I gladly would know.

PILATE Ah, such tales full soon would us irk,
If they were told so.

Harlot, what the hole from where thou [sprang
Amongst us with thy damned harangue?
Wend forth! High might thou hang,
Vile traitor!

CAIAPHAS Be off, before thou feel a bang,
And hold still thy chatter!

CENTURION Since your faith in me I must forgo, have [now good day!
God lend you grace to know the truth [alway.

ANNAS Withdraw thee fast, if fear thou heed,
For we shall well maintain our deed.

[CENTURION *withdraws.*

PILATE Such wonderful reasons were never to [read,
Now or before.

CAIAPHAS To say such things, even or morn, we need
Never no more.

But of more trouble to beware,
That afterwards might cause us care,
Therefore, sir, while ye are here
Among us all,

Let us no counsel spare
  What may befall.

CAIAPHAS Now Jesus said full openly
Unto the men that stood him by,
A thing that grieves all Jewry,
  And right so may,
That he should rise up bodily
  Within the third day.

If it be so, as might I speed,
Dread we then the latter deed
More than the first, if we take heed
  And tend thereto;
Advise you, sir, for you have need,
  What best to do.

ANNAS Sir, nevertheless if he said so,
He has no might to rise and go,
Save his disciples steal also
  His corpse away;
That were for us a bitter blow,
  A fearful fray.

Then would the people say each one
That he had raised himself alone;
Give orders then to guard that stone
  Which knights defend
Till these three days be come and gone
  And brought to end.

PILATE Now, certain, sir, full well ye say,
And for this same point to purvey
I shall, if that I may;
  He shall not rise,
Nor none shall win him thence away
  In no wise.

Sir knights, that are of deeds doughty,
And chosen chief of chivalry,
As I may herewith notify,
  By day and night
Go ye and guard Jesu's body
  With all your might.

And for what happen may,
Guard him well until the third day,
That no traitor steal his corpse away,
    Out of that stead;
For if they do, truly I say,
    Ye shall be dead.

1ST SOLDIER Yes, sir Pilate, for certain,
We shall guard with might and main;
No traitor tricks us, that is plain,
    To steal him so;
Get we what gear is for our gain,
    And let us go.

[*They go to the tomb.*

2ND SOLDIER No doubt we are the best in town
To guard him for your great renown;
Upon each side let us sit down,
    Altogether;
And straightway I shall crack his crown
    Whoso comes hither.

1ST SOLDIER Who should be where, that would I know?

2ND SOLDIER Even on this side will I go.

3RD SOLDIER And at his feet I sit me so.

4TH SOLDIER And I shall stay quite near!
Now by Mohammed, who dares to show
    Themselves in here

This corpse in treason for to take,
Though dragon from a burning lake,
Yet would I strike, make no mistake;
    Have here my hand;
This corpse, though for three days we [wake,
    Bides with our band.

[*Then the* ANGELS *sing "Christus resurgens" and then* JESUS *speaks.*

JESUS Earthly man, that I have wrought,
Lightly wake, and sleep thou nought!

With bitter bale I have thee bought,
To make thee free;
To this dungeon deep I am brought,
And all for love of thee.

Behold how dear I would thee buy!
My wounds are wet and all bloody;
Thee sinful man full dear bought I
With cares most keen;
Defile not now but fortify,
Now thou art clean.

Clean have I made thee, sinful man,
With woe and wandering I thee won,
From heart and side the blood out ran,
Such pain was mine;
Thou must love me that my life's span
Gave for thine.

Thou sinful man past me ye pace,
Swiftly to me thou turn thy face,
Behold my body, in each place,
How sore a sight;
Torn in this deep disgrace
Man, for thy plight.

With cords enough and coarse ropes tough
My limbs outdrawn by fell Jews rough,
For that I was not size enough
Unto the bore;
These deep wounds, man, and thy rebuff
Suffered I therefore.

A crown of thorn, that is so keen,
On me they set, me to demean,
Two thieves hung they me between,
For spite of old;
For this and these wounds here now seen
May I thee scold.

Behold my shanks and my knees,
My arms and thighs and these;

[*He holds out his hands.*

Behold me well, look what each sees,
But sorrow and pain;
This death I met to do thee ease
And for thy gain.

And yet more understand thou shall;
Instead of drink they gave me gall,
Mixed it with vinegar withal,
Those Jews fell;
Through my death may the fiend enthrall
No soul in hell.

Behold my body, how the Jews did it [wrong
With knots of whips and scourges strong;
My bright blood sprang out for long
On every side;
Knots where they hit, well may thou wit,
Made wounds so wide.

And therefore thou shall understand
In body, head, feet, and hand,
Five hundred wounds and five thousand
Here may thou see;
And thereto nine were dealt full even
For love of thee.

Behold in me nought else is left,
Before thou were from me bereft,
I should again bear each blow deft,
And for thee die;
Here may thou see that I love thee,
Man, faithfully.

Since I for love, man, bought thee dear.
As thou thyself the sooth sees here,
I pray thee heartily, with good cheer,
Love me again;
That it pleased me that I for thee
Suffered this pain.

If thou thy life in sin have led,
Mercy to ask be not adread;

The least drop I for thee bled
    Might cleanse thee now,
All the sin the world within
    Though done had thou.

I was more enangered with Judas
For that he would not ask me grace,
Than I was for his trespass
    That he me sold;
I was ready to show mercy,
    Of none would he be told.

Lo, how I stretch my arms out wide,
For thee safely to provide,
For thee my love shall ay abide,
    Well may thou know!
Some love again I would full fain
    Thou would me show.

Save love nought else ask I of thee,
And that thou try all sin to flee;
Strive thou to live in charity
    Both night and day;
Then in my bliss that never shall miss
    Thou shall dwell ay.

For I am very prince of peace,
From all sins I may thee release,
And whoso will from their sins cease
    And mercy cry,
Through mass I grant them ease
    By bread, of my body.

That very bread of life
Becomes my flesh in these words five;
Who it receives in sin or strife
    Is dead for ever;
Whoso it takes in righteous life
    Die shall he never.

[JESUS *retires and the three* MARYS *advance*.

MARY Alas! Death only may relieve my plight!

MAGDALENE In woe I long for endless night,
I droop and daze to see that sight
That I did see;
My Lord, magnificent in might,
Is dead for me.

Alas! That I should see his pain,
Him never shall I see again,
For every ill he could obtain
The cure for all;
Hope and help would all men gain
Who on him call.

MARY JACOBI Alas! How stand I on my feet
When I think of his wounds wet!
Jesus, that was in life so sweet,
And never did ill,
Is dead and buried, his defeat
Is with us still.

MARY SALOME Without reason these Jews each one
That lovely Lord they have undone,
And trespass did he never none,
Nor ever said;
To whom now may we, mourning, run,
Since our Lord is dead?

MARY MAGDALENE Since he is dead, my sisters dear,
Wend we will with full good cheer
With our anointments fair and clear
That we have brought,
For to anoint his wounds severe,
Which Jews on him wrought.

MARY JACOBI Go we then, my sisters free,
For sore I long his corpse to see,
But I know not how best it be;
We are alone,
And which shall of us sisters three
Remove the stone?

MARY SALOME Without more help we do not so,
For it is high and heavy also.

MARY MAGDALENE
Sisters, no further need we go
Nor make mourning;
I see two sit where we should go
In white clothing.

MARY JACOBI
Certain, the truth we may not hide,
The grave stone here is put aside.

MARY SALOME
Certain for what thing that may betide
Now will we wend.
To seek his love, and with him bide,
That was our friend.

1ST ANGEL
Ye mourning women in your thought,
Here in this place whom have ye sought?

MARY MAGDALENE
Jesu that unto death was brought,
Our Lord so free.

2ND ANGEL
Indeed, women, here is he nought;
Come near and see.

1ST ANGEL
He is not here, the sooth to say,
The place is void wherein he lay;
The clothing for his grave ye may
Clearly behold;
He is risen and gone his way,
As he you told.

2ND ANGEL
Even as he told so done has he,
And risen up most powerfully;
He shall be found in Galilee,
In flesh and fell;
To his disciples now wend ye,
And thus them tell.

[ANGELS *withdraw.*

MARY MAGDALENE
My sisters free, since it is so,
He has defied death's final blow,
And risen as said these angels two,
Such must we teach;
As ye have heard, where'er ye go
Look that ye preach.

MARY JACOBI
As we have heard, so shall we say;
Mary, our sister, have good day!

MARY MAGDALENE
Now very God, as he well may,
Man most of might,
He guide you, sisters, well in your way,
And rule you right.

Alas, what now shall become of me?
My caitiff heart will break in three,
When that I think on that same body
How it was spilt;
Through feet and both hands nailed was [he
Though free from guilt.

Though free from guilt yet was he ta'en,
That lovely Lord, they have him slain,
From sin he was without a stain,
Nor yet did amiss;
For my guilt he suffered pain,
And not for his.

How might I, as I loved him sweet,
Who suffered for me such defeat,
Since he is buried beneath my feet,
Such kindness tell?
There is no way till that we meet
Can make all well.

[*The* WOMEN *retire and the* SOLDIERS *wake.*

1ST SOLDIER
Out, alas! What shall I say?
Where is the corpse that herein lay?

2ND SOLDIER
What ails thee man? He is away
Whom we should guard!

1ST SOLDIER
Rise up and see.

2ND SOLDIER
Harrow! Thieves, for ay
Our lives are marred.

3RD SOLDIER
What devil ails you two
To make so loud to-do?

2ND SOLDIER
Why, he is gone.

3RD SOLDIER
Alas, but who?

2ND SOLDIER
He that here lay.

3RD SOLDIER Harrow! Devil, how got he away?

4TH SOLDIER What, could he so from us escape,
False traitor, make this tomb so gape,
And those clothes there neatly drape?
We are undone!
Our heads will roll, each from the nape
Wholly each one.

1ST SOLDIER Alas, what shall I do this day,
Since this traitor has won a way?
And safely, sirs, I dare well say
He rose alone.

2ND SOLDIER If sir Pilate hears this fray
Be we dead as stone.

4TH SOLDIER Believe ye well he rose indeed?

2ND SOLDIER I saw myself from hence him speed.

1ST SOLDIER When that he stirred we gave no heed
None could it ken.

4TH SOLDIER Alas, full hard shall be my need
Among all men.

3RD SOLDIER Yea, but knows sir Pilate he is fled,
That we were sleeping when he sped,
We must forfeit, without dread,
All that we have.

4TH SOLDIER We must tell lies, each for his head,
That he may save.

1ST SOLDIER I count that well, so might I go.

2ND SOLDIER And I assent thereto also.

3RD SOLDIER A thousand numbered all our foe
Well armed each one,
Forced us his corpse then to forgo,
Almost undone.

4TH SOLDIER Nay, certain, I hold nought so good
As say the sooth right as it stood,
How that he rose with main and mood,
And went his way;

Though slay us sir Pilate should,
Thus dare I say.

1ST SOLDIER Why, and dare thou to sir Pilate go
With these tidings and tell him so?

2ND SOLDIER So say I that we do also
We die but once.

ALL SOLDIERS Now he that worked us all this woe
Curse all his bones.

4TH SOLDIER Together may our fortunes mend,
Since we must to sir Pilate wend,
I trust that each remain a friend
Ere that we pass.

[*They come to* PILATE.

1ST SOLDIER Now I shall tell our tale to the end,
Right as it was.

Sir Pilate, prince without a peer,
Sir Caiaphas and Annas there,
And all the lords about you here,
To call by name,
Mohammed save and keep you clear
From sin and shame.

PILATE Ye are welcome, our knights so keen,
Much mirth for you we mean,
But tell your story us between,
How ye have wrought.

1ST SOLDIER Our watching, lord, as we have seen,
Has come to nought.

CAIAPHAS To nought? Alas, say you not so.

2ND SOLDIER The prophet Jesu, that ye well know,
Is risen and gone some time ago,
With main and might.

PILATE Therefore the devil death thee show,
Vile, recreant knight!

What! Cowardly curs I you call!
Yet let him pass among you all?

3RD SOLDIER Sir, what could we do withal
When forth he sped?

4TH SOLDIER Such fear we felt we down did fall,
And quake for dread.

1ST SOLDIER We were so dazed, each one,
When that he put aside the stone,
We quaked for fear, and durst stir none,
And could do no more.

PILATE Why, but rose he by himself alone?

2ND SOLDIER Yea, lord, of that be ye sure.

We heard never such, even or morn,
Nor yet our fathers, I'll be sworn,
Such melody, midday nor morn,
Was made before.

PILATE Alas, then are our laws forlorn
For evermore!

Ah, devil! what shall happen now?
By wisdom fares the world, I vow;
I pray you, Caiaphas, tell us how
To foil this fray.

CAIAPHAS Sir, if my book-learning would allow,
Fain would I say.

ANNAS To say the best forsooth I shall;
It shall be profit for us all,
Yon knights' words let us recall,
How he is missed;
We would not, for what might befall,
That any wist.

And therefore, by your courtesy,
Reward them generously.

PILATE Of this counsel well paid am I,
It shall be thus.
Sir knights, that are of deeds doughty,
Pay heed to us.

Hearken now how ye shall say,
Whereso ye go by night and day;

Ten thousand men of good array
    Came you to kill,
And stole from you his corpse away
    Against your will.

Look ye say this in every land,
And if ye keep to my command
Ten thousand pounds you have in hand
    As your reward;
And my friendship, ye understand,
    I shall spare not as your lord.

But look ye say as I intend.

1ST SOLDIER Yea, sir, as Mohammed me amend,
In every country where we wend
    By night or day,
Whereso we go, whereso we wend,
    This shall we say.

PILATE Mohammed bless you night and day!

[PILATE *and the* SOLDIERS *retire.* MARY *and* JESUS *advance.*

MARY MAGDALENE Tell me gardener, I thee pray,
If thou bore ought my Lord away;
Tell me the truth, say me not nay
    Where that he lies,
I shall remove him if I may,
    In any wise.

JESUS Woman, why weepest thou? Be still!
Whom seekest thou? Tell me thy will,
    Deny me not with nay.

MARY MAGDALENE For my Lord I pine full ill;
The place his body now may fill
    Tell me I pray;

And I shall, if I may, his body bear with [me,
Unto my dying day the better should I be.

JESUS Woman, woman, turn thy thought!
Know thou well I hid him nought,

Then bore him nowhere with me;
Go seek, look if thou find him ought.

MARY MAGDALENE
In faith I have him sought,
But nowhere him may see.

JESUS
Why, what was he to thee, in all truth now [to say?

MARY MAGDALENE
Ah! Dear he was to me that no longer [dwell I may.

JESUS
Mary, thou seeks thy God, and that am I.

MARY MAGDALENE
Raboni, my Lord so dear!
Now am I whole that thou art here,
Suffer me to nigh thee near,
And kiss thy feet;
Might I do so, no more I fear,
For thou art sweet.

JESUS
Nay, Mary, touch not thou me,
For to my father, tell I thee,
Ascended have I nought;
Tell my brethren I shall be
Before them all in trinity
Whose will that I have wrought.
To peace now are they brought, that im- [prisoned were in pain.
Wherefore rejoice in thought, that God has [come again.

Mary, thou must from me go,
Mine errand shall thou surely show,
In no temptation fall;
To my disciples say thou so,
That wretched are and lapped in woe,
That I them succour shall.
By name Peter thou call, and say I shall be
Before him and them all, myself in Galilee.

MARY MAGDALENE
Lord, I shall make my voyage
To tell them hastily;
When they hear that message,
They will be all merry.

This Lord was slain, certainly,
Falsely killed, no man knew why,
He did nought amiss;
But with him spake I bodily
Thereof comes my bliss.

My bliss has come, my care is gone,
My lovely Lord I met alone;
I be as blithe in blood and bone
As ever I might;
Our Lord has thrust aside death's stone.
My heart is light.

I am as light as leaf on tree,
For joyful sight that I did see,
For well I know that it was he
My Lord Jesu;
Lord, he that betrayed thee
Sorely may rue.

To Galilee now will I fare,
Call his disciples from their care;
With joy the risen Lord declare
That makes their bliss begin;
That worthy child that Mary bare,
He save you all from sin.

THE TWENTY-NINTH PLAY

The Pilgrims

CLEOPHAS LUKE JESUS

CLEOPHAS Almighty God, Jesu,
That born was of a maiden free,
Thou was a lord and prophet true,
Whilst thou had life and sought to be
Amongst us men:
Ill was thy death, and woe is me
That I it ken!

I ken it well that thou was slain
Wholly for me and all mankind:
The Jews readily caused that pain
Alas, why was thou man so blind
Thy Lord to slay?
On him why would thou have no mind
But him betray?

Blue thou beat him bare, his breast thou made [all black,
His wounds all wet they were: of pain there [was no lack!

LUKE As physician none could teach our Lord so [meek and mild,
Who so well could preach, by sin stayed un- [defiled:
Readily he taught each to leave ways rough and [wild,
His death has made a breach, for they him so [beguiled
This day,
Alas why did they so

To tug him to and fro?
From him they would not go
Till his life ebbed away.

CLEOPHAS These cursed Jews, on them cry woe!
They made our Lord his life forgo,
In innocence he was brought low
Upon the cross,
To beat his body blue, his foe
Thought it no loss.

LUKE Thou says the truth, they caused him pain,
And at that were they glad and fain.
They would not leave till he was slain
And done to death:
Therefore we mourn with might and main
With pain-drawn breath.

CLEOPHAS Yea, wretchedly we may it rue,
For him that was so good and true
That through the falsehood of a Jew
Was thus betrayed:
Therefore our sorrow comes anew,
Our joys must fade.

LUKE Certain it is a wondrous thing
That they would for no tokening,
Nor yet for his teaching,
Trust him as true;
They might have seen in his doing
Full great virtue.

CLEOPHAS For all that they to him did say
He answered never yea nor nay,
But as a lamb meek was he ay,
When they did bawl;
He spake never, by night or day,
No word at all.

LUKE As if he were in no such plight,
But meeting death before our sight,
As though he were of little might,
He suffered all;

He stood as still and upright
As stone in wall.

CLEOPHAS Alas, for dole! What was their skill
That precious Lord his life to spill?
And he served never none ill
In word or deed;
But prayed for them with all his will,
When more was his need.

LUKE When I think on his passion,
With tears I well nigh drown,
And his mother in compassion,
Did for sharp sorrow shake;
Under the cross when she fell down,
For her son's sake.

CLEOPHAS Methinks my heart was full of woe
When I saw him to death go;
The wicked Jews such spite did show
In rage so rough;
Blue was his body through many a blow
With strokes enough.

LUKE Methinks my heart dropped all in blood
When I saw him hang on the rood,
And ask a drink in full mild mood,
Right from on high;
Vinegar and gall, that was not good,
They brought him then truly.

CLEOPHAS Never no man had more need
That suffered half so great misdeed
As he, when death took him with speed,
Nor yet the care;
Therefore on sorrow I shall feed
Wheresoever I fare.

LUKE Whereso I fare he is in my mind,
But when I think on him so kind,
How bitterly they did him bind
Upon a tree,
Scarce my wits I then can find,
Such misery besets me.

[*Enter* JESUS *dressed as a* PILGRIM.

JESUS Pilgrims, why make ye this moan,
And walk so ruefully by the way?
Scold ye every stick and stone?
Or what ails ye, say!

What say ye as ye go along,
As ye your sad path do prolong?
To hear your grief full sore I long,
Your cares to know;
It seems ye are in sorrows strong,
Here as ye go.

CLEOPHAS What way, for shame, man, has thou taken
That thou know not of this affair?
Has thou all company forsaken,
To be of such news unaware?

JESUS I pray you, if it be your will,
Of such things to me speak your fill;
Ye are of heart so heavy and ill
Here in this way;
That you would show me now your will
I would you pray.

LUKE Art thou a pilgrim thyself alone,
Walking the country on thine own,
And know not what has come and gone
These last few days?
Methinks thou should make moan
And weep here in thy ways.

JESUS Why, what is done, can ye now say,
In this land this very day?
Has there befallen any fray
In the land anywhere?
If ye can, tell me I pray,
Before I farther fare.

CLEOPHAS Why, know you not who met his fate
Here at Jerusalem of late,
Whom the Jews killed in their hate,
Not long ago?

On the true prophet we meditate
And on his woe.

LUKE Yea, on Jesus, the Nazarene,
That was a prophet true and clean,
In word and work, full meek, I mean,
And that we found:
And so has he full long been
To all around.

To God and to the people too;
Therefore they thought his death was due,
And death the Jews without ado
Contrived his plight;
Therefore his fate so sad we rue
By day and night.

CLEOPHAS Him wicked Jews betrayed with guile,
To their high priests within a while,
And all began him to revile,
To curse and threat:
Upon a cross, not hence a mile,
His death he met.

LUKE We hoped it was he truly
Who his own death would defy,
As is told in prophecy
Of Christ's doing:
But certainly, that will not be
For nothing.

From off the cross he was ta'en,
And full soon laid low again,
In a stone grave to remain,
We saw him go:
Whether he be risen again
We do not know.

JESUS Pilgrims your speech is sad astray,
And I shall say directly why,
Your trust is merely in hearsay,
You cannot, surely, stand thereby,
The thing you hear:

And prophets told it openly
In this manner.

They said a child there should be born
To save mankind from sin and shame,
This same before had David sworn
And other prophets of learned fame,
And Daniel:
Some said he dead should be
And lie in earth days three,
And then as Lord almighty,
Rise up in flesh and fell.

CLEOPHAS Now, sir, forsooth, as God me save,
Women have scared us in our thought:
They said that they were at his grave,
And that instead they found him nought,
But said a light
Came down with angels, and up him [brought
There in their sight.

We would not trust them for nothing,
If they were there in the morning,
We said they knew not his rising
When it should be:
But some of us without waiting,
Went thither to see.

LUKE Yea, some of us, sir, have been there,
And found it as the women said,
Of any corpse that grave was bare,
Aside the gravestone also laid,
This sight we saw:
I wept for I was so dismayed,
My grief so raw.

JESUS Ye fools, ye are not stable!
Where is your wit, I say?
Both bewildered and unable
To reckon the right way,
For believe it is no fable
That has befallen this same day.

He knew, when at his table,
That Judas should him soon betray.

Methinks you little faith allow,
Nor with might and main
Heed what prophecies avow,
Which are not vain.
Told they not what wise and how
That Christ should suffer pain?
And so to his passion bow
To enter to his joy again.

Take heed of Moses and more also,
That were prophets true and good;
They said Jesus to death should go,
And be tortured on the rood;
And by the Jews be beaten so,
His wounds running with red blood;
After should he rise and go,
Such things the prophets understood.

Christ behoved to suffer this,
Forsooth, right as I say,
And after enter to his bliss
Unto his father for ay,
Ever to live with him and his,
Wherever is game and play:
Of that mirth shall he never miss
When he wends hence away.

CLEOPHAS Now, sir, we thank thee oft and well
For coming to us hither:
And so kindly us to tell
The prophecies altogether.

JESUS By your leave, sirs, for I must wend,
For I have far to journey.

LUKE Now, sir, we pray you, as our friend,
All night to abide for charity
And take your rest:
Then in the morning may ye be
For travelling best.

CLEOPHAS Sir, we pray you, for God's sake,
This night penance with us take,
With such cheer as we can make,
And that we pray:
We may no further walk nor wake,
Gone is the day.

LUKE Dwell with us, sir, if ye might,
For now it grows toward the night,
The day is gone that was so bright,
Let rest prevail:
Meat and drink is but your right
For thy good tale.

JESUS I thank you both for this good cheer,
At this time I may not dwell here,
My way to walk is still severe,
Where I must tread:
I cannot longer bide so near,
As ye have said.

CLEOPHAS Now, as I hope no more to smart,
At this time we shall not part,
Unless you thrust us through your art
Further away:
Unto the city with good heart,
Now wend our way.

LUKE Thou art a pilgrim, as we are,
This night shall thou fare as we fare,
Be it less or be it more
Thou shall assay:
Then tomorrow thou prepare
To wend thy way.

JESUS Friends, for to fulfil your will
I will abide with you awhile.

CLEOPHAS Sir, ye are welcome, though small our skill,
Such as we have lacks any guile.

LUKE Now are we here at this town,
Let us now go sit us down,
Our care in supper let us drown,
Here is our food:

We have enough, sir, by my crown,
By God so good.

[*They then prepare a table.*

CLEOPHAS Lo, here a board and cloth is laid,
And bread thereon freshly arrayed:
Sit down our care is well repaid
And make good cheer:
It is but penance, as we said
That we have here.

[*Then they shall sit down and* JESUS *shall sit in the midst of them: then shall* JESUS *bless the bread and break it into three pieces, and afterwards he shall vanish from their sight:*

LUKE Lo! Of this man what has become,
Right here that sat between us two?
He broke the bread and gave us some:
How might he hence thus from us go—
And leave this spot?
It was our Lord, it must be so,
And we knew not.

CLEOPHAS When went he hence, wither, and how,
Such knew I not in world so wide,
For had I known, I make a vow,
He should have stayed, what so betide:
But it was Jesus, that with us was,
Strange, methinks, the truth to say,
Thus privily from us to pass,
I knew not when he went away.
We were indeed full blind, alas!
And as I think beguiled for ay,
For speech and beauty that he has
Man might him know this day.

LUKE Ah, dear God, what may this be?
Right now was he here by me:
Again now all is empty,
He is away:
We are beguiled truly,
So may we say.

CLEOPHAS Where was our heart, where was our thought,
So far on way as he us brought,
Knowledge of him that we had nought
In all that time?
He was so like methought
To a pilgrim.

LUKE Dear God, why could we not him know?
So plainly seen by us below,
His words alone himself did show
One by one.
And now from us so soon to go,
Us now to shun.

CLEOPHAS I had no knowledge it was he,
Until he broke this bread in three,
And dealt it here to thee and me
With his own hand;
When he passed hence we could not see,
Nor understand.

LUKE We are to blame, yea, indeed.
That we took no better heed
When to come with us he agreed,
Where we were bound:
We might have known when we did feed,
Sitting on ground.

CLEOPHAS When he took bread full well I knew,
With his own hand he broke it true,
And gave it us, us to renew,
Right as he meant:
I knew him then as hitherto,
With good intent.

LUKE That we knew him, well he saw,
Therefore he did himself withdraw,
For us he would not overawe
Should he abide:
I wonder greatly by what law
Away that he should glide.

CLEOPHAS Alas, we were full murk in thought
Too prompt our own ideas to spread:

Man, for shame why did thou nought
  When he on board broke us this bread?

He told the prophecy more and less
  And spake it here with his own breath,
That to him so great distress
  Was done by Jews to bring him death,
    And more:
  We will go seek that king
    That suffered such wounds sore.

LUKE Rise, go we hence from this place,
To Jerusalem make we apace,
And tell our brethren of this case,
  Readily thus:
When he rose from death's embrace,
  He appeared to us.

CLEOPHAS In Jerusalem I understand
Our old friends will be at hand,
In that country and in that land
  We shall them meet.
Our words none shall withstand,
  Right in the street.

LUKE Let us not tarry for less nor more,
But fast on foot our way explore:
Our comfort soon he shall restore,
  A sign was this:
That blessed child that Mary bore
  Grant you his bliss.

[*They go out.*

THE THIRTIETH PLAY

Thomas of India

JESUS	5TH APOSTLE
MARY MAGDALENE	6TH APOSTLE
PAUL	7TH APOSTLE
PETER	8TH APOSTLE
3RD APOSTLE	9TH APOSTLE
4TH APOSTLE	10TH APOSTLE
	THE APOSTLE THOMAS

MARY Hail brethren! And God be here!
I bring news to amend your cheer,
  Trust ye it and know:
He is risen, the truth to say,
I met him going by the way,
  He bad me tell you so.

PETER Away, woman, an idle boast!
It was some spirit, or some ghost:
  Otherwise nought:
We may not trust in any wise
That dead men may to life rise:
  This then is our thought.

PAUL It may be truly for man's meed,
The Jews made him grimly bleed
  Through feet, hands, and side:
With nails on cross they hanged him long,
Wherefore, woman, thou says wrong,
  As might I bliss abide.

MARY Stop arguing and forget your loss!
I have seen him that died on cross,
  And spoken to him as I do now:
Therefore to both of you, say I,

Put away your heresy,
  Trust steadfastly as I avow.

PETER Away, woman! Let be thy fare,
  For shame and also sin!
If we mourned with heavier care
  His life may we not win.

PAUL And it is written in our law
No woman's judgement hold in awe,
  Nor too quickly show belief:
For with their cunning and their guile
They can laugh then weep awhile,
  When nothing gives them grief.

In our books thus find we written,
All manner of men have so been bitten,
  By women in this wise:
Like an apple ripe is she,
A joy, without a doubt to see,
  On the board as it lies.

If any take and start to chew
It is rotten through and through
  To the core within:
Wherefore in woman is no law,
For she holds nothing in awe,
  As Christ me save from sin.

Therefore we trust not easily,
Unless we saw it surely,
  And the manner how:
In woman's word trust have we nought,
For they are fickle in word and thought,
  To that I make my vow.

MARY As I am freed from all my care,
It is as true as you stand there,
  By him that is my brother.

PETER I dare wager with my head,
That before we go to bed,
  We shall hear some other.

PAUL

If it be truth and not hearsay,
And if this be the third day
Then shall we plainly see.

MARY

If no truth lies in my speech,
And it proved, ye I beseech
For false that ye hold me.

PETER

Out, alas! I think, my dears, as I stand in [this stead,
Such sorrow my heart shears, in a whirl is [all my head:
Since Magdalene this witness bears, that [Jesus rose from dead,
My poor eyes have wept salt tears, on [earth to see him tread.
But alas, that ever I awaked that dread [and doleful night,
When I for care and cold quaked by a fire [burning full bright,
When I my Lord Jesus forsook, for dread [of woman's might:
To righteous judgement will I look that I [lose not that seemly sight,

Alas for such mad hardihood, no man re- [pented faster:
I said, in need if he stood, to him none [should be truer:
I said I knew not that good creature my [master.

Alas! That we from thee fled, nor to thee [had turned again;
When thou among the Jews was led, none [dared thee to sustain,
But forsook thee that us fed, for we would [not be ta'en;
We were as prisoners sore adread by the [Jews for to be slain.

PAUL

Now Jesu, for thy life sweet, who hath [thus mastered thee?

That in the bread that we eat, thyself given [would be:
And later through hands and feet, be [nailed upon a tree:
Grant us grace, we entreat, thy light in [man to see.

[*Then comes* JESUS *and sings "Peace shall be to you shortly, this is the day which the Lord has made".*

This is the day that God made, and mirth [without alloy,
The holy ghost comes as our aid, God's [most gracious envoy:
In apparel red arrayed he brings us bliss [and joy:
Softly on earth he stayed our doldrums to [destroy.

4TH APOSTLE This deed through God is done, thus in all [our sight,
Mighty God, true King on throne, who in [Mary did alight,
Send us, Lord, this blessed boon: as thou [art God of might,
Surely to see him soon and have of him a [sight.

[*Again* JESUS *appears and sings "Peace be shortly with you".*

5TH APOSTLE Whoso comes in God's great name, ay [blessed must he be!
Mighty God shield us from shame, in thy [mother's name, Mary:
These wicked Jews will us blame: thou [grant us for to see
Thy very body and the same that died [upon the tree.

JESUS Peace be with you everyone! It is I, dread [thou nought,
That with you so much have done, and [dearly with death you bought.

Grope and feel flesh and bone and form of
[man well wrought:
Of such things ghosts have none: look
[whether ye know me ought.

That dead but now alive, no man that
[truth may hide:
Behold my wounds all five, through hands
[and feet and side:
To death did love me drive, my life blood
[to provide.
Of sin who will him shrive, these wounds
[shall be his guide.

For one so sweet a thing myself so dear
[had wrought,
Man's soul, my dear darling, to battle was
[I brought:
For that they did me ding, to force me
[from my thought,
Upon the cross to bring, yet love forgot I
[nought.

Love makes me as ye may see, sprinkled
[with blood so red:
Love made my heart so free, it opens in
[every stead:
Love so freely condemned me, and drove
[me to be dead:
Love raised me by power almighty, sweeter
[than mead I sped.

Know thou, man, to thee I cry, hold my
[father in thy fear;
Thine own soul keep cleanly, whilst thou
[art living here;
Slay it not with thy body, beguiled by sins
[severe,
On me and it have mercy, for I have
[bought it dear.

My dear friends, now may ye see, in truth
[that it is I,

That died upon that blessed tree and after
[rose up bodily:
And that the steadfast truth it be, ye shall
[see suddenly:
Of your meat give ye me, such as ye have
[ready.

[*A table is prepared, and the* 6TH APOSTLE *offers a honeycomb filled with honey and fish.*

6TH APOSTLE Lord, lo here a roasted fish and a comb of
[honey
Laid full fair in a dish and full honestly:
Here is no other meat but this in all our
[company,
But well are we that we have this to thy
[liking only.

JESUS My father of heaven dear, that made me
[born to be
Of a maiden kept most dear, and after to
[die on tree,
From death to life to appear, raised me by
[power almighty,
Speaking to allay fear, this meat thou bless
[through me.

In the father's name and the son and the
[holy ghost,
In three persons all in one glorious godhead
[steadfast:
I give this meat my benison, through words
[mightiest most
Now will I eat as anyone again my man-
[hood to taste
My dear friends come lay to, and eat for
[charity:
As my father bids me do I eat and so eat
[ye.
I eat that it may be true what is written of
[me
In Moses' law, that anew it fulfilled might
[be.

Remember ye what I you told in certain
[time and stead,
When I gave my power to hold to you in
[form of bread,
That my body should be sold, my blood
[be spilt so red:
This body buried dead and cold, the third
[day rise from dead?

Your hearts were filled with woe and dread
[while I have from you been:
My rising up from dead, no doubt can
[come between:
By truth your way be sped through stead-
[fast words and clean.
Dear friends, trust now the dead, that ye
[with eyes have seen.

Ye have disgrace and shame for your dis-
[severance,
I forgive you the blame, in me rest your
[assurance:
To folk whose sin them lame, preach them
[to repentance,
Forgive sin in my name, enjoin them to
[penance.

The grace of the holy ghost within receive
[here from me

[*At this he breathes into them.*

The which shall never cease within. I give
[you power almighty
Whom in earth ye cleanse of sin, in heaven
[cleansed shall be,
And whom in earth ye bind therein, bound
[in heaven be he.

[*At this he leaves them.*

7TH APOSTLE Jesu Christ in trinity to thee I cry and call,
That born was of a maiden free, save us
[sinners all!

For us was hanged upon a tree, drank
[vinegar and gall,
Thy servants save from vanity, in despair
[that we not fall.

8TH APOSTLE Brethren, be we stable in thought, despair
[put we away,
In unbelief that we be nought, for we may
[safely say,
He that mankind on cross has bought from
[death rose the third day:
We saw the wounds in him were wrought,
[all bloody still were they.

9TH APOSTLE He told us first he should be ta'en and for
[man's sin should die,
Be dead and buried under a stone and after
[rise up bodily;
Now is he quick from grave gone, he came
[and stood us by,
And let us see each one the wounds of his
[body.

10TH APOSTLE Death that is so keen Jesu overcome has,
As he told us, so we glean, from death how
[he should pass:
Jesu stood as witness between all with him
[that dwelling was,
All his disciples have him seen, save only
[Thomas.

[*Enter* THOMAS.

THOMAS If that I proud as peacock go, my heart is
[full of care:
If any sorrow might slay man so, apart my
[heartstrings tear:
My life worries me with woe, of bliss I am
[full bare,
Yet would I neither friend nor foe knew
[my deep despair.

Jesu, my life so good, than whom none
[better be,

No wiser man nor better food, nor none
[kinder than he:
The Jews have nailed him on the rood,
[nailed with nails three
And with a spear they spilt his blood,
[great sorrow it was to see.

To see the blood run down his skin well
[more than dole it was,
Such great pain for man's sin, such doleful
[death on cross:
My life has no more joy within since he to
[death did pass,
For he was fair of cheek and chin, for dole
[of death alas!

[*At this he goes to the* DISCIPLES.

Mighty God that stays alive, that never
[died, nor shall,
Woe and hardship from you drive, that ye
[not therein fall.

PETER He thee save with his wounds five, to Jesus
[Christ we call,
That rose from death to life and came be-
[fore us all.

THOMAS What, Peter! Art thou mad? Living who
[was him like?
For his death I am not glad, my heart deep
[sorrows spike,
Such torture from the Jews he had, his
[death stemmed their dislike:
Thou forsook him when most sad, for fear
[they might thee strike.

PAUL Those words, dear Thomas, unsay, such
[thoughts from thy mind drive,
For Jesus rose the third day from death in
[flesh alive;
With us he made short stay, and showed
[us his wounds five,

And eaten, as man may, honey taken from
[hive.

THOMAS Let be for shame! Clearly a phantom de-
[ceives thee!
Ye saw him not bodily, his spirit it might
[well be,
To gladden hearts so sorry in your ad-
[versity:
He loved us well and faithfully, therefore
[sorrow slays me.

3RD APOSTLE You know, Thomas, and truth it was, and
[often heard it say.
How a fish swallowed Jonas, three days
[therein he lay:
Yet God gave him might to pass, and safely
[win away:
Might not God that such might has, raise
[his son the third day?

THOMAS Man, if thou can understand, Christ said
[himself to you and me,
All might was in his hand, all one was God
[and he!
Full dark was all the land when he died on
[the tree.
I dread that none may stand his comforter
[to be.

4TH APOSTLE The holy ghost to Mary came, and in her
[maidenhead
God's mother she became, to manhood she
[him bred:
For love he went to claim his kingdom
[without dread:
Having fought, from human frame and
[human clothes he sped.

THOMAS If he skipped out of his clothing, yet you
[grant his corpse was dead:
It was his corpse that made showing unto
[you in his stead:

For to trust in your carping my heart is
[heavy as lead:
His death gives me great mourning, my
[wits whirl in my head.

5TH APOSTLE His spirit went to hell a space while his
[body lay slain,
And brought the souls from Satan's place,
[at price of Satan's pain:
His way the third day he did trace unto
[the body again,
God and man are raised through grace,
[and therefore are we fain.

THOMAS It seems you all conflict as you your rea-
[sons show,
But tell, no truth omit, each of you in a
[row:
When Christ came you to visit, as ye tell
[me this was so,
Whether as man or spirit, what gave ye
[cause to know?

6TH APOSTLE Thomas, unto thee anon, hereto answer I
[will:
Man has both flesh and bone, hue, hair,
[and hide as well:
Such things has spirit none, Thomas, your
[doubts to still:
God's son took flesh and bone, his purpose
[to fulfil.

THOMAS Thou has answered me with zeal and full
[skilfully,
But my heart is hard as steel to trust such
[mastery,
Say, bad he any of you feel the wounds of
[his body,
With flesh or bone to deal to assay him
[readily?

7TH APOSTLE Yes, Thomas, he bad us see, and with our
[hands him touch,

To find whether it were he, Jesu, that we
[might clutch,
That died upon a tree, flesh and bone and
[such,
It was the sharpest pity his bleeding
[wounds to touch.

THOMAS Out, alas! Ye are no good! Your reasons are
[defaced,
Ye are as women scared of blood, too easily
[solaced:
It was a ghost before you stood, like him
[in his blood laced,
His body that died on rood, for ever hath
[death embraced.

8TH APOSTLE Certain, Thomas, greater care, might no
[sinful woman have
Than weeping in her sad despair, the Mag-
[dalene at his grave:
Wrenched for sorrow her own hair and
[started so to rave,
When Jesus stood before her there from
[her deep sorrow to save.

THOMAS Lo, ye let your wisdom rust, wise men that
[should be,
That thus a woman's witness trust more
[than what ye see!
Your reasons are not right or just, your en-
[deavours fail ye:
If I see Jesus, my hand's thrust, not groping
[should decide me.

9TH APOSTLE Leave, Thomas, thy despair, and be not so
[misled,
Or else tell us when and where Christ
[cheated in any stead:
For he told us when thou was there, when
[he gave himself in bread,
That he should save us from our care, by
[rising from the dead.

THOMAS He was true in everything, that dare I [heartily say,
His way was righteousness to bring to each [and every day:
But since he suffered death's sharp sting as [on the tree he lay,
His life is brought to nothing, trust but in [death I may.

10TH APOSTLE Let not thy soul be severed by thy hard [heart within,
Jesus has death conquered, and washed us [all from sin.
May neither knife nor sword victory over [him win:
God's might in him appeared, reigning [evermore therein.

THOMAS God's spirit I trust full well came before [your sight,
But in body never a deal Jesus that [wounded wight.
My heart is hard as steel to trust in such a [might,
Unless that wound I feel, that him gave [Longeus, the knight.

PETER That wound have we seen, Thomas, and [so have more than we:
With Luke and with Cleophas he walked a [day's journey:
Each heart for him was sorry, which he [comforted with prophecy,
To Emmaus castle they did pass, there [hostelled they all three.

Jesu, God's son of heaven, at supper sat [between:
And the bread he broke as even as though [it cut had been.

THOMAS Nothing ye say even, would for me his [rising mean,

If ye told me such seven, it would but tax
[my spleen.

PAUL — Thomas, brother, turn thy thought, and
[trust what I tell thee:
Jesu so dear has bought our sins upon a
[tree,
Whose rising hath brought to heaven
[Adam and his company.

THOMAS — Let be your speech! Say it nought that he
[alive should be.

3RD APOSTLE — That must thou needs allow, if thou thy
[soul will save,
For what we saw we dare avow, the liv-
[ing Jesu rose from grave.

THOMAS — As I said once so say I now such words
[away I wave:
No risen Jesus saw thou, but beguiled ye
[rave.

4TH APOSTLE — For we say that we have seen thou doubt
[our wits hold good;
Jesus living came between, our Lord that
[with us stood.

THOMAS — I say ye know never what ye mean, a ghost
[before you stood;
Ye thought that it had been the corpse
[that died on rood.

4TH APOSTLE — The corpse that died on tree was buried in
[a stone;
Which laid aside found we, within that
[grave corpse was none:
His napkin there could we see, but he
[thence living gone.

THOMAS — No, but stolen is he by the Jews that have
[him slain.

6TH APOSTLE — Certain, Thomas, thou says not right, they
[would not him steal,

For they did watch him day and night,
[those knights they held most loyal:
He rose as we have seen despite what the
[Jews might feel.

THOMAS I believe not unless I might myself with
[him deal.

7TH APOSTLE He told us tidings, Thomas, that reminds
[me,
That as Jonas three days was in a fish in
[the sea,
So should he be, and has been in earth for
[days three,
So should he rise from death; as he said,
[done has he.

THOMAS Indeed, those words I heard him say, and
[so heard ye him all,
But for nothing trust I may that it should
[so befall,
That he should rise the third day who
[drank vinegar and gall:
Since he was God and dead lay, from
[death who might him call?

8TH APOSTLE The father that him sent, raised him that
[was dead,
He comfort in our mourning lent and coun-
[selled us in dread:
He bad us trust with good intent his rising
[in every stead:
Thine absence makes thy soul feel rent and
[makes thee heavy as lead.

THOMAS Thou says truth, right tardy am I to trust
[what to me ye say:
My hardness I trust wilfully, for he told us
[thus ay,
That his father was ever him by, for all
[but one were they:
That he rose up bodily, in no way trust I
[may.

9TH APOSTLE Trust thou not what we do know, forsooth
[that it was he?
Thomas, whereto should we say so? The
[truth we tell to thee.

THOMAS I know your hearts are full of woe and hurt
[through vanity;
Though all and more should swear this so,
[I trust it not until I see.

10TH APOSTLE Thomas, spurn this sin, and for us change
[thy mood:
He is risen from his grave within since he
[died upon the rood.
Save that place my finger win wherein the
[very nail stood,
And his side my hand put in whence shed
[he his heart's blood.

[JESUS *enters.*

JESUS Brethren all, be with you peace! Leave
[strife that now is here!
Thomas, from thine error cease, and true
[witness thou bear:
Put thy hand in my side, never fear, where
[Longeus put his spear:
And see my rising is no lie, there is no
[cause for your despair.

THOMAS Mercy, Jesu, pity me, my hand now bears
[thy blood!
Mercy, Jesu, for I see thy might which I
[never understood!
Mercy, Jesu, I pray to thee who for sin-
[ners died on rood!
Mercy, Jesu, of mercy free, for thy good-
[ness that is so good!

Cast away my staff will I and with no
[weapon go:
Mercy will I call and cry, Jesu, that suf-
[fered woe:

Pity me, king of mercy, let me not long
[cry so!
Mercy, for the villainy the Jews to you did
[show.

My hat will I cast away, my coat too I
[would shun:
Help unto the poor it may, for riches know
[I none.
In mercy will I dwell, and pray to thee
[Jesu, alone:
My sinful deed I rue for ay, to thee make
[I my moan.

Mercy, Jesu Lord, sweet, for thy five
[wounds so sore,
Thou suffered through hands and feet, thy
[seemly side a spear it tore:
Mercy, Jesu Lord, is meet for thy mother
[that thee bore!
Mercy, for thy tears, I entreat, thou wept
[Lazarus to restore!

My girdle gay and purse of silk, and coat
[away with all:
While I am wearer of such ilk, the longer
[mercy may I call.
Jesu, that sucked the maiden's milk, wear
[nought but raiment royal,
Thy clothes which from thee they did
[filch, left thee bare on cross withal.

Mercy, Jesu, honour to man, mercy, Jesu,
[man's succour!
Mercy, Jesu, pity thy darling, man's soul,
[thou bought full sour!
Mercy, Jesu, that may and can, forgive sins
[and be succour!
Mercy, Jesu, as thou us won, forgive, and
[give man thy honour.

JESUS None might bring thee to that state for
[ought that they might say,

But believe that I came straight from death
[to life away.
My soul and body mate in a knot that shall
[last ay:
Thus shall I raise, know well thy fate,
[each man at doom's day.

Whoso has not trusted right, to hell I shall
[them lead,
Where evermore is dark as night, and great
[pains give heed:
Those that trust in my might and love well
[alms' deed,
They shall shine as sun bright, and heaven
[have for their meed.

That bliss, Thomas, I promise thee, which
[is in heaven's city,
For thy tears that I see, on thee I have
[pity:
Thomas, thy wet tears for me, thy sin for-
[given be,
And so shall sinners pardoned be, that sore
[have grieved me.

Thomas, that thou felt me and my wounds
[bare,
My rising gave faith to thee, where earlier
[was despair;
All that trust but never see, and of my
[words take care,
Ever blessed may they be, a place in
[heaven to share.

[JESUS *disappears from their sight, and the* APOSTLES *withdraw.*

THE THIRTY-FIRST PLAY

The Ascension of the Lord

THOMAS	JESUS	MARY
APOSTLE JOHN	ANDREW	MATTHEW
SIMON	JAMES	1ST ANGEL
PETER	PHILIP	2ND ANGEL

THOMAS Brethren all, as ye have been,
Forget my Lord that may I nought:
I know not what it may mean,
But greater wonders will be wrought.

JOHN My Lord Jesus will work his will,
Plead we never against his thought,
For us he fashions by his skill,
The handiwork that he has wrought.

SIMON Upon his words will I rest
The which he said he would fulfil,
Steadfastly to trust is best,
Unbelief begets much ill.

PETER In heaven and earth his might may be,
His wit and his will also:
The holy ghost, brethren, meant he,
Thus will he never from us go.

Forty days now draw near
Since his resurrection complete:
And soon again he will appear,
Thus suddenly not leave us yet.

In Bethany here let us abide,
We know not yet what may befall:
Peradventure it may betide
He shall full well comfort us all.

[JESUS *appears to the* DISCIPLES.

JESUS Peace now, my dear friends!
Peace be with you ever and ay!
For peace all wrong amends:
Peace, brethren, to all I say!
Brethren, in hearts be nothing heavy
The time that I from you am gone,
I must go soon and speedily,
But nevertheless make ye no moan:

For I shall send to you anon
The holy ghost to comfort you,
And guide when you are on your own,
And I shall tell you the manner how.
You shall profit, I avow,
That thus for you I go:
It has been said ere now
My father's will is so.

With him must I abide and dwell,
For so it is his will:
For your comfort thus I you tell,
Be steadfast for good or ill.
Wait for me here right on this hill
Until I come to you again.
This first command ye must fulfil,
No longer here I will remain:
And in obedience be ye fain,
And also true and steadfast,
And live your lives without a stain
When that I am passed.

[*At this he departs.*

PETER Full heavy in heart now may we be
That our master thus shall go,
But nevertheless thus said he
He would not long stay so.
What wonder then if we feel woe,
Who suddenly our master miss,
And, masters, none of us can show
The wisdom that may comfort this.

He will pass forth to bliss,
  And leave us here behind,
No marvel now it is
  If we mourn now in our mind.

ANDREW In our mind mourn we may,
  As men that are amazed and mad,
And yet also it is no nay,
  We may be blithe and glad,
Because of tidings that we had,
  That himself to us did say;
He bad be blithe and nothing sad,
  For he would not be long away.
But yet both night and day
  Our hearts may be full sore,
By my faith, as I may say,
  For his words spoken before.

THOMAS Long before he said full openly,
  That he needs from us must part,
And to his master go on high,
  To heaven's endless joy depart;
Therefore we mourn with heavy heart,
  But merry also yet may be;
He bad us all our joy impart,
  Be glad and blithe in each degree,
And said that come should he
  To comfort us kindly;
But yet heavy are we
  Till we see him truly.

JAMES With eyes would we him see, our saviour [Christ, God's son,
That died upon a tree, yet such grace may [be won:
God grant to us each one, that with his blood [us bought,
To see him in his throne, as he made all of [nought:
His will now has he wrought and gone from [us away,

And forsaken in his thought therefore mourn
[we may.

PHILIP We may mourn, no marvel why, for we our
[master thus shall miss,
That shall go from us suddenly, and we not
[know what the cause is;
Nevertheless, the truth is this, he said that he
[should come again
To bring us all to bliss, thereof may we be
[fain.
That coming brings us much gain, and may
[our souls all save,
And puts us from that pain that we were like
[to have.

[JESUS *again appears.*

JESUS Hearken to me now, everyone, and hear what
[I will say,
For I must needs from you be gone, such is
[my father's way,
And therefore peace be with you ay, together
[and alone,
And save you from all fray, my peace be with
[you blood and bone.
I leave it with you one by one, but not as the
[world here knows;
It shall be true as any stone to defend you
[from your foes.

Let not your hearts be heavy, dread not for
[anything,
Ye have heard me say full plainly I go, and
[to you I am coming.
If ye therefore love me ye should be glad of
[this doing,
For I go full surely to my father, heaven's
[king;
The which without lying is more mighty
[than I,
Therefore be ye thus trusting, when all is
[ended fully.

Ye have been full of doubt, hard of heart and
[also of will;
The proof of my rising ye did flout, no cre-
[dence ye gave them still;
Mary Magdalene spoke my will, that I was
[risen, ye did but scold
Her, trusting not for good or ill the truth as
[she it told.
Such harms in hearts ye hold, unsteadfast in
[your prizing,
To believe none were ye bold, who bore wit-
[ness of my rising;
Therefore ye shall go teach in all this world
[so wide,
And to all the people preach who baptism will
[abide,

And believe truly
My death and rising,
And also my ascending,
And also my returning,
They shall be saved surely.

And who believes not this
That now repeated is,
He shall be shut from bliss,
Such vengeance on him wreak.
Tokens of truth be seen
In all believers I mean:
Devils shall they cast out clean,
And with new tongues speak.

Serpents shall they put away,
And venomous drink, by night and day,
Shall not annoy them, as I say:
And where they lay on hands
On sick men far and near,
They shall be whole and clear
Of all sickness and heavy fear,
For ever in all lands.

And therefore now I bid that ye
Bide in Jerusalem city,
But obey my father's decree
  Everywhere,
As ye have heard here of me:
For John baptized to his degree,
In water forsooth he baptized me:
  His task ye share:

But ye for sure on every coast
Shall baptize in the holy ghost,
Through his virtue that is the most,
  Lord God of might.
Within few days now following:
And at this marvel ye nothing.
For this shall be his own working,
  Shown in your sight.

[*He leaves them.*

PETER Wondrous ill now may we fare
In missing our master, Jesus:
Our hearts may sigh with laden care,
These Jews for wrath will seize us.

Us to betray they mean,
  They are about by night and day;
For Jesus that is so seldom seen,
  As mazed men mourn we may.

ANDREW Mourning makes us mazed and mad,
  As men that live in dread;
We are so comfortless and sad,
  Lacking him who has us led.

JAMES These Jews that follow their faithless will,
  And deemed our master to be dead,
With might and main they would him kill,
  If they knew how in town or stead.

JOHN Let us keep from their carping keen,
  And come but little in their sight;
When least expected our Lord will be seen,
  He will us rule and govern aright.

THOMAS
Of this carping now no more,
It draws near the time of day:
For meat I would we go before,
He send us succour that best may.

MARY
Succour soon he will you send,
If ye belief on him bestow:
Your moan meekly will be mend,
My brethren dear, this may ye know.

The pledges that to me were plight,
He has fulfilled in word and deed;
He lied never by day or night,
Therefore, brethren, not doubt ye need.

MATTHEW
Certain, lady, thou says full well:
He will us mend for us so he may:
We have found true, just as you tell,
All that ever we heard him say.

JESUS
Peter, and ye my darlings dear,
As men amazed methinks ye stare:
Wholly to you I have shown here
That I bring your hearts from care.

In care your hearts are cast,
And in your faith untrue;
In hardness your hearts are fast,
As men that nothing knew.

Sent was I for your sake from my father dear,
Flesh and blood to take of a maid so dear;
Since then for me ye sought and wholly fol-
[lowed me,
Of wonders that I have wrought some have
[I let you see.

The dumb, the blind as any stone,
I healed as I passed by,
The dead I raised anon,
Through my might truly;

And works of wonder many more,
I wrought wisely before you all;

My pain, my passion, I told before,
Wholly throughout as it should fall.

My rising on the third day,
As a token many have seen:
Your true sense had been cast away
Had not my blessed mother been.

In her did constant faith abide,
Your deeds should cause you bitter shame:
Here may ye see my sad wounds wide,
How that I bought you out of blame.

But, John, think when I hung on rood,
That I assigned thee Mary mild:
Keep her yet in stable mood,
She is thy mother, and thou her child.

Look thou her love, and be her friend,
And abide with her in well and woe,
For to my father now will I wend,
Need none of you ask whither I go.

PHILIP Lord, if it be thy will,
Show us thy father we thee pray:
We have been with thee in good and ill,
And saw him never, night nor day.

JESUS Philip, that man that may see me,
He sees my father full of might:
Trust thou not he dwells in me
And I in him if thou trust right?

In his house is many a place,
Which I go to prepare for you:
Ye shall all be filled with grace,
The holy ghost I shall send you.
He shall you guide, your heart possess,
In word and deed, just as I say:
With all my heart I you bless—
My mother, my brethren, have all good [day!

[*Then he goes to begin his Ascension.*

Father of heaven, with good intent,

I pray thee hear me specially:
From heaven to earth thou me sent
Thy name to preach and glorify.
Thy will obediently I have done,
In earth will I no longer be:
Open the clouds, for now I come
In joy and bliss to dwell with thee.

[*And thus he ascends: while the* ANGELS *sing "I ascend to my Father".*

1ST ANGEL Ye men of Galilee,
Wherefore marvel ye?
Heaven behold and see
How Jesus up did wend
Unto his father free,
Where he sits in majesty,
With him ay for to be
In bliss without an end.

And as ye saw him nigh
Unto heaven on high,
In flesh and fell in his body,
From earth now here,
Right so shall he surely,
Come down again truly,
With his wounds bloody,
To judge altogether.

2ND ANGEL Marvel no man might,
Nor wonder at this sight,
For it is through his might,
That all things may.
Whatso he will by day or night,
In hell, earth, or heaven's height,
Or yet in darkness or in light,
Without gainsay;

For he is God most grand,
Over heaven and hell, sea and sand,
Wood and water, fowl, fish, and land,
According to his will;

He holds all things in his hand,
No living thing may him withstand,
Then marvel not but understand.

1ST ANGEL And for this skill,

Right as he from you did wend,
So come again he shall,
In the same manner at the end,
To judge both great and small.

2ND ANGEL Whoso his bidding will obey,
And their lives amend,
With him shall win to bliss that day,
And dwell there without end.

And who that work amiss,
And themselves amend will never,
Shall never come to heaven's bliss,
But to hell be banished ever.

MARY A wondrous sight yonder now is,
Behold now, I you pray!
A cloud has born my child to bliss,
My blessing bears he ever and ay!

But, son, think on thy mother dear,
That thou has left among thy foes!
Sweet son, let me not dwell here,
Let me go with thee where thou goes.

But John, in thee is all my trust,
I pray thee forsake me nought.

JOHN Mary, look up without mistrust,
For thy will shall ay be wrought.

Here may we see and reckon so,
That he is God, most of might;
In him is good we know,
Wholly to serve him day and night.

PETER A marvellous sight is yon,
That he from us so soon was ta'en;

From his foemen he is gone
  With no other help is plain.

MATTHEW Where is Jesus, our master dear,
  That here with us spoke right now?

JAMES A wonderful sight, men may see here,
  My brethren dear, how think you?

THOMAS A wonder seems it all,
  That our master should thus go;
For his help I guess we call,
  That he might us some token show.

BARTHOLOMEW A greater marvel men ne'er saw
  Than now is seen among us here:
We saw a cloud to heaven him draw
  While angels sang with mirthful cheer.

From us, methinks, he is full long,
  Yet longer, I think, he will;
Alas! My heart it is so strong,
  That I may not weep my fill
    Anon.
A wondrous sight it was to see
When he climbed up so suddenly
To his father in majesty,
    By himself alone.

MATTHEW Alone, indeed, up he went, into heaven to his [father,
And no one knew what he meant, nor how he [rose in what manner,
But on climbing up was bent, in flesh and [fell from earth up here:
He said his father for him sent, that made us [all to harbour fear
  This night:
Nevertheless full well know we
As that he will so must it be,
For he has power almighty,
  And that is right.

MARY Almighty God, how may this be?
  A cloud has borne my child to bliss,
Save that I know now where is he,
  My heart would break, well know I this.

His ascension up to bliss on high,
  It is the source of all my joys;
My blessing, bairn, light on thy body!
  Let never thy mother be rent by the Jews.

Son so sweet, thy mother mind,
  Let me not suffer the Jews' harsh scorn;
Help, for my son's love, John so kind,
  For fear that I by the Jews be torn.

My flesh it quakes as leaf on tree,
  To shun the showers sharper than thorn:
Help me, John, if kind thou be,
  My son's missing makes me to mourn.

JOHN Your servant, lady, he me made,
  And bad me you in comfort keep:
Blithe were I, lady, thy joy to aid,
  And serve thee gladly without sleep.

Therefore be afraid for nothing,
  For ought that the Jews would do to you;
I shall be ready at your bidding,
  As my Lord bad, your servant true.

MARY Glad am I, John, while I have thee;
  More comfort, save Jesus, I cannot crave;
So calm thou my care, and quietly speak to [me,
  Whilst I thee see I feel most safe.
Was none, save my son, more trusty to me,
  Therefore his grace shall never from [thee go;
He shall thee requite, that died on a tree,
  If thou mend my mood, when I am in woe.

SIMON Let us hasten from this hill, and to the town [wend,

For fear of the Jews, that are pitiless and [proud:
To our dear lady our company lend,
And pray to her dear son, right here aloud.
To her obediently, I say, we bend,
Since her dear son from us is gone in a [cloud,
And heartily salute our gracious friend,
To our master is she mother, seemly in [shroud.

Ah, Mary so mild; thee missed we have;
Was never maid more gracious to behold
As thou art, and mother clean, but this would [we crave,
If this were Jesus, thy son, that Judas has [sold,
Show us the truth, it may us all save;
We pray thee, dear lady, that frankly [thou told,
Excuse us our asking but else might we rave,
But fain would we surely this mystery [unfold.

MARY Peter, Andrew, John, and James, I assent,
Simon, Judas, and Bartholomew the bold,
And all my brethren dear, to this now be at- [tent,
Give heed to what is said, until my tale [be told
Of my dear son, what I have meant,
That hence is heaved to his own hold;
He taught you the truth ere he to heaven [went;
He was born of my bosom as prophets [foretold.

He is God and man that unto heaven rose:
Preach thus to the people that most are of [price.

Ye Apostles eleven, look to the saving of those,
To the Jews of Jerusalem, as your way [lies,
To the whole city these tidings disclose,
Tell the words of my son in world most [wise:
Bid them in him their belief to repose,
Or else be they damned as men full of [vice.

[*The play is unfinished: there is a gap of twelve leaves in the manuscript.*]

THE THIRTY-SECOND PLAY

The Judgement

1ST EVIL SOUL	TUTIVILLUS
2ND EVIL SOUL	JESUS
3RD EVIL SOUL	1ST GOOD SOUL
4TH EVIL SOUL	2ND GOOD SOUL
AN ANGEL	3RD GOOD SOUL
1ST DEMON	4TH GOOD SOUL
2ND DEMON	

[JESUS *and the* ANGELS *in heaven, the* GOOD *and* EVIL SOULS *on earth.*]

2ND EVIL SOUL Full dark has been our deed, at his [coming our care;
This day we take our meed, for nothing [may we spare.

[*Trump.*

Alas, I heard that horn that calls us to [our doom,
All that ever were born, thither behoves [them come.
May neither land nor sea us from this [doom hide,
For fear fain would I flee, but I must [needs abide;
Alas, I stand in awe, to see that Justice [beckon,
Where no man may on law or legal [quibble reckon,
Advocates ten or twelve may not help [him in his need,
But each man for himself shall answer [for his deed.

Alas, that I was born!
I see my Lord's flesh torn
Before me with wounds five;
How may I on him look,
That falsely him forsook,
Most sinful wretch alive?

3RD EVIL SOUL Alas, careworn caitiffs may we rise,
Sore may we wring our hands and weep;
For being cursed and covetous,
Damned be we in hell full deep.
Gave we never to God in service,
His commandments would we not keep,
But ofttimes made we sacrifice
To Satan, when we stole from sleep.

[*Trump.*

Alas! That clarion calls our care,
Our wicked works can we not hide,
But on our backs we must them bear,
That give us sorrow on every side.
Our deeds this day will cost us dear,
Our judgement here we must abide,
And fiends, that fill us full of fear,
Will pounce upon us in their pride.
Boldly before us be they brought,
Our deeds that damn us as unclean;
That ear that heard, or heart that [thought,
Mouth that has spoken, or eye seen,
That foot that trod or hand that wrought,
At any time our lives between;
Full dear this day now be it bought;
Alas! Unborn that had I been!

[*Trump.*

4TH EVIL SOUL Alas, I am forlorn! A bitter blast here [blows!
I heard by yonder horn, I know whereto [it goes;

I would I were unborn! What may this [day dispose!
Now must be damned this morn we who [bewail our woes!
The evil that I did, alas, has left a stain
For which I am now chid, as ye shall see [full plain.
That would I fain were hid, my sinful [words and vain,
So that I may be rid this reckoning for [my gain.

Alas, fain would I flee for deeds that I [have done,
But that may now not be, my fate I may [not shun;
My hope was never to see this dreadful [day begun,
When on his throne to me he turns, where [shall I run?

Who can his wounds withstand! This is a [doleful case;
Alas! How shall I stand, or look him in [the face?
So courteous I him found that gave me [life so long a space;
My care is close at hand, alas! Where is [my grace?

Alas! Caitiffs unkind, whither was our [thought?
Alas! Where was our mind, so wicked [works we wrought?
See his suffering for mankind, so dear our [love he bought.
Alas! We were full blind, now are we [worse than nought.

Alas! My covetize, my ill will, and mine [ire!
My neighbour to despise, most was my [desire;

Ill deeds I would devise, methought high [to aspire,
I have been too unwise, now am I quit [my hire.

Where I was wont to go and speak my [words at will,
Now am I set full low and fain to hold [me still;
I went both to and fro, methought I did [never ill,
To slay my neighbours so, or harm them [through my skill.

Woe be to the father that begat me to be [born!
That ever he let me stir, that now am so [forlorn;
Accursed by my mother, and accursed be [the morn
That I was born of her, alas, for shame [and scorn!

ANGEL [*with a sword*]

Stand not together, part in two!
Together be ye not in bliss;
Our Lord of heaven will have it so,
For many of you have done amiss,
On his right hand ye good shall go,
The way to heaven he shows you this;
Ye wicked souls wend ye below,
On his left hand as none of his.

JESUS

The time has come I shall make end,
My father in heaven wills it so be,
Therefore to earth now will I wend
Myself to sit in majesty.

To deal my doom I will descend
This body will I bear with me,
It was made man's sin to mend
All mankind there shall it see.

[*Trump.*

1ST DEMON Out, harrow, out, out! Hearken to this [lord,
I was never in doubt ere now at this [morn;
So sturdy a shout, since that I was born
Heard I never hereabout in earnest nor [scorn;
A wonder!
I was bound full fast
In irons for to last,
My bonds broke with that blast
And shook all in sunder.

2ND DEMON I shivered and shook and shuddered for [fear,
I heard what I took for the doom of us [here,
But to swear on a book, I durst not [appear;
I durst not look, for all earth, either drear
Or pale;
But grinned and grimaced,
My fear I outfaced,
But all was but waste,
It might not avail.

1ST DEMON It was like to a trump, it had such a [sound;
I fell down in a lump, in a swoon I was [found.

2ND DEMON There I stood on my stump as to a stake [bound,
Though cramped by this clump yet held [I my ground
Half numb.

1ST DEMON Make ready our gear,
To welcome war here,
For now dare I swear
That doomsday has come.

For our souls all have fled and none are [in hell
If we stay we are sped, here let us not [dwell.

2ND DEMON It behoves us instead this rising to quell,
As Parliament peers said, whatever befell;
It is needful
To look to your own,
Where the wind shall be blown;
If the court practice be known,
The Judge is right dreadful.

1ST DEMON We have an empty home; our rout has [been complete,

2ND DEMON Let us go to our doom up Watling Street.

1ST DEMON I had rather go to Rome, yea thrice, on [my feet,
Than to grieve yonder groom, or with [him for to meet;
Wisely
Of things may he prate,
His power is great,
If he threaten his hate
He looks full grisly.

But first take our rentals, hie, let us go [hence!
Ere on us falls the great sentence.

2ND DEMON Here stand the thralls, we offer no de- [fence,
For all these damned souls, without [repentance,
As is just.

1ST DEMON Although we be crooks,
Examine our books

2ND DEMON Here is a bag full of looks,
Of pride and of lust,

Of wranglers and twisters, a bag full of [briefs,

Of carpers and criers, cutpurses and [thieves,
Of lubbers and liars, that no man believes,
Of a rout of rioters that robbed goods [receives;
These know I,
Of all estates
That go by the gates,
Their pride that God hates,
Twenty so many.

1ST DEMON Peace, I pray thee be still! I laugh that I [kink,
Is ought ire in thy bill, for then shall thou [drink.

2ND DEMON Sir, such mighty ill-will, that they would [sink
Their foes in a fire still, but nought that [I think
Dare I say,
Before him he praises him,
Behind him he abuses him,
Thus double he uses him;
Thus do they today.

1ST DEMON Hast thou ought written there of the [feminine gender?

2ND DEMON Yea, more than I may bear, of rolls for [to render;
They are as sharp as a spear though they [seem but slender;
They have ever sour cheer: and if they [be tender,
Ill-fettled;
She that is most meek,
When sick she seems to peak,
She can raise a shriek
If she be well nettled.

[*Trump.*

1ST DEMON Of rascals thou art best that ever came
[beside us.

2ND DEMON Yea, but go we now to rest, for fain
[would we hide us;
That blast blown with such zest, shows
[they will not abide us;
Let us dally not lest sorely they chide us
Together.

1ST DEMON Make ready our tools,
For we deal with no fools.

2ND DEMON Sir, all the clerks of our schools
Are ready to go thither.

1ST DEMON But, sir, I tell you before, had doomsday
[ought tarried,
We must have widened hell more, the
[world is so sullied.

2ND DEMON Now get we double store of bodies mis-
[carried
To the souls where they were together to
[be harried.

1ST DEMON These rolls
Are of backbiters,
And false indictors,
I had no help of writers
To list these damned souls.

Faith and truth, ma fay, have no feet to
[stand;
The poor people must pay, if ought be in
[hand,
The dread of God is away, and law out
[of land
This season.

2ND DEMON Sir, it is said in old saws—
Though near the dawn draws—
"Worse people worse laws."

1ST DEMON I laugh at thy reason.

All this was a token, doomsday to dread;
Full oft was it spoken, full few looked [ahead;
Our vengeance is woken, and devours [them instead,
Now the seal is so broken of deeds dark [and red
With ire;
All their sins shall be known,
Other men's and their own.

2ND DEMON And if this blast be well blown,
"Dick is in the mire."

[*Enter* TUTIVILLUS.

TUTIVILLUS Why ask ye not, sir, no questions?
I am one of your order and one of your [sons;
I stand at my station which each of you [shuns.

1ST DEMON Now thou art my own chorister, ye live [with the nuns;
Do tell me.

TUTIVILLUS Tax-gatherer in chief,
Court rollsman in brief,
Master lollard in belief,
As such none excel me.

I have brought to your hand of souls, I [dare say,
More than ten thousand in an hour of a [day;
Some at ale-houses I found and some at a [fray,
Some cursed to be bound, some yea, [some nay;
So many
Thus brought I to hell,
Thus worked I so well.

1ST DEMON All us ye excel
None such heard I any.

TUTIVILLUS Here's a roll of ragman of the round [table,
Of briefs in my bag, man, of sins dam- [nable;
Certainly I say, man, and weary of your [stable,
While I set my stag, man.

2ND DEMON Abide, ye are able
To take wage;
Ye know the court ways
Which your service repays,
I forecast foul frays
When ye come of age.

TUTIVILLUS Here be I guess many to mock at,
In care and curstness whom we may [knock at,
Gay gear and witless, his hood with a [cocket,
As proud as penniless, his sleeve has no [pocket,
Full senseless;
His shoes are trimmed soon,
He comes home with the moon,
And is out at high noon,
While his bairns are breadless.

A horn and a Dutch axe, his sleeve must [be flecked,
His hair fair as flax, his gown must be [specked,
Thus took I your tax, thus are my books [blacked.

1ST DEMON So great you may wax that what be [lacked
Be shown;
With words will thou fill us,
But now thy name tell us.

TUTIVILLUS My name is Tutivillus
My horn has blown;
Fragmina verborum, Tutivillus colligit [horum,
Beelzebub algorum, Belial belium [doliorum.

2ND DEMON What, ye know your grammary and [somewhat of art;
Had I but a penny to study I should start.

TUTIVILLUS Of females a quantity here find I a part.

1ST DEMON Tutivillus, let us see, God forbid we stay [apart!

TUTIVILLUS So jolly
Each lass in the land
Ladylike here at hand,
So fresh none may withstand,
Leads men to folly.

If she be never so foul a dowd, with her [nets and her pins,
The shrew herself can shroud, both her [cheeks and her chins;
She can caper full proud with japes and [with gins,
Her head high in a cloud, but not shamed [by her sins
Or evil;
With this powder and paint,
She plans to look quaint,
She may smile like a saint,
But at heart is a devil.

She is horned like a cow, and full secret [her sin;
Her side gaiter hangs now, furred with a [cat's skin,
All these are for you, they have come of [your kin.

2ND DEMON Now, the best body art thou that ever [came herein.

TUTIVILLUS In fact,
The fashion, I undertake,
Brings wedlock to break,
And sinful living for its sake,
And many a broken contract.

Yet a point not to shun, I tell you before,
More liars shall hither come than a thou-
[sand score;
Their swearing grieves God's son and
[pains him more and more,
Therefore with us they are one in hell for
[evermore.
I say thus,
That raisers of false tax
And gatherers of green wax,
Diabolus est mendax
Et pater eius.

A point of the new mode yet my tale I
[shall spin,
Of pranked up gowns and shoulders high
[set and moss and flock sewn within;
To have this fashion they would fret, they
[say it is no sin,
But on such fellows I me set and clap
[them cheek and chin,
No nay.
David in his psaltery says thus,
That to hell they be thrust,
Cum suis adinvencionibus,
For once and for ay.

Yet of these churchchatterers here is an
[army,
Of bargainers and usurers, and lovers of
[simony,
Of gossips and scandalmongers, God casts
[them out truly,
From his temple all such misdoers, I
[catch them to me
Full soon;

For written I know it is
In gospel without amiss,
Et eam fecistis
Speluncam latronum.

Yet of the sins seven something special
Now quickly to reckon that runs over all;
These lads strut even as lords most royal,
To be pictured even in royal robes withal,
As kings;
His tail may none dock it,
A codpiece like a pocket,
He scorns not to cock it
When he his tail wrings.

His buttocks they bulge like a fulling mill [clog,
His head like a stook bristles like a hog,
His blown up belly filled full like a frog,
This Jelian Jook drives he no dog
To shelter.
But with your yellow locks,
For all your many mocks,
Ye shall climb on hell's cross
With a halfpenny halter.

And Tess with trifles both crisp and of [silk,
Look well to your quiffles about your [neck as milk;
With ribands and bridals of Satan your [sire,
With his knacks and his idols for her gay [attire,
This wench knave;
It is open behind,
Before it is pinned;
Beware of a west wind
Your smock lest it wave.

Of ire and of envy find I more to show,
Of covetousness and gluttony, and many [more also;

They call and they cry, "Go we now, go!
I die I am so dry!" and there sit they so
All night;
They cackle and cavil,
Singing of evil,
These are hounds of hell,
That is their right.

In sleuth then they sin, God's works they [not work;
To belch they begin, and spue what may [irk;
His head must be held in, there in the [murk,
Then defies he with din the bells of the [kirk,
When they clatter;
The clerk he would hang
For he the bell rang,
But dares not him bang
For fear of a halter.

And ye gatemen of the stews, ye lechers [aloft,
Your bale now brews, adulterers full oft,
Your pleasures ye lose, but I shall set you [soft;
Your sorrow accrues, come to my croft
All ye;
All harlots and whores,
Each bawd that procures,
That fetches and lures,
Welcome to my see!

Ye lubbers and liars, and all ye who [thieve,
Ye foul-tempered knifers, who cause men [to grieve,
Wreckers, extortioners, my welcome re- [ceive,
False jurors and usurers, that to simony [cleave,

Here dwell;
Gamesters and dicers,
False deeds forgers,
Slanderers and backbiters,
Welcome to hell.

1ST DEMON Many had such a trick, both furious and [fell,
The good were few to pick, I had much [marvel,
And thought it drew near the prick.

2ND DEMON Sir, a word of counsel;
Souls came so thick of late now to hell
As ever;
Our porter at hell-gate
Is in so sad a strait,
Up early and down late,
Rest has he never.

1ST DEMON Thou art peerless of those that ever yet [knew I,
When I will may I go if thou be by;
Go we now, we two.

2ND DEMON Sir, I am ready.

1ST DEMON Take our rolls also, ye know the cause [why;
Do come
And hearken this day.

2ND DEMON Sir, as well as I may.

1ST DEMON *Qui vero mala*
In ignem eternum.

[*Trump.*

JESUS Each creature be intent
On the message I you bring,
This wicked world is spent,
And I come crowned as king;
My father of heaven has me sent
To judge your deeds and make ending;

Come has the day of judgement,
Of sorrow may every sinner sing.

The day has come for caitiffness,
All those find care that are unclean,
The day of battle and bitterness,
Full long a-coming has it been;
The day of dread to more and less,
Of joy, of trembling pain extreme,
For each creature's wickedness
May say, alas this day is seen.

Here may ye see my wounds so wide
That I suffered for your misdeed.
Through heart, head, foot, hand and side,
Not for my guilt but for your need.
Behold both back, body and side,
How dearly for you I did bleed,
These bitter pains I would abide
Your bliss to buy as was decreed.

My body was scourged with ill will,
My bitter fate I had to meet;
On cross they hung me on a hill,
Blue and bloody thus was I beat;
With crown of thorn thrusting full ill,
A spear into my heart they sent;
My heart blood spared they not to spill.
Man, for thy love I was beset.

The Jews spat on me spitefully,
They spared me no more than a thief;
When they me smote I stood meekly,
To them I gave no kind of grief.
Behold, mankind, this same am I,
That for thee suffered such mischief,
Thus was I slain for thy folly,
Man, loved I thee beyond belief.

Thus was I served thy sorrow to slake;
Man, thus behoved thy pledge to be;
In all my woe no wrath did wake
My will it was for love of thee.

Man, for sorrow ought thee to quake,
This dreadful day this sight to see;
All this I suffered for thy sake;
Say, man, what suffered thou for me?

[*Then turning to the* GOOD SOULS *he says to them:*

My blessed bairns on my right hand,
Your doom this day not dread ye need,
For all your joy is to command,
Your life in pleasure ye shall lead.
Come to that kingdom that ay shall stand,
That is prepared for your good deed,
Full blithely, there, ye understand,
Much joy in heaven is your meed.

When I was hungry ye me fed,
To slake my thirst ye were full free;
When I was naked ye me clad,
Ye would no sorrow on me see;
In prison when I was hard stead
On my penance ye had pity;
Full sick when I was brought to bed,
Kindly ye came to comfort me.

When I was worn and weariest,
Ye harboured me full easily,
Full glad then were ye of your guest,
And shared my poverty piteously;
Betimes ye brought me of the best
And made my bed where I should lie,
Therefore in heaven shall be your rest,
In joy and bliss to bide me by.

1ST GOOD SOUL Lord, when had thou such great need?
Hunger or thirst, how might it be?

2ND GOOD SOUL When was our heart free to feed?
In prison, when might we thee see?

3RD GOOD SOUL When sick or naked had thou need?
And when helped we to harbour thee?

4TH GOOD SOUL When had thou need of such a deed?
When did we all these things to thee?

JESUS My blessed bairns, I shall you say
What time these deeds were to me done;
When any that need had night or day,
Asked of you help and had it soon;
Your free heart said them never nay,
Early nor late, midnight, nor noon,
As often times as they would pray,
They need but ask and have their boon.

[*Then shall he speak to the* EVIL SOULS.

Ye cursed caitiffs of Cain's kin,
Ye gave no comfort to my care
Now ye from me apart shall spin,
And dwell for ever in despair;
Your bitter bales cease not therein,
That ye shall suffer once in there,
Thus be ye served for your deep sin,
For the dark deeds which ye all share.

When I had need of meat and drink,
Caitiffs, ye chased me from your gate;
When benched as sires and dressed in [mink,
Weary and wet I had to wait,
Yet none of you would on me think,
To have pity on my poor estate;
Therefore to hell I shall you sink,
Well are ye worthy to go there straight.

When I was sick and sorriest
Ye came not near for I was poor;
In prison fast when I was pressed
My plight ye all chose to ignore,
When I knew never where to rest,
With blows ye drove me from your door,
Your pride ye ever did attest,
My flesh, my blood, ye oft forswore.

Clotheless when that I was cold,
Though for you I had gone naked,
My miseries saw ye manifold,
But none of you my sorrows slaked.

But ever forsook me young and old,
Therefore shall ye now be forsaken.

1ST EVIL SOUL Lord, when had thou, that all has,
Hunger or thirst as God no less?
When was it thou in prison was?
When naked thou or harbourless?

2ND EVIL SOUL When did we see thee sick, alas!
And showed thee such unkindness?

3RD EVIL SOUL When did we thee helpless pass?
When did we thee this wickedness?

4TH EVIL SOUL Alas, for dole this day!
Alas, I ever thee annoyed!
Now am I damned for ay,
Nor may this doom avoid.

JESUS Caitiffs, alas, ye did forbid
The needful that asked in my name,
Ye heard them nought, your ears were [hid,
All help to them ye did disdain;
Ye me with that unkindness chid,
Therefore ye bear this bitter blame,
To the least of mine when ye ought did
To me ye did the very same.

My chosen children, come to me!
With me to dwell now shall ye wend,
Where joy and bliss ever shall be,
To live in pleasure without end.

Ye cursed creatures, from me ye flee,
In hell to dwell without an end!
There shall ye nought but sorrow see,
And sit by Satan's side, the fiend.

1ST DEMON Do now forth go, bustle and rush again!
Unto endless woe, everlasting pain;
Nay tarry not so, not here is our domain.

2ND DEMON Hie hitherward, ho, hurry this mob [amain!

Look out!
Nibble the alto shall ye,
Then the treble falls to me,
Now to the devil go we,
With this whole rout.

TUTIVILLUS Your lives are forlorn, and come has your [care;
Ye may curse ye were born, the bodies [ye bear,
And your fathers before, so cursed ye are.

1ST DEMON Ye may bemoan the morn and day that [ye were
Of your mother
First born for to be,
For what woe comes to thee.

2ND DEMON Each of you may see
Sorrow strike the other.

Where are the goods and the gold that ye [gathered together?
That merry company so bold riding [hither and thither?

TUTIVILLUS Gay girdles, dagged hoods that fold, [pranked gowns, whither?
Of your wits have ye hold, ye brought [nought hither
But sorrow,
And your sins in your necks.

1ST DEMON Curse them that ought recks
He comes too late that beckons,
Your bodies to borrow.

2ND DEMON Sir, I would give them a scold, and make [them be known,
They were haughty and bold, great [boasts have they blown;
Your proud prancing, behold, away has it [flown,

Of man's error ye told, but forgot quite [your own.

TUTIVILLUS Moreover,
Their neighbours they grudge,
Themselves them did judge,
But now must they budge,
Their saints' days are over.

1ST DEMON Their neighbours they rated with words [full ill,
The worst ay they stated, yet had no skill.

2ND DEMON With pence never sated, but stole and [kept still;
As misers calculated, but had no will
For heart's fare;
But rich and ill-deedy,
Gluttonous and greedy,
Ever nipping yet needy,
Your goods never spare.

TUTIVILLUS For the wealth that ye spared and did [extortion,
For your children ye cared, you hired [your son,
All to us now has fared and your years [are run,
In hell be it shared, lame malison
To bind it.
Ye set nought by cursing,
Nor no such small thing.

1ST DEMON Nought but praise at the parting
For now must ye find it.

With sweethearts and females your wed- [lock ye break;
Tell me what it avails so merry to make?
See so falsely it fails.

2ND DEMON Sir, I dare undertake
They will tell no tales, but see they so [quake

Like sheep;
He that to that game goes,

TUTIVILLUS Trots lamely on old toes.
The praise that ye grudge those,
From mind I did sweep.

1ST DEMON Sir, may they meet their doom which [long has been knelling;
Will ye witness their gloom.

2ND DEMON Thou art ay telling;
Now shall they have room in pitch and [tar dwelling,
Their grief they will groom and ay be [a-yelling
In our care.

TUTIVILLUS By your leave may we move you?

1ST DEMON If you can I shall prove you!

2ND DEMON Yet tonight to improve you
See a feat of ill fare.

TUTIVILLUS For those cursed and forsworn and each [that here wends,
Blow, wolfs-head and out-horn now, [namely my friends.

[*Trump.*

1ST DEMON Ill luck were ye born, your own shame [you rends,
That shall ye find ere morn.

2ND DEMON Come now with fiends
To your anger;
Your deeds damn you hither
Come, go we together,
We have you on tether,
Come, tarry no longer.

1ST GOOD SOUL We love, thee, Lord, in everything,
That for thine own has ordained thus,
That we may have now our dwelling
In heaven's bliss given unto us.

Therefore full boldly may we sing
As we mount up thus;
Make we all mirth and loving
With *Te Deum Laudamus.*

Notes to the Plays (Part Four)

THE TALENTS

This play is unique in medieval drama for the extended treatment of its theme which, when it appears in other cycles, is but an insignificant fragment of the drama of the crucifixion. Such a play at this stage of the Cycle might be inserted for tactical reasons. If actors and action are continuous *The Talents* certainly allows the actor playing the role of Christ a much needed rest. The play begins and ends with the familiar nine-line stanzas of the Wakefield Master and throughout it is informed with his characteristic bouncing vigour and skilful handling of dialogue. It forms the most striking contrast in tone, intensity, and subject matter to *The Crucifixion* which precedes it, and to *The Deliverance of Souls* which follows it. Its theme, its position in the cycle, and its treatment illustrate the deliberate art of an outstanding dramatist.

Tired tyrants getting into bed, leaving instructions for their menials not to disturb them, are such regular occurrences in medieval drama as to conform to a formula. However, this is the only instance in the Wakefield Plays when recourse is had to such a formula. Pilate's couch is probably positioned on the inner section of his pageant in front of which a curtain can be drawn, so that he at least seems undisturbed by the preliminary dialogue of the Torturers which is played on the fore part of his pageant (73–182).

The Third Torturer appears to yield the seamless coat too readily to Pilate, and, indeed, contrary to his previous stubbornness (353). Such a change can be made dramatically acceptable if Pilate's threats are interpreted as intending to transform the Third Torturer, who is free in the feudal sense, into a bondman (355–356).

A hint as to the manner of dicing the Torturers adopt is given by Pilate (346):

'Yea, but I play not the game with a puff or a blow.'

The Torturers hold the three dice in their cupped hands into which they puff and blow before throwing, a quirk of gaming unchanged by the centuries.

The moralizing at the end of the play (368–412), breath-taking in its sudden conversion of the seamiest villains of the cycle, nevertheless should be played straight. It is easy and superficially effective to play it tongue-in-cheek, with the Torturers leering at their own hypocritical piety ['How think ye of this?' (403)], but to treat their very last appearance in the Cycle cynically is to misrepresent the essential spirit of a great religious drama.

THE DELIVERANCE OF SOULS

The acting areas specified in this play are paradise, limbo, and hell. Dramatically it is important that Adam and Eve should be led by Jesus back to paradise; theologically the righteous souls cannot accompany Jesus to heaven until the Last Judgement. Limbo, by definition, is the region on the border of hell, the abode of the just who died before Christ's coming, and of unbaptized infants. It is therefore in limbo where Adam and Eve and the prophets are located, but a limbo which is part of hell's outer defences over which, until the Deliverance, Satan and his devils hold sway. Limbo might be represented dramatically as a fortress that guards hell-mouth. The contest between Jesus and Satan is conceived in heroic terms, and the conflict in hell with its frequent references to siege-warfare supports such a setting. That the Souls are 'sparred in a special space' (104) might indicate that they are confined by a stage portcullis. Ribald is later urged to spar the gates and 'set the watches on the wall' (120–121), which also strongly suggests siege preparations in a fortress. It is certainly these gates which crack and collapse (209), giving rise to Ribald's despairing cry 'Limbo is lost, alas!' (213). *The Last Judgement*, a painting by Stephan Lochner (c 1405–1451), depicts heaven and hell as two opposing towers. Hell's tower burns and the damned are being dragged to the lower left of the picture (stage left) to what one assumes is the pit of hell.

The main problem in Jesus leading the Souls out of a fortress rather than out of a gaping hell-mouth is that such a representation appears to be contrary to most early medieval iconography on the subject, in which Jesus holds out his hand to Adam and Eve who stand within the very jaws of hell. On the other hand, sparring the jaws of hell yet leaving sufficient room for its inmates to move, to speak, and to be seen, calls for a hell-mouth of very considerable dimensions, and even then it may fail to represent adequately the 'gates of hell' or 'the watches on the wall'. The illustration of the Valenciennes Mystery Play in K. Mantzius' *A History of Theatrical Art in Ancient and Modern Times* shows both the tower of limbo, with the Souls peering through prison-bars while a cannon engulfed in fire looms above them, and hell, stage left of limbo, with winged fiends watching from the walls above and others issuing from the jaws below. The Anglo-Norman *Resurrection* in its arrangement of mansions includes a limbo (jaiole) placed next to hell, the former opposing the sepulchre and the latter heaven (E. K. Chambers, *The Mediaeval Stage,* ii. 83), and in the fifteenth-century French *Resurrection* 'the aforesaid tower of Limbo shall be adorned all round with curtains of black cloth', which later are 'subtly drawn aside' (Allardyce Nicoll, *Masks, Mimes, and Miracles,* 204).

Hell-mouth or hell-pit, however, must be included, for such is certainly Satan's destination (360). That Satan speaks no more once he has fallen into hell-pit is a factor relevant to the main staging problem. His fall from limbo's tower to hell-pit, if so staged, may aptly recall Lucifer's fall from heaven.

The heroic element in this Wakefield play is emphasized by Jesus alone facing the combined forces of hell. In most other versions of *The Harrowing of Hell* Jesus is supported by a legion of angels, and it is Michael's specific charge to bind Satan and to lead the Souls to paradise (York,

Chester, and Cornish Plays). Satan's confrontation of Jesus, opposing his spear or trident against Jesus' tree-cross and banner, is the climax of the scene.

Sound effects are in this play particularly important, because on the one hand the deafening disharmony of hell must contrast with the defiant song of the hopeful Souls who, according to the original stage direction, sing the first verse of *Salvator Mundi* (44), and in their procession to paradise the *Te Deum.*

THE RESURRECTION

The two main playing areas are Pilate's Court and the sepulchre. The Centurion makes his entry on horseback [stage direction following (44) *Tunc veniet centurio velut miles equitans*], most probably in 'the place' and could pass by the sepulchre and address his first speech to the cross, which might, with considerable dramatic effect be left in position from *The Crucifixion* to *The Judgement.*

Pilate, Annas, Caiaphas, and the four soldiers are all located on Pilate's pageant at the beginning of the play. The soldiers are later dispatched (201) to the sepulchre where they take up their positions, one on each side of a rectangular tomb. The producer has the particular problem of making sure that the actor playing Jesus can get himself into the tomb unobserved by the audience between the end of *The Deliverance of Souls* and the beginning of *The Resurrection.* If in medieval times the two plays were performed by separate and mobile companies of guildsmen there would have been no great staging problem involved. If, however, it is wished to emphasize the continuity of place, action, and performer, then either a curtain must screen the tomb on the pageant, and Jesus after *The Deliverance of Souls* enters the tomb unseen, or before the dialogue of *The Resurrection* begins Joseph of Arimathea, Nicodemus, Simon of Cyrene, and John the Evangelist carry in the tomb containing Jesus and place it on the pageant. It is interesting to note that in the *Ludus Coventriae* while Jesus is still on the cross another actor plays the role of Christ's Spirit and descends into hell, and it is only subsequent to this action that Jesus is taken down from the cross and buried.

The Soldiers having propped themselves against the tomb go to sleep, but at least one of the Soldiers witnesses the resurrection (455), and evidence from art forms and other cycles representing this episode suggests that usually while two Soldiers are fast asleep two are staring, amazed and helpless, as Jesus steps from the tomb. The actual resurrection begins with the entry of two Angels singing, strongly supported by the heavenly choir, *Christus Resurgens,* they lay the stone aside and Jesus rises holding the cross-banner, the symbol of the resurrection ('With him a cross on his banner soon he displayed' *Ancient Cornish Drama, The Resurrection,* 527), and steps onto one of the Soldiers, a regular feature in the medieval iconographic treatment of this subject and specifically referred to in the Chester *Resurrection* (270–277):

1ST SOLDIER That time that he his way took,
Durst I neither speak nor look,
But for fear I lay and quook,
And lay in a sound dream.

He set his foot upon my back,
That every limb began to crack;
I would not abide such another shock
For all Jerusalem.

Jesus speaks from near the tomb and then withdraws. The two Angels sit on the tomb, one at the head and one at the feet and themselves withdraw after they have spoken to the three Marys (399). The Angels may have been played by boys as suggested by the Chester *Resurrection* (425/6):

1ST ANGEL Woman, why weepest thou so ay?
MARY MAGDALENE Son, for my lord is taken away.

A young boy's treble might equip him splendidly for the angelic choir, but it seems rather damaging to an Angel's dignity to be called 'Son'.

The Soldiers on waking are still half in a trance and are

slow to realize the full implications for them of the resurrection. Their first impulse is to lie to Pilate, but their later unanimous decision for truth approximates in dramatic feeling to the evangelistic zeal of the *Ludus Coventriae* Soldiers whose enthusiasm, however, is greatly moderated by Pilate's promise of meed.

The *Ancient Cornish Drama* and the *Ludus Coventriae* indicate that Mary Magdalene meets Jesus at a little distance from the tomb. Jesus, according to a stage direction in the Chester play (432), appears dressed in an alb and carrying a cross-staff. Certainly in this Wakefield play, as in the biblical version, Mary Magdalene mistakes Jesus for a gardener (563), and a gardener's costume together with a spade is accorded Jesus in the Lincoln misericord.

THE PILGRIMS

'fysher pagent' under the title in the manuscript indicates that the responsibility for staging the play was undertaken by the Wakefield Fishermen's guild, a powerful enough body in the days when the River Calder could be relied on for a rich yield.

The pilgrim's habit [*hic venit ihesus in apparatu peregrini* stage direction following (97)] might most simply be conveyed by scrip and staff. The stage directions give little help on Jesus' vanishing from the disciples' sight:

> *Tunc recumbent et sedebit ihesus in medio eorum, tunc benedicet ihesus panem et fanget in tribus partibus, et postea evanebit ab oculis eorum. . . .*
>
> [stage direction following (290).]

A trap-door near where Jesus is sitting might be a possible solution. There is ample evidence of there being trap-doors on the medieval pageants.

The action of the play takes place partly on the road between Jerusalem and Emmaus (1–278), and partly in the house at Emmaus (279–380). The first part, comprising the journey, is best portrayed moving in 'the place', the second part on a pageant, which in all the other Cycles is expressly referred to as the Castle of Emmaus.

THOMAS OF INDIA

The play is simply staged on a single pageant with most of the characters making their entries from behind, but perhaps Thomas, because of his initial soliloquy, making his entry from 'the place'. Mary Magdalene's part in the play appears to end at (64) and, although not indicated by any stage direction in the manuscript, it is appropriate for her to make her exit at this point. She is not present when Jesus appears to the disciples (83) nor when Thomas in turn answers the arguments of the disciples. Had Mary Magdalene been present Thomas would certainly have turned his attention to her in his refutation of the evidence for Jesus' resurrection.

Jesus makes three appearances in the play (83, 91, 311). The persistent use of a trap-door for these appearances would be damaging to the effect required; curtains might be used with greater dignity. As indicated by (86) Jesus is dressed in a red garment. He sings on his first two entries [*pax vobis et non tardabit, hec est dies quam fecit dominus* (83)], and although not specified in the original text his third entry should also be attended with music (311).

Thomas' first speech (168–179) is a soliloquy with the dramatic intention of conveying to the audience that although he may appear to strut as proudly as a peacock (168) and in the subsequent scene seem to be impatient with the disciples and scornful of Christ's power, he nevertheless has been profoundly moved by the tragedy of the cross. In effect he is saying 'I am not what I am', and with this the dramatic soliloquy has undergone a startling development.

There are two matters in this play which refer specifically to the previous play *The Pilgrims*. The term Emmaus castle (263) suggests the setting for the scene in *The Pilgrims* in which Jesus breaks the bread, and that the bread is broken cleanly in three as though cut by a knife is indicated by (265) and by the *Ludus Coventriae Christ's Appearance to Cleophas and Luke* (286).

THE ASCENSION

The play is incomplete, but the four hundred and eleven lines that remain represent the average length of the plays in the Wakefield Cycle, and indeed the main action is completed in *The Ascension* as it stands. However, both verse and dramatic structure are sufficiently tedious to dissuade most modern producers from taking further interest.

The most fascinating matter raised by the play is the stage management of the actual ascension. It takes place on a hill (45) or pageant, and when Jesus is ready to ascend he calls for the clouds to open (252), and it is enclosed in these clouds that Mary and the disciples watch him rise to heaven (300, 349). The stage cloud is apparently an extremely firm structure, worked by pulleys concealed above the acting area, made probably of wood as suggested by the miniature in the Chartres museum, which opens to allow Jesus to secure himself within it, leaving, below the cloud as he ascends, the bottom of his gown and his feet still visible to those looking up from the ground. The cloud is obviously a highly organized, smoothly working piece of stage machinery. In this play the Angels sing as Jesus ascends, but in the Chester play Jesus himself sings and stays suspended in mid-air for some considerable time. Most Ascension plays refer to Jesus' return to earth at the Last Judgement as being in the same manner as his ascension (York, 219; Chester, 160; Wakefield, 262).

This form of raising and lowering characters on the medieval pageant is common to all the cycles. Although the *Ludus Coventriae Ascension* is too fragmentary to yield evidence on this score, *The Assumption of the Virgin* from the same cycle makes repeated references to this two-way vertical movement. Most memorable perhaps is Jesus' plea in the York *Ascension* (175):

Send down a cloud, father! For
I come to thee, my father dear.

THE JUDGEMENT

The beginning of this play is missing in the manuscript. The producer has the choice of presenting it as it stands or of borrowing the first 144 lines of the York play. If the latter course is adopted, the whole Cycle may be given firmer shape by God's first speech: in *The Creation* God made man, in *The Judgement* man's life on earth will be brought to an end [York, *The Judgement Day* (56)]. There may, however, be stronger reasons for staging the Wakefield fragment as a play complete in itself. The York play is solemn and uniform in tone; the Wakefield play, which appears to be a zestful revision of the York play, or the revision of a common ancestor, abounds with interpolations which are the work of the Wakefield Master who imparts those indelible characteristics which might jar against rather than complement the uniformity of the York version. Undoubtedly the play can be effectively staged with the text as we have it. If at the very beginning the trump sounds, and the scattered Souls, Good and Evil, from their several entries move slowly into 'the place', which in effect will then be filled with nearly every actor taking part in the whole Cycle, a fitting prologue to the grand finale has been found.

Heaven, earth, and hell are the critical acting areas in the play. Paradise may also be included if the passage of the righteous Souls to heaven is to be shown. Jesus, after their deliverance from limbo, set them in paradise to await the Last Judgement.

More than in any other play there needs to be a very firm means of communication between heaven and earth. The Angel descends to part the Souls (73), Jesus descends to sit in judgement (83), and at the end of the play all the Good Souls are led into heaven by Jesus and the Angels, all singing the *Te Deum*. A stout staircase is called for, built either inside or outside heaven's tower.

So many medieval works of art depicting the Last Judgement show the Angels slightly above Jesus, holding in their hands the hammer, the nails, the crown of thorns, and sometimes the cross. This may be reproduced in the staging if, when Jesus descends to sit in majesty on earth, his throne should be placed immediately beneath heaven's tower from which the angels display the instruments of torture. A Chester stage direction, while supporting this arrangement of the Angels, suggests that Jesus, instead of being enthroned on earth, is suspended in mid-air on a cloud:

> *Finitis Lamentationibus mortuorum, descendet Iesus quasi in nube, si fieri poterit; Quia secundum Doctorum Opiniones in Aere prope terram iudicabit filius Dei. Stabunt Angeli cum Cruce, Corona Spinea, lancea, aliisque Instrumentis, omnia demonstrantes.*
> [Chester, *The Last Judgement,* following (356).]

If presentation is linear then hell will be opposed to heaven, that is to the left of Jesus as he sits in judgement. If presentation is in the round, and the usual conventions are being observed, then heaven will be to the east and hell to the north. At the parting of souls the good shall stand at the right of the throne and the evil at the left, and when the devils garner the Evil Souls into hell (612), they drag them from the east, probably through the south and west points, to hustle them north into hell-mouth.

The devils all carry scrolls on which are inscribed the names of the damned (183, 212, 224, 380), but these should be easily disposed of, tucked in a belt or a pouch, because the devils will need both hands to harry the Evil Souls into hell. Many medieval tympana and indeed also the Chester play (376) suggest that the devils carried their victims to the everlasting bonfire.

Perhaps no play in the range of medieval drama is richer in its references to the contemporary costume. Dramatic effectiveness is gained by dressing the Evil Souls in compliance with the suggestions in the text and directing the devils' speeches to the characters wearing the corresponding costumes. The producer may wish to include an even more august hierarchy of Souls, Good and Evil, which, as at Chester, will contain popes, emperors, kings and queens.